THE MAGNIFICENT MONARCH

The Magnificent Monarch
Charles II and the Ceremonies of Power

Anna Keay

continuum

Continuum UK, The Tower Building, 11 York Road, London SE1 7NX
Continuum US, 80 Maiden Lane, Suite 704, New York, NY 10038

www.continuumbooks.com

Copyright © Anna Keay 2008

First published 2008

British Library Cataloguing-in-Publication Data
A catalogue record for this book is available from the British Library.

Library of Congress Cataloguing-in-Publication Data
A catalog record for this book is available from the Library of Congress

ISBN 978 1 84725 225 8

Typeset by Pindar New Zealand (Egan Reid), Auckland, New Zealand
Printed and bound by MPG Books Ltd, Cornwall, Great Britain

For Simon

Contents

Illustrations

Maps and plans

Colour plates

Text illustrations

Acknowledgements

This book grew from the research initially undertaken for a PhD thesis, and thank yous are due to many people who have helped over a long period. John Nightingale at Magdalen College Oxford was an inspirational tutor and I am deeply grateful to him for both his patience and for introducing me to the world of the rituals of power. Professor John Miller guided me through the political landscape of Restoration England and read and commented on the book long after his duties as a supervisor had ceased. Edward Impey has been supportive of this endeavour, both as an employer and a friend, through my employment at Historic Royal Palaces and English Heritage. Andrew Barclay kindly read the book in draft and offered invaluable advice on the court and politics of the period. Many others have given help and encouragement; among them, Jeremy Ashbee, William Burlington, Bob Bucholz, Rod Clayton, Jeroen Duindam, Luc Duerloo, Ken Fincham, Susanne Groom, Gordon Glanville, Bruce Hunter, Lisa Jardine, Nancy Klein Macguire, Philip Mansel, Clare Murphy, Michael Questier, Florian Reinaud, Paul Seaward, Kevin Sharpe, Malcolm Smuts, Luke Syson, David Starkey, Andre Vandewalle and Giles Worsley. Particular thanks are due to Tony Morris for taking on the book at Hambledon and Ben Hayes for seeing it through at Continuum. I am grateful to my parents for their encouragement and sage advice. Sparing time he could not afford, my father set aside China for the court of Charles II to offer elegant and exhaustive editorial suggestions. No daughter could ask for more wonderful parents. Thanks, finally, to Simon Thurley for being mentor, colleague and friend in perfect combination; and who, as the last words were written, asked me to marry him. This, with everything else, is for him.

Abbreviations

Ailesbury, *Memoirs*	*The Memoirs of Thomas, Earl of Ailesbury written by Himself*, W. E. Buckley (ed.), 2 vols (London, 1890)
Angliae Notitia	Edward Chamberlayne, *Angliae Notitia or the Present State of England* (London, 1669)
BL	The British Library
Bod. Lib.	The Bodleian Library
Colvin, *King's Works*	Howard Colvin (ed.), *The History of the King's Works*, 6 vols (London: Her Majesty's Stationery Office, 1963–82)
CSPD	*Calendar of State Papers, Domestic Series*
CSPVen	*Calendar of State Papers and Manuscripts Relating to English Affairs in the Archives and Collections of Venice and in other Libraries of Northern Italy*, Allen B. Hinds (ed.) (London, 1916–35)
DRO	Dorset Record Office
Evelyn, *Diary*	*The Diary of John Evelyn*, E. S. de Beer (ed.), 6 vols (Oxford: Clarendon Press, 1955)
Hartmann, *Charles II*	C. H. Hartmann, *Charles II and Madame* (London: Heinemann, 1934)
HMC	*Historical Manuscripts Commission*
Lives of the Norths	*The Lives of the Right Hon. Francis North, Baron Guildford; The Hon. Sir Dudley North; and the Hon. and Rev. Dr. John North by the Hon. Roger North together with the Autobiography of the Author*, Augustus Jessop (ed.), 3 vols (London, 1890)
Magalotti, *Travels*	Count Lorenzo Magalotti, *Travels of Cosmo the Third Grand Duke of Tuscany through England during the Reign of King Charles the Second (1669)* (London, 1821)
NUL	Nottingham University Library, Manuscripts Collection
Pepys, *Diary*	*The Diary of Samuel Pepys*, Robert Latham and William Matthews (eds), 11 vols (London: G. Bell & Sons, 1970–83)
Reresby, *Memoirs*	*Memoirs of Sir John Reresby*, Andrew Browning (ed.), 2nd edn, Mary K. Geiter and W. A. Speck (eds) (London: Royal Historical Society, 1991)

Schellinks, *Journal*   *The Journal of William Schellinks' Travels in England*
                           1661–1663, Maurice Exwood and H. L. Lehmann (eds),
                           Camden Society, 5th Series, I (London: Royal Historical
                           Society, 1993)
TNA   The National Archives (formerly the Public Record
                           Office)
WRO   Worcestershire Record Office

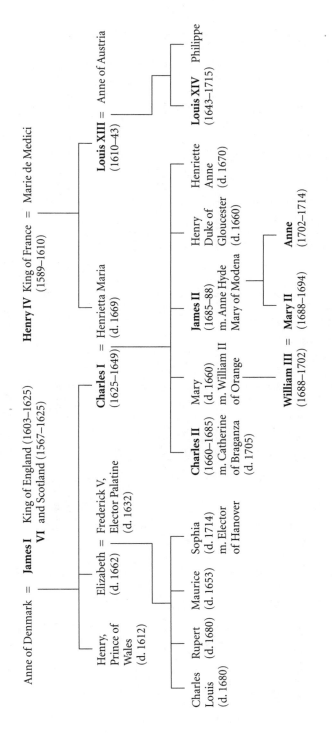

1. Family tree of the Stuart dynasty.

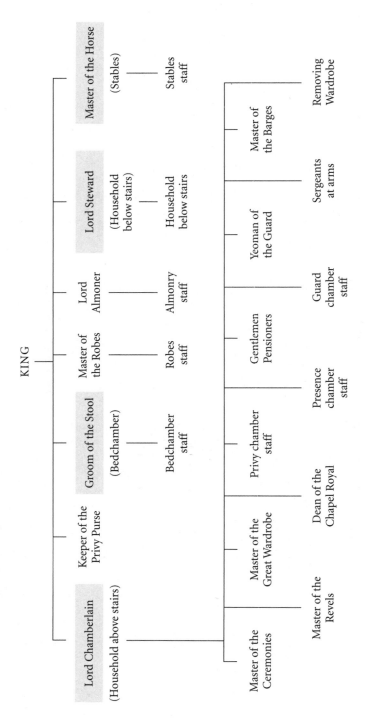

2. Household officers at the court of Charles II.

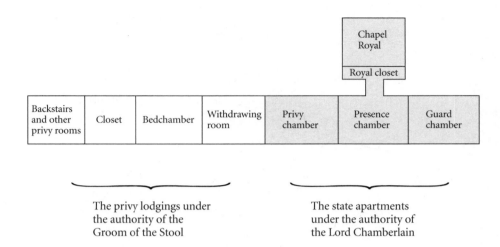

3. Diagrammatic plan of the sovereign's apartments in English royal palaces in the seventeenth century.

4. North-east France and the Low Countries in the seventeenth century.

Introduction

'A king that discourages ceremony, is like the carpenter that sawd off the pieces of timber upon which he stood.'[1]

(George Savile, Marquis of Halifax, 1684)

In the dead of night on 27 April 1646 King Charles I rode out of Oxford in heavy disguise. Protected by the darkness, he slipped through the east gate, over the Cherwell river at Magdalen Bridge and past the parliamentary forces camped outside the town walls. In so doing he abandoned the ancient city which for the last four years had been the headquarters of the Stuart court and nerve-centre of the royalist war effort. The king's escape was so secret that many of his closest friends and advisers were unaware of it. As well as deserting the city, he left behind him his twelve-year-old son, James, Duke of York. With Oxford now an easy target for the massed ranks of the New Model Army, the remaining royalists negotiated a swift surrender. The senior parliamentary commanders then entered the city and were taken to see the Duke of York. Though the boy was their prisoner, each seasoned soldier in turn leaned forward to kiss his hand in respect. What a poignant scene it must have been. One officer went further than his colleagues and as his turn came crumpled down onto his knees before pressing his lips to the prince's pale hand. This man was Oliver Cromwell.[2]

Why did these mighty parliamentarian officers perform these acts of deference to a child prince? Perhaps they were showing genuinely felt respect for a blameless member of a still vaunted royal dynasty. Alternatively, they might simply have been adopting a mode of behaviour so ingrained in them as men of their age that it was entirely instinctive. Or they may have been performing acts of calculated humility designed to play well in the propaganda war and perhaps win over wavering royalists. Whichever it was, this episode, like so many others, is a reminder that the seventeenth century was an age of allegory, one in which human relationships were articulated explicitly in physical gestures and modes of behaviour. These were not always straightforward representations of power relationships, indeed sometimes the reality of power was in fact the reverse of what a gesture seemed to imply, but they were nonetheless the language in which power was both expressed and exercised.

The subject of this book is how one man, Charles II, used this vocabulary of gesture and gesticulation, symbol and ceremony in his career as prince and king. How a whole range of forms of behaviour – many long-established, some innovations of the age – were maintained, managed and manipulated during his lifetime in ways that had fundamental and far-reaching effects for his regime.

There is no easy collective term for these modes of behaviour and courtly conventions. The term 'etiquette', sometimes used, is too flimsy and passive for such dynamic events, so throughout this book they are called 'ceremonies'. This has been taken to encapsulate the whole range of repeated and ritualized activities in which the king participated that expressed, in some way or other, royal authority. Almost everything a king did in the early-modern period spoke to some extent of his status, but this book is confined to those activities which were fundamentally about status rather than just tinged with it. For this reason royal theatregoing, hunting and court entertainments, pastimes in which the king participated principally for personal pleasure, are not examined. The main focus is instead on the ceremonies of the court, that is to say those events sometimes described in the French context as 'cérémonial domestique'.[3] Much of this is about the rituals of the day-to-day: the formalized aspects of how the king rose, dined and worshipped; the regular calendar of set-piece ceremonies he performed, such as healing the sick and the royal maundy; and the highly ceremonial exchanges which took place between the king, foreign princes and their representatives.

The days have now long passed when it would have been laughable to suggest the rituals of kingship as a serious area of study, and it is not necessary here to rehearse the historiography of this topic.[4] But one or two points are worth making. Though much lip-service has been paid to the importance of this field of enquiry for English history, still comparatively little has been published on it. There is as yet no monograph on ceremonial at the English court for any reign, and while lots of interesting and important work has been done on aspects of royal ceremonial it is still only a trickle compared to the torrent which the material would warrant.[5] In this context it is important to point out that while Charles II was sovereign of three kingdoms, this is essentially a study of English kingship.

The book follows broadly the narrative of Charles Stuart's life from birth to death, but it is inevitably a partial account and should not be read as a straight biography. Instead it examines in detail one facet of the king's life and as such has something in common with thematic biographies. So, like a literary biography of John Vanbrugh or a military biography of the Duke of Wellington, this, a ritual biography of Charles II, does not purport to present a complete picture of its subject but, rather, examines an important aspect of his career. Readers who want a rounded view of Charles II will need to read this book in tandem with others. However, it is argued here that no rounded understanding of the life and career of Charles Stuart can be achieved without considering this dimension.

This book is therefore intended as an addition to existing literature; a complement not a contradiction. Because this aspect of his life has been so little considered in the past an unbalanced view of Charles II prevails, one in which, in terms of his attitude to court ceremonial, he is still the 'merry monarch' and to which my title is intended as a corrective.[6] Historians have often been too quick to take at face value the king's occasional cavalier comments about royal rituals. He once complained to Samuel Pepys of the 'ceremoniousnesse' of the Spanish king, who 'doth nothing but under some ridiculous form or other; and will not piss but another must hold the chamber-pot', and in 1664 he wrote to his sister, Henriette Anne, recommending sleep as the best course to get through sermons.[7] But what Charles said and what he did were often quite different. Though he didn't require a servant to hold his chamber pot, he was attended by two senior officials when he relieved himself, one holding the candle and one the paper. Similarly, despite his dismissive words he attended royal services and sermons with remarkable regularity and not a single account of his nodding off in the chapel can be found.

There has been a tendency to assume that because Charles II enjoyed the corporal pleasures of life, because he was a hedonist who gambled and had multiple affairs, he must have been dismissive of royal rituals. He certainly had a way with people, a common touch that many a modern politician might envy, but it does not follow that he was careless of his status as king or of the modes of behaviour that expressed this. To some extent the nature of the sources for the period are responsible for the strength of the informal, 'merry monarch' view of Charles II. If Samuel Pepys had written his diary in the 1560s rather than the 1660s – the heyday of another young sovereign – what different views we might have of Elizabeth I and Charles II.

Accounts of Charles II's reign and the character of his court have also been influenced by their place in the English chronological narrative. The Restoration has always had something of an uneasy position in English history, trapped awkwardly between two revolutions, neither exactly *ancien régime* nor yet quite enlightenment.[8] The court of the early Stuart period, by contrast, with its stellar cast of politicians, painters and playwrights, has attracted lots of attention, leaving the Restoration something of an unsatisfactory afterthought, its court, surely, just a shadow of its pre-war predecessor. It has seemed unthinkable that Charles II, so different from his careful, ceremonious father, could have cared about the rituals of kingship to anything like the same degree.[9] There has been too hasty an assumption that Charles II's reign saw the mechanics of monarchy gradually malfunction, that its cogs and wheels – the rituals and conventions of English court life – were grinding to a slow halt even as the reign progressed.[10] The purpose of this book is to challenge this view and present, instead, a different King Charles II.

April 1661 was one of the wettest months in living memory. Rivers burst their banks, city streets turned to sludgy streams of mud and lead-grey skies pressed down bleakly on all of England. The ground was so saturated that even the precincts of the royal palaces became hazardous bogs, passable only by a network of planks laid in makeshift walkways across the mire. A battalion of carpenters battled the lashing rain to complete the triumphal arches which they had been building across the main east–west route through London since mid-February. As they and an army of others toiled away, royal officials gazed ever more anxiously from their windows, for each dreary dawn brought them closer to the feast of St George: the day they were to crown their king.[11]

On Monday 22 April the solemnities began. Early that morning Charles II, the 30-year-old king, was woken in his bedchamber at Whitehall Palace, at the far west of the capital. When the Groom of the Bedchamber drew back the thick crimson damask curtains he revealed an amazing scene: in place of the low, heavy skies of the previous weeks was a high unbroken expanse of pale blue, and in the privy garden below, the white marble statues threw long morning shadows across the gravel paths. As the king's barge carried him downstream to the Tower of London where the coronation procession was to begin, everyone marvelled at the dazzling day, a sure sign, they agreed, of God's blessing on the great occasion at hand.[12]

Charles II's coronation was an event of enormous expense planned down to every painstaking detail. The previous September a special committee had been appointed to oversee all the arrangements. The king himself was closely involved, leading the discussion at the committee meetings, and the whole occasion as it was staged was the embodiment of his own wishes. In his view, after a decade of republican government, England was tired of novelty. He ordered that 'the records and old formularies should be examined' and a coronation should be devised which in every way accorded with these, missing no opportunity to use ancient traditions 'to add lustre and splendour to the solemnity'.[13] One of the most important elements revived was the vast procession that carried the sovereign from the Tower of London (where kings often spent the days before a coronation) to Westminster Abbey, where the ceremony took place. The king's father, Charles I, had been happy to use the excuse of plague to cancel his coronation procession 35 years earlier. But his son knew the price his father had paid for underestimating the importance of such events in inspiring loyalty, and would not make the same mistake.

The magnificent procession snaked slowly through the London streets in the bright sunshine, passing under the four triumphal arches as it went and taking five hours to travel as many miles. Every window along the route was crammed with spectators, the victors of a bidding war for vantage points from which house owners turned a massive profit. The procession itself was many thousands strong; headed by the lowlier officials, each section was more illustrious than the last. It included almost the whole secular establishment of the kingdom: from the principal officials responsible for law, Parliament and finance through all the main officers of the royal household, to almost the whole nobility, among them over 50 barons, seven viscounts and 31 earls. The king was the apogee of the procession and carried off his role with aplomb: unusually tall and riding on a splendid horse, he was an immediately striking figure. His natural prominence was enhanced by his dazzling embroidered suit and the enormous plumed hat that distinguished him from the other participants – most bareheaded out of respect for their sovereign (*see* Colour Plate 1). As he passed through the streets, the king effortlessly combined majesty with the common touch, nodding graciously to individual members of the crowd, so spreading delight among those who felt themselves to have been singled out for favour.[14]

The coronation itself came the following day. The event was organized by the chief herald, Sir Edward Walker, Garter King at Arms. A fastidious 50-year-old, who had served as secretary to Charles I during the civil war, Walker had never been a popular figure. One contemporary sneered that it was no surprise that 'a herald, who is naturally made up of embroidery, should adorn his own services'.[15] But with the coronation, Walker came into his own, and he carried out to the letter the king's orders for continuity. The crown jewels had been broken up and sold by Parliament after Charles I's execution in 1649, so a new set of regalia had been required. Ordered from the goldsmith Robert Vyner, the new crown jewels so exactly replicated what had been lost that even objects whose functions were unknown were carefully re-created (*see* Figure 1). The king's own clothes were commissioned specially from Paris and these alone cost several thousand pounds.[16]

1. St Edward's Crown, 1661. Made for the coronation of Charles II this solid-gold crown is still used for royal coronations today.
The Royal Collection © 2007, Her Majesty Queen Elizabeth II

2. The coronation of Charles II in Westminster Abbey, by Wenceslaus Hollar.
© *Trustees of the British Museum*

Though the ceremony in Westminster Abbey did not start until 11 a.m., spectators started arriving long before dawn, keen to secure their seats. The king came upriver by boat from Whitehall to Westminster Hall where the procession assembled, and where it would later return for the coronation feast. Each element of the regalia – crown and orb, sceptres and swords – was carried by a specified nobleman, while the king wore a breathtaking gold and silver suit and a crimson velvet cap lined with ermine. Rich blue fabric was laid as a carpet from the high end of Westminster Hall to the door of Westminster Abbey. Here the ceremony was enacted, following closely the form that the ritual had taken since the early Middle Ages. This involved several discrete stages: the 'recognition', in which the king was presented to the people; the swearing of the coronation oath, in which he promised to rule fairly; the anointing with holy oil; the investiture with the robes and regalia; and finally the homage, in which the congregation pledged their loyalty. The beginning and end of the proceedings took place on the stage in the centre of the abbey and were easily visible to the delighted audience (*see* Figure 2). As the archbishop presented the king to the four banks of spectators they responded with a deafening bellow of support, and they had similar stadium

3. Charles II riding to Parliament, 1661. © *Trustees of the British Museum*

views of the bishops and nobility kneeling down to perform their acts of fealty at the end. In contrast, the anointing and investiture took place largely out of sight in the eastern arm of the church, so that when the crown was placed on the royal head, the cheers travelled down the building like a Mexican wave from the minority who could see to the majority who could not. So loud was the noise that most of the day's music was drowned out by the clamour.[17] Throughout the morning, the glorious weather held, sunshine streaming through the south windows of the church. Just as the ceremony drew to a close, and Charles passed out of the west door of the abbey – now the anointed and enthroned King of England – there was a terrific clap of thunder and the torrential rain returned.[18] For Samuel Pepys, like countless others, the memory of the occasion inspired real awe (though he had himself ended the day asleep in a slick of his own vomit); his diary entry for coronation day concluding with the solemn statement that he knew he would never on Earth see its like.[19]

The coronation of 1661 was the single most expensive and elaborate ceremony of Charles II's life. Though its ceremonial splendour was dazzling, it was much more than a pageant. For a prince who had spent 14 years in exile it was the concrete confirmation of both his restoration and his right to rule. If some kings considered coronations to be simply formalities, Charles II was not among them.

As Pepys recovered from his hangover and the debris from the day before was gradually swept away, the ceremonial did not cease. While the coronation per se was an exceptional occasion, an extraordinary one-off, the ceremony of kingship was not. Indeed the ritual of monarchy was more a *modus vivendi* than a calendar of events. A week before the coronation the location had been Windsor Castle, where the king had led three days of ritual in honour of the forthcoming feast of St George, the patron saint of the Order of the Garter.[20] Only days before that the court had celebrated Easter. As well as the ceremonies in the chapel royal, the king had performed the 'royal maundy', washing the feet of 31 paupers in front of a large crowd in the great hall at Whitehall.[21] The state opening of Parliament followed two weeks after the coronation (*see* Figure 3); again Charles donned his new state crown and rode in procession to Westminster to address his subjects. In the months between May and August almost 900 people received the king's touch in the ritual of healing the sick.[22] Each day had its own ceremonial timetable: the dressing of the king, the service of his meals, the form of his prayers, all following a regularized ritual pattern. The coronation might have been unusual in scale, but seen in the wider context of Charles II's life, it was not the exception but the rule.

2

Son and heir

Plague threatened like thunder in the warm summer air as the young queen of England entered the ninth month of an exhausting pregnancy. It was May 1630, and only weeks earlier well-ordered plans for the royal birth to take place at the Thames-side palace of Greenwich had been abruptly abandoned at the news of an outbreak of the epidemic there. The queen and her vast staff moved instead to the palace of St James's which, having started life as a leper hospital, enjoyed considerable isolation though it was only a stone's throw from Westminster (*see* Figure 4). Soon cases of the disease were being reported in the capital itself. Officials pleaded for the queen to be moved again but with stories streaming in of incidents of infection across England, it wasn't at all clear that she would be safer anywhere else. On the morning of Saturday 29 May, as the sky over the pastoral plain of St James's Park turned from black to inky blue and the horizon began to glow with hazy light, the queen's waters broke. The royal birthing corps, at the

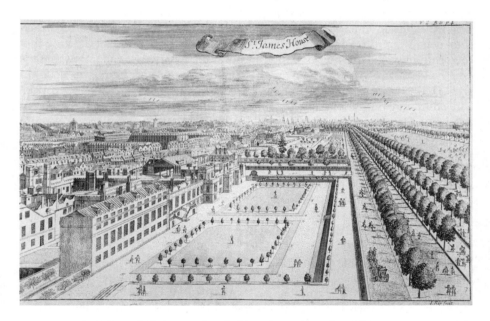

4. St James's Palace and park from the west, early 18th century.

ready for weeks, took immediate control. Drawing the heavy curtain across the great room, the ritual of the royal birth began.[1]

The young woman embarking on the agony of childbirth was herself just 20 years old (*see* Figure 5). Small in stature, with pale skin, sharp brown eyes and projecting front teeth, Henrietta Maria bore the names of both her illustrious parents. Her father had been King Henry IV of France, the Protestant prince who, considering Paris to be 'worth a mass', had converted to Catholicism to claim the French throne. Her mother, Marie de Medici, was daughter of Francesco I, Grand Duke of Tuscany, and shared some of the formidable character traits of her infamous forefathers. At just 15 Henrietta Maria had been engaged in marriage to the 25-year-old heir to the thrones of Great Britain, Charles Stuart. The sudden death of his father, James I, meant that when she finally sailed for England in June 1625, it was not as a mere princess but as Queen of England, Scotland and Ireland.

Her husband, Charles I, was not an easy man to know. Shy and acutely awkward as a child, he had spent his boyhood in the shadow of his brilliant older brother, Prince Henry, whose premature death had catapulted him unexpectedly into the limelight. Though he believed fervently in the sanctity of monarchy, he was naturally reserved, and as time wore on he increasingly shied away from the noise and disorder of public occasions, withdrawing into a refined world of high culture, painting and allegorical court drama.[2] His relationship with his bride was at first distant. The assassination of the Duke of Buckingham, to whom both Charles and his father had been deeply attached, changed everything, and the young king now turned to his wife for affection. Within months of the duke's death the couple conceived their first child. Joy turned to despair, though, when the queen went into labour just six months later. The doctors told the king that they could save the mother or child but not both. Charles was adamant that his wife be kept alive at any cost; given that all kings longed for heirs, this decision was taken as evidence of the king's extreme (and, to some, misplaced) devotion. The child they buried in 1629 had indeed been a boy, and the doomsayers now predicted that this second birth would be similarly cursed.

As the queen's attendants gathered around her at St James's early that May morning, the great men of the kingdom were also summoned to the palace. Royal convention dictated that the birth of a child be witnessed, in sound if not in sight, by the king's principal office-holders and most distinguished aristocrats. Accordingly, an illustrious party, headed by the king himself, trooped into the very room where the young queen sweated and strained, and there, separated from her by only a curtain, they mounted their vigil, their ears soon filling with her cries.[3]

The labour would last for 12 hours, managed by a small professional team brought over from the queen's native France especially for the event. The nurse in charge was Françoise Mounbadiac, working alongside an English physician (the king had drawn the line at a French doctor) and the midwife Madame Peronne, the most famous of the age; eight years later she would add Louis XIV

5. Charles I and Henrietta Maria with Charles, Prince of Wales and Princess Mary by Anthony Van Dyck *c.* 1632. *The Royal Collection © 2007, Her Majesty Queen Elizabeth II*

to her tally of royal deliveries. The screaming baby who took his first breaths the following afternoon never clenched his fist during the birth, a sure sign, said the nurses (not without ulterior expectations), that he would grow into a generous king. The relief at the arrival of a healthy son was palpable and those involved would indeed be handsomely rewarded: Madame Peronne received a gift of three hundred pounds from the king himself in gratitude for the prince's safe delivery, while Madame Mounbadiac would receive a cup and a pearl necklace. Presented at the christening, each was worth several hundred pounds.[4]

As soon as it was announced that a healthy son had been born, the king was reunited with his wife and remained with her for the rest of the day. Among those permitted to visit the child on the day he was born was the august Bishop of London, William Laud, who was ushered into the queen's presence before the prince was an hour old.[5] During the intimate hours the king and queen spent together, the news of the birth spread through London, and come the evening the diplomats of Europe were lining up at Whitehall to present their congratulations. The Spanish ambassador was so eager to be first that he ignored protocol and ambushed the king in the corridors of the palace.[6] Any expressions of emotion that may have taken place in the privacy of the queen's bedchamber on that Saturday afternoon were firmly under control by the following day. A constant stream of diplomats poured into the privy gallery at Whitehall to present their congratulations to the king, among them representatives from the United Provinces of the Netherlands, Denmark and Florence. When the Venetian ambassador took his turn, he noted that 'even on this great and extraordinary occasion he [the king] was as reserved as usual'.[7]

Charles I had brought real changes to the English court since his accession to the throne. Perhaps influenced by a visit to Madrid, where the Hapsburg kings led a highly closeted and ritualized existence, he instituted a new emphasis on decorum and order in the royal household. Regulations long flouted were now sharply enforced and within weeks of his succession, one contemporary noted, 'the king observes a rule of great decorum. The nobles do not enter his apartments in confusion as heretofore, but each rank had its appointed place and he has declared that he desires the rules and maxims of the late Queen Elizabeth.' Henrietta Maria, devout and serious minded, and educated in the stately surroundings of the convents and palaces of Paris, took naturally to these reforms and a new air of formality filled the corridors of the English royal palaces.[8]

The news of the arrival of a royal child was cause for both spontaneous and ceremonial celebration. Official declarations were issued to the civic and county officers across the kingdom announcing that a son and heir had been born, while envoys were sent abroad with the news.[9] As the despatches were delivered and read, bells were rung, bonfires lit and services of thanksgiving held.[10] This was partly the unprompted response of delighted subjects, but was also an act of loyalty required of all men of rank.[11] As the news reached the courts of Europe, festivities were staged there too: in Madrid and The Hague bonfires were lit in the courtyards of the royal palaces, and the English ambassador to Spain was specially honoured at a public bullfight.[12] In London, the king himself set a godly example by leading a procession to St Paul's Cathedral to give solemn thanks for the birth of a son.[13]

Within a fortnight, with the prince still strong, arrangements for the christening were being put in place. Usually more time was allowed for the recovery of the child and mother before a formal baptism, but with the plague still spreading (10,000 would die before the year was out), and with the chances of infection growing with every balmy day, the king did not want to wait. On 15 June, formal notification was given to members of the nobility that the event would take place in less than two weeks time, on Sunday 27 June. Their presence was not requested but required, 'all excuses sett apart'.[14]

So it was that the infant Charles took the lead role in the first major royal ritual of his life when he was barely four weeks old. The location of the christening was the Tudor chapel at St James's Palace (*see* Figure 6). The godparents were to be Henrietta Maria's brother, Louis XIII King of France; her mother, Marie de

6. Modern view of the interior of the Tudor chapel at St James's Palace.
The Royal Collection © 2007, Her Majesty Queen Elizabeth II

Medici, Queen Mother of France; and Charles I's brother-in-law, Frederick titular Elector Palatine and King of Bohemia. Such was the stature of these sponsors that it was universally hoped none would actually attend, for the costs of entertaining them with the appropriate magnificence would have been ruinous.[15]

The arrangements for the christening required considerable discussion. It was nearly a century since England had witnessed such an event – the last baptism of a prince of Wales had been that of Henry VIII's son, Edward VI, in 1536 – and since that time the kingdom had undergone a change of both dynasty and religion. The terms of the king and queen's marriage had laid down that any children should receive a Catholic baptism and upbringing. By 1630, though, other conditions of the treaty had already been broken, and the king felt little compunction in ignoring this particular stipulation altogether. It was distasteful to him personally and disgusting to an overwhelmingly anti-Catholic country. The baptism was therefore to be a Protestant occasion.[16]

The arrangement of royal ceremonial in England was divided between two senior officials. The Earl Marshal, head of the College of Arms, was charged with all out-of-doors royal ritual, including coronations, state entries and funerals (to this day the holder of this office organizes the state opening of Parliament).

The rituals and formal events which always took place within the palaces, in the 'chamber' or state rooms, were the responsibility of the Lord Chamberlain. State christenings were managed by the Earl Marshal with, in normal circumstances, the Archbishop of Canterbury officiating in the chapel. In 1630, however, the Archbishop was too ill to participate and so the role fell instead to the notorious Dean of the Chapel Royal: William Laud, Bishop of London.[17]

William Laud would be the most famous clergyman of the century, and 15 years later ended his life on the executioner's scaffold to the jeers of a blood-thirsty crowd. In 1630, though, he was enjoying sensational success: Bishop of London, head of the king's own religious establishment and Chancellor of the University of Oxford. In many ways he was an unlikely figure for such success: small and unprepossessing in appearance, he was a prickly character with few close friends, haunted every night by paranoid dreams. He owed his meteoric rise to the patronage of the late Duke of Buckingham, and through this most influential of figures he was introduced to the king, to whom his particular view of the church had appealed profoundly.

The Church of England had emerged from the Reformation as a hybrid institution, neither Calvinist nor Lutheran, but a uniquely English compromise form of Protestantism. In this there was always potential for schism, and so it would prove to be. Laud reacted strongly against the increasingly extreme views of the more Puritan, low-church elements of Anglicanism, and sought to reinvigorate what he considered to be the original form of the English church. For him this meant a greater emphasis on ritual and richness in worship, on beauty and decoration in church interiors and on ceremony and dignity in church liturgy, and he believed that a strong church arranged along these lines was a natural ally to a powerful and dignified monarchy. Charles I fundamentally shared Laud's outlook and it would be sharply reflected in their management of the Chapel Royal and, in time, the country at large.

Even before Laud's appointment, Charles I's Chapel Royal was being run with an increasing emphasis on ceremonial and sensual richness. With the appoint-ment of the arch-advocate of this view to the deanship, and the advent of a royal christening, a perfect opportunity presented itself to project an exemplary picture of royal worship. The christening was to take place in a blaze of publicity, and would follow two guiding principles: first it would be conducted with the formality and adherence to royal tradition appropriate to the status of the king's first-born son, and second it would set an example of the 'Laudian' view of proper worship.

The king, Bishop Laud and other senior and trusted officials pored over the details for the great event, and the surviving order of service bears marginal notes and corrections in Laud's own hand. No opportunity to demonstrate the holy beauty which Laud and Charles so believed should characterize the church was to be missed. The christenings of royal children consisted of two main components: the ritual of the baptism itself, in the chapel, and the great procession through the royal palace which came before and after it. Not only did the chapel need to be lavishly furnished for the occasion, but so did the entire route of the procession. This ran from the prince's own first-floor rooms downstairs into the open walkways of the ground floor and through the west door of the chapel. The walls were hung with tapestries, and rails were built on the open parts of the route to keep the crowds of spectators back. Within the chapel itself, also hung with tapestries, the font was placed on a raised platform, described – appropriately – as a 'stage', which was constructed by the royal surveyor of works, Inigo Jones, on as grand a scale as the space would allow. The top of the platform was enclosed by rails from which cloth of woven gold hung down to the ground. The floor of the platform, and the four steps up to it, were laid thickly with Turkish carpets and overhead a great canopy of state was suspended from the ceiling. On the platform stood the font, made of solid silver covered in gold, 'the best that may be had', with a cloth of the finest linen laid over it until the baptism itself took place. The original intention had been to erect this magnificent structure in the 'upper part' of the chapel, next to the altar itself. This plan was changed, though, in favour of a position in the 'midst' of the space, probably to ensure spectators had the best possible views of this baptism in the round. Especially for the occasion the Office of Works arranged for an organ to be installed in the chapel, and temporary galleries were erected around the interior of the building to accommodate musicians, for the occasion would be further enriched by rousing instrumental and choral interludes.[18]

The invitation list for the event was extensive and out of all proportion to the limited capacity of the Tudor chapel royal; as any visitor today can see, the room has the dimensions of a good sized reception hall but is a far cry from a cathedral (see Figure 6). As well as the presiding clergy and the British aristocrats standing proxy for the foreign godparents, the nobility, all the bishops and judges, and the Lord Mayor of London and his aldermen, were issued with invitations. In reality many of these can have done little more than line the route, as access into the choir of the chapel royal, where the font was set up, was restricted to the most senior guests.[19] All, however, added to the magnificence of the occasion both by their presence and by the splendour of their costume. Clerical dress was one of the sticking points in contemporary religious debate, puritans believing it ought to be plain and austere, and Laudians that rich robes were an essential reflection of the priest's holy status. At the prince's christening the clergy were specifically required to dress with splendour and to come wearing copes.[20]

After weeks of frantic preparation, on Sunday 27 June at 3 o'clock in the afternoon, the 'great bussines' of christening a royal prince began. The procession started in the prince's nursery on the first floor. Here the four-week-old baby lay in an elaborate cradle 'of estate', under a rich canopy. The queen's closest lady in waiting, or 'Groom of the Stool', the Countess of Denbigh, lifted the infant in her arms and carried him down the privy gallery to the waiting lords and ladies. Here, on the threshold of the state rooms, the procession formed, arranged in ascending order of seniority. At the front marched the aldermen of London, followed by the judges and the Lord Mayor; after the mayor walked, in rising order of precedence, the members of the nobility. After this large group processed the noblemen standing in for the two godfathers: the king's young cousin and Gentleman of his Bedchamber, the Duke of Lennox, and James, Marquess of Hamilton, head of Scotland's premier family and Master of the Horse. Then came the infant prince himself, borne in the arms of Hamilton's young wife, a Lady of the Queen's Bedchamber, who walked with the emblem of the event, the great basin for the font, carried before her. Lady Hamilton was flanked on one side by the Earl Marshal, the famous collector the Earl of Arundel, and on the other side by the Lord Treasurer, Sir Richard Weston, with the prince's nurse hovering close by. Behind the prince trailed a lengthy sable train which was carried by a group of noblemen, while others held a great canopy over the prince's head. Following the train-bearers was the grand and imperious Duchess of Richmond, standing proxy for the Queen Mother of France. A great beauty of an earlier age, the duchess had been married and widowed three times, each husband richer and more powerful than the last; she reputedly remarked that she would only marry a fourth time if the groom was a king. This grande dame was well suited to her role and – as one onlooker tartly commented – was more covered in jewels than Marie de Medici would have been had she attended in person.[21] The final part of the procession was made up of the ladies of the nobility, walking in pairs in descending order of rank. On the day, though, this section was embarrassingly thin as a last-minute rumour that they would be required to carry the Duchess of Richmond's train caused a large number to boycott the event rather than risk this humiliation.

When the procession reached the door of the chapel royal, Lady Hamilton passed the prince into the arms of Bishop Laud.[22] He then turned and stepped over the chapel threshold, so giving the musicians their cue. The air filled with the rich sound of the organ as he passed down the aisle.

Most spectators could at best only squeeze into the antechapel and, if tall enough, catch occasional glimpses of the ceremony. The more senior were seated in the chapel proper, with the men on one side of the aisle and the women the other, as was customary in all churches. As the organ played, the prince was carried to a small pavilion-like enclosure set up at the side of the chapel, which was decked out with thick carpets and a charcoal brazier to keep the child warm during the proceedings. Laud then started the service, which followed the normal form of evening worship in the chapel, but with the singing voices of the royal choristers chiming in to accompany the Dean's spoken words. Once the moment of baptism had arrived it was again Laud, in the absence of the Archbishop of Canterbury, who carried the prince up onto the stage to perform the sacrament, attended by the godparents, Lady Hamilton and Lady Denbigh. The baptism of a child, destined by divine will to be king, was a momentous occasion on any scale, and as Bishop Laud held the infant prince to the baptismal waters his hands visibly trembled.[23]

Charles and Laud gave further richness to the event by arranging for two of the baptismal prayers, once they had first been spoken by Bishop Laud, to be sung by the choir. Further anthems, which the king himself selected, were sung after the baptism had been concluded.[24] The infant prince was then taken to offer alms ceremonially at the high altar, which was done by placing him briefly in the great basin there. This done, the godparents themselves offered alms, followed by the great officers of state and the rest of the congregation in descending order of status.[25]

As the baptism itself had finished, the senior member of the College of Arms, the Garter King at Arms, stationed at the base of the stage, turned on his heel and proclaimed the title of the infant prince to the congregation. This was then passed by his colleagues through the palace, giving the prompt to the drums and fifes to strike up. They in turn were the signal for the flag on St James's Gatehouse to be raised. This was being awaited, across St James's Park, by the lookouts stationed on the roof of the Banqueting House at Whitehall Palace; they hauled up their own flag. The raising of the Whitehall flag was observed two miles to the east by the sentries on the parapets of St Paul's Cathedral, who raised their own ensign, itself the signal to the gunners standing ready on the roof of the Norman keep of the Tower of London to set off the great guns of the Ordnance Office – the booming shots telling the whole capital that the prince had been proclaimed.[26]

The ceremony completed, the procession which had borne the prince to the chapel reassembled and carried the infant back through the palace. On its return the cavalcade passed through the queen's apartments, into her bedchamber, to which Henrietta Maria was still confined, and there the baptized prince was presented to both his parents. It was not usual practice for the king to participate personally in christenings, his presence introducing an uncomfortable ambiguity to its focus. But Charles I had watched quietly from the royal closet overlooking the chapel, before returning to the queen's side to receive their son. Finally, the procession passed back through the queen's rooms to the nursery where the tiny prince was gently returned to his cradle.[27]

The majesty and magnificence which such an occasion projected is obvious even when peering at it through the fog of four hundred years. The reverence and awe shown to a four-week-old child created an instant aura of authority about his small body. The procession which formed around him was a perfect embodiment of the hierarchy of the realm with his person as its apogee, the sable trains and golden canopy emphasizing the inherent greatness of the tiny figure. The huge expense and splendour of the occasion had a prosaic as well as a poetic function, expressing the wealth and power of the regime and the potential rewards available to those who supported it – something further represented by the fact that the costly ceremonial props were distributed as gifts to participants after the event. To be allowed any part in such an occasion, from entering the palace as a spectator to taking a hallowed position in the heart of the procession, was, in abstract terms, to take a place somewhere in the upper levels of the great hierarchy and, in concrete terms, to feel the firm favour of the royal regime. But the event also demonstrates some of the subtler aspects of royal ceremonial. The careful management of its form by Charles I and Bishop Laud shows the extent to which occasions which might appear timeless and unchanging could be used as vehicles for sometimes quite specific political programmes. Even the peeresses' boycott concealed a serious truth: such events could only truly succeed if conducted on terms that suited the participants as well as the impresarios. While the ladies missed out on the prestige of taking part, they made a significant dent in the splendour of the day by leaving the procession to peter out in an undignified fashion. The chorus as well as the conductor could ruin the performance; both, in their way, had power.

As the cannon shots and revelry died away the people of London returned to the daily business of getting and spending. The year was 1630, the four lands of England, Wales, Ireland and Scotland ruled by one monarch and three parliaments. Thirty years earlier the Stuart King of Scotland James VI had inherited the English throne from his childless cousin Elizabeth I, and though much of the separate political infrastructure of two nations remained in place, the king and the national centre of gravity moved almost instantly to London. James and his family occupied a series of royal palaces built largely for Henry VIII in and around London, and set out on progresses around the south-eastern counties of England on a more or less annual basis. The Stuart dynasty was Protestant (though James's Danish wife would quietly convert to Catholicism) as were the majority of English, Welsh and Scottish people. In the wider European context Britain was in a minority. The two greatest European nations were Catholic, the Bourbon monarchs of France and the Hapsburg kings of Spain, and locked in constant competition for international supremacy; a competition in which the Spanish dominion of the Southern Netherlands (roughly modern Belgium) was a powerful weapon. After nearly a century of religious war, Protestantism was now confined almost entirely to northern Europe, with the British Isles, the breakaway political federation of the United Provinces of the Netherlands, Sweden and Denmark the most prominent players. Germany was a complex collection of small electorates, dukedoms and principalities held together principally by their collective overlord the Holy Roman Emperor, whose imperial court was at Vienna. Though technically elected by a series of prominent German princelings, the emperor was invariably a member of the powerful Hapsburg dynasty.

In 1630 parts of England were enjoying considerable prosperity and a burgeoning economy, of which the engine then, as now, was London. The population of the capital was almost 300,000, more than double its size a century before, and it would double once more before another century was out. The vast shopping emporia of the Royal Exchange in the City of London and the New Exchange on the Strand were among the largest in Europe. Open from before dawn until after dark they were crammed with boutiques that fuelled a thriving trade in luxury goods. Among the most sought-after commodities of the day were Chinese porcelain for ornaments and tableware, beaver fur for hats, and silk for every imaginable form of dress dyed a galaxy of bird-of-paradise colours. Since

Henrietta Maria's arrival in England, French fashions in dress had been in vogue, and shopkeepers competed to stock the latest Parisian styles. With wealth and population came buildings. In the year of the Prince of Wales's birth the Earl of Bedford, encouraged by the king, concocted a plan to build an ambitious new complex of town houses on the land behind St Martin's in the Fields. The enterprise was to take the avant-garde form of a 'piazza', the buildings ranged around an open square of land with a dramatic Tuscan church designed by Inigo Jones as its focus. Though most of the buildings are long gone, the age of Covent Garden's founding is still preserved in its street names: King Street, Henrietta Street and Charles Street.[28]

From the very first weeks of his life Prince Charles had both his own apartments and his own personnel, or household. Immediately after his birth the French nurses, who had been tolerated for the delivery itself, were sent back to Paris, and a staff of English attendants was appointed. At the head was the prince's governess, Mary Sackville, Countess of Dorset, wife of the Queen's Lord Chamberlain, the 4th Earl of Dorset. Much of the infant's establishment which she oversaw was made up of officials concerned with his physical well-being – all important in an age when infant mortality was horrifyingly high. These included his physician, Dr Chambers, a Gentleman Usher, John Ayton, and a team of nurses and 'rockers'. A laundress 'for the princes bodie' washed the child, while a 'coffer keeper' looked after the finances of this modest establishment.[29] Dr Chambers oversaw the prince's health with great care, writing reports, some to the king personally, of the boy's progress: his appetite, his stools, his teeth, and the prescription of medicines – such as the 'ointment to be applied to the circle of his neck' – were conscientiously documented.[30] The child's food was prepared from the outset in a separate kitchen with its own staff; this expanded to supply his brothers and sisters as they were born; by the mid-1630s they had between them some 18 'below stairs' officers.[31]

Like all royalty of the time, the infant prince never remained very long in one place. He retained apartments in St James's Palace, which was the usual London residence of the heir to the throne, and also had rooms alongside his parents at Whitehall Palace. But his principal home during his childhood was some ten miles west of London, at Richmond. Standing on the Thames between the river and Richmond Green, the palace was largely the work of the first Tudor king, Henry VII. In the late 1490s he had rebuilt an existing house and changed its name from Sheen to Richmond, after the Yorkshire town of which he had been Earl. The most prominent building on the site was the square stone structure that housed the royal lodgings. Standing several storeys high, this building was encrusted with exotic onion-domed cupolas and glittered with acres of leaded glass windows. It commanded wonderful views of the river and around its base clustered the courtyards and enclosed gardens of the palace. During the sixteenth century Richmond had been one of the sovereign's principal palaces and it was here that Queen Elizabeth had died. Under the Stuarts it was used instead as the

Prince of Wales's out-of-town residence. It was well suited for this purpose, being away from the disease and disorder that periodically infested the capital and provided with plenty of safely enclosed outside space for princely pursuits.[32]

At Richmond, Prince Charles would soon be joined by his siblings as the queen's confinements came thick and fast: Mary, the Princess Royal born in 1631 was followed by James, Duke of York (and future James II) in 1633. Large and active from birth, Charles looked a year old at only four months, and had a swarthy complexion of which his mother was ashamed.[33] At three years he was thought to have a melancholy temperament, serious and given to 'musing', but his being in the company of others had a positive effect, and saw him showing much more 'quickness'.[34] Though he lived largely apart from his parents, they were certainly not strangers to him. The royal children were frequently taken to them, and on many occasions the king and queen travelled to Richmond. Real affection developed between the Prince of Wales and his father; the Secretary of State recorded the toddler's response to seeing the king in July 1633, 'the Prince hath welcomed him home with the prettiest innocent mirth that can be imagined'.[35]

By 1634 the nurses and rockers had moved on to look after the prince's new siblings, and additional officials concerned with the education and ceremonial life of the prince took up their posts, among them Pages of the Backstairs, who waited on him in his bedchamber, and the Yeoman of Vestry who looked after his chapel.[36] The prince's nursery was refurnished as his bedchamber, and plans for his education were put in place.[37] In March 1635 Brian Duppa, Dean of Christ Church and one of Charles I's chaplains, was appointed as his tutor. Duppa was recommended for the post by Bishop Laud, and as a chaplain in the Earl of Dorset's household, would have been well known to the prince's governess. However, he was not the first choice. Another of the king's chaplains, the Dean of Salisbury, Edmund Mason, had originally been given the post, but died almost immediately. The unfortunate news reached the king as he was listening to Brian Duppa preach; it must have been an inspiring sermon as Duppa's appointment to the post followed just days later.[38] His suitability for this crucial early role in the prince's education was widely recognized. William Cavendish, Earl of Newcastle, who would take charge of the prince's household several years later, encouraged Prince Charles to make Duppa his role model as the perfect gentleman scholar. The admiration for one who combined so well the qualities of learned cleric and accomplished gentleman was universal, one contemporary eulogizing 'the comelieness of his Presence, the gentleness of his carriage the variety and smoothness of his learning'.[39] Duppa remained a constant presence in Charles's childhood until the early 1640s, and won the prince's enduring affection. At the Restoration Charles would reward him richly with the offices of Prelate of the Order of the Garter and Lord Almoner. When Duppa lay dying, Charles came to him and knelt at his old tutor's bedside to beg a final blessing, 'w[hi]ch he bestowed w[i]th one hand laid upon his master's head and the other lifted up to heaven' before passing away.[40]

As well as Duppa's own teaching, additional masters were brought in for specific subjects; Peter Massonnet received a substantial £60 a year for teaching the prince French, which, 'for the Q[ueen]'s respect', was thought the most important foreign language for him to learn, with Latin, Spanish and Italian secondary priorities.[41] It may be that the French page who attended the prince was employed partly to speak to his master in his native tongue.[42] Henry Gregory was paid the handsome sum of £50 a year from 1638 for teaching the prince to write, while a Frenchman, Guilaume le Pierrie, was engaged when Charles was just six to teach the vital royal skill of dancing.[43]

Part of the prince's time was certainly spent in the schoolroom at Richmond – which had been furnished in 1635 with two 'low Chaires' for the royal children's lessons. But he was also allowed to occupy himself with more lively pursuits.[44] At Richmond and St James's, plays and comedies were performed for his entertainment, with elaborate staging and scenery erected for the purpose. At the same time he developed his life-long love of fresh air and an interest in natural history. In 1637 the Office of Works erected a great aviary in the orchard at Richmond for the seven-year-old prince. Standing twelve feet high and with open wicker-work sides, it was painted bright green inside and out. The following year a section of the Pheasant Garden at St James's was fenced off to create 'a place for the Princes flowers'.[45] Physical exercise came in the form of tennis and horse-riding, both of which Charles genuinely enjoyed and continued throughout adult life.[46] The king was happy for his son to have playmates, so long as they were of the highest social standing, and Charles's Richmond childhood was a sociable one. As well as his brothers and sisters and numerous household officers, he also enjoyed the company of the two sons of the Duke of Buckingham, who on the king's instruction were brought up with the royal children to spare them a Catholic education at the hands of their mother.[47]

In 1638, on his eighth birthday, the prince's role in court life was put onto a different footing. In the spring of that year his household was constituted as the fully-fledged establishment of a prince, and so he began, in the words of one contemporary 'to hold his Court apart'.[48] Phalanxes of household officials were appointed to wait on him, with teams of attendants to be stationed in each of the rooms of his apartments.[49] The prince's finances were formalized and put into the hands of Sir David Cunningham, as Receiver General of the Prince's Revenues.[50] Most important of all, Lady Dorset was relieved of her post (going on to act as governess to the Duke of York) and William Cavendish, Earl of Newcastle, was nominated as his Governor and first Gentleman of his Bedchamber, his principal gentleman in waiting.[51]

William Cavendish, Earl of Newcastle, would serve as head of the prince's household for nearly four years, and was probably the single most influential figure in the prince's upbringing. On his appointment, Newcastle was given rooms at Richmond, and there he lived alongside his young charge; in the words of his wife, 'he spared no care and industry to discharge his duty' neglecting his own family and estates greatly in so doing.[52] The earl was one of the most distinguished and accomplished aristocrats of his age. Raised in the household of his aunt, Elizabeth, Countess of Shrewsbury (better known as Bess of Hardwick), he had been educated in the company of Henry, Prince of Wales – at whose side he was taught to ride by the great French equestrian Monsieur de St Antoine.[53] This set him on a course to become one of the most talented horsemen in Europe, but he would also win fame as a literary patron and lover of music and poetry. He built and entertained magnificently at his great Derbyshire houses, Welbeck and Bolsover, his legendary hospitality being the embodiment of his own idealized view of ancient English feudalism. The entertainments which he held for Charles I and Henrietta Maria, part of a concerted campaign to win a court position, had been grand spectacles on an Elizabethan scale, and his appointment in 1638 as the Prince of Wales's tutor was the sought-after result.

Newcastle's and Duppa's talents were very definitely complementary. Duppa provided the prince with a model of genteel learning, moderate religion and personal piety. Newcastle, on the other hand, showed little in the way of religious devotion (whether he even believed in God was only half-jokingly questioned by one contemporary), but he personified many of the secular accomplishments and qualities desirable in a prince. The position of governor allowed real intimacy to develop between Newcastle and his pupil: in the prince's rooms three types of lock were used, his household officers could enter some spaces with their 'single' key, the tutor and the prince's closest body servants could enter most with their 'double' key, but into the most private of the prince's rooms only the governor and the prince himself could enter using their exclusive 'treble' key.[54] A series of letters in careful boyish script from Charles to Newcastle survive, and show the love and admiration this child of ten or so developed for his dashing governor. In one of his periods of absence from Richmond, Charles wrote to Newcastle, volunteering 'to follow any … directions from you' and beseeching him to 'make haste to returne to him that loves you'. The relationship was warm on both sides: Newcastle commissioned the Italian sculptor Francesco Fanelli to cast a small bronze of the prince and ten years later would describe his pupil as set to be the most brilliant king of England since the Conquest.[55] Charles laboured to prove himself in the pursuits the earl thought most important, writing keenly, 'I ride every day' and in 1641 galloping his horse so hard in Hyde Park that he broke his arm from a fall.[56]

We cannot know what passed between the boy and his governor over the three-and-a-half years they spent together, or what precisely the subject of the many lessons and discussions were. However, light is cast on the subject by two extraordinary guidance notes for the prince written by Newcastle. The shorter dates to very soon after the earl's appointment, as indicated by an opening paragraph in which Newcastle pledges to try and fulfil the faith the king had shown in appointing him to the post. The longer second letter was written a decade or more later, during the period of the prince's exile. Though there is no proof positive that Charles read or studied these documents, the interest lies in the fact that they express so clearly Newcastle's own view of the world, and of the role he was preparing the prince to play in it. As such, they help explain how Charles developed into the sovereign he would eventually become.

In Newcastle's opinion, education was a dangerous exercise. Though he respected the study of history for the lessons it represented, and though he saw some merit in learning languages and various applied arts, he was deeply dismissive of the value of scholarship or bookishness, in which he detected only conceit and pedantry. In his view no bookworm had ever become a great states-man, and his pupil would do well to become 'a master of reading of men' rather than manuscripts. The prince's tutor, Duppa, was one of the few men of learning whom Newcastle genuinely respected, largely, he explained, because Duppa was wont 'discreetly to hide ye schollar in him'. Newcastle's view of the world was intensely conservative and patrician. Born in the Elizabethan age, he hankered after a time when each man knew his place and the social order was rigid and revered. Doubtless this outlook was sharpened by the events of the 1640s, and his second letter is particularly nostalgic for a lost age. However in both letters Newcastle counselled Charles to do everything possible to strengthen and shore up the natural hierarchy of being, a great pyramid descending down from God through monarchy, nobility, gentry and yeomanry to the common people. This picture of the world informed Newcastle's guidance on all matters. In religion, he instructed the prince to avoid too much devotion, which he considered inappropriate in a monarch ('one may be a good man but a bad king'), but on the other hand he was adamant that proper and dignified performance of divine worship was essential. For Newcastle the king's display of obedience to God was the perfect model for the loyalty and devotion which his subjects owed him. 'You owe as much Reverence and duty to him as we owe to you', he wrote, but 'if you have no Reverence at prayers, what will the people have think you, they go according to ye example of ye Prince ...' This was also, he explained, why orthodox Anglicanism was the only natural order of religious government: Catholicism would put the king in a struggle for authority with Pope, and Presbyterianism in a struggle with the people at large, 'They are both of them Destructive unto Monarcky.'

When Newcastle wrote the first letter, he acknowledged that the prince was an excellent pupil, noting in him a natural inclination towards the sort of religious observance of which he personally approved, and a disinclination towards books which pleased him equally, remarking approvingly 'you need no great labour to perswade you from the one, or long discourses to dissuade you from ye other'.

In his conception of a stable, hierarchical society, Newcastle considered the binding agent to be 'ceremony', by which he meant all aspects of the public representation of that order. For Newcastle ceremonies were the outward mani-festation of the correct order of things, part of the vital apparatus which 'keepes Everye man & Everye thinge within the Circle off their own Conditions'.[57] In his guidance to Charles he stressed above all things the importance of his role in reinforcing this as king, of reaffirming his own majesty and the delicately calibrated status of those around him. Performing the rituals of kingship was not courtly affectation but critically essential to the survival of society as it ought to be.[58] As Newcastle rhetorically enquired of his pupil:

> ... what preserves you kings more then Ceremony?, The Cloth of Estates, the distance people are with you, Great Officers, Heralds, Drums, Trumpeters, Rich Coaches, rich furniture for horses, Guards, Martialls Men making room, disorders to be laboured by their staff of office, and crie 'now the King comes' ... even the wisest though he knowe it & [be] not accustomed to it, shall shake of[f] his wisdom & shake for feare of it, for this is the mist [that] is cast before us ...'[59]

Newcastle's guidance on the subject of majesty did not end there. To him the most successful sovereign combined the force of absolute majesty with occasional gestures of gentlemanly humanity. 'You cannot put on to[o] much King, yet even there sometimes a Hat or a smile in the right place will advantage you', he explained. For example, he suggested, in the thick of the great procession to chapel, a word of recognition and thanks to the minor nobleman carrying the sword 'would infenitly please & oblige them' and so propagate just the sort of mixture of love and loyalty which a king most needed from his subjects. This 'civility' in the midst of ceremony was, said Newcastle, 'the thing y^t I have discoursed to you most'.[60]

For almost four years Charles was in the earl's care, receiving his counsel and striving to win his approval, and it seems impossible that Newcastle's tutelage did not fundamentally form him. That Newcastle practised what he preached with regard to the importance of ceremony and decorum is shown by his dealings with the Master of the Ceremonies, the official responsible for diplomatic ceremonial. In May 1638, only a matter of weeks after Newcastle took control of the prince's household, the ambassador extraordinary from the King of Spain came to visit the prince at Richmond. The Master of the Ceremonies expected the meeting to take place in the relative informality of the prince's withdrawing room, but Newcastle overturned his recommendation, insisting that such an arrangement was too casual and that a state reception room be used instead.[61] On another occasion in October 1639 the manner of the prince's reception of a mid-ranking Spanish diplomat was deliberately altered to ensure that the prince did not give him honours to which the Spaniard's position did not entitle him. Even during his absences from Richmond, the arrangements for the prince's ceremonial life were always referred directly to Newcastle, and the Master of the Ceremonies only proceeded with the earl's written consent. As a senior official of the prince's household at Richmond put it, Newcastle was 'the first wheel of all our motions'.[62]

Subsequent chapters will reveal the extent to which the future king was the product of Newcastle's epistolatory counsel. But that world of dignity and state into which the young Prince of Wales was born and over which Newcastle exercised such vigilance already portended both majesty and menace.

From the moment the infant prince drew his first breath he was playing a leading role in the drama of monarchy. At St James's Palace his apartments were a miniature royal suite, comprising, in sequence, a formal presence chamber, a semi-formal withdrawing chamber and the nursery or bedchamber.[63] As a baby, Charles's rooms were not equipped simply to suit the needs of a child, but were decked out with the splendour appropriate for a royal prince and the heir apparent to the throne. While still a few months old he was provided with a great blue damask bed, edged with silver lace and fringe on which he could be placed in his cradle under a quilted cover of matching fabric. Also upholstered in the same rich material were a high chair (for the prince), six folding stools (for high-status visitors) and four low stools (for second-tier visitors), as well as a 'swathinge' stool, a screen and rich covers to lay on tables, for wrapping and dressing the child.[64] As ever, his household attendants themselves were part of the image of princehood. On his first birthday, for instance, they were all given rich fabrics from which to stitch lavish costumes to mark the occasion: his Coffer Keeper a gown of satin with silver lace and his nurse and rockers gowns of lemon coloured satin with taffeta linings.[65]

The exquisite silk damask stools in the royal nursery were not for the ease of the nurses, but were the furniture of international diplomacy. Before his second birthday, the prince was already actively participating in the elaborate choreography of court life. When diplomats arrived at court, after formally presenting their credentials to the king and queen, they paid their respects to the royal children. Thus in January 1632, the day after his audience with Charles I and Henrietta Maria, the Venetian ambassador, Gussoni, was presented first to Prince Charles (aged 18 months) and then to Princess Mary (aged barely six months) in their respective apartments at St James's.[66] For especially important visitors, Charles would be brought out to receive alongside his parents. So in the month of his third birthday he was brought to Whitehall and stood at his parents' side in the privy gallery at the second audience of the French ambassador the Marquis de Fontenay.[67]

In an age when peoples and kingdoms were being riven by doctrinal conflict, the religious education of the heir to a throne was a matter of national interest and importance. At the age of five, the Prince of Wales was already participating in public royal worship in the chapels at St James's and Richmond. His spiritual life was the responsibility of his chaplain, Dr Andrew Claire, who ensured the chapels were furnished with all the equipment necessary for the dignified and reverential worship of which his father so emphatically approved.[68] One of the major matters of contention between the low and high movements within the Anglican Church was the question of the placement of the altar. For the Laudians Holy Communion, or mass, was the central act of all worship, the crucial sacrament at which the priest acted as a divinely inspired medium between God and man. Consequently the communion table needed to be treated with the utmost reverence, placed at the extreme east end of the church, raised up and railed off to express its sacred status. For the Puritans, hearing and heeding the word of God were more important activities than taking Holy Communion, which they viewed as a communal act of commemoration in which the presiding clergyman was more administrator than medium. For them the proper place for the altar was in the middle of the church placed long-ways to allow the congregation to gather round it, and treated with respect but not reverence.

In the prince's chapels a thoroughly Laudian arrangement was instituted. At St James's the altar was placed against the liturgical east wall, and a 24-foot balustrade was set up across the room to separate it from the congregation, with a similar arrangement at Richmond. The altar itself was richly dressed, covered with costly fabrics – an altar frontal and pall – and with a magnificent carpet laid before it. Two great gold candlesticks, two gold basins and a large Bible and Book of Common Prayer were placed on it. Gilt plates, additional linen and towels were provided for the service of communion, with rich vestments brought from the king's own vestry for the celebrants. The clergy wore surplices and copes, the latter much disapproved of by the puritans, and the congregation received the sacrament with the utmost reverence on their knees.[69] The full effect made the prince's chapels the physical embodiment of high-church Anglicanism: arranged to give richness and beauty to worship, and to ensure that the priest and the altar were dressed and equipped with the grandeur that reflected their special connection to God.

As well as worshipping in his own chapel, the prince would occasionally attend chapel alongside his father at Whitehall or one of the other royal palaces. The hierarchy of monarchy was strictly maintained and reflected on these occasions. The prince walked immediately behind the king in the procession to chapel from the royal apartments, and sat on his father's right hand in the royal closet in the tribune gallery. His great status was signified by the fact that, like the king, he wore his hat throughout the service whilst the rest of the congregation was deferentially bareheaded. When in October 1635, the king's nephew, Charles Louis – recognized in England as Elector Palatine – arrived in London, he joined the king and prince in attending chapel. As a foreign electoral prince, he came a close third in the royal pecking order, walking with the Prince of Wales behind the king, and sitting on the king's left as the prince occupied the more honourable right-hand position.[70]

With the formation of an independent prince's household, an 'establishment book' was drawn up setting out the entitlements of the members of the household, and stipulating how various aspects of his life should be arranged. That Newcastle was in charge of all things in the prince's household is clear from this book. He was first on the list of attendants, and all access to the prince was to be by his approval alone.[71] Ordinances for how the various rooms of the Prince of Wales's apartments were to be run had been issued for Charles I as a boy and for his elder brother Prince Henry. Now as king he decreed that these should be obeyed by his own son.[72] The orders stipulated how the prince's rooms were to be manned and managed by the fifty or so household officials who were

7. The 'circle' held in the presence chamber at St James's Palace for Marie de Medici, Queen Mother of France in 1638. © *The British Library*

stationed in them to ensure the heir to the throne's daily life was conducted with the appropriate decorum.

The year 1638 not only saw the Prince of Wales recognized as an independent figure but also witnessed a number of important public ceremonies in which he took a conspicuous role. In the autumn the prince's grandmother, the Dowager Queen of France, Marie de Medici, landed in England. Having been exiled from France by her son, her arrival for what would be a three-year stay was something of an embarrassment. Nonetheless, she was lodged at the king's expense, and treated with all the formalities that her rank required. Arriving with six coaches, 70 horses and a retinue of 160, her visit started with a grand procession through the streets of London. In the ceremonies of reception, Prince Charles knelt down at his mother's side in the courtyard of St James's Palace as his French grandmother alighted from her coach. The days that followed were filled with receptions and audiences, and the prince took an active part in these, including taking the position of honour beside his father's chair at the great circle in the presence chamber at St James's[73] (*see* Figure 7).

Also in 1638, Charles underwent one of the key rites of princehood: being formally initiated into the ancient English order of chivalry, the Garter. This exclusive brotherhood had been founded by Edward III in the mid-fourteenth century and ever since had been the king's own elite club.[74] Membership was highly prized and extended to only a privileged few: members of the king's own family, favoured foreign princes and a handful of the greatest aristocrats in the land. As a boy, Prince Charles shared his father's enthusiasm for the order and at seven he was already pleading to be allowed to join it.[75] To become a member of the Garter, all candidates needed first to have an ordinary knighthood. Initially the king wanted his son to be made a Knight of the Bath (the grandest variety of ordinary knighthood) and then to lead a procession to Windsor for his installation as a Knight of the Garter. In February 1638 this plan still stood, but it was soon after cancelled and instead the prince's elevation to the order was conducted entirely within the walls of Windsor Castle.[76] Though no specific reason was given for the change, the king may have been nervous about the possibility of disorder. He was naturally cautious about public ceremonial, and the account of Edward II receiving a knighthood, which was dug out by the officials in 1638, can only have worried him more: on that occasion the crowds were so great that two men were killed and the prince only avoided being crushed to death by climbing onto the altar for refuge.

Despite the curtailed plans, the occasion conducted within the privacy of the castle walls was nevertheless splendid. Having assembled in chapter, the knights, led by the king, elected the prince to the order and then invested and installed him as a member. The order of the prince's election was written by the king in intensely personal terms. Addressing the boy as 'our most dear, and entirely beloved son' the king expressed a wish that 'the Emulation of Chevalry will in your tender Years provoke and encourage you to pursue the Glory of Heroick Actions'. This dazzling initiation made a deep impression on the boy. At 11 he already owned six jewel-encrusted garters, and he would wear the insignia of the order about his neck for the rest of his life.[77]

The decision against a great public spectacle for the prince's installation as a Knight of the Garter was part of a wider trend in the later 1630s. The king had started to rein in the rituals of royalty. Instead of the great public events they had once been, he favoured smaller, more intimate occasions tightly focused on the royal family, and without the usual cast of thousands of participants and spectators. So while Prince Charles and James, Duke of York, had undergone lavish public baptisms in the early 1630s, by the end of the decade the king had changed the format for these occasions. In 1637, when Henrietta Maria gave birth to a daughter, Anna, the king decided that her baptism should be celebrated privately. So it was that the Prince of Wales and his sister, Mary, took leading roles in the ceremony, following 'a form newly devised by the king, as there is no memory of its ever having been done before'.[78] In 1640 when the third royal son, Prince Henry, was born, a private christening was again staged and the three sponsors who held the infant at the font were not noblemen and women of the realm, but his siblings the Prince of Wales, James, Duke of York, and Princess Mary.[79] A year later in May 1641 when Mary married William II of Orange, the king ordered that the ceremony should be performed with 'the greatest privacy that might be' in sharp contrast to the full formalities of state which had been staged when the king's sister Elizabeth had married the Elector Palatine in 1613.[80] In reality all these events were still highly formalized and attended by a good many onlookers, but the changes in scale instituted by Charles I in the late 1630s and early 1640s were still significant, and were influenced by the increasingly unstable and threatening political situation in the country as a whole.[81]

Despite his own peaceful routine of dancing lessons, riding classes and cere-monial duties, the decade of the prince's infancy and youth was far from calm in the nation as a whole. For the first decade of his life Parliament was not once called, such was his father's desire to govern without interference. The king's fervent belief in the form of high-church religious worship championed by William Laud – now Archbishop of Canterbury – and his expectation that his subjects would follow his lead in this as in all things brought the storm clouds gathering over the kingdom. The orders for the royal household spelled out the king's view that the role of the court was to set an example that the nation would follow. As the copes and kneeling cushions were being ordered for the Prince of Wales's chapels at Richmond and St James's, so the king and Laud were preparing to impose their chosen form of worship on the nation as a whole – including Scotland.

The Protestant reformation in Scotland had gone further than anywhere else in the British Isles, and the Scots felt great pride in their broadly presbyterian church. However the king, who believed that those who were opposed to bishops were opposed to kings, was deeply suspicious of Scottish forms of worship; so he began a mission to compel his northern kingdom to conform to his view of proper religious practice. In 1637 a slightly adapted form of the English prayer book was published in Scotland and met with instant and almost universal opposition. This set a snowball of protest rolling which saw the issuing of the National Covenant against the ecclesiastical reforms in February 1638 and, at the Glasgow Assembly of December, the articulation of a much more radical and presbyterian vision for the church of Scotland. A fierce standoff between the king and his Scottish subjects was the result. The king took the whole affair as an assault on the very institution of monarchy. The debate, he proclaimed, was not really about whether or not the prayer book was to stand, or even whether or not the Scottish church should be governed by bishops, 'but whether we are their king or not'.[82] A military expedition against the Scots was the dramatic outcome. The results were disastrous for the king. Running a military campaign without the extra money that Parliament normally granted for war was always going to be difficult, and so it proved. The conflict was brought to an end by the Treaty of Ripon, signed in October 1640, with the terms of the settlement held over for discussion in Parliament at Westminster. What would come to be known as the Long Parliament was accordingly summoned, and Charles I's troubles began in earnest.

During the summers of 1639 and 1640, the king was absent from London in Scotland for months at a time, and the pressure of maintaining royal dignity in England fell to the queen and the Prince of Wales. The threat in both years was felt to be strong enough for the king to provide them with dedicated military guards: in 1639 one hundred men for both queen and prince, and in 1640 two hundred at Richmond alone.[83] In March 1639, as a royal army embarked for the north, the king ordered that during his absence his eight-year-old son was to move from Richmond to 'keep his court' at Whitehall Palace. Here the boy was not to occupy his own rooms, some distance from the heart of the palace at the end of the long Stone Gallery, but was instead to take up residence in his father's apartments, as the living symbol of the absent king and of the stability of their dynasty. For three months the prince took a lead role at court, the Master of the Ceremonies bringing ambassadors and other diplomats to be received by him in the king's withdrawing room.[84] It is little wonder that Brian Duppa noted after the events of that summer that the prince 'hastens apace out of his childhood'.[85] Only a matter of days after the prince took these first solo steps in the dance of monarchy, his father demonstrated his own growing impatience with public royal events by refusing calls for a traditional, celebratory 'entry' procession through London. It was also a deliberate reprimand to the capital for its meagre contribution to the costs of the campaign, a means of showing them they were 'not … worthy of that honour'.[86]

In the autumn of 1640 the Long Parliament met and the men who gathered in Westminster were determined not to let their grievances go unaddressed. One of their first targets was Thomas Wentworth, Earl of Strafford, Lord Deputy of Ireland, whose steely management of Ireland was viewed by many as a trial run for England. Impeachment proceedings against Wentworth began in November 1640 and in the first week of May a bill of attainder was passed and the earl sentenced to death. The events of the trial sent the king into a wild panic but, despite his written promise to Strafford never to desert him, Charles put his signature to the bill. He was immediately racked with remorse, and the day before the execution tried desperately to persuade Parliament to commute the sentence from execution to life imprisonment. To deliver his appeal he sent his eldest son, the young Prince of Wales. The 10-year-old boy stood before Parliament and added his own anxious pleas for Strafford's life to those of the king. They cut him dead. Treating the prince 'with scant civility', the House of Lords refused even to open the letter and dismissed the petition outright. The following day a crowd of some 200,000 gathered on the rising ground outside the Tower of London, and roared with approval as Strafford was beheaded.[87]

As Prince Charles passed from childhood to adolescence his education continued alongside this growing involvement in the turbulent politics of the day. From the first his father had been strict that he was to associate only with children of appropriate rank, and as the prince grew older he acquired ever more symbols of his status.[88] He was transported in his own royal barge, specially built for

8. Charles II as Prince of Wales, in armour, by William Dobson, 1644. *The Royal Collection © 2007, Her Majesty Queen Elizabeth II*

his use when he was just six years old, and emblazoned with his princely coat of arms. He was attended daily by a drummer beating his royal presence, and he ate his meals from silver-gilt vessels made by the jewel house specifically to replicate the forms of tableware used by his royal parents.[89] At Richmond, under Newcastle's guidance, Charles learned the ancient and defining princely pursuits of which his tutor so approved: hunting, warfare and an appreciation of the arts. The conflict with the Scots, known as the First Bishops' War, can only have made an education in the arts of combat seem more urgent, and after Newcastle rode out against the Scots under the Prince of Wales's feathers, he returned to Richmond to institute daily military exercises for the prince. The prince's armourer carted around the full range of 'Armes, powder, Match shott, colors partizans, drums & halberts' for his training, which involved tuition in everything from the cross-bow to the pistol. This official was also responsible for looking after the prince's magnificent suits of armour, which were to be the very last made by the establishment of 'almain' or German armourers brought to

England by Henry VIII[90] (*see* Figure 8). As well as the stern arts of war, the prince learned the skills of the royal chase, and acquainted himself with the bewildering range of animals kept at Richmond among them spaniels, hawks, greyhounds, pheasants, pigeons, cormorants, antelopes and bears.[91] Newcastle's interest in the arts, and his belief that an appreciation of beauty was one of the necessary accomplishments of a prince, was also reflected in Charles's upbringing. The prince was given works of art by his governor as part of this education, including the 'brasse' statues for which Charles wrote a meticulous thank-you letter. As a result, by the time he was ten the boy had his own art collection including 'pictures statues medalls Books of Prints & drawings'. Thomas Chiffinch, one of the Pages of the Backstairs appointed in 1638, was given special responsibility for this collection, so taking on a role which he and his brother, William, would continue to fulfil until Charles's death almost fifty years later.[92]

The events leading up to Strafford's execution in May 1641 not only saw the prince dispatched on his humiliating mission to beg for Parliament's mercy, but would also lead to the departure of his charismatic governor. Newcastle was implicated in a failed plot to rescue Strafford from the Tower of London. The controversy which resulted gathered momentum over the following weeks and in July the earl decided it was politically necessary for him to resign the post of governor to the Prince of Wales.[93] In his place the king made a compromise appointment, choosing for this highly prominent position someone who would be acceptable to him and appease an irate Parliament. The man in question was William Seymour, Marquis of Hertford, who, despite his early disastrous marriage to the king's cousin, Arabella Stuart, and his own distant claim to the throne, was not a conspicuous royalist. In fact he was brother-in-law, and best friend, to the parliamentarian military leader, the 3rd Earl of Essex. He was also among the twelve peers who had signed a petition urging the king to recall Parliament in August 1640.[94] Hertford was installed at Richmond within weeks of his appointment, and began to fulfil the duties of a role which would soon see his political allegiances start to change.[95]

In August 1640 the Scots had invaded north-east England and Charles I had ridden out at the head of a military force to confront them. The following summer he travelled to Scotland to negotiate terms, leaving London in August and remaining away until November. With Strafford dead and Laud in the Tower on charges of high treason (accused, among much else, of promoting Catholicism) any notion of leaving the Prince of Wales alone in residence at Whitehall as had happened in 1639 was unthinkable. The royal children at first remained at Richmond, and then in September, despite the protests that it caused, the whole establishment, including Hertford and Duppa, moved to join the queen at her palace of Oatlands near Weybridge in Surrey.[96]

During the autumn of 1641 the king's approach to public ceremonial underwent a noticeable change. In 1639 he had stubbornly refused to participate in a public entry into London and was deliberately excluding the public from royal occasions. However, on his return from Edinburgh in 1641, with Ireland now also in rebellion, he seems to have recognized the impact such occasions could have in projecting a forceful image of monarchy.[97] In the first week of November the Prince of Wales was moved out of Oatlands and back into town and public view to take up residence at St James's Palace, where he would remain for the following two months. A few days later it was announced that the queen and Prince of Wales would ride to meet the king at the royal palace of Theobalds, just to the north of London, and then join him in a magnificent procession through the city of London to Whitehall.[98]

The decision to stage a ceremonial entry into the city of London on the king's return was taken in order to create a royalist spectacle that would encourage loyalty in its citizens. The king's principal Secretary of State, Edward Nicholas, repeatedly encouraged the king to agree to an 'entry', arguing that it was an excellent opportunity 'to shew yo[u]rself grac'ous to yo[u]r people, by speaking a short word now & then to them as you passe amongst them, to cheere & encourage them in their dutifull affec'ons'. In agreeing, the king and queen were recognizing the need to win public affection with the sort of public appearances that had been so successfully staged in the past.[99] It is not obvious how this shift in policy was arrived at. Nicholas was clearly important and the queen was also closely involved; indeed the king repeatedly referred aspects of the matter to her. But the role – if any – of the Prince of Wales is obscure. In October 1641, in the weeks before the entry was announced, the prince had been living with the queen at Oatlands and so must, at the very least, have been aware of the discussions that had been underway since September.[100] The decision to stage a grand, public royal ceremony in order to inspire loyalty in spectators and participants alike was an object lesson in the political expediency in which Newcastle had schooled his pupil. If the prince did not promote it, he must surely have recognized it as precisely the course of action that should be taken.

The triumphal entry was staged on Thursday 25 November under thunderous skies. Because of the recent wet weather, the roads and bridges had been boarded and cleared to provide a dignified route into the capital through the mud. The night before, the Lord Mayor and his vast train had ridden out to rain-drenched fields near Kingsland, north-east of the city, and there formed the encampment where the king was to be welcomed. The royal party, who set out at dawn from Theobalds in Hertfordshire, numbered seven: the king, queen, Prince of Wales, Duke of York, Princess Mary, the Elector Palatine and the Duchess of Richmond. The Lord Mayor sent out a troop of almost 80 men dressed in scarlet and silver to meet the royal coach en route and accompanied it to the door of the mayoral tent. There, on the threshold, the Lord Mayor and his senior officers knelt before their sovereign and, with a loyal speech of welcome, proffered the city regalia. The king returned the speech, remarking in what was doubtless a scripted aside, 'now I see that all these tumults and disorders have arisen only from the baser sort of people; and that the affections of the better, and main part of the City have ever been loyal'.[101] The parade into the capital then began. The king and Prince of Wales left the coach and mounted horses in order to show themselves more prominently to the onlookers. They took their places in a ceremonial line-up numbering over a thousand, which set off into the capital through Moorgate. The prince led the central and most prestigious section of the procession: riding behind the massed ranks of the nobility, with equerries and footmen alongside him, and directly in front of the Lord Mayor, who was himself directly before the king. The queen and the rest of the royal party trundled behind the king in the relative comfort of the royal coach. Though the precaution of stationing armed guards along the length of the route had been taken in case of the 'panique' predicted by some, the procession was greeted by loud and apparently loyal acclamations from the crowds of 'giddy people'.[102] The cavalcade stopped at the Guildhall for a grand ceremonial meal served to the royal party and 150 other diners, before travelling on to Whitehall by torchlight. As they passed St Paul's cathedral, the bells of 121 parish churches rang out while the cathedral choir sang from the south door. In the course of the proceedings the king knighted several senior civic officials, returned the 'joyful acclamations' of the crowds with 'great expressions of joy' and, at the end of it all, embraced the Lord Mayor and asked him to thank the whole city for such a glorious welcome.[103]

In spite of the rain and the predictions of disorder, the event seems to have been genuinely magnificent. The Venetian ambassador, who had no particular reason to spin the occasion to Charles I's advantage, wrote of its splendour and reported that the king and prince were met throughout the city with 'universal acclamations' of support. Not only did commentators consider the event to have passed off gloriously, but its success was such that a dramatic change in the king's waning political fortunes was immediately foretold. The Venetian ambassador gave a detailed report of the occasion. He explained to the Doge and Senate that it looked set to be of the greatest political significance: 'the pomp and circumstance in this connection give rise to hopes that the aspect of affairs here may yet change'.[104]

But all the hopeful predictions came to nothing. While the city officers had been putting in place the crowd barriers and bright hangings which lined the processional route, the House of Commons had been passing the Grand Remonstrance, a declaration which exhaustively listed the misdeeds of the reign and demanded that the king only appoint councillors with their approval. In the standoff that followed, the king rashly ordered the arrest of those MPs he held responsible for his troubles, and so brought matters swiftly to a head. In the midst of the crisis, the king lost his nerve. On the evening of Monday 10 January, without warning, he fled London with his wife and children, now desperate to escape those very crowds whose cheers of support had so lifted his spirits just two months before.[105]

3

War

The king, queen and royal children travelled from Whitehall to Hampton Court, a distance of some 20 miles, over poor and muddy roads in the pitch-dark on the night of 10 January 1642. Having given no notice of the move, they arrived to find the great Tudor palace cold, unlit and barely furnished. With no rooms ready, the royal family were forced to sleep together in one bed, huddled close for warmth.[1]

A few days later the king set off for the greater safety of Windsor Castle and began to make arrangements to evacuate his Catholic wife from the kingdom. This was done under the pretext of arranging an entourage to escort their elder daughter Princess Mary to the United Provinces of the Netherlands to join William II of Orange, the husband whom she had recently married. King, queen and princess travelled together to Canterbury and on to Dover, where on 23 February Charles bade Henrietta Maria a tearful farewell.[2]

During this time the Prince of Wales remained at Hampton Court, the subject of an escalating power struggle. Parliament was sure the king would send his son abroad at the first opportunity, and was determined to use his absence from London to gain control of the boy.[3] On his way back from Dover the king asked the Earl of Hertford to bring his son to meet him at Greenwich. Parliament, meanwhile, forbade Hertford from doing so and ordered him to remain with the prince at Hampton Court. Put in an impossible position, Hertford chose to obey his sovereign and the prince was taken to Greenwich. Parliament immediately despatched a delegation to retrieve the prince. When the king arrived from Dover moments before it reached the palace, the delegation quietly slunk away.[4] The king's relief was palpable: as he told Edward Hyde, having 'gotten Charles, I care not what answer I sent to them'.[5] From Greenwich, father and son travelled to the royal house of Theobalds. Parliament considered trying to snatch the prince from there, but decided against it when they heard the king had already left for Newmarket on 'a farther progress'.

So it was that the king and prince started to wend their way north on a journey that was to be longer and more arduous than any prediction. The king would not return to London for seven years, and then only to be tried and executed. The prince, who in his twelve years had never yet left London and its environs, would not see it again for almost twenty years, when after decades of weary exile he finally reclaimed it as king.

On 22 August 1642, in pouring rain, the royal standard was unfurled at Nottingham Castle and the king was formally at war with his subjects.[6] From their reunion at Greenwich, he and the Prince of Wales were together almost continually for three years – years that saw the prince grow from 12 to 15 and during which they crossed and recrossed the northern and western parts of the kingdom repeatedly. In 1642 alone, father and son covered little short of a thousand miles, so gaining a better first-hand knowledge of the kingdom than any of their predecessors since the Middle Ages.

Though the Prince of Wales was only 12 when the civil war began, he was to be personally present at a number of its battles. The first great encounter between the royal and parliamentary armies was at Edgehill, just south of Warwick, on 23 October 1642. Charles and his brother James watched the battle from the back of the royalist line under the supervision of Edward Hyde, a respected royalist lawyer, and a small unit of soldiers. As dusk fell, this little troop was returning to the camp when they encountered a detachment of enemy horse. Prince Charles, as one who was there later recounted to him, 'feared them not, and drawing a pistoll out of one of your [Charles's] holsters, and spanning itt, resolved to charge them...' Help came before any shots were fired, but the incident demonstrated that Newcastle's lessons had raised a thirst for battle in the young Prince of Wales. Two years later, he was no longer a bystander, and at the battle of Cropredy Bridge, he rode into combat alongside the king in the body of the royalist army.[7]

Though king and prince spent the years 1642–5 fighting for the kingdom, great care was taken to maintain the appearance and dignity of majesty in these adverse conditions. When the king arrived in York in the spring of 1642, he and his court plunged immediately into the royal cycle of Easter events. Among these was the service of the 'maundy', a long-standing royal ritual in which the feet of paupers were bathed in imitation of Christ's washing of his apostles' feet at the Last Supper. Though Charles I did not personally perform the ritual, it was in his name that the Lord Almoner sponged the feet of a collection of poor men at York Minster on 7 April.[8] Days later the feast of St George, the patron saint of the Order of the Garter, was celebrated with all the pomp and spectacle normally to be seen at its traditional home of Windsor Castle. The feast had not been held the previous year, and St George's day, 23 April, was still over a fortnight off; to avoid delay the king simply billed the event as the late staging of the 1641 feast. The officers of the king's household moved a huge amount of equipment up to York for the ceremony and a full list was issued of court officers whose attendance was required, which included, for instance, the Gentlemen of the Privy Chamber, who were to carry the king's canopy.[9] Also among those called to York were the king's musicians, who complained bitterly at being made to make the journey when they had not been paid for two years.[10] At the same time the king, keen to ensure no conspicuous absences from the great event, asked for the attendance or formal resignation of the prominent parliamentary leaders who held two of the most senior positions at court: Robert Devereux, third Earl of Essex, the Lord Chamberlain and Henry Rich, first Earl of Holland, the Groom of the Stool.

With civil war on his hands, the king turned to his family to reinforce his own and his dynasty's majesty and legitimacy. The Prince of Wales participated in the Garter feast as a knight of the order but, more importantly, the occasion was used for the induction of his younger brother, James, Duke of York. The nine-year-old James had until this point remained in London with the Marquis of Hertford but was now summoned to York for the great event. He arrived with his governor in a procession of almost a thousand horse, the citizens of York celebrating his entry by lighting great bonfires in his honour.[11] Shortly afterwards the duke and his first cousin, Prince Rupert, son of Charles I's sister Elizabeth, were duly elected knights of the ancient order. While James was invested with the insignia of the order in person, Rupert had yet to arrive from the continent. The king therefore held over this second investiture until it could be performed, with an equally dramatic sense of timing, four months later at Nottingham, as the royal standard was raised.[12]

In the autumn of 1642, with London firmly in Parliament's hands, the royalist base was established at the ultra-loyal city of Oxford. Here, over the following four years, life would comprise a curious combination of the momentous and the mundane. The royalist troops mustered on Bullingdon Green, huge new earthwork defences were erected around the city, and carts loaded with wounded soldiers periodically trundled in from the battlefields. The colleges became palaces, Merton for the queen, Christ Church for the king; and when they were not on campaign much of the round of royal life continued, the king and his sons attending chapel, playing tennis and dining with friends. The importance of maintaining dignity and decorum was always high in Charles I's considerations: special orders governing the royal household in Oxford were issued, chapters of the Order of the Garter met, and in the magnificent Tudor hall at Christ Church the Maundy Thursday foot-washing rituals were held.[13]

In addition to the king's court officials, the Prince of Wales was attended by a substantial corps of his own staff. Away from London, his household was overseen by one of the two Gentlemen Ushers of his Presence Chamber, the most senior officers concerned with the prince's household 'above stairs'. The two men who held this post, waiting on the prince in turns, were John Ayton and Henry Jay, both of whom had learned their roles under the Earl of Newcastle and were well versed in how the household should operate regardless of its location. They were assisted by one of the secondary ushers (known as 'quarter waiters' in reference to their cycle of attendance), and a series of more junior officials. So in 1643, for example, over 30 ceremonial officers were in attendance on the prince. These included Henry Jay, Gentleman Usher of the Presence Chamber, Robert Kilvert, the Quarter Waiter, Philip Palmer, the prince's cupbearer who served him at formal meals, and Philip Flood a more junior Groom of the Presence Chamber. In addition, teams of Grooms of the Privy Chamber and Great Chamber accompanied the prince, as did six footmen, eight yeomen of the guard and the grooms and ushers responsible for his clothes and furniture.[14] The last, the officers of the Wardrobe, had the difficult task of ensuring the lodgings which the prince occupied were appropriately furnished, often doing so under extremely tricky circumstances as the prince travelled rapidly from place to place.[15]

While the household officers toiled to ensure Charles was always attired and attended as a prince of the blood royal, a number of set-piece ceremonial events were staged that reinforced his status. After the Garter Feast of April 1642, on 2 October the prince had to take the lead in a ceremonial feast staged at Raglan Castle in the Welsh marches, where he had been sent by his father to rally support. The castle was decked out in magnificent hangings which depicted the stories of the 'ancient britons' from whom the Welsh were proud to claim descent. After a ceremonial entry and a great feast, the prince was presented with gifts ranging in value from a huge gold plate to a fat goat. He then made a speech of thanks in which he played on his title of Prince of Wales to make common cause with the assembled crowd. At Oxford, where king and court were quartered when not campaigning, the Prince of Wales and his brother were created MAs of the university in Convocation House, and in January 1644 they took their seats in a 'house of Lords' which the king assembled in the university's great lecture hall.[16]

Having chosen king over Parliament in February 1641, the Earl of Hertford went on to become one of the staunchest of the king's supporters.[17] In January 1644 he was appointed to the Earl of Holland's vacant post of Groom of the Stool. This ancient position had once entailed attending the king on his stool, or privy; by the early seventeenth century, though, a team of junior staff usually discharged such responsibilities, while the Groom of the Stool ran all aspects of the king's private apartments and acted as the king's closest senior attendant. Hertford's loyalty would remain firm to the last. On the icy morning of 8 February 1649, he would be one of those who carried the coffin containing the king's dismembered body to its burial place in St George's chapel. Yet, when appointed governor to the prince seven years earlier, Hertford had been neither a royal intimate nor even someone on whom the king could rely. He was to be a slight presence in the Prince of Wales's life, and once the civil war began in earnest the two were seldom in one another's company. According to one contemporary biographer, Hertford ensured the prince's education continued but at a remove; having been elected chancellor of Oxford in October 1643 he put the great minds of the university at the prince's disposal, providing 'for him severall worthy persons in the quality of Tutors for his instructions in all such languages and Sciences as were convenient for the accomplishment of a Prince'.[18] In 1644 a third nobleman would be appointed to the post of governor to the Prince of Wales. This was Thomas Howard, Earl of Berkshire, a boyhood friend of the king and second son of the great Earl of Suffolk, builder of Audley End. He had been Master of the Horse to Charles before his accession, and had travelled with him and the Duke of Buckingham on their trip to Madrid in 1623.[19] Berkshire may have spent more time with the prince than Hertford, but seems otherwise to have made little impression in the post. According to Edward Hyde, the decreasing calibre and influence of the prince's governors was not coincidence, but deliberate policy:

the king had decided to take his son's education into his own hands.[20]

Before the chaos of the civil war, the king had occasionally intervened in his son's tuition. In January 1637, for instance, when the Venetian ambassador was received by Charles I, the Prince of Wales proffered his hand to the ambassador in so formal a manner that the king corrected him: 'reproving the prince for having received me too stolidly', the ambassador recalled in his despatch.[21] In 1642, as the king and his entourage travelled north, one of their many stops was at Huntingdon, from which the royal party made an outing to the famous chapel at Little Gidding. Here a magnificent Bible was produced which the king showed to his son. Turning the pages and reading from it, he told the prince 'Charles, here is a book that contains excellent things, This will make you both wise and good.' After the lucky escape of February 1642, the king was determined to keep the Prince of Wales out of Parliament's hands at all costs, having 'no resolution more fixed in him, than that the Prince should never be absent from him'.[22] The war brought them together, both as mentor and pupil and as father and son. When they rode off from Little Gidding, the king shot a hare and the prince leapt from his horse to retrieve it; the creature was still alive and the prince chased it through several streams, before presenting it, laughing and breathless, to his father.[23] The king was prepared to reprove as well as indulge, and an onlooker later remembered him ticking the prince off for giggling during a service at the church of St Mary the Virgin, Oxford. It seems impossible that spending three full years in such close company with his father did not have an effect on the prince, not least in fostering a sense of the responsibility of the role he would inherit. Indeed, the royalist cause was increasingly seen not just as the king's but as the king's and prince's together. In January 1642 Charles I ordered a gold medal to be struck to commemorate the loyalty of his subjects, which was to feature not only his own image but also that of 'our dearest Sonne Prince Charles'. The following year the mint at Oxford was asked to produce silver badges to be awarded to soldiers for distinguished acts in the royalist cause; they were to bear the image of both the king and prince, identified as 'Charles R' and 'Charles P'.[24] Standing before the massed troops at Kingsmore in Somerset on 23 July 1644 the king promised the crowd that their loyalty would be rewarded, remarking, with calm foresight: "'If I live not to do it, I hope this young Man, my son (your fellow Souldier in this expedition) will, to whom I shall particularly give it in Charge"'.[25]

The civil war was not going well for the king. Parliament's stronghold was in East Anglia and the south, while the north and west (including Wales) were the royalist heartlands. After inconclusive engagements in the first months, 1643 saw the royalist army in the ascendant, defeating their enemies at a series of summer battles, with Prince Rupert taking the great city of Bristol after a dramatic siege in July. As Parliament's forces became better organized and disciplined, however, fortunes began to shift. In 1644, though they reclaimed territory in the south-west, the royalists suffered the terrible defeat of Marston Moor, which effectively lost them much of the north, and come the following year their hold on the west would start inexorably to weaken.

After keeping his son with him for three years, the king decided in the early months of 1645 that the risk of their both being taken captive was growing too great for the arrangement to continue. This was an idea with which the king had been toying for some time, but it was in March 1645 that 'his majesty told them he found it absolutely necessary to pursue his former resolution of separating the Prince his son from himself, that the enemy might not, upon any success, find them together, which, he said, would be ruin to them both'. The move was not just one of political expediency, though. He told Edward Hyde some months earlier that 'it was now time to unboy him, by putting him into some action and acquaintance with business, out of his [the king's] own sight'.[26] At 15 the prince was swiftly becoming his own man, and was starting to strain at his father's authority. When one of Oliver Cromwell's officers was arrested and brought to Oxford, Prince Charles asked the soldier in charge what they were going to do with their prisoner. On being told that he was being taken to the king, the prince replied 'Carry him rather to the gallows and hang him up, for if you carry him to my father hee'le surely pardon him.'[27] In December 1644, when negotiations had been going on in Oxford, one diarist observed that the prince was far from following his father's lead, noting instead that 'Prince Charles made some overtures ... which did much startle the king'.[28]

Now encouraged by this show of independence, Charles I gave his son nominal charge of the royalist forces in the west country in the early spring of 1645. Based in Bristol he was advised by a distinguished council, including his governor, Lord Berkshire, the royalist general, Lord Hopton, three peers (Lords Capel, Brentford and Culpeper) and a man who was to feature large in the prince's life for the next 20 years: the Chancellor of the Exchequer, Sir Edward Hyde. Hard work, intellect and an advantageous marriage had propelled Hyde from relatively modest origins into the king's inner circle. But he was no fawning courtier; an accomplished lawyer, Hyde was both a critic of some of the royal policies of the 1630s – which he considered to disregard the legal structure of the land – and a staunch supporter of the king as the country melted into civil war. He was brilliant, if short-tempered, with a disciplined mind and an unshakeable belief in the need for political and religious stability within the framework of the law. Hyde's tendency to be both pompous and prudish would irritate the young Charles, but his loyalty to royal father and son was absolute.

With his own council and command, Prince Charles now considered himself master of his own destiny. In May 1645 he decided to appoint a Gentleman of the Bedchamber, one of his corps of close aristocratic attendants. His choice was the 17-year-old Sir John Grenville. Son of a powerful Cornish family, Grenville had been dramatically wounded at the second battle of Newbury when he was just 15 years old, for which he was subsequently knighted. It is easy to imagine why the Prince of Wales would have wanted this charismatic boy two years his senior in his household. However, such appointments required his father's approval, and he duly wrote to the king for permission. Before doing so, though, the prince announced the appointment so widely that the king was left with little discretion in the matter. Charles I was furious. As he explained to the queen, he had no objection to Grenville's appointment per se, but was unhappy that the prince had forced his hand. Like many parents, the king encouraged the theory of his son's independence but struggled with the reality.[29]

In the event Prince Charles had little time to exercise the command with which his father had charged him. On 14 June 1645 the king's forces were all but obliterated by the New Model Army at the battle of Naseby in Northamptonshire. This was followed by an unstoppable parliamentary march west, which saw the royalist towns of Wessex tumble like dominoes: in July and August Bath, Bridgwater and Sherborne fell, and on 10 September Prince Rupert surrendered the great power-base of Bristol after only six days' resistance, bitterly disappointing the king who wrote of his disbelief that 'one that is so near me as you are, both in blood and friendship, submits himself to so mean an action'.[30] By Christmas the Prince of Wales and his council had been pushed into the furthest tip of the mainland and were sheltering at the great sixteenth-century fortress of Pendennis Castle on the southern Cornish coast.[31] Since September the king had been convinced that the only safe course was for the prince to sail for France; though it was not until March that the Prince of Wales and his entourage finally boarded *The Phoenix*, and cast anchor from mainland Britain. They made, first, for the Scilly Isles and, after an alarmingly close brush with the parliamentary fleet, sailed on for the island of Jersey.[32]

The prince and his council spent three months in Jersey lodged at the coastal stronghold of Elizabeth Castle, a late Tudor fortress built to replace the medieval Mont Orgeuil. Early in the civil war this small but strategically vital Channel Island had fallen into parliamentary hands, but in 1643 the royalist naval officer and Jersey-man, Sir George Carteret, succeeded to the post of bailiff of the island, and swiftly recaptured it. This tough but hugely capable man would keep the island in royalist hands by sheer force of will for almost a decade in the face of fierce parliamentary attempts to reconquer it. He would, in time, be richly rewarded for his loyalty and among his prizes would be an island off Virginia that he would christen 'New Jersey' in honour of his home. Not surprisingly, it was to his offshore haven of cast-iron royalism that the embattled Prince of Wales took himself in the spring of 1645.

A detailed description of the Jersey visit left by one Jean Chevalier casts a light on the sometimes murky issue of how the Prince of Wales's court operated during these years. Chevalier's account makes it clear that, though its presence was in itself a sign of the royalists' dismal fortunes, the court of the Prince of Wales was almost as ordered and magnificent at St Helier as it would have been at St James's. Despite their unhappy situation the prince and his ministers did not behave like beleaguered refugees. The princely entourage numbered some 300 when they reached Jersey, principally comprised of his council and household officers (both 'above' and 'below' stairs), many of whom had their own attendants in tow. Additionally, the usual parade of ushers and grooms of his formal apartments had been augmented with a corps of military officials to maintain personal security and a troop of suppliers and tradesmen, among them his shoemaker and tailor, to maintain personal splendour.[33]

While in Jersey the prince performed the formal royal ceremonies that defined and expressed his status, regardless of the fact that he was only a stone's throw from exile and his father was at that moment adopting an elaborate disguise to escape capture by his own subjects. Among these ceremonies were the rituals of dining and attending chapel 'in public', which were witnessed by substantial crowds of spectators. The formal dinner on 16 April 1646 took place within the castle itself. The crowds jostled in to see the Prince of Wales sitting alone at the table, wearing his hat while all others present were respectfully bareheaded. The prince sat facing the spectators on the long side of a table, with his chaplain standing on his right to begin and end the meal with a prayer. The carver, cupbearer and sewer (or server), messrs Smith, Palmer and Duncombe, waited on their master in the most formal fashion, performing their duties on bended knee. First the prince washed his hands in a silver-gilt bowl, then the various dishes were served up. This was done by the carver, on the other side of the table, cutting pieces from whichever of the many meat and fish dishes Charles chose to eat, first tasting them and then presenting them. The bread, along with everything else, was served on silver or silver-gilt dishes. The cup was also presented on bended knee after its bearer had tasted the contents, and a silver bowl was held under the royal chin as Charles drank to prevent any drops falling on his clothes. Following dessert the officers undressed the table and cleared any remnants of food onto a silver plate; finally Charles rose, the priest gave a closing prayer and the meal ended. The occasion deeply impressed Chevalier, who approved of the decorum and dignity of the royal table. He noted in his diary: 'So that the king's table would be well kept, it was ensured that each official knew his office, and the dishes were laid out in an orderly manner; as a result each officer was prompt to carry out his duties and everything was seen to be done in a harmonious and pleasing fashion.'[34]

While in Jersey, as doubtless had been the case through the civil war, Charles and his entourage attended church with royal formality every Sunday. The importance of the prince being, and being seen to be, an exemplary Anglican was something his father had taken great pains to stress. As the prince left his care, he repeatedly emphasized that though he was to obey his mother in all things, this was to exclude religion, in which the prince was always to defer to his old tutor, Brian Duppa, now Bishop of Salisbury. There is every reason to believe that Prince Charles took the matter of the correct and public religious performance seriously. At Pendennis in the winter of 1645/6 he declared his intention to build a chapel within the castle in an attempt to stave off the 'madness and outrage of those enemies that seeke nothing more than ye spoyling and destroying of such houses'.[35]

In this context it is not surprising that Jean Chevalier should have observed such dignity and grandeur in the prince's religious observance during his stay in

Jersey. He saw Charles attending church in St Helier on two occasions in 1646, on Sunday 26 April and three weeks later on Sunday 17 May, and his descriptions reveal much about how these occasions were conducted. The prince travelled from Elizabeth Castle to the parish church of St Helier in a great procession formed of his own principal officials and local dignitaries. They passed through the streets with drums beating and colours flying, watched by a great crowd of spectators keen to catch a glimpse of the heir to the throne. Once inside the prince was seated on a chair of state set right at the front of the congregation near the altar. The chair stood on a rich carpet and before it was placed an elaborate kneeler, with a long cushion on the lower section to receive the royal knees and another on the upper part to receive the elbows. Here the prince sat through the service, during which one of his own chaplains preached in English. On Sunday 17 May the occasion was conducted with additional grandeur, as it was Whitsun, one of only three occasions a year when the royal family took public communion. By this time Sir George Carteret had repaired and furnished a chapel within Elizabeth Castle for the use of the prince and his court but, regardless, Charles travelled to the parish church to take communion within full view of the local population. As was normal the junior household officials received communion during a morning service, while the prince and his senior officers came separately in the afternoon. The altar was adorned with valuable plate brought by the prince, including a vast altar-plate made of solid silver covered in gold, the like of which Chevalier had never seen. In addition there were two great silver vessels containing the communion wine and two chalices and two patens, on the last of which was the communion bread, cut into long pieces in a form usually reserved for clergymen. The ceremony of offering gold alms at the altar happened first, the great plate being presented to the prince by the minister on bended knees, before being offered up at the east end. The communion service itself followed. The prince was first after the clergy to receive the sacrament which he did kneeling alone before the rest of the congregation came forward. This order of receiving communion was a long-standing tradition which gave visual form to the royal family's claim, as God's elect, to be more than other mortals. The whole occasion greatly impressed Chevalier, who described the prince and his courtiers' reception of the sacrament as being done 'a vecq grand devotion'.[36]

The relative calm of the prince's stay in Jersey came to an end in June, when news reached him that his father was in the hands of the Scots. In an attempt to escape the now all-powerful parliamentarian army, the king presented himself to the Scottish leaders, hopeful of being able to strike a bargain for their support. In the event, neither side would be prepared to accept the terms that the other offered, and the Scots eventually just handed the king over to the English parliamentarian leaders. The queen had been asking Prince Charles to join her in France since he left the mainland. Now with his father's fate hanging in the balance, he decided to delay no more. Most of his council saw a reunion with his mother as defining the end of their authority, so it was largely without them that the prince boarded a ship off the Jersey shore and set sail for France.

4

The shadow of a king

The moment Charles, Prince of Wales, set foot on the soil of France his public persona changed. Though he and his family had suffered considerable hardship during four years of war, fighting bloody battles and living a sometimes cold and uncomfortable existence, few had yet questioned that they were the sovereign family of the kingdom. As soon as the prince's ship weighed anchor from the Channel Islands, all this would change: his personal safety was secured but his princely status was in question.

Visits abroad by members of royal families were, under normal circumstances, rare and carefully planned events. Other than the obvious practical and financial reasons for this, there was a more intangible consideration. The absolute status of a sovereign or prince in his own dominions was beyond dispute. He was treated and addressed by his subjects in ways that properly reflected his position: no one from a commoner to a duke would be likely to claim superiority to their king. However, things were altogether less clear when a prince travelled abroad. When two royal leaders met, who then was superior? And how should this be reflected in protocols of dress and speech? At first glance such questions appear to be ceremonial niceties; but in reality they were the polite exterior of bitter and relentless international power struggles. No European sovereign would learn the truth of this more personally than Charles II.

All personal dealings between princes were, fundamentally, about hierarchy. That the King of Spain was superior to the Elector of Brandenburg was uncontroversial; both parties would agree on this and arrange affairs accordingly. Matters became much more complex when the people or nations in question were closer in standing. Should the King of Spain treat the King of France as an equal? How did the sister of the King of Portugal rank in relation to the daughter of the King of England? Normal procedure in the event of a planned meeting between any two sovereigns or their families was for endless discussion and consultation about precedent to take place between their officials before a single bag was packed. Only when complete agreement had been reached would any visit go ahead. Sometimes negotiations failed and royal visits were abandoned for precisely this reason. What was clearly disastrous was for a trip to be undertaken without any such prior discussions, as once abroad the visiting prince would be virtually powerless to negotiate. In July 1646 this was precisely the situation in which the Prince of Wales found himself. As the Venetian ambassador put it, however hard things had been for Charles in England, it was at least his own country, while 'in France he would be a foreigner, begging his bread and subject to the will of others'.[1]

This, then, was the challenge of the exile. How, without an army or administration, palaces or patronage, to maintain the mystique of majesty? In short, how to be king without a kingdom?[2]

After Charles I had seen his beloved wife Henrietta Maria onto a ship at Dover in 1642, she had first sailed to the United Provinces with her daughter and then journeyed on to France. Here she took up residence in Paris as the guest of her brother, King Louis XIII of France. A year later, when Louis died suddenly, the crown of the great kingdom passed to his four-year-old son, Louis XIV. The boy's mother, Anne of Austria, became Regent, with her every decision overseen by her powerful first minister and lover, Cardinal Mazarin.

Charles, Prince of Wales, arrived in France in July 1646 and would spend the next two years under his mother's eye at this complex court. In the summer of 1648 plans were afoot to invade England and rescue his father, attacking from either Scotland or Ireland; to prepare for the expedition, Prince Charles moved to the court of his sister and brother-in-law, the Prince and Princess of Orange, in the United Provinces. This prosperous little nation was a republic but periodically elected an overlord, or stadtholder, usually from the powerful Nassau dynasty, princes of the small territory of Orange. Mary Stuart's marriage to Prince William gave the Stuarts rich and powerful allies just across the Channel. The Dutch sea-ports were ideal launch pads for an invasion of England, and Prince Charles based himself a few miles from the coast at the Dutch capital of The Hague. As the autumn wore on, Charles I's fate became ever more uncertain and at the end of the year Parliament decided to try the king for treason, charging him with making war on his own subjects. The prince was still in The Hague, his invasion plans unrealized when, on 30 January 1649, his father stepped calmly onto a timber platform on the main public street of Westminster and, before an almost silent crowd, lay down to receive the blow of the executioner's axe. Charles received the terrible news three days later. Tears poured down his cheeks: a son weeping for the loss of his father, and a king for the kingdom which he had both gained and lost.[3]

With Charles I dead, the English Parliament swiftly abolished the monarchy altogether, as well as the House of Lords; bishops and the Book of Common Prayer had been outlawed a few years earlier. As the new republic set about trying to decide what exactly it wanted instead, Charles II, as he now called himself, moved uneasily between Paris, Holland and the Channel Islands. Various schemes for invading Britain and recapturing the throne were entertained, then abandoned, until eventually, in the summer of 1650, Charles made his move. Signing terms with the presbyterian Scots that would have horrified his father, he embarked for the north and on 23 June sailed into the Moray Firth. Although he was greeted with bonfires and bell-ringing, he was in reality little more than a political pawn in the hands of the puritan Scots. His coronation at Scone Palace on 1 January 1651, which might have shored up and celebrated his regal status, verged on the humiliating: before being crowned he was forced to ask public forgiveness for the sins of his family, while the hour-long sermon painstakingly catalogued the misdeeds of his father and grandfather. The occasion was held at Scone, near Perth, as Edinburgh was already in Cromwell's hands and the days of Scottish independence were numbered. With their backs against the wall, Charles and the remaining Scottish army made a mad dash for the south, making it as far as Worcester before being annihilated in the decisive battle fought there on 3 September 1651.

After a daring escape from the battlefield, Charles spent the next three years at the French court. But French enthusiasm for sheltering a refugee was already wearing thin. Finally in 1654, keen to sign a profitable treaty with the English republic, Cardinal Mazarin paid Charles to leave France. Professions of literal and metaphorical brotherhood notwithstanding, the brutal realities of national self-interest prevailed. As one observer remarked, Charles II left Paris 'with the sympathy of all France, as they know full well that the ties of blood are sacrificed to policy and that this compels a king, related to this crown, to wander as an outcast for the sake of flattering Cromwell'.[4]

From France, Charles II travelled to Germany, where he was the guest of a series of princes of the Holy Roman Empire. With the recent death of his brother-in-law, William II of Orange, Holland became an unrealistic refuge, though his sister Mary visited him in Germany and tirelessly promoted his cause. Just as his options were narrowing as nation after nation signed alliances with England, Cromwell snatched Jamaica from the Spanish, and a powerful ally hoved into view. Philip IV of Spain now had an interest in the downfall of Oliver Cromwell and anyone who might accomplish it; he agreed to give Charles II support for an invasion. The Stuart court moved from Cologne to the Spanish Netherlands, and here it would remain from 1656 until Charles was invited to return to England as king four years later.

Sixteen when he first crossed the Channel, Charles would be 29 when he made the final return voyage. The experience of exile brought him striding into adulthood. Even in the salons of Paris he immediately cut a striking figure. At over six foot he was unusually tall, and with his distinctive black hair and handsome face, he always attracted attention.[5] Without the infrastructure of the Wardrobe of the Robes, he still dressed with all the splendour and fashion of a prince. He kept a tailor, John Allen, on his permanent household staff throughout the exile, and at times his own shoemaker as well.[6] Dressing a prince was an expensive business, and in one year alone his officials ran up substantial bills with mercers, tailors and shoemakers, leaving debts for the king's clothing soon standing at a massive 10,000 guilders.[7] In the budget devised in 1654, almost 10 per cent of the funds available for running the royal household was allocated to his clothing.[8] Though much of the king's day-to-day wardrobe was made up by John Allen, his most splendid costumes always came from Paris. Charles cared about clothes and wrote in person to his officials with his sometimes fastidious requirements.[9]

It was also during exile that he grew the slender pencil moustache that he sported for much of his life, carefully clipped and trimmed by his barber, Mr Folliart, who used the freshest whipped egg-white for shaving his master and applied scented essence, powder and pomade afterwards.[10] But Charles was more than a dandy: dressing the part he played was a political as well as a personal act. When he moved to the Spanish Netherlands in 1656, he was keen to ensure he had the clothes needed to make the right impression on the Governor General, and wrote anxiously to Paris for shoes, hats and clothes to create the required effect.[11] Royal dress took on additional significance when it came to bereavement. A long-standing convention dictated that kings should wear the sombre clothes of mourning not just for deceased members of their own family but for those of other royal and princely families. This provided Charles with opportunities to reiterate his claim to regal status. The whole exiled court adopted black costume in 1649 to mourn the death of Charles I, with his heir dressing in deep violet, the mourning colour reserved for kings alone, for an entire year.[12] The death of the Holy Roman Emperor, Ferdinand III, in 1657 provided another opportunity for Charles to don regal costume, and for his court at Brussels to enter a formal term of mourning.[13]

Though he spent a decade and a half in exile, Charles II was never unattended. Out of love, loyalty or sheer lack of an alternative, a stream of royalists, some noble, many not, came to the continent to pay court to him.[14] The size of this group is not easy to pin down (see Appendix 5). As ever, the court was made up of several different though overlapping collections of individuals. One discrete group of people held official positions that involved personal attendance on the king (largely members of his household and privy council); another distinct category comprised those who did not hold such positions but came to court to enjoy its attractions and to try and win influence and favour. These two groups of people themselves brought with them a third group, made up of their families and servants plus tradesmen and other hangers-on, who swelled the numbers attached to the court still further. When Charles arrived at Jersey in September 1649 his entourage, made up of all these groups, numbered around 300.[15] Eight years later, a list of those attached to his court made by the Bruges civic officials named 156 individuals attending the king. As this list does not record the third category of people described above (it contains no women, for example), it would indicate that the exiled court had not substantially contracted since 1649, and may well have been rather bigger.[16] Of the 150 or so named in the Bruges list, only about half were actually in the king's employ, and of those there was a core of about 30 whom the king would take with him on important visits.[17]

The most powerful men at the court-in-exile were Charles II's privy council. This body was made up of a combination of senior royalist noblemen, such as the earls of Bristol, Norwich and Rochester, and of distinguished men of business, notably Sir Edward Hyde and Sir Edward Nicholas. These last two were old friends as well as colleagues and had much in common, though Nicholas was as reticent and self-deprecating as Hyde was short-tempered and stubborn. A brilliant administrator, Nicholas had risen to the important post of principal Secretary of State in 1641, just in time to see its authority crumble with the rest of royal government a year later.

In 1654 members of the council were officially entitled to a monthly payment of 150 guilders as 'boardwages' (payments made in lieu of meals), over twice the amount allowed to the next best rewarded officials. As well as the councillors themselves, there was a small band of council clerks, responsible for paperwork relating to its deliberations, and the porter of the council chamber. Outside the council, the paid employees of the court were all members of the royal household.

Under normal circumstances the royal household was divided into four distinct departments responsible for the different geographical areas of a royal palace: the Bedchamber under the Groom of the Stool, responsible for the king's private apartments; the Chamber under the Lord Chamberlain, responsible for the rooms of state; the Lord Steward, responsible for the kitchens and the household 'below stairs'; and the Master of the Horse, responsible for the stables and royal transport. In exile the separation of the departments remained, but with very few appointments to the senior roles. Having been Charles I's Master of the Horse, Prince Rupert nominally held the position under his first cousin, Charles II. In reality Rupert spent almost no time with Charles during this period, and in any case resigned the office after the two men fell out in 1653.[18] Patrick Ruthven, Lord Brentford, was given the post of Lord Chamberlain in 1649, but on his death in 1651 it was left vacant for several years. In 1653, to general surprise, Charles appointed Lord Henry Percy to the position. But given that Percy was a long-standing member of Henrietta Maria's circle and that Charles II was preparing to leave France permanently, there can have been little expectation on either side that Percy would exercise many of the responsibilities of the position, and indeed there isn't any real evidence that he did so. If Edward Hyde is to be believed, the appointment was simply a tactic by the king to stop Percy from lobbying to be made Master of the Horse, a post to which he considered himself entitled as he had held its equivalent in Charles II's household when he was Prince of Wales.[19] No appointments to the posts of Lord Steward or Groom of the Stool were made during the exile.

The Bedchamber was the most complete of the royal household departments in exile. In the late 1650s there were four Gentlemen of the King's Bedchamber: the Earl of Rochester, the Marquess of Ormond, Lord Gerrard and Lord Wentworth, plus four Grooms of the Bedchamber and two pages. The staff of the king's state apartments was much diminished, a reflection, in part, of his relatively modest living arrangements during much of the exile: a handful of men were appointed Gentlemen of the Privy Chamber, while the four officers attached to the presence chamber in 1649 had dwindled to one by 1657.[20] Religious life at the court, and the king's own devotions, were the responsibility of the Dean of the Chapel, a post held by Dr Richard Steward until his death in 1651 and thereafter of the two royal chaplains, Dr John Earle and Dr Robert Creighton.[21] The kitchens were overseen by a cook (John Sayers), assisted by an under-cook (Giles Rose), a baker, a sommelier and his assistant. The stables were well staffed, as might be expected of an establishment which was so often on the move, with some twenty officials, ranging from the senior equerries to the sumpter-men who looked after the packhorses. A small coterie of men was charged with the king's physical health and appearance: two wardrobe officers, a tailor and shoemaker, a doctor, a surgeon and a barber. A number of miscellaneous other posts also existed including Keeper of the Privy Purse and the king's trumpeter.[22]

Of the 150 or so people listed as part of the exiled court in 1657, a handful had been members of Charles's household before the civil war. Two pages of his Bedchamber, Thomas Chiffinch and Hugh Griffith, had been with him from childhood: Chiffinch had been appointed a Page of the Backstairs in 1638 and Hugh Griffith was already a Yeoman of the Prince's Vestry in 1635. Richard Harding, Groom of the Bedchamber in 1657, had been part of Charles's household for almost as long, having been made a groom when his patron, the Marquis of Hertford, became the prince's governor. Others who remained from before the war were the footman James Jack, the groom Henry White, and George Barker, who had been keeper of the prince's pheasants at Richmond, and now served in the stables. The one other survivor was the king's old French master Peter Massonnet, who now served as a clerk to the Secretaries of State, a role for which this professional linguist must have been well suited.[23] It is noticeable that, with the exception of M. Massonnet, all of these men were very junior officials. At the Restoration many would complain of the influence wielded by such 'little people' who served the king in his privy apartments, but given their constant service over so many troubled years it is hardly surprising that he should have come to trust them.[24]

Much of the routine of court life continued during the exile. The traditional round of 'waiting weeks', the periods when officers were in service, was maintained for the Gentlemen of the Bedchamber at least, though it is unlikely that there were enough staff to allow the usual rotation of weeks 'on' and 'off' for the more junior staff.[25] These junior officials, including the grooms and footmen, were dressed formally in royal liveries, which one of the king's grooms of the Bedchamber was instructed to buy in The Hague and to have made up according to a specific royal pattern. The king's scarce finances had to be stretched to pay for these, and as an economy measure the suits were carefully altered for new officers when members of the household left their posts.[26]

The buildings over which these officials presided, and the style that they were able to maintain, varied considerably. There were two distinct phases to Charles II's exile: the period until 1654 when he was able to enjoy the hospitality of his cousin, Louis XIV, in France and of his brother-in-law, William II, in Holland, and during which he was usually lodged in royal palaces; and the period after 1654 when Mazarin's treaty with Cromwell and William's premature death left him without a powerful royal patron and he was forced to fend for himself.

Though in 1656 Philip IV of Spain agreed to give him aid for an invasion, his support never stretched to the provision of royal lodgings for the exile and his court; indeed the Spaniard refused Charles II's request to live at Brussels with the disingenuous excuse that if he did so they would have to treat him with such magnificent gestures of respect that the cost would be more than Spain could bear.[27]

It is possible to get only a general sense of Charles II's life in the early years of his exile, as the surviving household accounts that contain the requisite detail do not begin until 1654. In 1646 Henrietta Maria had been allocated the great sixteenth-century palace of St Germain en Laye as her residence, plus the use of apartments in the Louvre; so it was in these palaces that Charles II lived when he was in France.[28] However, between June 1648 and his return from the Scottish expedition in October 1651, he was largely itinerant, moving between Paris, the United Provinces and the Channel Islands and occupying a variety of accommodation. When he arrived in the United Provinces in the autumn of 1648, he was immediately allocated 'very good' rooms within the palace of the Binnenhof in The Hague alongside his sister Princess Mary and his brother-in-law William II.[29] When, during that stay, the awful news of his father's execution broke, Charles's status as king was swiftly recognized and within a fortnight he was occupying new apartments.[30] When he had passed through the Spanish Netherlands in June that year he was again lodged in royal houses – at both Antwerp and at Brussels – and was entertained at the expense of his hosts.[31] For just over a year between 1650 and 1651 Charles was in his own kingdom of Scotland. Soon after his arrival Cromwell invaded Scotland from the south and, partly as a result, the court seldom stayed in one place for more than a few days. During the Scottish expedition, though, he lodged partly in his own royal palaces, notably at Stirling and Falkland, and partly with his senior subjects.[32]

Once Charles left France in 1654, he no longer had royal palaces at his disposal and was forced instead to acquire and pay for his own lodgings. Given that it was lack of money which had prevented him from leaving France sooner, it was clear that if he had any chance of living in a dignified manner thereafter, the finances of his court would require extremely careful management.[33] Charles recognized this himself, and wrote to his friend, the Earl of Rochester, on the subject of money in July 1654 explaining that 'I am now putting my Family into some order'. Crucial to this was the young Stephen Fox, protégé of Lord Percy and younger brother of John Fox, a junior household official since 1638.[34] In the summer of 1654 Stephen Fox was given charge of the finances of the exiled court, with the demanding task of supporting that court on an allowance of 6000 guilders a month. The meticulous accounts that he kept testify to the great care with which he carried out his responsibilities.[35] During the next six years the king was much on the move. He travelled from town to town – Cologne, Spa and Aachen in the mid-1650s, on to Bruges and then Brussels in the later years of the decade – and he often moved lodgings within those places as his fortunes allowed. Keen to live in the very grandest establishments he could afford, he was quick to trade up when instalments of his various pensions arrived. In December 1659, for example, when he returned from his trip to Spain having successfully extracted some money from Philip IV, the king immediately gave up his house in Brussels, rented from a civic dignitary, Monsieur de Vig, for 500 florins a year and moved into a far grander establishment belonging to Count Basseny, for which he paid four times the price.[36] When a move to a new location was planned, household officials were dispatched ahead to seek out the best possible accommodation.[37] The search for sufficiently fine lodgings was often a tricky one; when the court moved to the affluent but provincial town of Bruges in the spring of 1656, the king stayed at the house of Lord Taragh for over a month, until the 'handsome accommodation' he wanted could be found.[38]

It is quite clear from the surviving accounts that Charles configured these buildings, however big or small, as English royal palaces. The accounts for equipping the king's house in Bruges in 1656 refer to the royal presence chamber, prayer room, withdrawing room, bedchamber and backstairs – a royal suite of precisely the kind that was be found at one of the smaller royal palaces in England.[39] A decade of exile and a love of French fashion had not persuaded Charles to make any change to the nomenclature, sequence or composition of English royal apartments. At Cologne in 1654–5 the king's apartment comprised a presence chamber, prayer room, withdrawing room, bedchamber, closet and backstairs.[40] The new house in Flanders into which the king moved in January 1659 was grander, arranged with a five-room royal suite, now including a privy chamber and eating room in the sequence.[41]

Given that the plate and linen used in the rooms, and even the staff who manned them, all bore the king's cipher, it seems highly likely that the furnishings were also royal in character.[42] When the king moved into Count Basseny's house in 1659, carpenters and plasterers were called in to put up lath and plaster partition walls and to erect pillars in the royal bedchamber to create a bed alcove. This was almost certainly inspired by the alcove which his grandfather Henri IV had had installed in the bedchamber of the royal pavilion at the Louvre. The teenage Louis XIV had taken up residence in this suite in 1652, on his return from a brief exile from Paris brought about by the political disturbances known as the 'Fronde', and Charles would have known the room well.[43]

Tobias Rustat and his assistant, the staff of the royal Wardrobe, were responsible for the tricky task of furnishing the royal suite on a tight budget and for overseeing the frequent movements of the king from house to house. They worked to equip the king's rooms as finely as limited money would allow, buying and hiring the furniture to do so. The hangings that adorned the walls in most rooms could be rolled up and packed in trunks when the court moved, which was presumably the fate of the Turkish leather hangings bought in 1655 and hung from a series of rods in the king's bedchamber in Cologne.[44] The king's bed could be disassembled into sections that fitted into specially made packing cases, for which Charles himself – having an eye for ingenious inventions – suggested a special wheeled carrying cart be made.[45] Paintings were also to be found in the king's apartments, among them the great picture that hung in the presence chamber at Bruges. It was on loan from a Mr Vouters of Antwerp, and so cost the king only the price of porterage.[46] The king's closet in Cologne was furnished with handsome striped curtains, which could be taken down when he left for the Spanish Netherlands, but the bookshelves of the king's library had to be built anew when the court moved house in Bruges. The books themselves and the other items of the royal cabinet were packed carefully in trunks by the closet keeper, Thomas Chiffinch – among them the locked casket containing the king's personal papers, for which Charles kept the only key.[47]

Despite the best efforts of his household officers, the king's apartments in these rented houses were not as grand as Charles II would have liked, and he did not use them for ceremonial occasions. This may have been personal preference, but it was also proper procedure. Strictly speaking a prince not on a state visit could never receive anyone in his state rooms (presence chamber or privy chamber, *see* p. xv), since his private status prohibited it. It is quite possible that adherence to this rule was the reason Charles seldom, if ever, used his state rooms for royal rituals during the exile, though it may well also have been convenient to enforce this and so avoid the embarrassment of being found in sometimes insufficiently regal state.

Informal meetings within the private rooms were quite a different matter. When princes travelled privately, or 'incognito', this was how all business was conducted. When the Scottish deputation came to Breda to negotiate with the king in 1650, they were shown into the king's bedchamber, with Lord Wentworth formally conveying them in; and in 1660 when the Dutch Estates wanted an audience with Charles II, it was again to a Gentleman of the Bedchamber that they applied. During the exile, Charles grew used to receiving visitors and transacting business in his bedchamber, and would continue the practice when back in England after the Restoration.[48] In this context, the balance of staff in the king's exiled court, with six grooms and pages attached to the Bedchamber and only one to the state rooms, makes perfect sense.

During the dark days of exile, there was a brief period when much that Charles II wished for materialized and he was accepted and inaugurated by his own people, the Scots. When Charles II arrived in Scotland in June 1650, having brokered a disadvantageous deal with the presbyterians, he found a nation divided. After repelling Charles I's attempts to impose Anglicanism on them in the late 1630s, the Scots had been able to insist on a constitutional settlement that gave them a significant degree of independence from royal authority, including the power to elect the executive and judicial officers of state. During the civil war itself, they had first sought to prevent Charles I from crushing the English Parliament and then, when the strength and radicalism of the parliamentary army became clear, many had joined an initiative known as 'the engagement', invading England in 1647 to try to restore Charles I to power. The crushing defeat of the engagers saw the rise to power of the more militant Kirk party, of which the Marquess of

Argyll, the leading Covenanting nobleman, was the most prominent member. Though the Kirk party was strictly presbyterian, its members, like their fellow countrymen, retained both their belief in monarchy and loyalty to the Stuart dynasty. All Scotland was therefore profoundly shocked when news broke that the English had executed their king. On 5 February 1649, less than a week after the event, they proclaimed Charles II King of Scotland.

Charles's experience in Scotland would be bruising. While he had not enjoyed signing the pledges to Presbyterianism with which he had bought the kingdom, the rapturous welcome he had received when he landed must have made him feel that the price had been worth paying. To avoid being intercepted by Cromwellian warships, the king and his followers had sailed far up the east coast of Scotland into the Moray Firth, and there on 23 June 1650 they cast anchor, disembarking at the mouth of the river Spey. From the Earl of Huntley's great fortified manor house Bog of Gight (later called Gordon Castle), where they spent their first nights, the party travelled south, reaching Aberdeen four days later. Here they were lavishly entertained by the magistrates of the town and lodged at their expense in a handsome merchant's house opposite the Tolbooth (to which the hand of the executed royalist leader, the Marquis of Montrose, was gruesomely nailed).[49] From Aberdeen they set out towards Edinburgh. In the capital the news of the king's landing had been greeted with wild celebrations: bells tolled, the dancing in the streets continued until daybreak and even the poorest traders tossed their furniture onto the bonfires to feed the flames. As the king travelled south, the heralds, dressed in their dazzling cloth of gold tabards, processed to the Edinburgh mercat cross and formally proclaimed that Charles II had been admitted to the exercise of his sovereign power.[50] On 2 August the king rode into the city, passing through Canongate and processing up the hill to Edinburgh Castle where the canons fired in his honour.

But despite the clamour of celebrations, Scotland was preparing for war. With the monarch proclaimed and installed in Scotland, Cromwell foresaw that it was only a matter of time before an invasion to reclaim the English throne would be launched, and he decided to stage a pre-emptive strike. As Charles was making his triumphant tour, the English army was marching north and by the autumn most of the south-east corner of the country, including Edinburgh, was in their hands. The Scottish forces had mounted a valiant defence, and Charles himself did much to spur them on with morale-boosting visits to their encampment at Leith, but they were in the end no match for Cromwell's fighting machine.[51]

As blows were being exchanged in south-eastern Scotland, the rest of the country was relatively peaceful and Charles moved back and forth between the great royal and courtier houses of Fife and Perthshire. As formally proclaimed king, he enjoyed all the ceremonial reflections of status that he would spend so much of the 1650s seeking. He lived in his own palaces with their state rooms handsomely furnished; he received his meals in the royal fashion, the dishes served by kneeling officials; and he rode out to hunt and hawk, regally attended on the finest horses.[52] But despite all this, with no role in the exercise of executive authority he was, in reality, almost powerless. In the words of one contemporary he was 'at best but the shadow of a King'.[53] Still worse, he found himself imprisoned by the very conventions that were supposed to elevate him. The Scottish Parliament appointed a Committee of Estates charged with advising the king, but in reality they governed entirely without reference to him. In effect the whole episode was an elaborate charade. The king pretended to be a presbyterian, enduring endless prayers and fasts – on one occasion sitting through six sermons on the trot. Meanwhile the Scots pretended to respect his authority, scraping and bowing in deference while excluding him entirely from government and delivering bitter diatribes against the deeds of the Stuart dynasty from the pulpit.[54]

About ninety people had travelled from the Low Countries with the king, most holding positions in his household.[55] For obvious reasons he could not be seen to be travelling with Anglican chaplains, though in reality two came in his party as secretaries.[56] Within days of landing, the Scots tried to dismiss most of these royal servants as unsuitable 'malignants'. Over time, many were removed and the king, increasingly isolated from those he trusted, was kept under constant surveillance.[57] The prime mover of this regime was Archibald Campbell, Marquess of Argyll. A committed presbyterian of diminutive stature and with a disfiguring squint, Argyll's unprepossessing appearance masked a politician of rare skill and the nobleman who had taken the hardest line on negotiating with the king in the late 1640s. Charles I had known well the ways of this wily Campbell, and when Argyll assured him he would be safe and honourably treated in the Scots' hands, the king had remarked – with a powerful premonition of the fate that would later befall his son – that this meant he could be 'put into prison provided he be served by persons on their knees'.[58]

Although Argyll believed monarchy was the proper form of government, he also believed that monarchs had to be closely managed to ensure they ruled in the interests of their subjects. When Charles II came to Scotland in 1650, Argyll was in the ideal position to put this doctrine into action: as the de facto leader of the Kirk party, he could manage the king politically, and as hereditary Master of the Royal Household in Scotland, he could control the king personally. In the royal apartments, Argyll used the rules of access to prevent the king from meeting anyone he considered unsuitable. Though the moderate noblemen who had joined the 'engagement' were Charles II's natural allies, they had been excluded from power. When these old engagers tried to visit the king, Argyll and his cronies loitered menacingly in the royal apartments to prevent it; with his son, Lord Lorne, serving as Captain of the King's Guard, there was little Argyll did not see. In July 1650 the Earl of Carnwath managed to slip through to visit the king in the privy chamber at Falkland Palace but Argyll quickly had him escorted out of the building and threatened him with execution if he ever returned.[59] The terrible truth was that rules of access only worked in the king's favour if he was genuinely powerful, in which case it was in the interests of those operating them to serve him. When the king was a pawn, the rules of access were a gift to those who wanted to control him. The regulations for access to the king of January 1651 were issued ostensibly to ensure orderliness in the household of the newly crowned monarch, but in reality they increased even further the control that the ruling party had over him.[60]

During the exile, Charles grew accustomed to receiving visitors in his bed-chamber, which, as he was travelling in a 'private' rather than a 'state' capacity, he could not avoid doing.[61] Now that he was in Scotland, though he could (and did) legitimately receive visitors in the state apartments, he used his bedchamber even more, as it was the only place where he had anything resembling privacy. It was in the bedchamber that he had meetings and discussions of any sensitivity, with visitors being brought in discreetly by the king's servants without the Scots intercepting them.[62] The Scots recognized that the Bedchamber was the area in which the king had the most control over his own activities, and in August 1650 they insisted he accept the appointment of a series of their nominees to his Bedchamber staff.[63] This room now being too closely watched for Charles to feel comfortable, he started holding meetings instead in obscure corners of the grounds, meeting Lord Dunfermline secretly in the gardens and Lord Ogilvy in a summerhouse by the river.[64]

Three months after the arrival of the king, the Committee of Estates demanded, again, that most of his household should be removed. The king finally rebelled. On the afternoon of 3 October, he set out, ostensibly for an afternoon's hunting, with a small coterie of his household officers. In fact he was making an escape, probably in the hope of leading a royalist uprising, though he may have intended to make a dash for Holland. He rode almost 50 miles that day, but the initiative soon faltered and two days later he was found in a filthy cottage sleeping on a straw mattress, exhausted and afraid. After this, even hard-line Scots like Argyll realized they were pushing too hard. On his return, he was finally invited to attend the meetings of the Committee of Estates, which now took place in the king's own apartments, and a date was at last set for the coronation.[65]

Coronations were the ultimate expression and endorsement of the legitimacy of a ruler. For Charles, as he sailed for Scotland in June 1650, the prospect must have been extremely appealing. He eagerly anticipated the show and splendour of such events and, soon after his arrival, he took Sir James Balfour, the senior Scottish herald, aside at Falkland and dictated to him in great detail what he wanted the heraldic devices of each rank of the royal guards to be. Arrangements for the coronation were to have begun immediately the king landed, but the event was repeatedly postponed, first to August, then September and then indefinitely – the English invasion providing an unanswerable excuse for the delay.[66] In October a new date was agreed: 1 January 1651.[67] Over the course of that summer, it had become clear that no amount of formality could redress the weakness of his position; in fact the rules of formality might actually be exacerbating it. As it was for the king's daily life in his palaces, so it would be in the coronation: the conventions of kingship could all too easily be manipulated to oppress the one they were supposed to elevate.

The organization of the coronation was put into the hands of a committee formed of Scottish noblemen and ceremonial officers, who duly considered what form the occasion should take. The last Scottish coronation, that of Charles I in 1633, had taken place relatively recently, and so there was little trouble in establishing the form of the event. The committee proposed an essentially traditional ceremony, but with a number of exceptions. These were almost all adjustments to make the occasion more presbyterian: there was to be no Eucharist during the service, there would be no singing, the king would not be crowned by a clergyman, and – crucially – there would be no anointing.[68] Because Edinburgh was in the hands of the English, the event could not take place at Holyrood Abbey and it was decided, instead, that it should be held at Scone. Here the ruins of Scone Abbey had been transformed into a fashionable new house by Sir David Murray some forty years before.[69] But the real attraction was its association with the inauguration of Scottish kings in the Middle Ages, most famously Robert the Bruce. The king took up residence in Murray's house some days before the event and from his bedchamber there he processed in his princely robes towards the chapel on Wednesday 1 January 1651.

The ceremony lasted several hours. It started with a procession, in which the king was flanked by the great noblemen of the kingdom carrying the Scottish regalia, and which conveyed him from Murray's house to the chapel on the moot hill at Scone (see Figure 9). Inside, Charles sat, with the Scottish regalia laid out on a table beside him, while the sermon was read. Once this was completed he swore his commitment to the Covenant. He was then 'presented' to the congregation, who signalled their approval of his accession and willingness to obey him by crying out 'God Save King Charles the Second' – a section of the ceremony known as the 'acclamation'. After the king had sworn the coronation oath, and thus the mutual commitments of monarch and people had been made, the moment came for the investiture itself. Charles ascended the great stage erected in the middle of the church to take his seat in the chair of state. One by one, senior noblemen bestowed on him the symbols of sovereignty: the Lord Great Constable gave him the sword, the Earl Marshal the spurs, the Earl of Crawford and Lindsey the sceptre, and the Marquess of Argyll placed the crown on the king's head. After receiving the homage of the congregation, Charles walked out onto a viewing platform and showed himself to the assembled people, before returning to parade in full dress back through the crowd to Murray's house.[70]

On the face of it the event was a great success. Even Edward Hyde, a stickler for ceremonial niceties, described it as having happened 'with great solemnity and magnificence', and reports of it were soon carried abroad. But for Charles himself, the undoubted satisfaction of being invested as king by his people must have been tainted by the way the event was conducted. The traditional days of fasting and prayer before a coronation were, in this instance, turned into opportunities for the Scots to enumerate the wrongs of his father and grandfather.[71] At the event itself, the sermon, which lasted over an hour, was preached by Robert Dowglas, one of the most distinguished clergymen of his day; his subject was the crowning

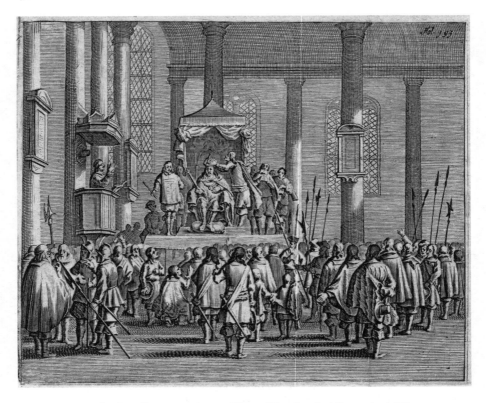

9. Charles II's coronation as King of Scotland at Scone in 1651.
© *Trustees of the British Museum*

of kings in troubled times, but he allowed himself to muse at length on the sins of the house of Stuart, describing Charles I in particularly critical terms, as one who was responsible for perverting religion 'all the dayes of his life'. The lecturing was not just confined to the sermon: at the moment of coronation, as Argyll lowered the crown onto the king's brow, he asked publicly that God should purge it of 'the sins and transgressions of them that did reign before'.[72] Charles II had complained before of what he considered to be unwarranted and unnecessary criticism of his father's actions, asking the Scots to be 'sparing of his fathers name and memory', but even on this great occasion he was forced to endure it, and it must have left him smarting with indignation.[73]

Nine months after his Scottish coronation, Charles left Scotland. The parliamentary armies had advanced with such determination that by the summer of 1651 the king felt he had no choice but to lead a Scottish army to invade England. He crossed the border with almost 20,000 men and marched south with amazing speed, reaching Worcester by the end of August. On 3 September he faced Oliver Cromwell across the battlefield. The young king led his forces with real bravery and charisma: riding up and down the battle lines rallying troops and officers alike, and risking his own life as much as any other in the thick of battle. Though the royalists fought valiantly, they were outnumbered two-to-one by their opponents, and defeat was inevitable. Slipping away from the devastation of the battlefield, Charles spent the next six weeks on the run, a fugitive in his own country. He came very close to capture on several occasions, among them the day he passed hiding in a large oak near Boscobel House, from which he could see the parliamentary soldiers searching for him in the dense woods below.[74] But thanks to the efforts of a network of royalists, among them many Catholics, he survived. At 8 a.m. on 15 October a boat bearing the king left Shoreham on the Sussex coast for France.

Back in Paris, Charles cut a heroic if rather tragic figure, telling tales of his life on the run after his army's defeat at Worcester. But it was not just the battle that had been a failure; though he had gained a crown, bestowed in a formal coronation – unquestionably a symbolic advantage to an exiled king – the whole experience had been deeply disillusioning. In the course of it he had learned what terrible torture it could be to reign without ruling, and that without power the rituals of royalty could actually be the braces and manacles of royal authority. Little wonder that when his glamorous French cousin asked him about the expedition, his flirtatious mood turned temporarily to thunder as 'he spoke of the miserable life he had led in Scotland'. He soon remembered himself and explained playfully that the memory of the horror faded in such charming company as hers.[75]

Charles II's overriding concern throughout his exile was raising the money and men he needed to recapture his kingdom. Though some aid was expected – and a little received – from within Britain, it was from other European rulers that the decisive assistance would need to come. In this context, the question of whether the princes of Europe were prepared to treat him as the sovereign he considered himself to be, or as the private individual that the English republic had branded him, was not just a matter of ceremonial protocol, but of political life or death.

Charles II's battle for recognition by his European counterparts was in part a matter of endless diplomacy and correspondence managed by the king's advisers and councillors, but also a matter of face-to-face dealings between the king himself and the rulers of Europe. The question of how he was received and treated by his sibling princes was vital, embodying, as it did, his standing in their eyes. Their approval and support could bring two things: first practical resources – money, ships, men and arms – and second the less tangible but crucial aura of legitimacy that was so vital to persuading all concerned of the strength and justice of his cause.[76]

In the weeks before her son landed in France, Henrietta Maria had visited her sister-in-law the Queen Regent frequently, recounting the family's many woes in pitiful sobs, and pleading for assistance. Henrietta Maria's entreaties bore fruit: Charles was granted a French pension of 8000 crowns a month and given permission to lodge with his mother at court. Negotiations soon began on the question of how Charles would be treated by the eight-year-old king.[77] In a manner of which his father and Newcastle would certainly have approved, Charles immediately pushed for the highest possible honour for himself in the meeting: though Louis XIV was a sovereign and Charles, at this stage, only the son of a sovereign, Charles audaciously asked to be treated as an absolute equal to the French king, quoting his father's reception at the Spanish court in 1623 as a precedent. Unsurprisingly this proposal did not find favour with the French officials, who remarked haughtily that 'France did not need to take example from others'. However, by starting the bidding so high, and thanks to Henrietta Maria's careful cultivation of Anne of Austria, Charles managed to achieve a remarkable coup: the French agreed that while they would not formally consent to the King of France treating the Prince of Wales as an equal, in practice he would do so.[78] Crucial to such an arrangement being feasible was that the prince had declared his visit to France to be 'incognito', and so rather than being a full state visit with the complete panoply of ritual – starting with a royal entry into Paris – it was an informal visit by one prince to another. Since claiming incognito status was common practice – indeed most visits between members of royal families in the seventeenth century (other than those in which a marriage was involved) were conducted in this manner – it implied no dishonour to either party. In any case a state visit would have been impractical as well as inappropriate. The prince would have struggled to marshal the full range of officials, gifts, costumes, coaches and horses required, and the French would have had to make a huge and unnecessary financial outlay to stage it with the necessary splendour.

So it was that during the months that followed, the eight-year-old Louis XIV and the sixteen-year-old Charles II conducted a careful and formal dance around one another at court events and receptions designed always to express the parity that existed between them. The quiet reserve of these two boys, who would grow into such charismatic and forceful men, was remarked upon. Both doubtless felt the responsibility of a situation in which a single word or movement could have a significant effect on the standing of their nation. Louis relinquished his chair of state on all occasions when Charles was present, electing instead to be seated in the same manner as his cousin. At the magnificent ball held at the Palais-Royal in the winter of 1646/7, the great throne, which was set on the dais overlooking the ballroom, remained empty throughout the evening. Seeing the unoccupied chair, the boys' wonderfully conceited cousin, Anne-Marie-Louise, daughter of their uncle Gaston d'Orleans, seized the moment and enthroned herself, remarking proudly that 'I saw two princes and all the princesses of the court at my feet'.[79] One of the Queen of France's ladies remarked of the relationship between Charles and Louis at this time, that 'nothing was forgotten in each rendering to the other the honour due to their birth and to the closeness of blood and kinship between them'.[80] Few commentators described the Prince of Wales's treatment at the hands of the French in 1646 as anything other than completely cordial. The exception was Edward Hyde who, in his *History of Rebellion*, complained of

Charles's unworthy and dishonourable treatment.[81] However Hyde's account cannot be taken at face value: he was not present in Paris to witness the events he described, having chosen to remain in Jersey when the prince decided – against his advice – to leave for France. Furthermore, he did not write his account of these years until much later, and it seems likely that when he did so, he was influenced both by a personal view of the French, and by events that would follow in the 1650s and serve to confirm that view. It would not be long before the sweet relations between the two cousins started to sour.

Aspects of this first period of the exile and the reception arrangements that were then made would recur throughout the following years. Charles never ceased to push for the best possible terms in his meetings with foreign authorities – terms that would bring honour to his person and to the institution and cause he represented – employing every available ruse in so doing. He took great care that the details of any meeting were discussed and agreed at the outset, and that none were allowed to proceed if they did not meet with his approval. The situation in Paris in 1646 was saved by Henrietta Maria's personal discussions with Anne of Austria; but as Hyde himself commented, it would have been 'fitter to have been adjusted in Jarsey, before he put himself into their power', and Charles was to learn from this mistake.[82] In 1649, when he was poised to journey to Ireland from his sister's court in Holland and wanted to travel via France to see his mother, Charles would not leave Breda and so cross into the Spanish Netherlands until Lord Cottington and Edward Hyde had secured him 'a courteous passage' and settled in advance 'all particulars in Flanders in order to his reception there'.[83] The results were worth the wait: the Prince of Orange rode with Charles to the border at the head of a great procession of 40 troops of horse. Here, the king was met by the agents of Archduke Leopold, Governor-General of the Spanish Netherlands, and was presented with a fine coach and six horses, to be followed by a gift of 25,000 gold crowns. Charles was installed in the coach and 'with great magnificence' entered the ancient city of Antwerp. The royal cavalcade was welcomed with such exuberance that the young Stephen Fox, riding behind the king in the procession, was peppered with burning gunpowder from the celebratory gun salutes. Only the painstaking ministrations of Richard Pyle, the king's surgeon, in picking out every grain saved him from permanent disfigurement.[84] Charles had a meeting with Archduke Leopold himself at Valenciennes and later, having arrived in France, he was met by the Duc de Vendome, uncle of the King of France, and invited to travel onwards in the French state coach. Vendome accompanied Charles to Compiegne where Louis XIV himself rode out over a mile to meet his cousin, before acting as host at a royal dinner. As was remarked upon at the time, these gestures of honour demonstrated that, his lack of a kingdom notwithstanding, Charles II was indeed a great prince.[85]

Despite the impression given by the cheering crowds and the gracious receptions, the regal treatment Charles enjoyed on that journey from Breda to Paris was anything but spontaneous. In fact it was the result of intense and shrewd manoeuvring in the six months since his father's death. The news of the execution of a king by his own people sent shudders of horror down the spines of the crowned heads of Europe, and the first impulse of many was to denounce it in the most uncompromising terms. However the regicide was also an impressive demonstration of the strength and determination of the English Parliament. Throughout the courts of Europe the feeling grew that it might be unwise to make an enemy of this new power, and loyalty to the fraternity of kingship was swiftly toppled by political expediency. The king's sister, Mary, and her husband William of Orange expressed their complete rejection of Parliament's action by immediately according Charles royal status, but the weeks passed and the anticipated wave of official condemnations of Parliament's actions did not follow. Instead there came a slow trickle of vague and ambiguous gestures. The Dutch States General treated Charles with respect, but carefully avoided addressing him as a sovereign. According to one contemporary, a Dutch official may once have referred to Charles as 'King', but he had muttered the word so indistinctly that no one was quite sure, and his subsequent refusal to use the term in writing added to the confusion. The Portuguese ambassador did visit Charles to express his support, but explained that he came only in a personal capacity as he had no instructions to recognize him on behalf of his master. Philip IV of Spain decided that the solution was for official letters of condolence to be sent to Charles II, but for these to be backdated to before Parliament's declaration that the Stuart succession was defunct, leaving him with a convenient excuse if Parliament objected. From the young Louis XIV, Charles's cousin and supposed ally, came terrible silence. In Paris Henrietta Maria lobbied furiously for her son's recognition, pressing all her friends to do the same, but to no effect; even the Spanish ambassador to London was amazed, writing in disbelief that '... the King of France has not yet written a single letter to this poor devil (the Prince of Wales), nor made the slightest manifestation for six months that his father's head has been struck off'.[86]

Come the summer of 1649, therefore, not only was Charles suffering from a conspicuous scarcity of international support, but having heard nothing at all from Louis XIV, he could not honourably set foot in France on his voyage to Ireland. So when Cottington and Hyde had set off to negotiate his 'courteous passage' they were facing a serious challenge. Rather than continuing to petition Louis XIV, which was obviously not working, they decided on an alternative approach. To reach France without hazarding capture by the hostile ships of the Channel, Charles would have to travel through the Spanish Netherlands; and if an honourable reception from the Spanish there could be secured, it would be extremely difficult for the French to avoid treating him in a similar manner. Furthermore, Charles II had reason to think that agreeing a regal passage across the Spanish dominions might indeed be possible. First, the governor-general of the territory had made his personal support for Charles known months earlier, telling him that as an archduke of the Holy Roman Empire, he considered Charles's sovereign status indisputable, 'conferred on him by birth and descent from so long a line of Kings'. Second, the King of Spain's ploy to undermine his recognition of Charles's sovereignty by backdating his letters had misfired. He had overlooked the crucial fact that the post from Brussels to The Hague took only two days, making it impossible for Leopold to deploy this trick convincingly, and a furious English Parliament had published the correctly dated letters of recognition in disgust.[87]

So when Charles II asked Leopold to allow him a dignified passage through his dominions, the Archduke felt compelled to agree. But the Stuart negotiators were not content to leave matters there: they wanted more, including 6000 doubloons of Spanish gold in financial assistance and agreement to a face-to-face meeting between Charles and the Archduke. Lest the meeting prove the final straw, the English offered soothing reassurances that Charles would come 'incognito, accompanied only by twenty persons, not looking to be received with the usual ceremony or any éclat and solely with the view of seeing his Highness'.[88] On these gentle terms it was agreed; but at the last moment, with the Archduke absent in the field, the English dramatically altered tack. As was afterwards explained to Philip IV: 'the English entirely changed what had been agreed upon, by declaring to his Highness that they wished the king to be publicly received, the citizens to be under arms, salute of guns and other ceremonies to be observed with great pomp'. With the arrangements so far advanced, Charles II's regal status already publicly recognized, and on Spanish territory too, the Spanish caved in and the whole trip was conducted with the greatest ceremony. When asked by an angry Philip IV to explain how this had come to pass, Leopold wrote bitterly that he had been given little choice: 'The honours due to the rank of King have been rendered him, which it was impossible to avoid from the moment your Majesty wrote to him according to that title.'[89] As soon as all this was in train, the French could no longer hold out, and they agreed to accord Charles a similarly formal reception on his arrival in France.[90] The young king had played a poor hand with consummate skill.

In the years that followed, great care and planning ensured that all the meetings which took place between Charles II and his fellow princes or their senior representatives were conducted in a fashion that brought him honour. His reception at Cologne in 1654, for instance, was staged 'with all the respect, pomp, and magnificence that could be expected, or [the city] could perform', while at his meeting with the new governor of the Spanish Netherlands in 1656 he was welcomed 'with every sign of courtesy and respect'.[91] These triumphs never materialized by chance, but were always the result of meticulous preparation. Books of ceremonial protocol were consulted, precedents sought and talks conducted. As the journey of 1649 shows, the English were tough negotiators. When Philip Wilhelm, Duke of the German territory of Pflaz-Neuburg, invited Charles and his sister Mary of Orange to be his guests at his palace in Dusseldorf in 1654, no acceptance was given until detailed discussion of the arrangements of the meeting had taken place. Though Charles's prospects were woeful at the time – he having just been pushed out of France – he and Hyde stood firm on a whole range of details. In the end they conceded on only two points: that the duke would be allowed to bow to Princess Mary, and that on their first meeting only, Charles would address him once as 'highness' – something the king only accepted when it was confirmed that the Holy Roman Emperor himself always addressed the duke in this way.[92]

Nor were these matters of the king's reception simply handed over by Charles to his officials; they were the subject of his own close attention. When the governors of Ghent suggested the exiled king lodge at one of the local inns, the royal officials took the best rooms at the Golden Apple. On discovering he was to occupy such common lodgings the king erupted with rage, and refused to receive any visitors or accept any of the presents the city worthies subsequently sent him.[93] On another occasion Charles crossly reprimanded Hyde for failing to bring him a book of titles and etiquette, which he particularly wanted so that he could correctly address the son of the King of Spain.[94] Given what a precise gauge such events were of Charles II's standing and the prospects of his cause, this is perhaps not surprising. When he travelled to Spain to attend the talks between Cardinal Mazarin and the Spanish first minister, Don Luis Mendez de Haro, in 1659, Charles clearly felt profoundly gratified by the honourable manner of his reception there. The great Spanish minister, nephew of the Duke of Olivares, stepped from his coach and, despite the driving rain, knelt before Charles and humbly kissed his hand. News of this treatment, which saw Charles waited on 'as if he were the King of Spain', spread fast and Hyde received reports of it from six or seven separate sources, among them the king himself who, though he hated writing letters more than anything, sat down to describe in his own words the 'great kindness' he had received.[95]

As well as having an understandable interest in how he was to be treated by the princes of Europe, Charles brought considerable personal attributes to the business of international diplomacy: notably a gift for behaving with spellbinding regality when occasion required, and the personal charm and charisma to inspire genuine affection in those he met. In 1646, when he first arrived in Paris as Prince of Wales, the Venetian ambassador noted that, despite his poor fortunes, he showed 'all the sentiments of a generous and prudent prince' and similar remarks about his princely behaviour would follow.[96] Throughout his exile, Charles's amiability was often commented upon, his excellent manners and courtesy impressing even the haughtiest Parisians, and his good humour and pleasant nature winning many friends.[97] His move to Spanish territories in 1656 brought new challenges, as Hapsburg court culture was the most formal and restricted in Europe. The style of princely behaviour he had mastered in France was no longer appropriate. His council urged him to 'take on more majesty' and Charles heeded this advice, soon winning the admiration of the Spanish for his personal bearing and conduct at formal meetings.[98]

There was, of course, another side to this tale of decorous audiences and magnificent receptions. When they happened, they provided a vivid demonstration of his status and legitimacy, but the trouble was that for considerable periods they did not happen, and Charles remained alone and unvisited, the private individual he so dreading becoming. This happened either because he could not come to a satisfactory arrangement as to the form of such a visit, or, worse by far, because no meeting was sought. Despite his initially warm treatment by the Bourbons, the great families of the French court were less convinced of the advantages of acquaintance. The reason was clear: in the words of Madame de Motteville, 'ill-fortune was its cause; they [the exiled Stuart family] had no favours to bestow. Theirs were crowns without power.' With requests for audiences uncomfortably infrequent on his return to Paris in 1649, Charles chose to limit the damage by absenting himself from court, remaining instead some miles away at the palace of St Germain en Laye.[99] When he came to the Spanish Netherlands in 1656, with the crucial promise of Spanish military support already agreed, he still pushed for conspicuous and ceremonious meetings between himself and the new Spanish governor-general, Philip IV's illegitimate son Don Juan José, as affirmation of the strength of Spanish support for his cause. The two men had a number of audiences over the following year, which were conducted with such formality that royalists started to brag publicly of the Spaniard's 'civilities'.[100] Regardless, Charles lobbied for yet more, using his meeting with Don Juan José in December 1656 to 'press for more open recognition and for more civility from the Governors'.[101] His concern was understandable: the eyes of Europe were trained on such meetings, diplomats writing to their princes and Cromwellian spies to their masters with meticulous descriptions of who had and had not visited the Stuart king: all were waiting and watching for signs of changing fortune.[102]

Back in August 1646, as the terms of the then Prince Charles's first reception were being thrashed out, his father had written from Newcastle-upon-Tyne and instructed him to appoint Richard Steward as head of his chapel royal. In his letter he reminded his son that if monarchy had one greater weapon than the sword, it was the church: 'as the Church can never flourish without the Crown, so the dependency of the Church on the Crown is the chief support of maintaining regal authority'.[103]

Other than his treatment by foreign princes, the most closely watched aspect of Charles II's life in exile was his form of worship. The manner of his religious devotions could communicate to observers both his majesty or otherwise and, crucially, his confessional status. Given the central role religion had played in the civil war, the question of the religion of the heir to the throne was of huge interest to contemporaries. Charles's own allegiances were clear to those close to him: he believed absolutely in the importance of following the form of Protestant worship for which he believed his father had given his life. The strength of his words to his brother the Duke of Gloucester, when rumours of Gloucester's conversion to Catholicism emerged, are striking: 'If he do not observe the last words of his dead father to be constant to his religion', Charles told the young duke 'he must never think to see England or the King again.'[104]

Charles was therefore careful to maintain a conspicuously Laudian Protestant form of worship throughout his exile.[105] Dr Steward duly took up his post as

Dean of the exiled Chapel Royal in 1646 and continued to perform this role when the Prince of Wales became king. After his death in 1651, various senior clerics who had also followed the king into exile effectively took over from him. Notable among these were Dr John Cosin, the committed Laudian who oversaw worship among the Protestants in Henrietta Maria's household until the Restoration, and Dr John Earle, who would be confirmed in his post as the king's Clerk of the Closet (responsible for the king's personal devotions) in 1660. Earle was a brilliant Oxford cleric who had come to Charles I's attention as chaplain to the University Chancellor. His gentle manner disguised a talent for acid observation, and his *Microcosmographie*, a series of witty caricatures of moral and personality types, had been a national bestseller. Earle married the diarist John Evelyn to Mary Browne, daughter of Sir Richard Browne, when the court was in Paris and in 1654 accompanied Charles II to the Low Countries. Following Charles I's instructions, he and Cosin referred particularly sensitive religious questions, by letter, to the prince's erstwhile tutor Brian Duppa, who was passing a quiet retirement in Richmond upon Thames.[106] In addition to these senior churchmen, a series of junior chapel officials supervised the practical aspects of running the Chapel Royal in exile, among them Thomas Haines, formally sworn Serjeant of the Vestry in 1660, who oversaw the provision of all the physical equipment necessary for royal worship, while others, among them John Harding, appointed a Gentleman of the Chapel Royal by Charles I before the civil war, carried out other tasks including dispensing money for the king's offering.[107]

While Charles was living in Paris in the late 1640s and early 1650s, he worshipped in a room at the Louvre specifically assigned to the exiled English Protestants by the French Queen Regent, Anne of Austria. The generosity of the French faltered at allowing the Protestant sacraments to be celebrated within the royal palace, and so the room at the Louvre was used as an oratory, for morning and evening services of readings and prayer. On holy days the king travelled to the house of the Stuart representative in Paris, Sir Richard Browne, where a chapel was set up at which Cosin, Stewart and Earle celebrated the sacraments with the king and his brother.[108] After Charles's departure from Paris in 1654, a room was always set aside in the various houses he occupied to serve as a 'chapel' or a 'prayer room'.[109]

These rooms used by Charles for worship were decked out in Laudian splendour or, at least, with as much splendour as circumstances would allow.[110] The prayer room at the Louvre, an English Protestant enclave within the French royal palace, was secured under Dr Cosin's own key and he ensured it was 'decently furnished and kept' in a high Anglican manner for the king's devotions.[111] Though the prayer rooms that Charles's staff set up after his departure from France in 1654 were a far cry from the grandeur of the Louvre, they were nonetheless handsomely equipped. The rooms were provided with fine gilded plate, including chalices, patens, alms dishes and other communion plates, and a wealth of candles both 'greate and small' to illuminate proceedings.[112] Upholstered stools and benches were laid out for the attendants, and a supply of bread and Muscadet wine was maintained for the Eucharist itself.[113] Charles told the presbyterian deputation that visited him in May 1660 that the Anglican clerical surplice had been used in his chapel throughout the exile, and this is borne out by the household accounts, which contain many references to the cleaning and mending of surplices by officers of the Chapel Royal.[114]

In these ceremonious settings, the exiled king meticulously maintained high-church Anglican worship according to the prescriptions of the Book of Common Prayer – copies of which were carefully stowed in boxes at the end of the services.[115] The annual calendar of devotion described by the Prayer Book was carefully followed, along with the many conventions that governed royal worship. Like his father, Charles took Holy Communion on three occasions during the year: at Christmas, Easter and Whitsun.[116] In December 1651, John Evelyn watched Charles receive the sacrament in Paris, almost certainly at Sir Richard Browne's chapel, while the household account books include allowances of money for the king to offer at the altar before taking communion on Easter Sunday and Whit Sunday 1658 and Easter Sunday 1659.[117] Not only was the English royal calendar of receiving and offering adhered to throughout the exile, but so too was the particular royal manner of taking communion. Charles received the host on his knees immediately after the senior clergy and before all other communicants, with two noblemen holding a towel beneath the royal chin. On occasions other than the great feasts, his visits to chapel were regular and frequent, and daily services of prayers were held in his lodgings throughout the exile.[118] When the delegation sent to negotiate terms for Charles's proclamation in Scotland had arrived at The Hague on Good Friday 1649, they were told it was not worth coming to court until the following Tuesday because the king was occupied in his Easter devotions.[119] The religious calendar was also followed outside the chapel rooms: Fridays were set aside as fast days on which the king and royal household dined on fish, while on key festival days the king distributed alms to the poor, all part of a clear determination 'to serve God after our old English manner'.[120]

Charles probably believed that regular Anglican worship would improve his prospects of salvation, and he certainly believed it would improve his prospects of restoration to his father's throne. Edward Hyde was often frustrated by the king's conduct and moral elasticity, but he had no fears for his master's Anglicanism, 'confident that all the world cannot move the King in his religion'.[121] Given that he was living in Catholic countries and was in the pay of a series of Catholic kings, smouldering rumours of Charles's conversion were to be expected, and with the encouragement of a rampantly anti-royalist puritan press in England, these were periodically fanned into flames. In January 1654 reports were circulating that the king and his entourage were now worshipping with the Jesuits, while two years later even the printing presses at The Hague were churning out news of the English king's conversion.[122] Such gossip was not dampened by the fact that Charles certainly did visit Catholic churches: in September 1654, for example, he attended evensong at the cathedral at Aachen, staying behind to handle their treasured Charlemagne relics. But these were not the visits of a religious apostate; they were in part the polite house calls of a visiting dignitary and in part the sightseeing expeditions of a traveller with time on his hands. On arriving at Cologne in 1654, Charles visited all the city's major religious establishments in turn so that they could formally perform their ceremonies of welcome: the Jesuits, the Carmelites, the Franciscans, the Dominicans and the Carmelite nuns.[123] These could be spectacles in themselves: during the ceremonies of welcome staged at the Jesuit College, he was met at the refectory door by seven boys of the order dressed in splendid robes. In their hands they held brightly coloured shields each of which they revealed, in turn, to be decorated with a large letter, spelling out the king's name: Carolus. Every boy made a short speech congratulating the king on his arrival, and then, simultaneously, they spun their shields around to spell out the name of their city 'Colonia'. With further songs of welcome and fanfares of trumpets, the performance ended with the boys prostrating themselves before their distinguished guest. Charles did not just visit Catholic establishments: in Frankfurt, for instance, he was taken both to two Lutheran churches and the great synagogue, and commented on the scale and grandeur of each with interest.[124] Regardless of their real purpose, such visits added fuel to rumours of the king's conversion, and Charles was convinced that only by his own behaviour could they be scotched: as he wrote of his Anglican faith: 'the world cannot but take notice of Our constant and uninterrupted profession and exercise of it in those places where the contrary religion is only practiced and allowed'.[125]

So it was that Charles took every opportunity to demonstrate his absolute conformity and commitment to his father's brand of Anglicanism. This was not simply a question of worshipping in a particular way, but of being seen to do so. When the king attended Richard Browne's house in Paris, it was not in quiet privacy – huge crowds of people were ushered in to witness the event.[126] In April 1656, when Charles travelled to Brussels to negotiate moving his court there, he left Secretary Nicholas with strict written instructions for the household in his absence, stipulating that 'it is our express will & pleasure they frequent the publick prayers att the usuall times … as if we were there in person'.[127] Even a break of a matter of weeks in royal chapel attendance was a matter of concern to all; and as soon as the deal for the court's move had been brokered, Dr Earle was sent to join the king ahead of the rest of the household, 'to conduct the public devotion, which he has now been a long time without'.[128]

The king's expedition to Scotland was the one episode in which Charles failed to follow his own maxims on religion, and it served only to strengthen his resolve thereafter. When the Scots had come to Breda in the spring of 1650 they had made it clear that they would accept Charles as their king only on strict conditions. These required him to sign the presbyterian manifestos of the National Covenant of Scotland and the Solemn League and Covenant, committing him to the establishment of Presbyterianism throughout his lands and to following that form of religion himself. With a kingdom just a signature away, Charles had not been able to resist and agreed to every one of the Scots' demands – though it meant conceding what Charles I had died to prevent. It was no one's finest hour: even the Scottish delegates admitted they had left him with no other choice. Alexander Jaffray, the MP for Aberdeen, wrote mournfully in his diary that 'we did sinfully both entangle and engage the nation and ourselves, and that poor young prince to whom we were sent, making him sign and swear a covenant, which we knew, from clear and demonstrable reasons that he hated in his heart'.[129]

As he had signed away his Anglicanism on paper, Charles was, by his behaviour in the chapel royal, keenly signalling that this was only a political move. At the beginning of the negotiations he had discussed with the Scots his personal faith in 'Episcopacy and ceremonies'. As the conference wore on, and Charles gradually conceded on every single point, making ever more bloodcurdling commitments to Presbyterianism, he insisted that the Book of Common Prayer continue to be used in his own chapel at Breda. Come the first week of June, all the terms were agreed and a date the following week was set for his departure for Scotland. The intervening Sunday was Whitsun, and Charles took the opportunity of this great holy day to demonstrate once again his personal devotion to high-church Anglicanism despite his promises to the contrary. At four o'clock on Saturday 4 June the Scots delegation heard that the king was to take communion the following day in the full Anglican manner, including receiving the host on his knees before the altar. The Scots were horrified. That this was Charles's preferred method of worshipping was no surprise, but that he intended to stage such an audacious act of Anglican conformity after having agreed to lifelong Presbyterianism made a farce of all the promises they had extracted. The Scots complained desperately to the king, and were admitted late that evening to his presence. They found him unshakable; as one of the delegates recalled, 'He said "His father always used to communicate at Christmas, Easter and Whitsunday, and that he behoved to do likewise; and that people would think it strange of him if, having resolved to communicate, he should forbear it"', adding, in a wonderful sting, that anyway 'he did it to procure a blessing from God on his intended voyage'. Nothing the Scots said could dissuade him, and the following morning he entered chapel and, exactly as his father had always done, knelt before the altar to receive the holy sacrament.[130] Though the king later dined out on tales of his escapades after the battle of Worcester, there was no escaping the fact that the Scottish enterprise as a whole had been an abject failure. The experience clearly had an effect on his view of religion; when his confessor emerged from a heart-to-heart with the king immediately after his return, he reported with quiet confidence that 'there is no more danger of Presbytery'.[131]

The way in which Charles II worshipped was designed to demonstrate that he was a loyal Anglican, but it was also meant to show that he was a divinely sanctioned king. The particular form of royal worship in which the king received communion alone directly after the priests had long been used by English kings to show that they, as God's chosen rulers, were not as other men. If the divine authority of the king was implicit in the rituals of the chapel royal, it was unmistakably explicit in another of the king's ritual activities: the royal healing of the sick. The ceremony of 'touching for the king's evil' saw sufferers of scrofula, a common glandular condition of the period, come to court to be cured simply by the touch, or 'stroke', of the sovereign of England.

Throughout his reign Charles II undertook the ritual healing of the sick in good times and bad. In December 1649, within a year of his father's execution, the teenage king touched 11 people in the chapel at Elizabeth Castle on Jersey, and ten years later, days before his departure for a triumphant return to England, he held three consecutive days of healing at his sister's court at The Hague.[132] The author of the description of the events at The Hague was at pains to explain that it was not just the prospect of a return to power which prompted the king to heal, but that he had successfully healed the sick since his accession, 260 touched between 17 April and 23 May that year and before that many more at Brussels and Bruges.[133] One of the king's surgeons would later note that the king had 'exercised that faculty with wonderful success, not only here, but beyond the seas in Flanders, Holland and France it self'.[134] The royal household accounts from the 1650s period bear out these testimonies, recording payments made to officials for attending the healing ceremonies and for the gold medals and ribbons distributed to those the king touched.[135]

News of the effectiveness of the king's touch was clear evidence of his divine right to rule and can only have been encouraged by his supporters. Such stories certainly circulated: in 1652, for instance, it was reported in England that 'our king had of late healed a ppasent [peasant] which was most desperusly roten with the evell'. As well as shoring up the king's claim to legitimacy, such reports gave further opportunity for the king to demonstrate his miraculous abilities as each brought more of his afflicted subjects to the continent to receive his healing touch.[136] Among the travellers who came for this purpose was the daughter of Sir Richard Atkins, who was advised by London's most eminent physicians that her best hope of a cure was to receive the healing stroke of the exiled king, and a poor man with a hideously swollen neck who travelled from England to Bruges especially to be touched.[137] As well as these independent travellers, organized groups of scrofula sufferers were brought to the Low Countries by enterprising merchants. As one contemporary later recalled, 'There was a Scotch Merchant, who made it his business every Spring and Fall to bring People from Scotland and Newcastle, troubled with the Evil, to the King where ever he was in his Troubles.'[138]

For the success of the royal healing ceremonies, it was crucial for all concerned that the king was seen to cure those whom he touched, and to increase the likelihood of this happening, even in exile the events were very carefully organized. Before anyone was allowed to receive the touch, he or she had first to be examined by one of the king's surgeons. Only if scrofula was positively diagnosed – for the king could only heal this particular condition – was the patient allowed to apply to be touched. If the diagnosis was positive the surgeon notified the sufferer of a particular day and time when they were to present themselves to the king in his chapel (if it was negative the ailing applicant was advised to present himself at a hospital instead). The ceremony itself was presided over by the king's personal chaplain, the clerk of the closet. Not having the royal mint at his disposal, Charles could not present the traditional healing medals and so ten shilling pieces or, when times were really hard, coins of the sufferers' own providing were substituted.[139]

The great set-piece ceremonies of healing and of royal worship were the most conspicuous occasions when the exiled Charles II could publicly demonstrate the regal status he claimed. However, they were far from the only ways this was done. English sovereigns had long participated in a series of cycles of royal events and activities, each embodying and expressing the regality of the sovereign, and reflecting and rewarding the bonds of loyalty between subject and ruler. In exile, again, such occasions took on a stark new significance, as both the regality of the sovereign and the loyalty of his subjects was seriously in question.

After the Reformation, when much of the religious calendar had been stripped out, English sovereigns became increasingly concerned with celebrating dynastic anniversaries and other significant days associated with members of the royal family. Among these was the birthday of Elizabeth I, which would remain a totemic date for many Anglicans throughout the seventeenth century. Another was 5 November, marked since 1606 as a day of thanksgiving for the delivery of the royal family from the Gunpowder Plot. With the execution of Charles I on 30 January 1649, another date entered the royal dynastic calendar. On the first anniversary of his father's death, Charles II was in Jersey. The day was declared one of prayer and mourning and everyone on the island fasted and abstained from manual work until five o'clock in the evening. In church the furniture was draped in black and the sermon was on the lamentations of Josiah: mourning for the exile of the people of Israel.[140] Everyone prayed for the restoration of the king to his throne. The following year the occasion was again 'solemnly kept', and for every year for the rest of his reign Charles would similarly remember the day of his father's execution.[141] As well as marking this new date, Charles II continued to celebrate publicly other Stuart dynastic anniversaries. Festivities were staged for his own birthday and for those of his siblings, with gun salutes fired and feasts served. In addition he continued to commemorate the other secular high-days, including 5 November, which saw the preaching of special sermons and great cannon sounding a five-gun salute.[142]

As Madame de Motteville had tartly remarked in 1649, one of Charles's most debilitating problems during the exile was that, without a kingdom or funds, he had no favours to distribute. He did not command a vast royal bureaucracy with countless paid positions with which to reward loyal subjects. The wages of loyalty during the exile were meagre, exiled courtiers usually suffering severe financial loss by supporting this king. However, one of the things that Charles could and did continue to distribute during the exile was status. Elevation to the

Order of the Garter, which the young Charles II had so clamoured to join in 1638, remained the pre-eminent honour in the king's gift. His patronage of the order during the exile was conspicuous, as he was never seen without its insignia.[143] Perhaps part of the importance of the Garter during the exile was the fact that while Charles's status as sovereign of England was controversial, his role as head of the Order of the Garter went unchallenged.

Sixteen new Knights of the Garter were created in the eleven years before the Restoration. As had always been the case, a number of foreign princes were appointed, Charles understandably favouring those with the greatest connection and attachment to his own family; in 1649, therefore, his first cousins Prince Maurice and Prince Edward of the Palatinate (brothers of Prince Rupert) were made Garter Knights, and in 1653 his nephew, the young William III, Prince of Orange, was also appointed. Many of the king's own countrymen lobbied to be elevated to the Garter, but very few were successful.[144] Charles II's creations were seldom the result of whim or favouritism, but clearly reflected the political priorities of the moment. Many were designed to cement absolute loyalty when he needed it most. For instance, the Marquis of Newcastle and Earl of Derby, the most powerful royalist noblemen of the north, were made Garter Knights on the eve of the king's Scottish expedition in 1650, as was the young Duke of Hamilton. Likewise James Butler, Marquis of Ormond, the premier nobleman of Ireland, was elevated to the order in September 1649 when Charles was set on reconquering his kingdoms from Ireland. Jean Ferdinand de Marsin, Comte de Granville, the Spanish nominee in charge of the force being gathered for the English invasion in 1658, was another whom Charles used the Garter to flatter and charm into loyalty.[145] Even without the elaborate ceremonies of installation at St George's Chapel, Windsor, being elected a Knight of the Garter could still bring with it real prestige, and Charles and his entourage went to considerable efforts to cultivate the atmosphere of status.[146] When Ferdinand de Marsin was initiated into the order in February 1658, the insignia was conveyed to the gathering in Antwerp in its own coach. The king himself, flanked by two other Garter Knights, placed the collar round the Comte's neck, and the Garter King at Arms knelt to affix the other emblems of the order. The effort paid off, Marsin was 'much transported with the honour', and days later happily accompanied Charles on a mission to Don Juan José in Brussels to try and raise the money that would keep the Stuart court from destitution.[147] Wisely, Charles rarely appointed new Knights of the Garter as soon as places fell vacant; in fact three or four years usually elapsed between the death of one knight and the election of another. Since the number of Garter Knights was limited, this ensured that the possibility of appointment was always there as a lure to inspire loyalty in his followers.[148]

As well as in conspicuous acts of kingship, royal status could also be demonstrated by the way a king performed otherwise mundane activities, and of no activity was this more true than dining. Before the civil war Charles had periodically taken meals with his parents at which the English form of royal dining was followed.

Broadly, this meant the king would eat only with those of royal status (usually his immediate family), the seating plan would meticulously reflect the hierarchy of the diners, and the dishes would be ceremoniously served by court officers on bended knee, following a prescribed order of service. The meal began and ended with prayers read by the king's personal confessor, the clerk of the closet. Charles II followed this form of royal dining precisely from the very beginning of his exile, as we know from Jean Chevalier's detailed description of royal dining on Jersey. As the exile wore on, huge care was taken to ensure that when the king dined in public he always did so in royal fashion. When Charles returned to France in 1649, and was finally recognized as a king by Louis XIV, it was by dining with his cousin that Louis unequivocally acknowledged Charles's regal status. When Charles reached Compiegne, Louis and Anne of Austria 'received him with all the marks of affection their Majesties owed to so great a prince'. For the great feast that followed, the table was set for royalty alone; here Charles was invited to take his seat as a sovereign next to Louis XIV, and was provided, like King Louis and Queen Anne, with a chair of state. As Madame de Motteville explained, it was not the food or the surroundings, but the princely company that made this 'a truly royal dinner'.[149] In the United Provinces in 1648, when Charles was still Prince of Wales, he ate his meals together with his sister, while William of Orange, her husband, ate apart. When the news of Charles I's execution broke, this arrangement ceased and Charles II was given his own table, at which he took his meals in regal solitude.[150]

The style in which the king was to dine was one of the questions that had to be settled before he visited another prince. When he was received by the Duke of Pfalz-Neuburg, this was discussed in advance, and the result – that Charles and his sister sat at the dining table alone with the Duke and Duchess – was the satisfactory outcome.[151] When Charles went to Scotland, dining-room protocol was also a key question, and though the king had much to complain of once he arrived, the form in which he was served his meals could not be faulted: 'the King's table was well served, and there he sat in majesty, waited upon with decency'.[152] The surviving painting in the Gruuthuse Museum in Bruges, though executed some years after Charles returned to England, bears witness to the importance of regal dining to the image of the king, even, or perhaps especially, in exile (see Colour Plate 1). Charles is shown with his two brothers in a civic hall, seated at a dining table placed on a fine Turkish carpet under a canopy. The king's elevated status is indicated by the central position he occupies at the table and by the hat he wears, while his brothers and the spectators remain bareheaded. The dishes were brought in by a stream of richly dressed officials, who served the royal party on bended knee. A detailed description of the feast held at The Hague in May 1660 (see Figure 10) makes it clear that, on this occasion at least, every care was taken to ensure the form of service reflected perfectly the delicate distinctions in hierarchy of the diners and celebrated the majesty of the king.[153]

The tableware Charles used in exile was both handsome and regal, reflecting the importance of dining to royal identity. His napkins, cupboard cloths and

10. Charles II dining at The Hague in May 1660. The king, at the head of the table, is surrounded by his immediate family, while members of the States of Holland are seated on the long spur table adjoining it.

tablecloths were all embroidered with the letters 'CR' surmounted with a royal crown, and he kept a fine collection of silver and silver-gilt plate, including a number of large dishes weighing three or four pounds each, a set of silver Italian trencher plates, a great salt cellar, ten silver spoons and forks and four gold trencher plates, valued altogether at some 2000 rix dollars.[154] As well as this considerable collection, the tables were adorned with additional pewter dishes and trenchers hired at a six-monthly rate.[155] Ensuring the king could dine in style was a priority in Stephen Fox's management of the household accounts. When the court was in Cologne in 1655, for instance, about 21 guilders was spent every day on the king's meals. Looking at it on a larger scale, of the 6000 guilders per month allocated for maintaining the court in 1654, a third was to be spent on the king's own table and the royal stables. Though there were periodic complaints that finances were so parlous the king would have nothing to eat within a matter of days, in reality Charles II was well, if not extravagantly, served during the exile.[156] On Thursday 5 November 1655, for instance, dinner comprised roast chicken and partridge, veal, stewed quinces and fruit, and supper was roast mutton with gravy, pigeon, lark and crayfish, with stewed apples and fruit for pudding. Royal breakfasts were also hearty affairs at which various cooked meats were accompanied by eggs, sometimes served with bacon or sausages, and at other times served sweet with lemon and sugar.[157] Expenditure on the royal table remained fairly constant through the year, though more lavish meals were served on feast days. On Christmas Day 1655, for instance, the king dined on a festive meal of roast beef, collar of boar and chicken served with plum pudding, followed by fruit tart, plum broth and mince pies, at a cost of almost twice a normal day's fare.[158]

Food also figured in Charles's dealings with other princes as the subject of royal gift giving. The exchange of presents between men of broadly similar status was a long-standing form of princely behaviour, and one in which Charles II participated as much as his finances would allow. After his move to Cologne, courteous exchanges took place with the German princes of the surrounding territories. The Duke of Pfalz-Neuburg sent Charles a great boar, while the Elector of Cologne signified his contentment with Charles's residence in his city with the gift of three boars.[159] When Charles moved to the Spanish Netherlands, he keenly dispatched gifts to the Governor-General, Don Juan José, in an attempt to emphasize their princely brotherhood and win his support. As soon as it was established that the Spaniard lacked a decent pack of hounds, one was immediately found and sent to him as a gift.[160]

In many of these rituals Charles himself performed the lead role, and for the required effect to be achieved it was vital that he played it perfectly. To this end his appearance was carefully managed to ensure he cut a sufficiently regal figure.[161] As the English regalia had been left in London in 1642, and seven years later was sold by Parliament to the highest bidders, Charles did not have any of the more formal emblems of kingship to hand. However, he did have the insignia of the Order of the Garter and, as discussed, these he wore constantly. On public occasions he sported the great garter star on his coat, a blue sash across his chest, and the garter itself fixed below his knee, while on all other days he wore the lesser George around his neck.[162] With his coronation in January 1651 he had finally acquired a crown, but his hasty departure from Scotland meant he was soon parted from it. The advantages of possessing such definitive emblems of majesty, and ones with which he had actually been invested at a coronation, were obvious. Once Charles was safely back in Paris, he wrote to the keeper of Dunottar Castle asking him to hand over the 'Crowne Scepter, and other the Hono[u]rs of that our ancient Kingdom' to the captain of a ship which he was sending to Scotland for that purpose.[163] Unfortunately for Charles, Scottish reluctance to dispatch their 'honours' abroad meant his request was not fulfilled and he would have to wait until 1660 to feel the weight of a crown once again.

Charles II spent a good deal of his exile making and receiving visits, engaging in complex diplomacy and maintaining the ritual activities of a king. Nonetheless he often had time on his hands. Some of the idle hours he spent engaging in traditional kingly past-times. In his first summer of exile he hunted extensively in the royal forests around Fontainebleau, and he continued to enjoy this energetic pursuit during the years that followed, hunting daily in Jersey in the winter of 1649 and frequently in Scotland during the summer of 1650. He also enjoyed hawking and kept his own birds of prey at the exiled court. When one bystander caught a snatch of the conversation between Charles and Louis XIV in July 1649, the young kings talked only of horses, dogs and hunting.[164] Charles's own love of dogs continued; spaniels had been his favourite breed since Richmond days, and his footman, James Jack, was given special responsibility for looking after his own pack in the Low Countries.[165] In addition, Charles swam regularly and played any number of games including tennis, golf and billiards. A fencing master came with the court when it moved from Cologne to Bruges, and presented himself at the king's lodgings every day to give lessons to the royal brothers.[166] Tennis was a long-standing royal pursuit in England and France – as the surviving tennis courts at Fontainebleau and Hampton Court attest – and one that had formed a part of the education Newcastle devised for him. The household accounts for the exile record payments for kit (including the king's tennis socks), for the 'marker' or umpire, and for the hire of courts – such as the bill of 60 florins he incurred for the use of tennis courts in June 1658.[167] In addition to these princely sports, Charles II enjoyed dancing, plays and music.[168]

Henrietta Maria, among others, had made efforts to find her son a suitable bride – someone one who could bring money and powerful friends to the Stuart cause – but an outcast king wasn't much of a proposition for the princesses and infantas that she picked out for him, so he remained a bachelor. Feminine company, though, was something in which Charles took real pleasure. This was a matter not simply of sex, though that clearly played its part, but also of affection and companionship. Many of Charles's strongest relationships during his life were with women: he formed a close friendship with his nurse, Christobel Wyndham, which continued into the civil war and beyond, and, despite the occasional quarrel, he was on excellent terms with his sister, Mary, Princess of Orange.[169] It was also during the exile that he developed an adoring friendship, the most loving platonic relationship of his life, with his youngest sister. Fourteen years her brother's junior, Henriette Anne was born at Bedford House near Exeter in June 1644 as the guns of war opened fire across England. She would never meet her father, and within days of her birth, her mother escaped to France without her. Two years later, Lady Dalkeith disguised Henriette as a boy and, slipping past the authorities at Dover, boarded a waiting ship, which carried her to safety. The young Princess grew up at the French court. She was only nine when her brother left Paris, but the two were reacquainted on his journey back from Spain in 1659 and an intimate and enduring bond developed between them. In his first surviving letter to Henriette, Charles described himself as 'a brother that loves you more than he can expresse', and such sentiments would be repeated endlessly in the correspondence the two kept up over the following years. When Henriette died in 1670, Charles II would be heartbroken and withdraw to his bedchamber for days, his old friend the Duke of Ormonde remarking that the king had never known such grief.[170]

It was also during the exile that Charles began the first of a succession of sexual liaisons. At 18 he became involved with Lucy Walter, a girl of about his own age, the daughter of a Welsh gentleman called William Walter. The affair, which seems to have been relatively brief, resulted in a son, born at Rotterdam in April 1649. The affection between the couple soon waned and by 1656 Lucy had had three children by three different lovers and was blackmailing Charles for money. In a drastic move by any standards, the king ordered that the boy, James, be taken from his mother and, after a disastrous first attempt, he was successfully seized and became the ward of one of Charles's retinue, Lord Crofts.[171] Though his relationship with Lucy turned spectacularly sour, Charles was undeterred and during the 1650s was linked with a number of other women. He later acknowledged a second child from this period, Charles FitzCharles (known as Don Carlos), born to Catherine Pegge in 1657.

Reports of his 'devotion to pleasure' circulated widely and his enemies elaborated them to great propaganda effect, their hostile reports of 'fornication, drunkenness and adultery' at the exiled court dripping with vicarious excitement.[172] While the Lucy Walter affair showed they had some basis in fact, there was nothing particularly scandalous in a bachelor king having a sexual relationship with an inconsequential unmarried woman. Furthermore, much of the social activity of the exiled court was of the ballroom rather than the bedroom variety and as such provided opportunities for Charles to cut a princely figure. Formal balls, for instance, could be a powerful demonstration of status. A painting of Charles dancing at The Hague shows him taking the floor with his sister (*see* Figure 11),

11. Charles II dancing at a ball during the 1650s by Hieronymus Janssens.
The Royal Collection © 2007, Her Majesty Queen Elizabeth II

and by his dress and hat he is unquestionably the most senior person in the scene. When his old governor Lord Newcastle hosted a ball at his house in Antwerp in 1657 (a building now famous as the home of Peter Paul Rubens) it was more ceremony than revel. Only once the guests had assembled and taken their places did the king enter the room, his arrival announced with a musical fanfare. Before the dancing began, pre-prepared verses of poetry were read aloud in his praise, and halfway through the evening a great supper was served, borne into the room with a flourish by the king's senior officers carrying the large platters in pairs. After further dancing, the event ended at midnight with a formal speech 'prophesying his Majesty's re-establishment'.[173]

In general, Charles enjoyed himself much as other men did. Since as early as the 1650s, though, this aspect of his exile has dominated accounts of the period to such an extent that he is given credit for little else. He may well have learned to game and gamble, flirt and fornicate, but this was never his main concern or the salient feature of his character. In exile he learned to trust his closest servants, to dislike Presbyterianism and to master the rudiments of court politics. He also learned how demanding the role of a monarch-in-exile was, and how far he would go to reverse it. He perfected skills in diplomacy and deal making, and no one learned better the art of cutting a regal figure, of never giving an inch in ceremonial precedent, and of using the rituals of kingship to maximum effect.

On 3 September 1658, after several days of delirious fever, Oliver Cromwell died of pneumonia at Whitehall Palace. The rejoicing at the Stuart court in Bruges quickly turned to disappointment as, instead of the predicted political collapse, Cromwell's son Richard was immediately proclaimed his successor as Lord Protector. But the event brought about a shift in power that prompted movement in another quarter. In the months that followed, Sir John Grenville, the young man whom Charles had personally appointed Gentleman of his Bedchamber in the west country 15 years earlier, made contact with the king. Having valiantly held the Scilly Isles for the Stuarts until 1651, Grenville had lived quietly in England for seven years, feeling he could do little more for the cause. But in April 1659 the army forced the abolition of the Protectorate, so ending Richard Cromwell's rule. This left military power in Britain overwhelmingly in the hands of one man, and as he was Grenville's cousin, Grenville felt he could offer to approach him on Charles's behalf. The man in question was General George Monck.

Now in his fifties, George Monck was every inch a career soldier: he had signed up at 16 and in the intervening years had seen as much service as any senior officer in the land. Born to a gentry family in Devon, he had joined Charles I's doomed campaign to relieve the French Protestants at La Rochelle in 1627 and, despite some ambivalence towards the royalist cause, fought for the king again in the civil war. After his capture by the parliamentarians at the siege of Nantwich in 1644 his allegiance waned. When he was released to fight the Irish rebels, he found the royalist cause in tatters, and fell to fighting for Parliament with remarkable ease. His outstanding abilities as a soldier were swiftly recognized by Oliver Cromwell, who gave him command of a regiment. It was Monck whose battering of the strongholds of south-east Scotland during the winter of 1650–1 kept Charles II constantly on the move, and it was his occupation of Edinburgh – of which he was made military governor – that necessitated the relocation of the coronation to Scone. During the 1650s Monck remained the dominant figure in Scotland, in both military and political terms, and when news of Cromwell's death reached him, he had immediately declared his allegiance to Richard. But as a believer in strong government and political stability rather than any particular model of authority, Monck became increasingly uneasy as Richard was deposed and the English army grew ever more radical and volatile. When Charles made an approach through Grenville, the general did not at first respond, but his opposition to the stance of the English army was clear and with deft manoeuvring he was soon commander-in-chief of all the British forces. In February 1660 Monck marched into Westminster and by the end of the month was persuaded that the only way to end the instability was for the moderate MPs who had been excluded from Parliament for their defence of the monarchy in 1648 to be readmitted and for new elections to be held. In early March, Monck and the king corresponded in earnest: Monck claimed that he had long been working for the Stuart cause and the king agreed to his terms for a restoration, which were concerned principally with ensuring order in the process. In the new elections, the exhausted and war-weary electorate returned a moderate house, which swiftly revived its upper chamber. The two houses took the view that Monck had already formed, and together they turned to the only figure whose status and position would enable him to unite a battered and divided country: King Charles II.

5

England reclaimed

On the afternoon of 23 May 1660 at the port of Scheveningen on the Dutch coast, Charles II boarded the English flagship the *Royal Charles*. The great vessel, known as the *Naseby* until it was judiciously rebranded for its new role, had been sailed over from England with the best ships of the fleet by Admiral Edward Montagu, sent to bring the king home. The day was wonderfully warm, with a clear, cloudless sky and mirror-calm sea. Thousands of spectators gathered on the long sandy beach and high dunes to witness the historic event; the sea was thick with vessels, the king's ship surrounded by a flotilla of almost a hundred more. The air rang with the sound of trumpets; gorgeous streamers and banners glimmered in the dazzling sunshine and as the *Royal Charles* weighed anchor for England, 29 Dutch cannons sounded a thunderous salute to which the English fleet made a deafening reply. Charles's return was as joyous as his departure had been fraught, and when night fell the wind rose up and a bright moon lit the inky waters as the great convoy cut across the Channel. In one of the smaller boats sailed the Admiral Montagu's young retainer, Samuel Pepys, pressed in beside the king's faithful footman James Jack and his favourite spaniel. The Kent coast was sighted at 3 a.m. on 25 May, but the royal party waited until all was ready before disembarking. The three royal brothers, Charles, James, Duke of York and Henry, Duke of Gloucester, boarded the state barge and were rowed ashore, watched by thousands of onlookers. As Charles finally stepped onto English shores as undisputed king, he knelt down and gave thanks to God. George Monck, the man who had brought the Restoration to pass, was on his knees on the pier to meet him; Charles immediately ordered the kneeling soldier to stand, kissed him, and addressed him gratefully as 'father'.[1]

As Charles had been preparing to leave The Hague, in London arrangements were hastily being made for the royal return. On 8 May the chief herald, William Ryley, Garter King at Arms, had formally proclaimed Charles II in New Palace Yard, Westminster. He then travelled through London, part of a great procession, to repeat the proclamation at Temple Bar, the Royal Exchange and Chancery Lane. Each time he read out the words 'King Charles the Second', the crowds roared with approval – the shouts were loud enough to be heard all across London, drowning out even the booming toll of the Bow Bells.[2]

A week or so later Arthur Annesley, President of the Interim Council of State, received Charles's instructions for his arrival in London. Time was by now so short that Annesley felt sure errors of protocol would arise, for which he apologized in advance, reassuring the royal party that what might be missing in detail would be made up for by the clamour of jubilant spectators. The route was to be from the south, with the king travelling from Rochester to Blackheath and there taking his place in the procession that was to pass through London. The event was to be sooner than the council had realized, it was to be 'hastned' to just four days after the king landed, Tuesday 29 May, his 30th birthday – too good an anniversary to miss.[3] During that last week London hummed with industry as Whitehall Palace was made ready, glorious costumes were prepared and the streets were swept and rails erected to hold back the crowds.[4] The form of the occasion seems to have been the result of a mixture of official planning by a committee for the king's reception, guided by the king's own instructions, and more popular initiatives: for instance a group of young women asked, and were allowed, to meet the king when he entered the city, dressed in white dresses and crimson petticoats. Meanwhile the citizens of London vied with one another to lay the most spectacular bonfire; pyres several storeys high were prepared across the capital, one in Covent Garden being built around a ship's mast, others surmounted with large timber crowns or painted images of Charles II, and one in Southwark so high it dwarfed even the tallest house.[5]

The moment Charles stepped ashore at Dover the choreography of majesty began in earnest. As he walked up the beach with Monck, a canopy was borne over both their heads and the chair of state, which had been conscientiously provided in case the king wanted a moment of regal repose, was carried alongside them. After being formally welcomed by the mayor and aldermen of Dover, the king, his brothers and General Monck boarded the royal coach and, taking their seats in strict order of precedence, were drawn through the town and out towards Canterbury. Once they were in the open countryside the four men left the coach and mounted horses but still rode in ceremonial formation: the king wearing his hat in the centre, with the Duke of York and Monck, bareheaded, flanking him. Dover Castle was not in a fit state for royal occupation, so the king's first night was spent at Canterbury in St Augustine's Abbey, where the former abbot's lodgings, converted into a handsome royal palace by Henry VIII, now belonged to Lord Campden. The following day, in public and with great formality, Charles asked Monck to kneel before him and the general was invested with the insignia of the Order of the Garter. The Duke of York fastened the garter around the general's knee, while the king himself placed the chain of office, the 'George', around his neck, with the royal brothers 'joyning unanimously together to honour him'.[6] On Sunday the king attended Canterbury Cathedral and healed the sick – running up considerable bills for gold and ribbons in the process. On Monday 28 May he rode to Rochester, where he spent the afternoon inspecting the ships in the docks at nearby Chatham, and lodged on the last night before his grand entry into the capital.[7]

On the morning of his 30th birthday, Charles woke long before dawn and by 4 a.m. the royal party was on the road from Rochester to Blackheath nine miles from London. The Kentish militia lined the route along which they travelled, which, according to one onlooker, was so thronged with spectators that it looked like one continuous busy street. Boys dangled from the branches of trees to catch a glimpse of the king, and householders hung sheets from upstairs windows in celebration of the great day. It was past noon by the time the king reached the great open plain at Blackheath. Here General Monck stood at the head of his army, numbering over 50,000 infantry and cavalry, to welcome the king. Impeccably equipped and dressed, the soldiers waited in orderly formation as each of the senior officers was brought forward, introduced to the king, and allowed to kiss his hand. As ever, Charles played his part perfectly, charming the officers with smiles and thanks, and drawing loud cheers from the soldiers with his words of address. At St George's Fields the Lord Mayor and aldermen awaited the king, and on his arrival knelt down before him and offered up the sword of the city as a gesture of loyalty. The king knighted many and stayed a while to take refreshment with the Mayor before the great procession formed.

The extraordinary cavalcade that accompanied the king home numbered well over ten thousand and was largely made up of companies of soldiers and the civic dignitaries of London. The involvement of the army meant it had a strongly military character, though the splendour of the soldiers' uniforms impressed spectators more than any weaponry they carried. Right at the front of the procession marched twelve troops, each numbering several hundred men. First came Major-General Browne's men, dressed in silver doublets; then, among others, a troop of Londoners in buff coats with bright green scarves and the Earl of Cleveland at the head of a troop of 300 men dressed in blue fringed with gold. Between each section of the procession were trumpeters and drummers, bearing the king's arms and sounding triumphant salutes. Next came the sheriffs of the city of London, the city companies and 600 citizens; the royal life guard followed, separating these junior city figures from the civic officers. The city marshals headed this section of the procession, in which rode the aldermen of London in their scarlet gowns and a wealth of other civic officials culminating with the Lord Mayor himself, bearing the city's sword. Behind him came the principals: General Monck and the country's most senior nobleman, the Duke of Buckingham, rode together in front of the king's two brothers, who flanked the king himself, a strikingly tall figure even on horseback, wearing a magnificent plumed hat. Behind the royal party were numerous other companies of soldiers, including Monck's own life guard and five whole regiments. The girls in the white skirts and crimson petticoats strewed their petals in the path of the procession, while the windows on the route were crammed with spectators, framed with flowers and hung with bright woven fabrics. As the procession passed, the musketeers who lined the route fired their guns in loud celebratory salutes. The rejoicing was universal and the noise so great that nothing like it had been heard in living memory. In the thick of this extraordinary scene, the king turned to one of his companions and remarked wryly that it must be his own fault he had been in exile so long, since clearly there was no one in England who hadn't longed for his return.[8]

But the real irony was that, despite his painstaking cultivation of the princes of Europe – his sibling sovereigns – ultimately it was to the army raised to fight his father that Charles II owed his restoration. No one was more aware than he just how great his debt was to the war-weary soldier who waited for him on Dover shore; and the ceremonies of welcome were arranged so that as well as celebrating the return of the king, they heaped honour on General Monck. It was Monck who greeted the king on behalf of his subjects. He rode in the state coach with the royal party, seated as a prince of the blood, while the Duke of Buckingham, a nobleman of the first rank, travelled outside. The general's investiture as a Knight of the Garter took place in full public view and was conspicuously performed by the royal brothers themselves. In the procession that bore the king into London the most numerous participants were again soldiers; and directly before the king rode General Monck. By arranging the ceremonies of welcome in this way, much was achieved: the king could publicly thank and reward Monck for his role in bringing the Restoration to pass; his army, whose loyalty was all important, could play a part in the rituals of restoration, and a public statement was thus made that the most powerful figure in the land was as close to the king as a brother.

On his return to England, Charles II took up residence at Whitehall Palace (*see* Figure 12). This great complex of buildings would be burnt almost to the ground before the end of the century and as a result is much less well known and understood than comparable buildings of the period. Historians have tended to complain of its warren-like confusion of rooms, though this probably says as much about their own confusion over the layout of this long-lost complex as it does about the buildings themselves. The palace stood on two sides of the great thoroughfare running north–south between Charing Cross and the Palace of Westminster. The road is now called 'Whitehall', but in the seventeenth century Whitehall was the palace which enveloped it and the road was known simply as King Street. The palace had started life as the London residence of the archbishops of York, but had passed into royal hands with the fall of Cardinal Wolsey. Henry VIII had undertaken major building works there and successive English sovereigns had made their own changes; the result was that Whitehall was not one grand architectural set-piece, but the product of centuries of additions and improvements. Two great gateways, known as the Holbein and King Street gates, spanned the main road and provided first-floor access between the two halves of the palace.

Though there had been no sovereign in London since Charles I's nocturnal flight in 1642, Whitehall had not been left unused. Initially its administrative function had continued, with a host of parliamentary committees meeting within the palace. This conformed to prior practice as royal administration had also operated from here, with the council meeting in the king's apartments and the Treasury and Secretaries of State operating from elsewhere in the palace. Following Oliver Cromwell's elevation to the office of Protector in 1653, he and his family had taken up residence within the royal apartments and it had

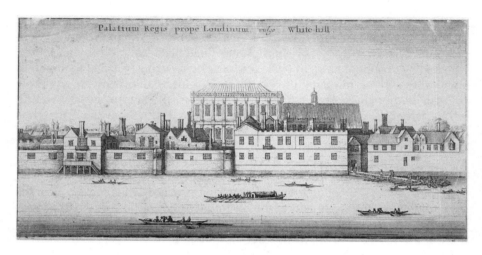

12. Whitehall Palace from the River Thames, mid-seventeenth century, by Wenceslaus Hollar. The most prominent structure, in the centre, is the Banqueting House.
© *RIBA Library Drawings and Archives Collections*

again functioned as a residential palace. Though much used, Whitehall was not fundamentally altered during the 1640s and 50s, and what Charles II found on his return was largely as he would have remembered it from boyhood. On the east of King Street between the road and the Thames, were the king and queen's own rooms, including the king's state apartments. Among these were the statuesque 'Banqueting House', built by Inigo Jones for James I, as well as the large enclosed privy garden adorned with classical statues and an elaborate sundial. To the west of the street stood the royal mews or stables and the palace entertainment complex; here the Tudor tennis court was still in use but the sixteenth-century cockpit was now a court theatre. In addition to providing the royal family with accommodation, Whitehall had well over 1000 rooms, which were allocated to court officers.[9]

The distribution of offices in the new royal administration was a burning concern for the entire political elite in May and June 1660. A torrent of petitions poured into Whitehall for every imaginable position from avenor to yeoman of the woodyard. Charles had difficult choices to make. As well as those angling for new posts, he was lobbied hard by those who had formed part of his household as Prince of Wales and those who had held positions under his father – whom he had declared he wished to accommodate.[10]

The various officials who successfully secured court positions at the Restoration deserve treatment in the context of their departments. However, it is worth, first, making some general points about the composition of the household Charles II appointed on his return. The most prestigious posts, awarded to senior noblemen, were the Gentlemen of the Bedchamber and the four great court offices of Lord Chamberlain, Lord Steward, Master of the Horse and Groom of the Stool. These positions Charles spread between those who had been loyal to him, and those who had once opposed him but whose loyalty he now most needed to maintain – an approach that mirrored the careful mix in his appointments to the privy council. Two of the posts were given to senior aristocratic royalists: Ormond – the Irish nobleman impeccably loyal to the king throughout the exile – was appointed Lord Steward, and the old Marquis of Hertford, Charles's governor and holder of the post under his father, Groom of the Stool. Two positions went to their former enemies: Monck was made Master of the Horse, and the Earl of Manchester, the Speaker of the House of Lords, Lord Chamberlain.

The picture was rather different below this most senior 'white stave' level of the royal household. Appointments to the key middle-ranking positions in the king's household above-stairs were overwhelmingly of the king's exile companions. Of the eleven grooms of the Bedchamber appointed in 1660–1, seven had served Charles on the continent during the 1650s, as had six of the seven pages of the Bedchamber. Raphael Folliart, the king's barber, Richard Pyle and Richard Wiseman, his surgeons, John Earle his chaplain and many more who were listed in the king's household before 1660 were confirmed at the Restoration.[11] There were, of course, some who had not been in exile: notably those who survived from Charles I's household and managed to secure reappointment in 1660, plus those who had powerful enough friends to secure a post without a previous claim. However, the positions of influence in the royal apartments, both private and state, were overwhelmingly held by those who had served Charles II for many years. They were men who knew the king's preferences and peccadilloes well, yet who had learned a rather unusual model of monarchy, having exercised their responsibilities in rented rooms rather than state apartments, and this was to have significant consequences for the character of the court that now assembled in the great rooms of Whitehall Palace.

Two household departments ran the vast majority of royal ceremonial, the Bedchamber (under the Groom of the Stool) and the Household above Stairs (under the Lord Chamberlain) (*see* p. xiv). To understand how the ceremonial world of the Restoration worked, it is necessary to look closely at those establishments, their staff and responsibilities. The old Marquis of Hertford, who had been born the year the Spanish Armada sailed, lived just long enough to see the monarchy restored and to be made Groom of the Stool before dying quietly in October 1660.[12] To replace him at the head of the Bedchamber, Charles turned to Sir John Grenville, who had opened the correspondence with Monck that had been so important to the Restoration. Grenville had been Charles's first personal appointment to his Bedchamber back in 1645 and would run the department for the next 25 years. His appointment was probably due partly to Monck's influence, partly to his prior tenure as Gentleman of the Bedchamber in the 1640s, and partly to the king's desire to reward him personally. The Groom of the Stool was certainly a post worth having: it brought an income of up to

£5000 per year and influence worth much more, having responsibility for all the king's private rooms, including, crucially, control over access to the sovereign when he was within them. Interestingly, though, Grenville – or the Earl of Bath as he soon became – does not seem to have made a great deal of this. He was the leading royal servant in the south-west and both before and after 1660 most of his concerns were there. Within two years of the Restoration he was Lord Lieutenant of Cornwall and Governor of Plymouth, which city he went on to refortify; and in 1666 he organized the Devon and Cornwall militia for the defence of the region. There is little evidence that he enjoyed special intimacy with the king after the Restoration, and until a dispute with the Lord Chamberlain arose in the 1680s, he exerted little influence in his oversight of the king's privy lodgings. Even his apartments at Whitehall were at one remove from the rooms for which he was responsible, being located nearer the Duke of York's rooms than the king's own.[13]

The positions of Gentlemen of the Bedchamber, the aristocrats who waited on the king in his private apartments, were almost all given to established royalists. Indeed several of those appointed had been fulfilling the responsibilities for many years in exile, among them the newly elevated Marquis of Ormond, the king's childhood companion the Duke of Buckingham, Lord Gerard and Lord Wentworth. Charles's old tutor, Newcastle, now a marquis and soon to be a duke, was also given a Bedchamber post. The lone exception to this royalist line-up was George Monck who, as Duke of Albemarle, now joined this blue-blooded band.[14]

These great men were charged with the most privileged aspects of the personal attendance of the king. The Groom of the Stool, as Chief Gentleman of the Bedchamber, headed the establishment, and so had ultimate responsibility for all that happened in the king's private apartments, including the enforcement of the written rules for the rooms. He also enjoyed the eponymous privilege – if that's the word – of attending the king at his close stool (though in reality this was exercised by his junior staff) and with the Gentlemen, who 'waited' in cycles, he dressed and undressed the monarch and served his meals within the privy lodgings. The Groom of the Stool, or the Gentleman of the Bedchamber on duty, spent the night in the bedchamber with the king, sleeping on a temporary bed assembled every evening.[15]

Below the Gentlemen in seniority were the Grooms of the Bedchamber, who also numbered about 12, and who were explicitly not to be any grander than gentlemen. Grooms were responsible for providing the king's linen, being in constant attendance in the rooms to do the king's bidding, and aiding the Gentlemen in their service of the king at his private meals; they too slept in the privy lodgings, but on the floor of the adjacent withdrawing chamber.[16] Again, almost all appointments made or confirmed in 1660 were of men who had served in Charles's household for many years. Seven had held comparable posts at the exiled court, while another had been a household officer to Charles I. At least two of the Grooms confirmed in 1660 had travelled with Charles to Scotland in 1650, including Harry Seymour, who had been a Groom of the Bedchamber since Charles was eight years old and was one of the few who was with him on his clandestine dash from Perth in October 1650.[17]

The most junior staff of the privy apartments were the six Pages of the Bedchamber (sometimes also called Pages of the Backstairs). These men, who were paid only £80 per year compared to the £500 earned by the Grooms, were, in reality, responsible for much of the day-to-day operation of the privy lodgings. They were charged with ensuring 'that every thing be ready', which included mundane tasks such as lighting fires, making the beds, keeping the rooms clean and running errands. To make certain order and timeliness prevailed in the king's private rooms they were issued with 'watches with alarums', despite the fact that the king's rooms were full of clocks that ticked and chimed noisily throughout the night. They were also, crucially, responsible for the day-to-day manning of the doors. In the absence of an assertive Groom of the Stool, it was they who, in reality, operated many of the rules of access – something that gained them notoriety then and since. Of the seven men confirmed as Pages of the Bedchamber in 1661, four had been Pages of Charles's Bedchamber since he was Prince of Wales, while a fifth, Theodore Randue, had been a member of the Duke of Gloucester's household. Among them was Thomas Chiffinch, who retained his additional responsibility, held since the 1630s, for the king's private sanctum or 'cabinet' closet.[18] Through the 25 years of the king's reign, there was remarkably little change in the people who served as pages, only 11 men ever holding posts. One other position was effectively part of the Bedchamber, the Keeper of the Privy Purse, responsible for the king's personal expenditure. This post was given in 1660 to the ambitious and urbane young courtier, Henry Bennet, who had represented the king at the Spanish court during the interregnum, and who would soon be appointed to the powerful political position of Secretary of State.[19]

The grooms and pages of the Bedchamber were Charles II's daily companions and the means by which those desirous of private access to the king might be brought into the royal lodgings by the back stairs. There was nothing particularly sinister in this; it had always been within their remit. But the experiences of his exile led Charles to rely particularly on this band of loyal and long-serving staff. Moreover the restrictive life they had all lived in Scotland in 1650–1 had taught the king and his servants to circumvent the state apartments when necessary, and to use the bedchamber and backstairs instead. Indeed, the appointment as Groom of the Stool of someone with major commitments a long distance from London, and who was not an overbearing or controlling presence in the royal household, may have been deliberate. Charles had learned from painful experience the discomfort of having the rules of access managed against him, and in the bedchamber as he established it in 1660–1, he may have been purposefully ensuring such a situation would not arise again.[20]

The responsibilities for running the royal household were distributed on a largely geographical basis (*see* p. xv). So while the Groom of the Stool oversaw all activities within the king's private rooms, the Lord Chamberlain was answerable for the state rooms – the guard chamber, presence chamber, privy chamber, privy gallery and the chapel royal. By definition these rooms were the location of all the public or state ceremonies performed within the palaces, and the Lord Chamberlain was the most important ceremonial officer in the kingdom. On 1 June 1660 Charles II gave this highly influential position to Edward Montagu, second Earl of Manchester. Manchester was 58 at the time, and would hold the post until his death at the age of 69 in 1671. The earl's days of action had been in the mid-1640s, when he had fought vigorously as a general of the parliamentary army. His ardour soon dulled, though, and by the late 1640s he was defending the House of Lords, of which he was speaker, and opposing the trial of the king. Having lain low during the Commonwealth and Protectorate, Manchester played an important part in the run-up to the Restoration, and as Speaker of the House of Lords welcomed the king on his return. He was therefore an appointment likely to be acceptable to both royalists and parliamentarians. Although not a flamboyant Lord Chamberlain, he was well liked and his ministry would be characterized by general harmony in the king's household, despite the retrenchment that would soon be forced on him by the deteriorating state of the royal finances. In describing Manchester's term as Lord Chamberlain, Clarendon later reported that he 'complied very punctually with all the obligations and duties which his place required, never failed being at chapel, and at all the king's devotions with all imaginable decency; and, by his extraordinary civilities and behaviour towards all men, did not only appear the fittest person the king could have chosen for that office in that time, but rendered himself so acceptable to all degrees of men, that none, but such who were implacable towards all who had ever served the king, were sorry to see him so promoted'.[21]

To assist him in his work, the Lord Chamberlain was aided by a Vice-Chamberlain. To this post Charles appointed the Jerseyman Sir George Carteret, who had been host to the exiled household in the Channel Islands for two prolonged periods and whose loyal defence of Jersey won him almost universal admiration. As a deserving royalist who had been notionally appointed to the post in 1647, Carteret was the obvious candidate.[22] With his assistance, Manchester was responsible for a huge staff of almost 900 people. Of this multitude, over half were members of one of the discrete sub-departments, among which, with varying levels of autonomy, were the Chapel Royal, the Great Wardrobe (responsible for furnishing the royal palaces), the Revels department (responsible for drama and entertainment at court) and the Office of Ceremonies (responsible for diplomatic protocol). Around 300 other members of the Lord Chamberlain's department were attached to one of the state rooms and performed their duties directly in those rooms.[23] Each of the principal chambers of the state apartments had a substantial staff who answered ultimately to the Lord Chamberlain. To the guard chamber, the outermost room in the sequence, was attached a corps of more than a hundred Yeomen of the Guard, responsible for the overall security of the rooms. On duty in batches of as many as forty, these formidable functionaries – they were required to be tall and strong – dressed in a red and gold uniform that had changed little since Henry VII's day, were a striking sight for any newcomer to court. At the Restoration, George Goring, Earl of Norwich, who had been one of the king's court in exile from at least 1654, was given the lucrative post of Captain of the Guard. In addition to the military staff, the guard chamber was also manned by a yeoman usher, who supervised access, and a team of grooms and messengers who ran errands and kept the room clean.[24]

The adjacent presence chamber was the most important ceremonial room in the state apartments and had the largest staff. At Whitehall there were in effect two presence chambers, the room of that name in the royal apartments and the Banqueting House, which also served that function. The primary officers of the chamber were the Gentlemen Ushers Daily Waiters, who stood next in seniority only to the Vice Chamberlain, and so had authority under him over all the officers of the state apartments.[25] Unlike the posts in the Bedchamber, which had been substantially filled during the exile, the positions in the state apartments had mostly remained empty. So while many of those appointed in 1660 had long been part of Charles II's household, few had actually performed the duties that they were now appointed to undertake. The exception was John Ayton, who was appointed to Charles's household when the prince was only three months old, and served as his Gentleman Usher Daily Waiter from childhood.[26]

Under direct control of the Gentlemen Ushers Daily Waiters were the Gentlemen Ushers Quarter Waiters, who manned the doors, and the Pages of the Presence who kept the rooms clean and furnished with fuel and candles.[27] In addition to being used for the most formal audiences, the presence chamber was where the king dined in state and so where the carvers, cupbearers and sewers (or servers), who waited on him, were stationed. On top of this host of administrative officials, the presence chamber had two great bands of ceremonial guards attached to it, the Gentlemen Pensioners and the Sergeants at Arms, who accompanied the king on ceremonial occasions, notably when he attended the chapel royal.[28]

A door at the end of the presence chamber led into the privy chamber. This room had once been part of the sovereign's private apartments (hence its name), but since James I created the institution of the Bedchamber, the privy chamber had been subsumed into the state apartments. As a result the room had lost its defining function, and now served as a less formal alternative to the presence chamber for royal audiences. The once-powerful Gentlemen of the Privy Chamber, who in the previous century performed the duties now undertaken by the Gentlemen of the Bedchamber, were still required to be on duty in the room in batches of 12, but as Charles II rarely used the privy chamber and never ate there, they had few if any actual duties. In reality the room was run by the Gentlemen Ushers of the Privy Chamber assisted by the more junior Grooms of the Privy Chamber. Of the four men appointed ushers in 1660, three had nominally been staff of the Privy Chamber during the 1650s, while at least one of the six grooms had served Charles since his father's death. The privy gallery was also within the domain of the Privy Chamber, and additional gallery keepers were appointed by the Gentlemen Ushers to man the doors and keep order there.[29]

As well as all the men who staffed the royal apartments, appointments were quickly made to the subsections of the Lord Chamberlain's department. Gilbert Sheldon, who had met the king at Canterbury on his return and fast became his trusted adviser, was made Dean of the Chapel Royal, a post which had remained vacant since the death of Richard Steward in 1651. Soon after created Bishop of London, Sheldon was a highly influential churchman. One of the principal architects of the conservative religious settlement of 1662, he would disapprove vociferously of the king's adultery, reputedly refusing him communion on one occasion.[30] John Earle, who had overseen the king's religious life in exile, was confirmed in the post of Clerk of the Closet, responsible for the king's private oratory and his personal devotions. The Great Wardrobe was given to Admiral Montagu, now Lord Sandwich, who had been responsible for the navy's support for the Restoration and had collected the king from Scheveningen; the office of the Robes was given to Newcastle's son Viscount Mansfield, with Tobias Rustat who had performed the role on a shoestring in exile, confirmed as yeoman of the department. The Jewel House was put under the mastership of Sir Gilbert Talbot, a long-standing exile companion, who was notionally a Gentleman of the Privy Chamber in the 1650s, while Sir Charles Cotterell, who had briefly been assistant Master of the Ceremonies before the civil war, and who had been secretary to the Duke of Gloucester during the exile, was made Master of the Ceremonies.

Overall it is noticeable that while the most senior officers and heads of department or sub-departments were a mixture of royalists and former supporters of Cromwell, the core holders of these offices were men who had performed these roles during the exile. Though most would be unfamiliar with the palaces that they now occupied, they knew their master well and had proved their loyalty to him in ways with which no newcomer could compete.

6

The clamour of kingship

The cavalcade which had carried Charles II through London on his 30th birthday was just the beginning of the ceremonies of arrival. Once inside the royal palace he had taken his seat on the throne at the south end of the Banqueting House and, his ears still ringing with his subjects' cheers, received their representatives, the members of the House of Lords and the House of Commons. To them he promised that his commitment to the welfare of his people would be second only to his faith in Christ. That done, an evening service was held at which the king 'made his oblations unto God', an event that took place in the presence chamber, as the chapel royal would not be ready for use for a fortnight.[1]

During the following weeks Whitehall throbbed with activity. Charles was so busy seeing visitors, attending meals and performing ceremonies, that he barely had a moment to himself. Every day he dined in public in the state apartments, watched by hundreds of his curious subjects who flocked to Whitehall. In the evenings he supped at the houses of members of the aristocracy, both those he knew well and those with whom he was only slightly acquainted. In the month after his return he ate, on separate days, with the Earl of Pembroke, the Duke of Buckingham, the Earl of Shrewsbury, the Earl of Manchester, Lord Lumley, Lord Berkeley, the Lord Mayor of London, the Speaker of the House of Commons, the Earl of Middlesex and the Countess of Devonshire.[2] On 5 July he rode in a great procession to a magnificent state feast hosted by the Lord Mayor of London; torrential summer rain poured down throughout the day and both the participants and the carefully prepared pageants along the way were drenched.[3]

Deputations of visitors poured into Whitehall to present themselves, all anxious to be among the first to court the king's favour. Within a month of his arrival he had received visits from the Lord Mayor and Aldermen of London, the Chancellors and senior officers of the Universities of Oxford and Cambridge, the ministers of the French, Dutch and Italian churches, and delegates from towns and cities up and down the kingdom. Among them came the Marquess of Argyll, boldly presenting himself in the belief that among so many who had displeased the king over the past decade, he would not be singled out for disfavour. But he had overestimated the king's clemency; he was immediately arrested for treason and soon ended his life on the executioner's block.[4]

John Evelyn, the bookish son-in-law of Sir Richard Browne, the royalist agent in Paris during the exile, was among those eager to introduce himself to the king. A week passed after the entry and Evelyn looked on in disbelief at the sheer volume of people who swarmed through Whitehall vying for the king's attention. The numbers were almost beyond counting; the desire of people to see their sovereign was in Evelyn's opinion so great as to be 'intollerable, as well as unexpressable', leaving him wondering how the king had time to eat. But what struck the diarist most was the king's reaction. Rather than recoiling from the hordes, he ordered that no one be kept away and showed himself just as eager for the attentions of his subjects as they were for sight of their sovereign.[5]

Once the officers had been appointed and the coronation completed, the main concern of Charles II's household, and of royal ceremonial in the 1660s, was this clamour for access to the sovereign.[6] To some extent it was characteristic of the first years of any reign, but in this case many of those who now courted the king had spurned him in the preceding decades. Most, from European princes to the English gentry, had ground to make up with Charles II. There was, too, a national hunger for stability, which manifested itself in almost unprecedented enthusiasm for monarchy in general, and for this monarch in particular.

On Saturday 15 September 1660, James Wynstanley of Gray's Inn travelled to Whitehall Palace. He came in his capacity as the Recorder, or the senior legal adviser, to the town of Leicester and travelled with a large deputation of the aldermen of that town. Their purpose was to present their compliments and congratulations to the king in the hope of securing royal favour for Leicester. Many towns had done the same over the course of the last few months, from great cities like London, Exeter and Nottingham to much smaller settlements such as the town of Eye in Suffolk. At Whitehall the Leicester-men had secured an introduction via a minor nobleman, Lord Loughborough, and a day and time had been appointed for their visit. On arriving at Whitehall they were brought through the royal apartments to the door of the king's bedchamber. Here they were ushered into the presence of the king himself, the heir to the throne, the Duke of York, and a collection of senior household officials. Wynstanley then delivered his carefully prepared speech, congratulating the king on his restoration and thanking him on behalf of the corporation of Leicester for his clemency to those who had opposed him, which had shown that Charles was indeed God's representative on earth. Then, presenting the king with £300 in gold, the Recorder and aldermen knelt to kiss the royal hand and departed.[7]

Dozens if not hundreds of visits like this took place during the early years of Charles II's reign (see Colour Plate 3). They followed the sort of pattern that such visits would have taken in either his father or grandfather's reign, with times prearranged, a senior figure effecting the introduction, and formal exchanges of greeting and thanks between the participants. They were, however, fundamentally different from the events James I or Charles I would have known in that they no longer took place in the state apartments but in the privy lodgings, and in many cases within the king's own bedchamber.

To understand what this change meant, it is necessary to look more closely at the geography of the royal palaces and of Whitehall, in particular. In the year of his return from exile, Charles II was in almost continual residence at Whitehall. His very first concern in terms of the decoration of his principal rooms was the fitting out and arrangement of the chapel royal (of which more later). Once this was done, the department responsible for the building and repair of the palaces, the Office of the King's Works, turned its attention to the king's bedchamber.

Since the days of Henry VIII, the sovereign's apartments at Whitehall had formed a roughly L-shaped range of rooms on the east and south sides of the open courtyard at the heart of Whitehall Palace. The main entrance to the palace was in the north-west corner of the courtyard, the state rooms were on the east side, and the private rooms opened off a privy gallery along the south side. Entering the lodgings from the north-east corner the visitor would pass south through the state apartments: the great hall, the guard chamber, the presence chamber, the privy chamber (*see* Figure 13). At the junction of the two ranges,

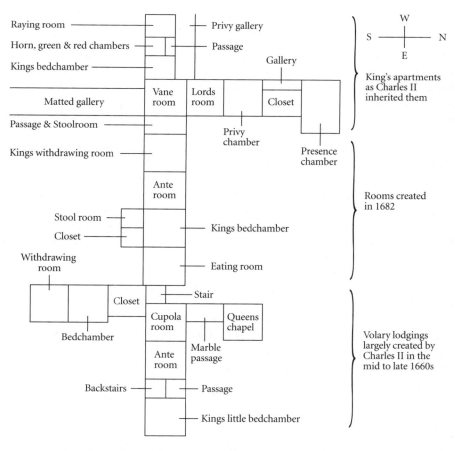

13. First-floor plan of the king's apartments at Whitehall Palace in 1682.

in the south-west corner of the courtyard, was the withdrawing room, known since the early seventeenth century as the 'Vane' Room after the weather vane that James I had had mounted above it, connected to a device in the room that showed the direction of the wind. The private apartments then ran west, with the king's bedchamber immediately adjacent to the Vane Room and a series of private closets and chambers beyond; this range projected over the road in a bridge formed by the Holbein Gate and terminated in a set of stairs leading down into St James's Park. It was into these rooms that Charles II moved in May 1660.[8] The bedchamber was essentially that created by Charles I, and Charles II knew it well, both from his father's residence there, and because he had himself occupied these rooms as a boy, when he had been left as royal figurehead while his father had journeyed north to fight the Scots.[9]

Following the frantic activity of the six months after the Restoration, Charles II ordered a series of physical changes to be made to the royal bedchamber during the winter of 1660–1. The building accounts reveal that the space was to be reconfigured to incorporate a large alcove, in which the royal bed was to stand, measuring 19 foot across by 12 foot deep, opening off the body of the room. The floor was to be laid with fashionable parquet, while the alcove was to be separated from the rest of the room by a low carved screen, with sections opening as gates at either end (see Figure 15). The alcove was given a theatrical treatment, its opening framed by two great curtains carved in wood, each pulled back by a winged cherub, revealing at the centre two eagles flanking a carved head.[10] Sadly no image survives of this magnificent confection, and it is not known whose head was represented. However, the arrangement described matches almost exactly the alcove in the bedchamber at the Louvre built for Henri IV.[11]

Soon after the building work was complete, the redecoration of the room was taken in hand. For the ceiling the English artist John Michael Wright painted an allegorical canvas, which does survive (see Figure 14). It shows the mythical figure of Astraea, daughter of Zeus, whose life on earth heralded a golden age that ended when she ascended to live among the stars. Astraea is shown flying back down to earth. To make sure that the message was absolutely clear, a portrait of Charles II adorned the heavens while a whole squadron of flying cherubs bore an oak tree skywards – not a subtle metaphor for the glories of Restoration, perhaps, but certainly a clear one.[12]

Following the reconfiguration of the room, new furniture was ordered; in keeping with the first fashion of the day, it was all upholstered in the same opulent fabric: a rich crimson damask edged with a deep gold and silver fringe. The bed itself, supplied by the royal upholsterer John Casbert, and the accompanying six chairs, were also covered in this gorgeous fabric. Nor did it stop there: the walls were hung with framed panels of the same material, the curtains for the two windows were also made from it, and even the carpet on the parquet floor was crimson damask. Charles personally chose the regal crimson and the price of the materials was equally princely: the fringe for the wall hangings alone came in at little under £200 (something like £14,000 in modern terms).[13]

14. *Allegory of the Restoration of King Charles II* by John Michael Wright. This painting
was part of the ceiling of Charles II's bedchamber at Whitehall.
© Nottingham Castle Museum

15. Gilded rail or screen made for Charles II. The carved letters 'CR' were later adapted to read 'GR' for one of the Hanoverian sovereigns.

This was not the only alcove bedchamber which Charles II planned. During the early years of the reign, he embarked on an ambitious scheme to rebuild the Tudor royal palace at Greenwich. Though the money ran out before the scheme could be completed, drawings were made for the interiors, including the royal bedchamber. Here the king planned a very similar arrangement to Whitehall, though in this case the alcove was to be given an exotic palm tree treatment, with the arching palm fronds framing the opening[14] (*see* Figure 16). While the Greenwich bedchamber was never realized, the great bedchamber at Whitehall continued in use right through the reign, periodically re-hung and redecorated.[15]

The works to the Whitehall bedchamber in 1660–1 created a room that was, in decorative and functional terms, an innovation in England: the king's state bedchamber (*see* Figure 17). It was something that would have been completely alien to Charles I and James I, who would never have countenanced receiving a civic deputation in their bedchambers.[16] Charles II created a room laid out not for rest and repose but for formal meetings and events, with the bed ceremonially cordoned off in the alcove. In administrative terms the room was still part of the private apartments, as was the Vane Room next door to it; but in functional terms within weeks of the Restoration both these rooms and the galleries that ran from them had become semi-public spaces.

There were essentially three reasons for this change. The first was purely practical: in the early months of the reign Whitehall was awash with carpenters, plasterers and other craftsmen modifying the royal apartments to Charles II's taste. In the inevitable disruption, rooms temporarily served a variety of functions that blurred the boundaries of public and private space. The presence chamber, for instance, was briefly used as a chapel, and a throne was set up in the matted gallery for audiences, both transient arrangements made to accommodate the building works.[17] The second reason the private apartments were used for formal events, and so for the creation of a state bedchamber, related to Charles II's own use of space. As already discussed, the king while in exile had grown used to using his supposedly private rooms for all manner of business and meetings, partly because, living abroad as a prince, convention required it and partly because experience in Scotland, in particular, had given him reason to prefer this arrangement for the greater control it gave him. The third reason was one of geography. The layout of the apartments at Whitehall and the separation of private and public space worked on the basis that visitors passed into the rooms from north to south, from the great hall through the state apartments. Crucially, the privy gallery, which formed the spine of the east–west inner rooms, was supposed to be a private space, and the steps from the west end of it that led down into the park were private stairs. However in the years since Charles I's occupation of the palace, this arrangement had been eroded, and, come the Restoration, it was not unusual for visitors to enter the privy gallery from the park or indeed up the backstairs from the privy garden, so reversing the original axis and throwing the sequence of rooms into confusion.[18]

16. Design for Charles II's bedchamber at Greenwich Palace by John Webb, 1665.
© *RIBA Library Drawings and Archives Collections*

CONNE LE NY LORD NAIOR ACONPAIGNEDE SES COLLEGVES
VIENT SALVER LA REYNE LVY FAIRE SES PRESENS

17. Marie de Medici, Queen Mother of France, receiving visitors in her bedchamber
at St James's Palace in 1638.

When, for instance, the deputation from the University of Oxford came to
Whitehall on 13 June 1660, they *should* have come in by the main gate from
King Street, and then passed through the state apartments, starting with the
guard chamber. In fact they came into the palace from the south, directly into
the supposedly private area of the privy garden, walked north along the stone

gallery, cut across a courtyard to reach the top end of the state apartments, and then retraced their steps at first-floor level through the state apartments to reach the privy gallery, where their audience was to take place.[19] Others came into the privy gallery up the stairs from the park, while many wandered in the long matted gallery that ran south from the Vane Room.[20]

The reordering and refurnishing of the king's bedchamber as a reception room created a space fit for the function it would continue to perform. Not just in the early months, but throughout the reign, the king used the room for a whole range of events. The most ceremonious diplomatic audiences still took place in the state rooms, but a whole host of events of middling formality happened in the bedchamber. Among them were official introductions, as in April 1665 when John Evelyn – now on familiar terms with the king – presented the young Dutch captain, Everse, to the king in his bedchamber.[21] When the king knighted his subjects, he often did so in the bedchamber, as for instance in November 1674 when the Director of the Dutch East India Company received this honour at Whitehall.[22] In the summer of 1681 the inventor, engineer and arch self-publicist, Sir Samuel Morland, successfully demonstrated how water could be pumped from Windsor park into the castle; delighted with this work, Charles summoned him into the royal bedchamber and there, in the company of Prince Rupert, the Lord Chamberlain and a host of other dignitaries, conferred on him the title of 'Master of Mechanicks'.[23] Marriages, too, sometimes took place within the royal bedchamber. In the spring of 1663 the king provided his illegitimate son, James, with both the dukedom of Monmouth and the most eligible heiress in the country, the 12-year-old Anna Scott, Countess of Buccleuch. The two were married in a ceremony conducted in the king's bedchamber, though their youth spared them the semi-public consummation ritual.[24] In April 1666, as part of the proceedings relating to the trial of Lord Morley and Mounteagle in Westminster Hall, the king presented the staff of the Lord High Steward to Lord Clarendon in the bedchamber.[25] Very occasionally chapters of the Order of the Garter were held in the bedchamber and on at least one occasion the privy council met there.[26]

In the early months of the reign, the king had encouraged the tide of people pouring into Whitehall; after the isolation of exile he had welcomed it, and was determined to keep 'all doors open to all persons'. But he soon came to see that such an approach had its shortcomings; for while the once-private rooms at Whitehall were being used for meetings and receptions, the king was still trying actually to live in them. As a result the French ambassador would stride in as he was dressing, and it was almost impossible to escape the daily clatter of aldermen's boots.[27] So, in November 1662, the king asked for a second royal bedchamber to be created at Whitehall, to be located east of the Vane Room in the gallery built for Cardinal Wolsey towards the river, known as the Turk's Gallery.[28] Four years later this initiative was taken further and the king had a whole new building constructed in this area to contain a suite of private rooms. The new lodgings were three storeys high with hipped roofs, and stood on three sides of an open-sided courtyard that contained an aviary or 'volary garden'. The fourth side was open to the river, giving the rooms spectacular views framed by ingenious new sash windows.[29] Here the king was provided with a range of rooms over which he and his staff could genuinely keep control; they included, amongst others, a new bedchamber, withdrawing room, backstairs and closets.[30]

Although the staff of the Bedchamber were still nominally in control of the Vane Room and alcove bedchamber as well as the new rooms in the Volary lodgings (as they were called), in reality the Vane Room and alcove bedchamber formed a semi-public section of the king's apartments while those in the Volary were genuinely private. This is made quite clear, for instance, by the descriptions of the mourning fabric in which the king's apartment was draped on the death of his mother, Henrietta Maria, in 1669. Purple fabric covered the rooms into which visitors might pass: the guard chamber, presence chamber, privy chamber, the Vane Room, the privy gallery and the king's bedchamber. The private rooms in the Volary lodgings were out of bounds.[31]

While Charles II's subjects flocked to ingratiate themselves with their restored king, the princes of Europe, whose condemnations of the regicide had, with only one exception, been so muted as to be almost inaudible, also had ground to make up. Little thanks to them, Charles II had regained his kingdom, and it was in many ways a kingdom enhanced; its naval power had improved considerably since the days of his father and British trading links were fast expanding. Throughout 1660, diplomats sailed for London to present their masters' compliments on the king's restoration. Special embassies of congratulation, the grandest led by 'extraordinary' ambassadors, came from the kings of Spain, France and Denmark, the Doge and Senate of Venice, the Grand Duke of Tuscany and the United Provinces. Such was the enthusiasm with which these leaders greeted Charles II's restoration, that it seemed almost unthinkable that they had paid so little attention to his accession ten years earlier.[32]

Though Charles II was no longer fighting for his political existence, the handling of international diplomacy required great care if the nation's standing was to be maintained. The arrangement of diplomatic ceremonial was part of the responsibilities of the Lord Chamberlain, but with the creation of the position of Master of the Ceremonies in 1603 its day-to-day management had been delegated to this official – an arrangement that had existed at the French court since the 1580s. Under the Master of the Ceremonies a small department was formed, comprising an assistant master and a marshal.[33] Sir Charles Cotterell had been given the senior post in 1660, and to him fell the task of organizing the reception of diplomats and all other aspects of protocol relating to their visits. Cotterell was well suited to the post. He was an excellent linguist, and having spent much of the exile abroad he was well acquainted with several of the nations with which he now regularly dealt. During the interregnum he had acted as secretary to the young Duke of Gloucester, but he had also worked extensively for the king's aunt, Elizabeth of Bohemia, and so had first-hand experience of the reality of European diplomacy. Much more than a bureaucrat, he was also temperamentally suited to the job, being both urbane and astute, as well as enjoying considerable fame in literary circles for his popular translations of romantic and political works.[34]

The Master of the Ceremonies' role was to act as intermediary in arranging the formal contact between foreign ministers and the royal family. The actual cut and thrust of foreign affairs was not his responsibility – the powerful secretaries of state had this job – but all aspects of the rituals of diplomacy were. He was to liaise between the diplomats and the Lord Chamberlain or the king to agree the time and location of meetings. It was his job to ensure that the form of ceremonies accorded with past practice, and that the privileges allowed to any given minister were appropriate to his status, his embassy, precedent and the treatment given to English agents at his home court.[35] It is clear, not least from the frequent reiteration of the need to consult him, that diplomats often tried to make arrangements via the Lord Chamberlain or one of the secretaries of state without reference to the Master of the Ceremonies. It was his job to ensure this did not happen, and that no procedural nicety was overlooked.[36]

Diplomatic ceremonial was punctiliously observed in the seventeenth century, and the evidence for it is copious, precisely because its importance warranted a permanent staff of officers to keep detailed records.[37] The subject can now seem both arcane and archaic, but at the time it was considered of the highest importance. As a contemporary diplomat remarked, 'nothing is more natural nor more deeply founded upon every good reason of state than that the good or ill relations between kings and government should depend upon the good or ill reception and treatment of foreign ministers in the courts'.[38] The way one ruler treated the representatives of another mirrored the attitude and approach of one nation to another. As a result, all those involved with diplomatic ceremonial took meticulous care to ensure that it reflected precisely the appropriate levels of respect or deference required by the relative status of the participant nations.

It was not only the diplomatic corps who set great store by diplomatic ritual. As ceremonial receptions were universally believed to reflect national dignity, men and women of all classes took real personal pride, or offence, in the manner of their performance. In 1663, for instance, a dispute arose between Charles II and Louis XIV about the order of the coaches in the entry procession of the English ambassador into Paris. Louis XIV wanted to alter the usual sequence in his favour, by putting French princes of the blood ahead of the ambassador. A six-month stand-off followed, which was only broken when Louis's brother agreed not to attend. When the news reached England, Timothy Allsop, the king's brewer, ranted to Samuel Pepys at length about how 'our Embassadour had, it is true, an Audience; but in the most dishonourable way that could be, for the Princes of the Blood (though invited by our Imbassador, which was the greatest absurdity that ever embassdor committed these 400 years) were not there, and so were not said to give place to our King's imbassador'.[39]

To appreciate Charles II's own approach to diplomatic occasions, it is essential to understand how this area of royal ceremonial functioned. Diplomats came in different ranks. At the top of the scale were ambassadors proper. These were either 'ordinary' ambassadors, permanently resident at a foreign court, or 'extraordinary' ambassadors, dispatched on a special mission that seldom lasted more than a few weeks. Below ambassadors in status were the lowlier grades of envoys and residents. All meetings between Charles II and diplomats at his court were to some extent governed by ceremonial protocol; but by far the most important ceremonial occasions were the rituals associated with the arrival and, to a lesser extent, the departure of a foreign agent. The procedure for diplomats arriving at a foreign court and presenting their credentials was highly formalized across Europe.[40] The first act of a diplomat reaching his destination was to make himself known to the Secretary of State responsible for relations with his home country. Having satisfied that official with the authenticity of his credentials, he was then directed to the Master of the Ceremonies, who made all arrangements for his formal introduction to the king.[41] For the less grand diplomats, residents and envoys, this just involved arranging an official meeting, but for the senior diplomats no meeting could take place before their ceremonial entry into London.

By definition, ambassadors had usually already arrived in London before their 'entry', as it frequently took several weeks of discussion with officials in the capital to agree the details of the occasion. Once the time and date were fixed, the ambassador would quietly leave London, travelling back downriver to Greenwich or Gravesend, to set forth on the ceremony of arrival.[42] These entries took the form of great processions from the diplomats' notional point of disembarkation from their ships to Whitehall Palace. The Master of the Ceremonies met the ambassador with the royal barge, accompanied by a nobleman representing Charles II and a clutch of household officers, and invited him to travel in it to the royal palace.[43] The journey normally involved being transported by river to the wharf at the Tower of London, and then by coach through the streets of London and Westminster.[44] At the Tower a great procession formed behind the royal coach, composed (in the early 1660s at least) of the coaches and entourages of other diplomats as well as those of the nobility. The numbers could be enormous: there were regularly over forty coaches in such processions, while more than sixty accompanied the Spanish ambassadors on their entry in May 1665.[45] The procession included a great baggage train containing the ambassador's possessions – or at least that was what the vehicles appeared to carry. In reality, the diplomats' bags had usually been unpacked weeks before and beneath their bright covers the numerous carts were completely empty.[46] The procession passed westward, down thoroughfares cleared of people and vehicles by royal officials, to New Palace Yard in Westminster. This was the location of the house belonging to one Lady Williams where, by long arrangement, ambassadors were entitled to be accommodated by the king until their public audience. Here they would be met by the officers of the king's household who were to attend them during this period and various further arrangements were made.[47]

There was intense competition between nations about the way in which these entries were conducted, ranging from concern about the general level of splendour at an ambassadorial entry to the precise details of the event. Diplomats contended to outdo one another in 'gallantry and entertainments' to the extent that in 1669 Jan Boreel, the Dutch ambassador, lobbied to dispense with an entry altogether rather than risk the sniggers of onlookers disparaging its scale and splendour in comparison with the recent Danish entry.[48] The extent to which the detail mattered just as much as the overall effect is clear from the endless correspondence on seating within the royal coach, the identity of the nobleman sent to greet the new arrival, and the order of the procession.

Its sheer importance to contemporaries is nowhere more vividly illustrated than in the scenes of extraordinary aggression that erupted in the city of London at the entry of the Swedish ambassador in September 1661. At this time both the French and the Spanish ambassadors considered themselves the most senior diplomats in London, and so claimed the honour of travelling immediately after the royal coach at the entry. This was not just a matter of Whitehall protocol, but was a symptom of an ongoing struggle between France and Spain for European supremacy. Violence was in the air in the morning of Monday 30 September 1661, the day of the Swedish ambassador's entry, with both Spanish and French diplomats determined that they and their entourages would follow immediately after the royal coach. Charles II had extracted a promise from each that they would not carry firearms, but no one was in any doubt that blood would be shed before the day was out. The French ambassador, D'Estrades, looked certain to come off best: he had conscripted several hundred Frenchmen resident in London to join his entourage and, despite his promise, secretly armed them with muskets and pistols. In contrast the Spanish ambassador, Batteville, had only a small number of men from the Low Countries in his troupe, armed with just swords and sticks. As soon as the blameless Swedish ambassador climbed into the royal coach and set off for Whitehall, the French attacked the Spanish head-on and a brutal skirmish raged on the narrow wharf between the Thames and the Tower of London. Though the French were better armed and more numerous than the Spanish, Batteville had taken two crucial precautions: first, he had visited the site a few days earlier and had strategically positioned his coach; and second, he had had the leather harnesses that joined his coach and horses lined with strong chains. As a result when the royal coach set off he was able to swing easily into pole position and, cutting the harnesses on the French horses, sent his adversaries into immediate disarray. Undaunted by the loss of four of their six coach horses, the French pursued the Spanish through the streets, with bricks and stones being thrown, pistols fired and the habitually anti-French crowd baying in favour of the Spaniards. At the end of the day six or seven men were dead and dozens more injured; among them was D'Estrades own son, horribly wounded when a great rock collapsed his chest, and his brother-in-law, who had been slashed ferociously across the leg by a sword. However, Batteville's victory was to be brief and pyrrhic. Louis XIV was incandescent with rage when he heard what had happened, especially when it emerged that Batteville had paid Londoners to attack the French. Following threats of war, Philip IV of Spain was forced to make the ignominious concession that he would never again contest French supremacy on such occasions.[49]

The splendour with which these entries were normally conducted reflected more than the status of the visitor. Charles II's own entry into The Hague in 1660 was described by Hyde, significantly, as 'answerable to the pomp, wealth and greatness of that State'. Part of the job of the Master of the Ceremonies, Sir Charles Cotterell, was to ensure that a great and grand audience of English people turned out to witness them.[50] To make certain this happened, he would notify all the nobility in London of the date of an entry, encouraging them to come personally, or at least send their coaches, to add to the magnificence of the occasion. The day before the event a drum was beaten through the streets of London as a reminder to all citizens to be ready to cheer the new diplomatic arrival.[51]

Once their entries were over, ambassadors were entitled to be lodged and fed by the king for three days, pending their first formal audience.[52] Though it clearly left a little to be desired, Lady Williams's house in New Palace Yard, where they were normally put up, was conveniently located for Whitehall.[53] Important ambassadors were sometimes given much grander lodgings in houses specially furnished for the occasion. In the autumn of 1660, for instance, the Prince de Ligne, extraordinary ambassador from the King of Spain, was lodged at Campden House, while the Comte de Soissons, who came in the same capacity from the King of France, stayed at Somerset House.[54]

At their highly formal first public audience with the king, ambassadors offered their letters of appointment and presented gifts.[55] On the agreed day, the Master of the Ceremonies and a member of the nobility collected the ambassador from his lodging in the royal coach.[56] The diplomat in question was usually accompanied by members of his own household, often dressed in gorgeous livery, and with them travelled to Whitehall.[57] On arrival at the palace, the ambassador was taken to the council chamber, where he would wait for word that the king was ready to receive him.[58]

These receptions were among the grandest and most conspicuous ceremonial occasions of any reign, and for the reception of extraordinary ambassadors the vast Banqueting House was specially prepared. It was reached, like the presence chamber, from the guard chamber, though in this case via a long spur corridor, and was administered by the presence chamber officials. For public audiences the room was perfumed and the walls were hung with one of the Great Wardrobe's most magnificent suites of tapestry.[59] After his marriage, Charles II usually received ambassadors with his consort, both seated on chairs of state placed on a dais of three steps, beneath a great canopy of state, with important and favoured courtiers and councillors standing behind them.[60] Separating the dais from the rest of the hall was a rail, which diplomats were taken through via a small gate, when presented.[61] Members of the household guard, the Gentlemen Pensioners and Yeomen of the Guard, lined the route from the door to the dais and musicians played from the gallery (*see* Figure 18).[62]

On arrival, the diplomat was met at the door by the Lord Chamberlain and led up to the high end of the room. Here, following a speech and much bowing, he offered his letters of credence to the king, who swiftly passed them on to the Secretary of State.[63] The king and queen would then rise, the king removing his hat out of respect for the ambassador's position and the ruler he represented. The diplomat might then be invited to come forward on to the royal dais, where the king would usually invite him to put his hat on, doing the same himself.[64] Conversation on the general amity and good relations between the Stuart kingdoms and the ambassador's nation would follow, with the king and ambassador raising their hats whenever mention was made of their respective prince or republic. When the ambassador turned to address the queen, he would usually remain bareheaded, ceremonial rectitude being carefully maintained where the consort was concerned.[65]

At the grandest of these audiences gifts were given, usually appropriate to the country of origin of the embassy; so the Dutch ambassador gave fine paintings, furniture and sculpture, the Russians sable and ermine furs, the Venetians gondolas and the Moroccans lions and ostriches.[66] Where feasible, these were delivered with considerable flourish; the Russian ambassador had his presents brought into the Banqueting House by members of his vast retinue, among them dozens of ferocious-looking hawks and a group of magnificent Arab horses.[67]

18. The reception of the Prince de Ligne, extraordinary ambassador from the King of Spain, by Charles II at the Banqueting House in September 1660.

As was the case with so many aspects of these ceremonial occasions, the flamboyance and generosity of the presents was intended to reflect the status and power of both the giver and the receiver.[68]

Before the end of the audience, the king would invite members of the company to kiss his hand, and the most important of them, usually just the ambassador, to kiss the queen's.[69] On exceptional occasions, the king might embrace the diplomats, as he did the extraordinary ambassadors from Venice in August 1661, as a special sign of friendship.[70] Credentials and presents delivered, and professions of amity exchanged, the ambassador would take his leave. He withdrew without turning away from the king and queen, walking the hundred or so feet to the door backwards.[71] The nobleman who had accompanied the ambassador to the audience then saw him either to a second audience with the Duke of York and his family, or back to his house.[72] At the end of an extraordinary embassy a virtually identical state audience of departure, or congé, would be held. The departing ambassador would be collected from his house by the Master of the Ceremonies and a nobleman, be taken to court in the king's coach, repose in the council chamber, and be received by the king in the Banqueting House.[73]

Being grand and often exotic affairs, the public audiences in the Banqueting House were well attended. The guards who lined the route to the dais were not just for show, and sometimes had difficulty maintaining the dignity of the occasion; the combination of a sizeable diplomatic retinue, the usual battalion of household officers and a substantial crowd of onlookers could be overwhelming and the guards frequently struggled to keep order in the crush and the heat.[74] There seems to have been little close scrutiny of those who came. Samuel Pepys was able to push through the crowds right up to the dais without being challenged.[75] With the crowds flocking in, even the balconies of the Banqueting House were filled with spectators, so many on some occasions that it was feared the structure would sheer off and come crashing to the ground.[76]

Diplomats below the status of ambassador would have neither a ceremonial entry nor a great public inaugural audience in the Banqueting House. Nonetheless, they were given a carefully arranged first audience with the king and queen, to which the Master of the Ceremonies conducted them. On the appointed day, the residents or envoys in question would be met by the Master of the Ceremonies from his lodgings. Residents were always brought to court in the Lord Chamberlain's coach; envoys and envoys extraordinary might sometimes be brought in the king's coach; while ambassadors were always brought in the king's coach.[77] A nobleman would accompany the Master of the Ceremonies to collect an ambassador, but for lesser diplomats Cotterell travelled alone.[78] On alighting from the coach at Whitehall, the visitors were received by the Marshal of the Ceremonies. These first audiences would take place in the royal apartments, but never in the Banqueting House. The diplomats would be escorted through the state apartments, where, in the case of envoys, the Yeomen of the Guard would stand to arms as they crossed the guard chamber. Like extraordinary ambassadors, they would usually have to wait for the king to be ready to receive them, though in their case they were left in either the privy chamber or the Lord Chamberlain's lodgings during this time.[79]

Unless the Banqueting House was being used, when the king and queen received formally together in the royal apartments they usually did so in the queen's apartments. The first audience of the Russian envoys in August 1667 took place in the queen's presence chamber, as did that of two other Russian envoys in November 1682.[80] However, according to the Master of the Ceremonies, when the royal couple received separately the king's presence chamber was not used at all; instead, the king received 'sometimes in his Antechamber ... & sometimes in the Bedchamber'. At the door to whichever was being used the visitor would be met by the Lord Chamberlain, or Vice Chamberlain if it was in the state apartments and a Gentlemen of the Bedchamber if it was the bedchamber. In the latter case the Master of the Ceremonies would walk on the left hand of the visitor into the audience.[81] Though diplomats should, technically, have been received by the king sitting and with his hat on, Charles II usually conducted such audiences standing and hatless.[82] Having seen the king, handed over his credentials and exchanged pleasantries, the diplomat would be conducted to the queen, usually in her withdrawing room, where he was met at the door by her Lord Chamberlain or Vice Chamberlain, and where she would receive him sitting.[83] Very much the same procedure was followed in these first audiences as those in the Banqueting House: the diplomat's credentials were handed over, compliments and declarations of good intent were exchanged, and royal hands were proffered for kissing.[84]

After the first formal meeting there would be many others of a less ceremonious variety, and indeed there had frequently been a 'private' audience in the days before an entry.[85] Although much of the real business was conducted between the diplomats and the king's ministers, the king encountered the foreign agents in London on a more-or-less daily basis in the galleries and withdrawing rooms of Whitehall, and further audiences might be requested from time to time when occasion merited it.[86] These private audiences were usually conducted in the king's bedchamber or closet, without the formal trappings of dais and canopy of state. Indicative of their private character was the diplomats' approach, not through the state apartments, as for a public audience, but through the privy gallery from St James's Park or directly from the privy garden into the privy apartments.[87] However, though the king usually conducted the interview standing and bareheaded, the Master of the Ceremonies would still (in principle, at least) officiate, even bringing the diplomat to court in the royal coach, and great notice was always taken of the sovereign's smallest physical gestures.[88]

In the early months of 1660 there was a scramble among the diplomats based in London to win favour with the new regime, for which they had to secure amended letters of accreditation from their masters. Desperately keen to demonstrate their support for the Stuart Restoration, they sponsored extravagant fireworks, threw parties and paid for fountains of wine to run in the streets in celebration.[89] As was the case with his own subjects, the king's first reaction to this clamour for access and favour from the diplomatic corps was overwhelmingly receptive. In fact he went out of his way to be utterly charming to many of those he met. To residents, the lowliest rank of diplomatic representatives, he dispensed with the usual convention that the king should neither stand up nor remove his hat when they entered the audience room, and instead he flattered them by doing both. After being received in this manner in July 1660 a Venetian diplomat wrote home breathlessly of this young king who 'excels all other potentates in humanity and affability'.[90] To the dismay of Cotterell, who like all Masters of the Ceremonies hated change, the new king not only received some relatively minor visitors standing and bareheaded, but conducted private audiences with diplomats in the alcove bedchamber, rather than in the withdrawing room. Cotterell acknowledged that Charles did this without making any alterations to the precedent books, and he admitted that he did not take kindly to anyone expecting to be treated with undue honour. He nonetheless clearly disapproved.[91]

While Charles disposed with some of the relatively minor conventions of diplomatic ceremonial, it was generally agreed that when it came to grander events of greater substance, he displayed a powerful and insistent majesty which could be spellbinding to behold. His old governor Newcastle, now a duke in his dotage, must have smiled to himself at the sight of his erstwhile pupil practising exactly what he had preached. The comment of the extraordinary ambassadors from Venice about the king's style of majesty was Newcastle's advice epitomized: while the king enjoyed the pleasures of court, 'on great and noteworthy occasions he does not forget to uphold the royal majesty, though it is combined with a pleasing suavity whereby he has won the respect and affection of the common people ...'[92]

Beneath the affability and charm, universally commented upon throughout the early 1660s, the young king had a steely streak and a long memory. Despite the fireworks and the fountains of wine, a whole slice of the diplomatic corps resident in London were refused access to the king: the Dutch ambassador was turned away, as the king was 'ill pleased with him personally owing to his behaviour during the late incidents', while the French ambassador, Bordeaux, was similarly excluded from court for what he had 'done and spoken to his [i.e. the king's] disadvantage'.[93] On the other hand, he went out of his way, within the basic structure of diplomatic protocol, to demonstrate his gratitude to others. Francesco Giavarina, the Venetian Resident, was among those who had dashed down to Dover to meet Charles II in May 1660. Introduced to the king at Canterbury, Giavarina was thrilled to be treated so graciously: Charles addressed the diplomat in his native Italian and expressed delight that he was among the first to whom he was introduced. The Resident wrote back to Venice explaining this kindness: 'He told me he knew that I was the only minister who had not recognised the Parliament.' In a similar spirit, Charles arranged for the Russian ambassador to be received with every demonstration of pomp and splendour, as 'the *Emperor* his Master having not onely been kind to his Majestie in distresse, but banishing all Commerce with our Nation during the Rebellion'. Some years later, Charles insisted that the young son of the Duke of Pfalz-Neuburg, in England on an educational visit, be treated with much greater attention and ceremony than would usually have been the case in recognition of the duke's reception of him at Dusseldorf in 1654.[94] Just as he would make regular payments from his own purse to those who had hidden him after the battle of Worcester right up until his death, so he did not forget which nations had given him succour during the dark days of the 1650s.

Charles was not, as a man, a natural pedant or a lover of ceremonial conventions for their own sake. In another existence he would have made a poor herald or Marshal of the Ceremonies; as Cotterell himself remarked, the king was instinctively 'willing to escape anything of trouble or ceremony'.[95] But Charles knew from both education and experience the value of the rituals of majesty and made it his business to take them seriously. He was personally involved in the negotiations over how senior diplomats and other high-status visitors would be received. Arrangements regarding the reception of the French extraordinary ambassador, Verneuil, were, for example, conducted by letter directly between Charles II, his wife, and the king's sister, the Duchess of Orléans.[96] Offers and counter-offers were made, and trade-offs proposed; they were as rigorously negotiated as war and peace. In such discussions it was Charles himself who made the crucial decisions. In fact a procedure developed to reflect this. The Lord Chamberlain and Master of the Ceremonies worked out their recommendation for the form of any given reception based on past precedent, and highlighted any areas of contention or ambiguity for referral to the king. These were then put to Charles as a list of questions, which he went through, returning considered answers to each. So the form of the reception of the Grand Duke Cosimo III of Tuscany and queries regarding the treatment of Mary of Modena and William of Orange were all the subject of detailed discussion with the king.[97] The question of how William of Orange, on a visit to London, ought to receive the foreign diplomats stationed there was resolved with reference to 'the King's pleasure' in the matter, while when Prince Rupert raised a question about how the Duke of York would receive the Elector Palatine, the answer was simple: the duke would ask the king.[98]

Charles II's refusal to agree to the changes Louis XIV wanted to make to the entry of the English ambassador into Paris demonstrates his tenacity in matters which he considered to involve the reputation and international standing of his nations, and therefore of himself as sovereign.[99] He explained to his sister, Henriette Anne, who had married Louis XIV's brother, the difference between 'trifles', or 'points of honour' of negligible importance ('not worth his [Louis XIV's] anger or myne') and things which were of genuine importance, such as the treatment of his official representatives. As he put it 'I never did nor never will permitt my ambassadore to give the place to any whatsoever.'[100] When the French ambassador to London made his entry into the capital in 1677, he was instructed by Louis to prevent the Duke of York's coach going immediately after the royal coach in the entry procession. However after months of argument, Louis XIV eventually 'sat down and acquiesced' to Charles's insistence that this would indeed be the order of the procession, having been driven 'to his wits end' by Charles's absolute stubbornness on this point.[101] So while Charles II was not, like Louis XIV, personally fascinated with the details of ceremonial receptions, he was acutely concerned with receiving the honours that were due to him as a sovereign, and as a sovereign of England, Scotland and Ireland.

While Whitehall reverberated with the footsteps of the men and women who came to introduce themselves to the long-absent king, another group of people, largely of lesser social status, also clamoured for access. It had been almost twenty years since royal healing ceremonies had been held in London and many saw the return of the king as offering the chance of relief from a painful and disfiguring condition.[102] As discussed, Charles had touched regularly throughout his exile, and continued to do so unabated with his restoration. He healed the sick on the way from Dover to London, and within a month of his return to Whitehall was holding massive healing ceremonies in the Banqueting House, at which hundreds were touched.[103] In the remaining six months of 1660, Charles II touched almost seven thousand of his subjects (*see* Appendix 1). Clearly these occasions needed to be managed if utter chaos was to be avoided. A proclamation was therefore issued that stipulated that the king would heal only on Fridays, that no more than 200 would be admitted for the royal touch in one sitting, and that even they would have to secure their places by the proper means.[104]

Much of the procedure for being touched had been established by Charles's father. Instinctively private and ill at ease with crowds, Charles I had not much enjoyed the event, but its divine symbolism appealed to his sense of kingship so he periodically performed the ritual and did much to bring order to how it was conducted. In 1625 a proclamation had been posted up in all market towns in England that the king would touch only at Easter and Michaelmas, and that no one would be allowed to apply for the cure without a certificate from their parish testifying that they had never been touched before. JPs were warned not to allow anyone to travel to London for the cure without such a certificate. This requirement was augmented by another by 1638: that before any journey was made the sufferer should have been seen by both a doctor and a surgeon and should carry a second certificate from them verifying that the bearer had scrofula or 'the king's evil'.[105] Charles II would institute similar measures: on 4 July 1662 a proclamation was issued requiring all those seeking the royal touch to bring with them a certificate confirming that they had not been touched before, a requirement that continued to be reiterated throughout Charles II's reign.[106] A copy of such a certificate survived in Grasmere Church, Oxfordshire; signed by the rector and churchwardens, it declared 'That David Harrison of the s^d Parish aged about ffourteen years is afflicted as wee are credibly informed with the disease comonly called the King's Evil & (to the best of o^r knowledge) hath not heretofore been Touched by His Majesty for ye s^d Desease'.[107] The inference that unscrupulous types forged certificates demonstrates that these documents were essential for admission to the ceremony of touch. John Browne, one of Charles II's surgeons, noted that extra vigilance was required by all concerned against the 'Cheats by counterfeit Certificates and the like', and recommended that printed certificates be introduced to prevent their activities.[108] However, the fact remains that people were still able to gain the touch more than once: one Mrs Astley and her son were both touched for a second time at Windsor in 1681, while William Vickers, who developed his own medical cure for the disease after failing to find relief in the royal touch, recorded, 'I was stroaked twice by King Charles II and thrice by King James II.'[109]

The popularity of the royal touch was due, in part, to the fact that it was widely recognized to be an effective cure for a painful and disfiguring condition, and many contemporary accounts testify that those touched did indeed get better. There may well have been a psychological aspect to the cures effected by the king's touch – the power of belief somehow effecting the cure. More practically, however, the glandular inflammation known as scrofula in this period naturally waxed and waned. If the sufferer had recently received the royal touch any remission could easily be attributed to it.[110]

As was the case with the other ceremonial activities that took place in the state apartments, touching for the king's evil was ultimately the responsibility of the Lord Chamberlain. In reality, two groups of officers in his department oversaw the ceremony: the three sergeant surgeons and the Clerk of the Closet. The former, as men of medicine, were responsible for vetting and admitting the sick, the latter, as a man of God, for administering the readings and prayers that accompanied the royal touch.[111] The Yeomen of the Guard attended to keep the proceedings in order. Though he occasionally stepped in to settle disputes and assert order, the Lord Chamberlain left the day-to-day running of the healings very much in his juniors' hands.[112]

Having acquired a certificate, those seeking the cure would make their way to court to try and gain admission to the ceremony itself. There were several stages to this: first the afflicted was to obtain further verification from the king's surgeons or physicians that he or she was indeed suffering from the king's evil.[113] They then needed to obtain a ticket of admission to a particular touching ceremony. The dispensing of the tickets was the job of the Sergeant Surgeon in waiting, who gave them out in exchange for certificates from a house in Covent Garden.[114] As was explained in the newspaper *Mercurius Publicus* in 1660, those seeking the cure were 'to repair to Mr Knight his Majesties Chirurgion, living at the Cross guns in Russel-street, Covent-garden, over against the Rose Tavern, for their tickets'.[115] The three sergeant surgeons worked in monthly shifts, during which time they issued the tickets for those healings that were to take place during their time of waiting.[116] The days when the Sergeant Surgeon received applicants – usually Wednesdays and Thursdays from two till six in the afternoon – were published in the press. The issuing of tickets was to be done strictly without bribery, as the Lord Chamberlain's order commanded 'nothing be demaunded of the people by the Surgeon as his fee'.[117]

Despite these apparently orderly arrangements, procuring a ticket for a touching was far from easy.[118] Endless waiting won the surgeons a very poor name, even one of their number describing the 'ill opinion the Chirurgion goes under at the continual and tedious waitings at his House'. When the surgeon actually began dispensing tickets, boredom gave way to frenetic activity, with potentially disastrous effects. On one occasion in 1684 the crowd at the surgeons' door was so great that six or seven people were killed in the crush.[119] No doubt partly because of the unappealing prospect of endless waiting in Russell Street, ways were found of obtaining a ticket without having to attend. One of these was to send someone to obtain a ticket on your behalf. This was certainly frowned upon by the Lord Chamberlain, but complaints against the practice indicate that it continued to happen.[120] Those grand enough could send for the Sergeant Surgeon, who, with reasonable notice, would visit them at their lodgings.[121] There were yet other ways of easing the process and sometimes, it seems, of bypassing it altogether, by persuading some prominent courtier to speak to the surgeon, or one of the other presiding officers, on your behalf. Marmaduke Ling of Somerset, for instance, wrote to his old school friend, Mr Stephens, who worked at the king's backstairs, to ask him to procure him a ticket.[122] The Clerk and Keeper of the Closet, who officiated at the healing ceremonies, were also frequently asked to 'get a touch' for friends and relations.[123] Although the Sergeant Surgeon was in charge of dispensing the tickets during his month in waiting, he gave his two fellow surgeons a small allowance of tickets for them to dispense directly, which were doubtless also the target of many requests and petitions.[124]

It was the job of the Sergeant Surgeon to inform those to whom he had issued tickets of the appointed healing day and it was generally agreed that the most auspicious day of all was Good Friday. This may have resulted in Fridays being assigned for healings in 1660, a practice that continued for the rest of his reign[125] (see Appendix 2). In 1662 Charles stipulated just two annual periods of public healing: the two months immediately before Christmas and the month before Easter.[126] But he later added additional winter months to these published times and, in reality, he often touched outside these periods. John Browne, one of Charles II's surgeons, wrote an account of the royal touch, in which he included the monthly figures recorded by the keeper of the closet. These show that though there was a definite drop-off in numbers over the summer months, and peaks in the autumn and early spring, of the 21 years covered by the published registers, there were only four in which a month passed without the king healing.[127] April was consistently the month of the year in which the largest number of people received the touch, reflecting the recognized view that those touched at Easter had the greatest chance of being cured, and the fact that April was frequently the last month of regular public healing before the summer.

In reality, Charles II touched people whenever he wanted to.[128] This meant there was always considerable uncertainty about healing times. Many letters passed between court and country on the subject, like that from Richard Sherlock to Robert Francis, in April 1669 requesting information about healing times for his ailing son so that he could bring him down from Oxford to London.[129] Even the physicians of the royal household were often unsure when the next session would be and sometimes only ascertained its date from reading news of it in the *Gazette*.[130] Many cure-seekers suffered considerable hardship from the delays. One Joseph Jackson, who travelled 200 miles to be touched by the king, found himself detained in the capital unable to support himself and had to petition the governors of St Bartholomew's hospital for succour; another who had travelled 110 miles had to borrow 20 shillings from one of the physicians to pay for the journey home. As Browne put it, these unfortunate people were 'kept so long in Town till both their Money and Credit is gone'.[131]

Numbers at healings varied considerably, reflecting, in part, the difference between the official public healings and 'private' healings that the king also held. No more than 200 were supposed to be admitted to public healings and though the numbers were much greater in the early months of the reign – up to 600 in a session – they soon settled to around that figure.[132] Private healings happened on a very small scale, often only six or seven being healed at a time – though occasionally just one person might receive the royal touch.[133]

People came many hundreds of miles to receive the cure, travelling from places as far afield as Cumberland and Plymouth, sometimes in organized groups.[134] Almost all social classes were represented. Those mentioned as cure-seekers included an impoverished seaman, 'a poor Girl who came out of the North' and a servant maid from Enfield, as well as the daughter of the king's builder from Portsmouth, the wife of John Hebden Esq., the daughter of Captain Wilkes, the son of the mayor of Wycombe and the son of the Earl of Stirling.[135] The free-to-all aspect of the royal touch was noted, with comments that the king 'never makes any exceptions of Persons, being either Young or Old, Rich or Poor, Beautiful or Deformed'.[136]

Having secured their tickets and received notice of a healing day, the sick assembled outside the relevant building for the ceremony, which was usually held after the king had attended morning prayers.[137] The Gentlemen Ushers came in to prepare the room, ensuring 'Odorofferous parcells' were provided to combat the stench of the poor and the sick, and rosewater so the king could wash his hands.[138] The Yeomen of the Guard ushered the ticket-holders in and marshalled them into the order in which they were to be taken to the king.[139] Charles then entered and took his seat on a chair of state, where he remained, hatless, throughout the ceremony. On one side of him stood his personal confessor, the Clerk of the Closet, attended by his assistant, the Closet Keeper, with the gold medals or 'touch-pieces' hanging on their ribbons on his arm, and on the other side one of the royal chaplains[140] (*see* Figure 19). Nearby, the prayer book, from which the service would be read, was placed on a cushion.[141] Two royal surgeons waited with the assembled sick some distance from the throne, keeping them in order and poised to bring them up to the king in sequence; the order of their approach reflected how far they had travelled, those who had come the furthest being brought up first.[142]

With everyone in position, the surgeon in waiting came forward with the first person to be touched; approaching, he made three bows to the king, and then led the sufferer by the hand to the throne. Here, both the surgeon and the patient kneeled before the king. This procedure was made slower and more complicated by the fact that many of those who came to be healed needed considerable assistance to move: some came on crutches, while others had to be supported or even carried forward; some were wrapped in bandages, others completely blind

19. Charles II touching for the king's evil. © *The British Library*

or so incapacitated that they had to be 'brought in a chair' to their sovereign.[143] It is clear, too, that there was, on occasion, squabbling between the surgeons about procedure and precedence, causing the Lord Chamberlain to scold them for making 'a disturbance in His Ma^ts Pr[e]sence at ye tyme of Healinge'.[144]

With the sick person kneeling before the king, the chaplain, also kneeling, read aloud from the Bible, recounting Jesus's appearance to the Apostles after he had risen, and his words to his followers that: 'They shall lay their hands on the sick and they shall recover'. As this line was read, the king reached forward and stroked the scrofula-sufferer under the chin with both hands.[145] This done, the second surgeon led the touched person away, and the next person to be healed was brought forward and the procedure was repeated. Once all the sick had been touched, they were each brought forward a second time to be presented with the touch-piece. Again the surgeon in waiting accompanied each person forward, making three bows, and kneeling down before the king. The chaplain then read aloud from John 1.1–13, and at the words (verse 9) – 'That Light was the true Light which lighteth every man which cometh into the World' – the king placed over the head of the ailing person the piece of gold on a ribbon that had been handed to him by the Clerk of the Closet, also on his knees. The chaplain continued to repeat this verse as every person was presented, and then, once all had been touched, finished the reading. Everyone being then in the positions in which they had started the ceremony, the chaplain concluded with prayers, during which all bar the king knelt, finishing with a prayer asking God's blessing for the ceremony.[146] The ceremony proper over, the Lord Chamberlain and two other noblemen came forward holding between them linen, a ewer and basin. Kneeling before the king, one held the basin, one poured the water over the king's hands and the third proffered the towel. They then made their obeisances and withdrew.[147] The king then followed and the ceremony was complete.

Healing ceremonies were public in both the ceremonial and the literal sense, and the Lord Chamberlain announced the dates in advance to encourage spectators to attend.[148] To see the king cure the sick was an impressive sight by any measure, and contemporary accounts and engravings show that crowds gathered to witness the ceremony. Only the kings of England and France claimed the gift of healing, and the most important foreign visitors to England were taken to watch the ceremony, albeit discreetly so as not to blur the focus on the king. In 1673 the Duchess of Modena and her brother came with Catherine of Braganza, all 'incognito'; they entered the Banqueting House from the door behind the canopy of state, and they were placed in an inconspicuous seat to the side to watch the event.[149] In 1669 Cosimo III of Tuscany was taken to watch the king heal at the modest royal house at Newmarket, and viewed the proceedings from an open side door.[150] Ambassadors, too, were encouraged to attend, and on 29 January 1682 the Moroccan ambassador watched the king conduct a 'general touch' at Whitehall.[151] As well as these visitors, who were effectively the king's own guests, many others were able to crowd into the Banqueting House, or elsewhere, with relative ease. Samuel Pepys and his friend Tom Guy came to

Whitehall just three weeks after the king's return to see the healing ceremony on 23 June 1660; though the pouring rain delayed the occasion, and soaked the poor sufferers waiting outside, both men gained access to the building and witnessed the whole event with ease.[152]

A much less formal and elaborate version of the ceremony was followed for private healings. Though still the responsibility of Clerk of the Closet, these occasions involved far fewer royal officials and were sometimes overseen by a single royal surgeon.[153] One of the functions of private healings was to allow people access to the touch at times when there were no public healings; in October 1669, for example, one of the royal surgeons reported, 'I do not think the King hath healed since summer but privately'.[154] This is also suggested by the enquiry made of Secretary Williamson in March 1666 asking whether it would be possible to obtain a private touch if there were to be no public healings.[155]

Even after the initial rush of the Restoration, Charles II continued to heal on a vast scale – at least 3000 a year received the touch for the rest of the decade. In the words of one contemporary, Charles 'cureth more in any one year, than all the Chirurgeons of London have done in an age'.[156] From the Restoration to his death he touched somewhere in the region of 100,000 people; with an English population of a little under five million, that figure amounts to 2 per cent of the entire population[157] (see Appendix 1). Only very seldom, perhaps once every three years, did a month pass in which the king failed to heal; he touched well over a thousand people most months almost every year of his life as restored king.

Healing on such an extravagant scale required considerable dedication. Even if the presentation and touching of each sufferer took less than one minute, a session in which just 100 people were healed (bearing in mind that every sufferer was presented twice) must have lasted at least three or four hours. Given that many more might be healed in one session, the ceremony must often have lasted most of the day. Charles was by all accounts a restless person, not given to sitting still for long, but he performed these ritual healings with extraordinary patience. He never hurried the chaplains through their offices or bent the rules. There are no complaints from the officials that the king was opposed to the traditional form of the ceremony, or wanted to shorten or simplify them. Instead he conducted the ceremonies with majesty and patience.

The Earl of Newcastle had counselled his pupil that without grand displays of regality, kings were no more than ordinary men. Nothing embodied the superiority of kings more that the royal power of healing, and touching for the king's evil was the quintessential regal ceremony. Its message was unequivocal: the king was not as other men, but a priestly, quasi-divine being. Charles II's constant and enthusiastic performance of this ceremony, both in exile and after the Restoration, is testimony to his belief in its importance to his power and authority. Little wonder the royal officials were ordered to encourage spectators to crowd into the Banqueting House. The king's hope must have been that those who came to watch would respond as the Moroccan ambassador did. After seeing Charles heal, the diplomat begged the king's forgiveness for not having brought him a more magnificent gift, he had understood from his masters that the King of England was only a minor prince, but having watched him exercise his divine powers, 'now he found him to be the greatest monarch in Europe'.[158]

The first years of Charles's reign saw the doors of Whitehall thrown wide open. No king better appreciated how much he depended on the goodwill of the crowds who had cheered him through the streets of London and who packed the audiences in the Banqueting House to watch the theatre of monarchy. The grandest ceremonies, those that reflected his royal status most conspicuously, he performed with the utmost care and attention from the first. In less public arenas he was not always so fastidious. Tall and energetic, he found composure difficult, and often chose to stand rather than sit at private audiences. As well as suiting him personally, it could be read as a winning gesture of respect to the diplomat or dignitary who visited him. In these early years, described by Edward Hyde, now Earl of Clarendon, as a time when the 'rules or formalities' were yet to be established, the king did not always resist his personal inclination towards familiarity and ease. As the 1660s wore on, though, things began to change. Pressures from all sides caused a slow but inexorable modification in the king's circumstances, and so in the way he lived and ruled.

7

Reform and retrenchment

The universal joy that had greeted the restoration of the monarchy did not take long to abate. The return of king and court, ever magnets of conspicuous consumption, had delighted the city merchants; but as the spending gathered pace, others looked on with growing disapproval. Extravagance alone caused disquiet in some quarters, but this was exacerbated by the mania for all things French that gripped the Restoration court. The king wore French clothes, danced French dances, slept in French beds and listened to French music; the royal library was filled with French books, French was widely spoken at court and even sermons were occasionally delivered in French.[1] After the soirées and masquerades Charles had attended at the Louvre, the gatherings at Whitehall in 1660 had seemed parochial and unsophisticated. There was no mistaking where he looked for his model of perfection. As he wrote to his sister in December 1663, the ball just held in the privy chamber was a great improvement, so much so that 'the assembly would not have been disliked for beauty, even at Paris it selfe'.[2]

The English population at large was instinctively xenophobic, and this courtly craze for all things French did the king's popularity no favours. As the packing crates poured in from Paris, the shopkeepers and city merchants grumbled loudly at their loss of trade and even some courtiers shifted uncomfortably at the 'servility of imitation'. The king was not unaware of this, and made some rather flimsy gestures of amelioration, for instance by introducing a new form of jacket called the vest explicitly 'to leave the French mode, which had hitherto obtained to our greate expense & reproch'. The new style notwithstanding, French fashion in dress remained in the ascendant, though calls for the king to set an example by 'buying English' did not cease.[3]

Behind the king's fading favour with his subjects as the 1660s wore on, and not unrelated to his francophilia, lay worries about the moral tone of the court. While his father's faults had been many, licentiousness had not been among them. Charles I's devotion to his wife had been constant and unquestioned; given her unpopularity, many probably wished his attentions had wandered. But in place of a shy family man, a virile and gregarious bachelor now occupied the throne. Charles II's reputation for frivolity and the pleasures of the flesh resurfaced and was again the subject of heated metropolitan gossip. Two figures in particular embodied this: his illegitimate son, James, and his mesmerizing mistress, Barbara.

After being parted from his mother in 1658, the king's illegitimate son, James, had lived a peaceful and unstructured life in France in the care of his father's friend, William, Lord Crofts. Four years later, at the age of 13, he was brought to England and his obscurity abruptly ended. On being reintroduced to his son, Charles's fatherly instincts instantly flowered. Keen to secure the boy's future, he swiftly married him to an heiress and by the end of the year gave him a string of titles, the greatest of which was Duke of Monmouth. The king did everything he could to demonstrate his affection for his illegitimate son, but was always clear that he was just that. His title was grand, but not one of those reserved for royalty, and while he was made a Knight of the Garter, he took his place alongside the other knights while the stall reserved for a Prince of Wales remained eloquently empty.[4]

The existence of an illegitimate child was not, in itself, a cause for scandal: the king was unmarried and royal bastards were not an unknown phenomenon. However Monmouth's appearance at court coincided with the rise to power of the king's newest mistress, the ravishing and rapacious Barbara Palmer. Born into the Villiers family, a dynasty of spectacular social climbers, Barbara was a cousin of the king's boyhood companion, George, second Duke of Buckingham. She first met Charles on the eve of the Restoration, as the 19-year-old bride of the royalist lawyer Roger Palmer. Even those who despised her (and there were many) conceded that she was a dazzling beauty with alabaster skin, long black hair and startling blue eyes. She was smouldering and scheming in equal measure and exuded an almost irresistible sexual allure, bewitching even minor court figures like Samuel Pepys, who was haunted by erotic dreams that 'my Lady Castlemayne [was] in my armes and [I] was admitted to use all the dalliance I desired with her'.[5] Barbara's affair with the king was well known by the end of 1660 and the following February she gave birth to a daughter, Anne, whom he later recognized. That autumn, Roger Palmer was elevated to the nobility as Earl of Castlemaine, 'the reason whereof everybody knows'; though the humiliation of the affair led to the couple's separation in 1662, Barbara was now a member of the nobility and her influence with the king was at its strongest. Over the next five years she would bear him a further four children and for the gossip-mongers each birth served as a living confirmation of the moral vacuum at the heart of the kingdom.[6] With national disapproval mounting fast there seemed to be one clear course of action: the king must marry.

While Charles had been a doubtful commodity in the marriage market of the 1650s, the Restoration had instantly transformed him into a highly eligible prospect. After some discussion, the bride chosen was the Portuguese Princess, Catherine, daughter of the late King John IV of Portugal, and sister of the reigning Alfonso VI. The match was an excellent one by any reckoning. Catherine was from no obscure German duchy but the daughter of a crowned head and she came with a spectacular dowry, including Tangier, Bombay, various valuable trading rights and a cool £330,000. The marriage treaty was completed in June 1661, and in April 1662 the 24-year-old princess left Lisbon on an uncomfortable and stomach-churning voyage across the Bay of Biscay to marry a man she had never met in a country she had never visited. The royal fleet that carried her was bound for the bustling naval port of Portsmouth, where the wedding was to take place. Though home to the vast royal docks and numerous forts and blockhouses, Portsmouth had never had a royal palace, and so to accommodate the royal couple, Lord Manchester, the Lord Chamberlain, had to improvise. The most important house in the town was the residence of the Governor of Portsmouth; his establishment, hard on the waterfront, was a sprawling complex that had been built out of the remains of the 'Domus Dei', a pilgrims' hospital founded by a wealthy Bishop of Winchester in the thirteenth century. The house was requisitioned and its various rooms were swiftly arranged into royal apartments, with suites carved out for the king and queen, and lavishly dressed by the Great Wardrobe.[7] The medieval church, the only part of the complex that still stands today, became the chapel royal. The full complement of ceremonial staff on duty at Whitehall, plus various others not 'in waiting', were summoned to this makeshift palace on the docks. Over 100 royal officers were to be on duty in the king's apartments alone, including 20 Yeomen of the Guard, 16 Gentlemen Ushers, 12 Gentlemen of the Privy Chamber, all the carvers, cupbearers and sewers and two Gentlemen of the Bedchamber.[8] Whatever the Governor's House lacked in architectural splendour it compensated for in the extent of the retinue that shuttled down from London to staff it.

When the royal fleet was sighted, the king himself was still in London trying to coax various bills through Parliament. It thus fell to the Duke of York to greet his brother's bride. At sunset on the evening of Sunday 11 May 1662, the duke was carried across the now calm waters of the Solent to welcome the princess – a mark of honour to which she was entitled as the daughter and sister of a sovereign. A week later, when the final bill passed at Westminster, Charles immediately took to the road, his coach travelling south-west at furious speed to reach Guildford in just three hours and Portsmouth by two o'clock the following afternoon.[9] On Wednesday 21 May 1662, in sweltering heat, Catherine and Charles were married. The official ceremony was a Protestant one, to which the Catholic Portuguese had only agreed to ensure there would be no question as to the legitimacy of any children. Gilbert Sheldon, as Dean of the Chapel Royal, officiated. The wedding party assembled in the king's presence chamber where a rail had been erected separating off one end of the room. Charles, Catherine and two witnesses passed within the enclosed area; with the couple seated on thrones beneath a canopy of state, and with a crowd of the nobility and household officers looking on, the Dean conducted the ceremony according to the rites of the Book of Common Prayer.[10] The use of a secular space for the wedding ceremony was a long-standing convention of royal weddings. Henry VIII had married none of his six wives in the chapel royal and none of the weddings of members of Charles's immediate family – those of his brother, son and two nieces – took place in a church. In fact, while royal weddings have been perhaps the most extravagant and public of all royal ceremonies in the modern age, in the sixteenth and seventeenth centuries they were often treated as family occasions, usually attended by only a handful of people other than immediate kin, and without any public procession or state ritual.

After the wedding, Charles and Catherine travelled north to take up residence for the summer at the great Tudor palace of Hampton Court, arriving there, by a bit of neat choreography, on 29 May: the king's birthday and second anniversary of the Restoration. The voyage and the shock of a new country and married life had left Catherine ill and weak. She had been bedridden throughout her first week in England and as soon as the ceremony of marriage was complete she retired to bed once again. The door of her chamber was firmly closed in the king's face when he presented himself there on their wedding night, and it would be four days before the union was consummated.[11] Her recovery was not helped by the oppressive heat that continued through the summer months of 1662 and for which the English royal palaces were not at all well equipped. When she dined with the king on their arrival at Hampton Court she was visibly suffering: the great warmth of the day combined with the noise and clamour of

20. *Catherine of Braganza* by Dirk Stoop. © *National Portrait Gallery, London*

the crowds caused sweat to run from her temples, carrying with it her makeup. Her discomfort was such that she was hurried out of the hall halfway through the meal.[12]

While no beauty, Catherine was agreed by all to be an attractive woman, small and shapely with dark hair and deep, appealing eyes. First impressions had been good, and Charles had written rapturously from Portsmouth: 'she has as much agreeablenesse in her lookes altogether as ever I saw'. But regardless of her royal blood and natural charms, the Infanta found the culture and fashions of the English court hopelessly alien.[13] The Portuguese court dress that she and her ladies wore appeared ridiculously antiquated to English courtiers draped in their Parisian finery, and the long fringes the Portuguese wore in scooping curls across their foreheads (captured in Dirk Stoop's portrait of Catherine – see Figure 20) provoked audible sniggers from the English. Thrown into the hedonistic culture of Whitehall, with the career of Lady Castlemaine at its height, Catherine was bound to suffer. What affected her position most, though, was her inability to bear the king a child and to wield the influence of the mother of an heir. The queen's childlessness haunted her and was made ever worse as each new baby was born to one of the king's mistresses. In 1663, when an illness caused her to fall into a delirious fever, she became convinced she had given birth three times and when she briefly regained consciousness she anxiously asked those around her 'how do the children?'

At the time of his wedding, Charles had told Clarendon that he would have to be the 'worst man living' not to make a good husband to such a blameless bride, but he did on occasion treat her with cruelty. Most notably he insisted that Barbara Castlemaine be made a Lady of Catherine's Bedchamber in the face of her desperate pleas to be spared the humiliation. However, the affection for Catherine that he expressed in that first letter from Portsmouth never deserted him. He was with her throughout her illness, and when it was at its worst he knelt down at her side and begged her to live for his sake. Though many around him would urge him to consider divorce, he never abandoned her.[14]

After two months at Hampton Court, the king and queen travelled to London on 23 August 1662. The Lord Mayor of London arranged an extravagant waterborne procession up the Thames to collect the royal couple. Charles and Catherine travelled in a glorious vessel in the shape of a large floating temple, seated beneath a gold canopy of state wreathed in bright garlands of flowers.[15] When they arrived at Whitehall, the queen's apartments were brought into use for the first time since the outbreak of the civil war and England once again had a royal consort in residence.

As queen, Catherine had her own household, which was in many ways a reflection of the king's, and she participated with him in various aspects of court ceremonial: together they received diplomats, dined in public and took part in civic processions. Some ceremonies were by their nature the territory of the sovereign alone – notably, touching for the king's evil and the rituals of the Order of the Garter – while those that involved religious worship did not exclude the queen per se, but being Catholic, Catherine took no part in them. There were, however, a small number of ceremonial occasions at which the queen herself took the lead, the most important of which was the evening gathering known as 'the circle'.

In the autumn of 1660 the king's mother, Henrietta Maria, had briefly visited England, and 18 months later she returned for a stay that would last three years. Though she did not have use of the consort's apartments at Whitehall, the Queen Mother re-established herself at her old London palace of Somerset House and at the Queen's House, Greenwich. There she swiftly revived the evening 'circle', which had been a feature of court life before the war (*see* Figure 7). On her first arrival in London, Catherine of Braganza dutifully attended her mother-in-law's gatherings. On 7 September 1662, for instance, a fortnight or so after the court returned to London, Samuel Pepys was taken to the circle at Somerset House by the royal surgeon James Pierce. Henrietta Maria was the hostess of the occasion, with her daughter-in-law sitting immediately next to her. Everybody who was anybody at court was present, including Barbara Castlemaine and James, soon to be Duke of Monmouth. As the evening progressed, the king himself, the Duke of York and his wife, Anne, daughter of Edward Hyde, also attended. Pepys stayed until after dark, marvelling at the ease with which he was able to pass so familiarly among the English royal family.[16]

Unsurprisingly, Queen Catherine was reluctant simply to sit silently at her mother-in-law's side, and before the end of the year she had instituted her own circles at Whitehall. These were at first sombre occasions, presided over by Catherine with suffocating formality. Attendances were unsurprisingly poor (laughter was not a feature of Catherine's circle) but as the new queen gradually adapted to her surroundings, the events became more relaxed and attendance soon improved. Henrietta Maria's departure for Paris in 1665, never to return, brought the rival gatherings to an end, and Catherine's circles were confirmed as the principal court meeting place for courtiers, visitors and members of the royal family.[17]

As before the civil war, the venue for Henrietta Maria's evening assemblies had been her presence chamber, and when Catherine established her own events she followed suit and held these in her Whitehall presence chamber.[18] The grandest reception room in the queen's apartments, the presence chamber brought a certain inherent formality to the gatherings. The queen sat on a throne placed on a raised platform beneath a velvet canopy of state embroidered with the royal arms.[19] However, at some point in her first years as queen, Catherine made a significant change and moved the circle from the presence chamber to the more intimate withdrawing room. While the presence chamber was a room of state, overseen by her Lord Chamberlain and used for the most ceremonious audiences, the withdrawing room was one of the 'private' rooms, overseen by her Mistress of the Robes (the female equivalent to the Groom of the Stool).[20] For the rest of the reign, the evening circles took place in the queen's withdrawing room at

Whitehall, and soon the room and the event were synonymous, so much so that the royal 'drawing room' would remain the key social event at the English Court well into the twentieth century.[21]

Thus, though the king's marriage to Catherine was in many senses unsuccessful, and Lady Castlemaine continued to reign supreme while the queen was left with neither issue nor influence, she did not slip into dusty obscurity but presided almost daily over the most important and well-attended social gathering in the land. As the thin showings at her first circles show, courtiers were not courteous enough to attend simply as a matter of form. But within just a few years the French ambassador was writing to Louis XIV that no self-respecting member of the court was ever absent from Catherine's circle. All the world, 'the public ministers and the private gentlemen', flocked to her rooms every evening.[22] Given that her power was at best limited and her company unremarkable, it begs the question of why and how this came to pass.

The answer lies in an understanding of how the circle or drawing room worked. The event was typically held at Whitehall towards the end of the day, coming to a close sometime after eight when people went their various ways for supper.[23] The queen's Whitehall withdrawing chamber faced the Thames on the east side of the palace, and on warm summer's evenings the guests spilled out of the room onto the great terrace overlooking the river.[24] The walls of the room were hung with tapestry, and the two windows with white taffeta curtains. For specific activities such as the playing of card games, the necessary items of furniture, including leather stools for the players, would be brought in. Otherwise the room was sparsely furnished, with two royal chairs and six stools all upholstered in sky-coloured velvet. As the circles took place in the evening, the room was supplied with extra coals and candles to keep it warm and well lit as darkness fell.[25] It was the same at Windsor where the major building works of the mid-1670s reconfigured the queen's withdrawing room, installing a large ceiling canvas by Antonio Verrio depicting, appropriately, a great assembly of the gods.[26]

The format for the occasion was relatively simple: visitors were ushered into the drawing room where the queen was seated against the wall in her chair of state, with guests standing around her in the curved formation that gave the occasion its name.[27] As new people entered they bowed respectfully to the queen who would acknowledge them with anything from a frosty nod to an affectionate embrace.[28] Once or twice Catherine co-hosted the circle with another female member of the royal family. However, if there was any ambiguity about the status of the other hostess, this could cause difficulties. In 1673, for instance, she presided over the drawing room with the new Duchess of York, Mary of Modena. Mary's mother, the Duchess of Modena, was also then at court, but was specifically asked to avoid the event because the English ladies were refusing to defer to her (insisting that she was no grander than they), and had she attended they would have boycotted the occasion – humiliating both the queen and the Duchess of York.[29]

The French ambassador's statement that everyone who was anyone would be at the queen's circle seems to have held true. Well over one hundred people usually attended from a surprisingly wide range of backgrounds.[30] Both the king and the Duke of York were habituees, frequently dropping into the gathering at some point during the course of the evening.[31] Catherine's own ladies invariably attended, including her Maids of Honour – unmarried beauties of the aristocracy who were an attraction in their own right – and any noblewomen then in London.[32] The great men of the land, too, presented themselves at the door of the queen's drawing room, everyone from consummate courtiers like the second Duke of Buckingham or the Duke of Monmouth, to men of business such as the Earl of Sandwich, vice-admiral of England.[33] Mingling with these British luminaries were foreign diplomats resident in London and visiting dignitaries from overseas.[34] As well as such grandees, all sorts of gentlemen and ladies who simply looked respectable enough to pass the ushers' eye could gain access.[35] For instance, both Pepys and his friend John Evelyn, reputable but not grand, attended the queen's circle on a number of occasions.[36] For an event to which no invitations were issued, appropriate dress was almost the most important qualification for entry, and the finery of the guests was much commented upon. Pepys was astonished by the beauty, both natural and sartorial, that he encountered there, Lady Warwick was dazzled by the 'great gallantry of jewels', and even the visiting Grand Duke of Tuscany slipped away to change his clothes before putting in an appearance.[37]

What was it that drew so many to Catherine's drawing room? On the simplest level, these occasions were one of the few organized events in the royal apartments in which the men and women of the court might mingle freely. The meetings, audiences and levées of the king's apartments were almost exclusively men-only occasions; but the drawing room, being in the queen's domain, was filled with women and doubtless this in itself held an attraction for both sexes. Certainly, they were occasions on which much rumour and news was exchanged and court gossip was hotly discussed: on 2 December 1668 the king regaled the assembled company with the tale of Lord Rochester's clothes being stolen while he was seducing a girl, while on 20 January 1677 Sir Carr Scroope was berated by a young woman who had been the victim of 'some lampoone made of her that she judged him as the author'.[38]

Beyond the purely sensational, information of a more serious nature, 'of the news of the day', was exchanged on these occasions, relating to politics, diplomacy and international relations.[39] Pepys claimed he attended to keep abreast of affairs – 'in order to my hearing any news stirring'; as an occasion for meeting people, extending invitations and securing introductions, the drawing room must have been extremely useful for a young man on the make.[40] Though the Grand Duke of Tuscany's secretary claimed business and affairs of state were not discussed in the drawing room, he was clearly being disingenuous; such matters were often talked of in the relative informality of the queen's withdrawing room, albeit with some discretion.[41] In fact the drawing room was an ideal gathering for unofficial discussions on just such subjects, and in the bustle and conversation the king or Duke of York often took individuals into a corner for a quiet word on some point of politics or patronage. In the weeks before the arrival of William of Orange in 1677, the king was anxious to reassure the French ambassador, Barillon, of the continuing strength of Anglo-French relations. Hence, at the queen's drawing room on 17 September, he took the Frenchman into a window embrasure and whispered quiet words of encouragement into his ear.[42] On another occasion, the Duke of York took one of Barillon's predecessors aside from the 'cercle' into an adjoining gallery to discuss with him the poor state of English finances. When the king arrived at the gathering, all three slipped out into the queen's bedchamber where the king pressed the point further.[43] So while some certainly attended the queen's drawing room in part to hear the news and ogle Lady Castlemaine, it was also a time for real business.[44]

Over and above providing a forum for social and political conversation, the occasion served useful ceremonial and symbolic purposes. The gathering was perfect for public demonstrations of loyalty, favour and inclusion. Attending at all was a way of 'shewing ... respect to their majesties and their royal highnesses': merely by being there, a courtier or diplomat was demonstrating both recognition of the legitimacy of the regime and that he or she was, to some extent, in royal favour.[45] As the one regular gathering that could be attended by more or less everyone at court, exactly who came and what passed at the drawing room was an extremely useful gauge of people and politics. The great regard with which, for instance, the jockeys at Newmarket were held by the king in 1677 was typified by one observer with the remark that they 'command as formerly, both in the drawing-room and bed-chamber'. Charles Hatton noted tellingly, on the Duke of York's return to England after a period of enforced exile in September 1679, that attendance at such occasions was 'ye mesure ye disafected personns take to judge how other personns stand affected'.[46]

The drawing room was used, in turn, by the royal family to demonstrate publicly whom they favoured and whom they shunned. Immediately after the 1673 marriage of James, Duke of York, to the Catholic Mary of Modena, the duke brought his wife 'forth into the withdrawing room'. By appearing here, 'at that first Circle' and being introduced to members of the court by the heir to the throne, Mary's elevation as Duchess of York, sister-in-law to the king and member of the royal family, was forcefully displayed to the assembled court.[47] While the status of the Duchess of York was not normally in question, others with more ambiguous positions could benefit enormously from public displays of royal favour at the queen's drawing room. In the early part of Charles's reign the Duke of Monmouth had been a regular presence there. After a period of estrangement in the early 1680s, the duke and the king were reconciled, albeit briefly, in 1683. Following an emotional reunion, the king immediately came 'to the Queen's circle as usual before supper time', where he told members of the company 'that James had surrendered himself', and the duke was once again welcome at such court gatherings.[48] How the queen and members of the royal family treated those who came to the drawing rooms was hugely important. When the Duke of York was introducing his bride at the circle in 1673, he remained with her throughout 'telling her to whom she should rise up & what ladies she should salute'. Crucially he instructed her to kiss the sons of Barbara Castlemaine, now Duchess of Cleveland, showing his wife and, just as importantly, the assembled company, the level of respect he accepted as due to his brother's illegitimate children.[49]

Interestingly, Charles II was regularly to be found transacting both political and social affairs in a variety of rooms in the queen's apartments. In the autumn of 1666, for instance, shortly after the great fire of London, John Evelyn came to court with a survey of the charred city and proposals for rebuilding. The king called him into the queen's bedchamber where he and the Duke of York pored over the drawings for over an hour.[50] On 19 May 1669, Pepys, loitering in a gallery at court, met the Duke of York, who recounted a story that the Duke of Buckingham had just been telling the king in the queen's bedchamber in the presence of 'much mixed company'. The participants in these informal gatherings were mostly men, though Catherine of Braganza often paused before entering her own dressing room in case the king had slipped in there with one of his amours.[51]

In 1670, after Lady Castlemaine's influence had waned, the king fell in love again. The subject of his affections was a 21-year-old French woman, Louise de Kéroualle, daughter of a minor French nobleman and maid of honour to his beloved sister, Henriette, wife of Louis XIV's brother, Phillippe duc D'Orleans (*see* Figure 21). Louise accompanied her mistress to England in May 1670, on the visit associated with the sealing of the Secret Treaty of Dover. Shortly after their return to France, Henriette, still only in her mid-twenties, died unexpectedly. The news left Charles heartbroken, and it may be that his desperate sadness for the loss of his sister was at the root of the strength of feeling he developed almost instantly for her lady in waiting, who arrived back in England a few months later. Louise was another striking beauty with black hair and pale skin and within a year she was established as the king's principal mistress and – like Barbara before her – was given extensive apartments at Whitehall Palace. Though Charles would have other liaisons, not least with the colourful Nell Gwyn, Louise's position was never seriously threatened and she retained his affections for the rest of his life. When Charles died, a full-length portrait of Louise hung in his bedchamber at Windsor Castle.[52]

Louise was created Duchess of Portsmouth in her own right in 1673, and within a few years her apartments were serving as an extension to the queen's for meetings and assemblies that brought the king into contact with his favoured subjects.[53] In March 1677 the diarist and MP Sir John Reresby 'entertained the King in the Duchess of Portsmouth's chamber with the Marquis of Worcester', and from then on her rooms were regularly used in this way.[54] The gatherings in Lady Portsmouth's lodgings were not simply attended by the king and his boon companions, but diplomats and politicians were also to be found there.[55] So, for example, in January 1682 the Moroccan ambassador, whom the king was at

21. Louise de Kéroualle, Duchess of Portsmouth, by Pierre Mignard, 1682.
© *National Portrait Gallery, London*

some pains to please, was 'invited to a splendid entertainment at the Duchess of Portsmouth's lodgings' also attended by the king.[56]

The principal reason people flocked to both Catherine's drawing rooms and Louise's soirées was fundamentally the same: it was because the king was there. Charles's passion for his mistress, combined with the obvious informality of gatherings in her rooms, is sufficient explanation for the use of Louise's apartments for unofficial discussions. However, in the case of the queen, affection was not enough to bring him to her side every evening. What her gatherings offered, though, was a happy hybrid: a respectable court gathering at which even the most disapproving dowager duchess could appear but one that gave Charles far greater freedom than he would have had if conducting meetings in his own apartments. When Cosimo III, to whose secretary we owe much of our knowledge of the detail of Catherine of Braganza's drawing rooms, came to England, he was travelling as an unofficial visitor. Though he refused to take part in any of the ceremonial events of the state apartments, he appeared every evening in the circles hosted by the queen. The explanation he gave was that it enabled him to meet the great company of court without jeopardizing the unofficial status of his visit. Just as he was able to meet foreign diplomats so long as it was in a ceremonially neutral space (such as the lodgings of a third party), 'his highness appeared at different times [in the queen's circle] as in the third place'. Similarly because the queen's drawing room was neither part of the king's apartments nor one of the queen's outer rooms of state, Charles himself could appear there without having to insist on the great gestures of respect and status that would have been required had it been a more stately space.

In this respect, it is worth considering the change to the location of the circle in Catherine's first years as queen. As noted, the circle had traditionally been held in the queen's presence chamber, but in 1664 or thereabouts Catherine moved her circle two rooms along the enfilade into her withdrawing room, the first space in the sequence that was technically outside the control of her Lord Chamberlain and the state ceremonial over which he presided. By moving this formal event of the circle into the technically 'privy' space of the withdrawing room, Catherine of Braganza's drawing rooms were a sort of crossbreed occasion, combining the old formality of the circle with the relative informality of activities, such as card-playing, that had always been conducted in the withdrawing room.[57] This hybrid has a direct parallel in the king's use of his own privy apartments, notably his bedchamber, into which he moved a whole range of ceremonial events, among them many of the formal audiences that had previously been conducted in the king's state apartments. If Catherine of Braganza had conducted her circles in the highly formal presence chamber as her mother-in-law had done, the king would not have been able to saunter in and out and disappear into corners as he was to do in the withdrawing room. It is quite certain that the 'incognito' Cosimo III of Tuscany would never have appeared there. But by using the withdrawing room, a flexibility was immediately introduced that would never have pertained in the presence chamber.

In the queen's drawing room the king and duke could be found 'divesting themselves awhile of the restraint of royalty' while also participating in a respectable court event.[58] Here too, the king was not the host; he did not need to spend the entire evening seated with a circle of courtiers standing around him, or patiently playing cards – all of which was left to his wife. Instead he could wander in at whatever time suited him, tell amusing stories, whisper promises in the ears of aspirant courtiers and hold political discussions in window embrasures, before sloping off elsewhere. He was not the conductor of the event, trapped on the chair of state, caged by the circle of courtiers and bound by the conventions of the occasion. For the king to have this freedom of movement it was necessary that he should not be the host. By attending his wife's gathering he could resign the formalities largely to her without leaving the walls of his own palaces.

While Catherine's drawing room provided a respectable forum for the king to mingle with the court, her arrival did not solve the court's reputation for loose morals, or the king's faltering reputation. On 29 May 1668, Charles II's 38th birthday and the eighth anniversary of the Restoration, he was striding with characteristic energy through the corridors of Whitehall. As he passed down a gallery his eye was caught by a piece of elaborate graffiti on a wall and he stopped abruptly to examine it. There, in an elegant hand, was sketched a royal crown and the king's initials. Under this came the vicious couplet:

> Hobbes his Religion, Hyde his Moralls gave
> And this day birth to an ungrateful knave

The king gave no reaction. He walked on, later asking for the graffiti to be scrubbed off; but the point must have hit home: he was losing the love of his people.[59]

As the coffee house gossip wore away at the reputation of the restored regime, a wave of almost biblical disasters swept over the kingdom. In the spring of 1665 black rats scurried ashore from Dutch ships onto docks along the southern coasts of England; it was a common enough sight in itself but this time their mangy fur teamed with minute fleas that, with every bite, transmitted a catastrophic disease: the bubonic plague. Within hours of being bitten by the fleas, humans developed unsightly blotches on the skin, which swiftly bloated into agonizing pustulating sores; unimaginable pain was often relieved only by death, which could follow just days later. Within a matter of months the disease had established itself in south-east England in epidemic proportions. By June 1665 hundreds were dying every week, and just a month later it was thousands. Londoners poured out of the capital to escape infection, but for many it was already too late. Throughout the city the fatal sign of contamination spread: a barrier nailed across the door, daubed with a red cross and the words 'Lord Have Mercy upon us'. Among those who fled, though not by any means the first, was the king and his entourage. In the last days of June, Whitehall Palace was a frenzy of packing as court officers marshalled hundreds of wagons and travelling trunks. The king went first to Hampton Court, but as the scale of the epidemic emerged it became clear that this was not nearly far enough. At the end of July he travelled west, first to Portsmouth, then on to Salisbury and Weymouth, before settling at Oxford towards the end of September. The disease only subsided when the cold weather of the winter months slowed the multiplication of the fleas. By then some 100,000 people had died at its hands.[60]

The king returned to London in February 1666 and within seven months tragedy struck again. On the morning of Sunday 2 September a fire broke out at a bakery in the south-eastern corner of the city of London near London Bridge. The building was soon alight and the flames roared across the narrow lanes to neighbouring houses. These, with their timbers bone-dry from a long hot summer, caught alight immediately and a real inferno soon raged. Later that morning, Samuel Pepys travelled by boat from his house near the Tower of London to Whitehall to attend the Sunday service at the chapel royal. News of the fire was just breaking at court and, as one who had seen it with his own eyes, he was rushed into the king's chapel closet. The king was horrified to hear that unless houses were actually torn down to create a break, the fire was probably unstoppable. He sent Pepys to the Lord Mayor to tell him to spare nothing to halt it. Despite all efforts, including those of the king and the Duke of York, who later that day had joined those fighting the blaze, the fire raged on. It burned for days, taking with it over 13,000 houses, 93 churches, the Royal Exchange, the Guildhall and the mighty St Paul's Cathedral. The city, England's commercial engine, was left a smouldering wreck.[61]

The trinity of calamities was completed in June 1667. For two years England and the United Provinces of the Netherlands had been at war. The conflict had been sparked by the English capture of the Dutch colony of New Amsterdam (swiftly renamed New York after the Duke of York), but the war was in essence about commerce and had so far comprised a series of inconclusive naval battles. Then, in early June 1667, the Dutch fleet sailed quietly into the Thames estuary and slipped up the Medway River on the north coast of Kent. It passed unchallenged through the narrow neck leading to the Medway basin, capturing the half-built fort of Sheerness on the way, and pushed forward to Gillingham Reach. Here, close to the royal naval dockyard at Chatham, the principal ships of the English navy were moored. In a spectacular and audacious coup, the Dutch opened fire. The effect was devastating: three of the greatest ships of the whole fleet were completely destroyed, including two that had formed part of the Restoration convoy from Scheveningen in May 1660. The *Royal Charles*, the very vessel that had carried the king home, was captured and towed away as a prize. Of the five principal flagships of the fleet, four were completely lost by the end of the day; worse than this, the attack was a spectacular humiliation, a body-blow to English national confidence. The news was greeted with disgust across the kingdom, and the blame laid firmly at the door of the government.[62]

As well as damaging English pride and morale, these disasters had a serious impact on the wealth of the kingdom and on the financial condition of the monarchy. The royal income, on which the royal household depended, was made up of the traditional sources of revenue (including customs and excise, the hearth tax and income from royal lands) and additional money granted by Parliament. At the Restoration, Parliament had given the king what had seemed like a handsome financial settlement, totalling £1.2m a year, even Edward Hyde calling it 'a noble revenue'.[63] However, before long it became clear that there was a serious gulf between the king's expenditure and his income. First, the sources of the king's 'ordinary', or non-parliamentary income, were yielding far less money than had been anticipated, with royal lands much depleted and the estimates of 1660 hopelessly optimistic. Second, Charles's outgoings were huge. His outstanding debts from the exile were being called in, but the real drain came from his determination to reinstate the royal household in all its former magnificence, and it was this, rather than trips to the theatre and keeping mistresses, that sapped the royal income dry.

Since the Middle Ages, one of the sights of the English court had been that of all its officer-holders, from minor grooms to the king himself, eating together in the state rooms of the palaces. The act of feeding your entourage was still a defining gesture of lordship and majesty in early-modern Europe, and in England this meant providing two meals a day for a whole complement of court officers.[64] During the summer of 1660 the practice, known as the 'bouche of court', had been revived and within a year all the senior, and most of the middling, court officers were receiving their meals at court. At the same time the king himself began dining in public several times a week. Hospitality on such a grand scale impressed those who saw it. As a contemporary guide to the kingdom, explained:

> The Magnificence and abundant plenty of the Kings Tables hath caused amazement in all Forreigners ... This prodigious plenty caused Forreigners to put a higher value upon the King, and caused the Natives who were there freely welcome, to encrease their affection to the King, it being found as necessary for the King of England this way to endear the English, who ever delighted in Feasting; as for the Italian Princes by Sights and Shews to endear their Subjects, who as much delight therein.[65]

However within three years of the Restoration it became clear that the king simply could not afford to continue to pay for dining at court on this scale. In 1660 the royal practice of purveyance (the right to purchase food at a fixed low rate) had been abolished, and as a result the costs of feeding the court soared. The obvious solution was to commute office-holders' right to meals into a fixed cash payment, known as 'board wages', a practice that had begun before the civil war. In December 1662 a whole series of court officers lost their meals on this basis but the costs were still well above the money available to pay for them. In August 1663, things were looking so bleak that the king had no choice but to agree to a radical emergency measure: all court meals would be abolished so that, other than the immediate royal family, only Prince Rupert and the Queen's Maids of Honour would be entitled to the bouche of court. Furthermore the payment of all board wages was temporarily to cease.[66] The impact of this was enormous not least because for many officials board wages made up a substantial portion of their income. A year later, in October 1664, the moratorium on board wages was lifted but, with the exception of the Gentlemen Waiters, the bouche of court remained at a restricted level and so it would continue for the rest of the reign. The king's stated desire to feed his household and so conform to 'that antient and [laudable] hospitality for which the court of our royal progenitors have ever beene famous amongst all nations' had buckled under the weight of financial necessity. A significant strand of courtly magnificence was thereby permanently terminated.[67]

The cost of the king's own dining arrangements was also being closely questioned, but to this his response was tellingly different. The care taken to ensure Charles ate his meals in regal fashion during the exile had reflected the role of royal dining as a defining behaviour of kings, and this care did not subside with the Restoration. It too had been marked by a succession of formal meals: from the state dinner hosted for the king by the States General of the Netherlands at the Mauritshouse in The Hague (*see* Figure 10), to the public meal the king ate at Whitehall on his arrival and the great dinner hosted for him by the Lord Mayor of London in July 1660.

Like so much of court life, royal meals fell into two separate categories: some were eaten in public in the rooms of state, others were taken elsewhere and were designated private. Breakfast and supper were always private, while dinner, eaten in the mid-afternoon, was often taken in public and as such was much the most important royal meal. When James I had arrived in London from Scotland in 1603, he immediately adopted the English style of dining and regularly ate in state in the presence chamber, served 'on the knee' by important courtiers from the finest royal plate.[68] The dignity of formal dining had appealed to Charles I, who – with specific reference to Henry VIII's household orders – reinstated the obligation of senior household officers to dine in the great hall and guard chambers on high days. He also reintroduced the 'board of state', an ancient practice in which a formal dinner was served at the sovereign's table in the presence chamber regardless of whether or not the king was actually present.[69]

As soon as Charles II arrived at Whitehall in 1660 he revived the practice of regularly dining in state in his own apartments and if anything, made these meals more majestic than they had been before the civil war. When he dined in state he did so, by definition, within the state apartments, either in his presence chamber or, on especially grand or well-attended occasions, in the Banqueting House in its capacity as a second presence chamber.[70] After his marriage, he often ate in public with the queen, and when this happened he usually travelled to the queen's presence chamber to do so.[71] On 21 September 1662, shortly after the king and queen returned to Whitehall, Samuel Pepys went to the queen's presence chamber to watch them dining in public together; when the queen decided to stay at St James's rather than join the king, 'they were forced to remove the things to the King's presence, and there he dined alone'.[72]

The most formal and grand dinners held at Whitehall during Charles II's reign were staged in the Banqueting House itself. On his birthday and the anniversary of his restoration to the throne in 1669, for instance, he attended chapel and then was to be seen 'dining in public, with the princes of the blood, in the banquetting room at Whitehall'.[73] It was also in the Banqueting House that the Knights of the Garter had their great dinner when their feast was celebrated in London in April 1667[74] (*see* Figure 22). In terms of their ceremonial status, their attendants and their decoration, the king dined in rooms that radiated the eminence and

22. Charles II dining at the feast of the order of the Garter in St George's Hall, Windsor, by Wenceslaus Hollar. The appearance of this room would be dramatically transformed in the early 1680s. © *The British Library*

glory of the English monarchy.[75] Neither the Banqueting House nor the presence chambers were normally equipped with dining tables. Instead – following contemporary practice – these were set up for the occasion and packed away afterwards. The king's seating arrangement, however, was a permanent feature of the rooms. Each of these state chambers was furnished with a canopy of state, made of rich red silk and embroidered with the royal arms in gold and silver thread. Sometimes reaching twenty feet or more high, the canopies shaded the royal throne, which stood on a raised platform below, placed on a Turkish carpet and flanked by stools and cushions upholstered in matching fabric.[76] The presence of a canopy over the head of the king was a defining feature of royal public dining. When William of Orange visited England in 1670 to try and recoup some of the money Charles had borrowed from his father, he was treated with countless marks of respect. As Prince of Orange, he was even permitted to have his own canopy of state in his lodgings at Whitehall. However, that honour was allowed on one highly significant condition: that he would not sit beneath it when he dined, as this would accord him a truly regal status to which, as a prince and a stadtholder, he was not entitled.[77]

When the king dined in public, people flocked to watch; they came in such numbers that a barrier was set up in front of the table. One onlooker explained of the royal birthday dinner in 1669, that the dais was 'traversed by a balustrade, to prevent the people who resort thither from flocking round the royal table'.[78] In addition, the room was equipped with a great cupboard or buffet for the storage and display of gold and silver plate, which itself might be surrounded by a rail to protect the plate from inquisitive, and sometimes acquisitive, spectators.[79] At the far end of the room was a 'traverse' curtain which was drawn back during the day but which was pulled across the room to enclose the area where the night guard, the Esquires of the Body, put down their pallet beds.[80] From the first weeks of the reign, the royal musicians played in the presence chamber when the king ate; the quality of their playing provoking widespread admiration.[81]

The same formal manner of dining that Charles had followed during his exile (*see* above, pp. 73–5) continued after the Restoration. The one full set of household orders that survives from the reign gives some information about the procedure for serving the king when he ate in the presence chamber. The food was to be brought up into the state apartments from the kitchens below by the Yeomen of the Guard, some of whom remained in the presence chamber while the king ate.[82] Once the salt cellar was placed on the table, everyone other than the diners themselves had to stand. After the king had taken his seat, he was waited on by the carver, sewer (server) and cupbearer then in waiting, who were to present themselves by ten o'clock every morning 'to receive directions from the Gentleman Usher concerning the Service'.[83] These ancient posts were not to last long in England, and by 1714 the carver and cupbearer had ceased to serve the king when he dined in the state apartments, the staff of the Bedchamber performing the service instead.[84]

The detailed descriptions of Charles II's coronation banquet indicate that the rituals of tasting and serving on the knee continued after the Restoration.[85] This is also borne out by Samuel Pepys's description of the king and queen dining at Whitehall in September 1667. Pepys was particularly struck by the 'formality' whereby all those who served a dish tasted a morsel of it before it was placed before the king and queen.[86] The Clerk of the Closet attended the king at dinner, saying grace before the meal as had happened at Elizabeth Castle in 1646.[87]

The practice of serving a royal dinner in the presence chamber even though the king was absent continued during the reign of Charles II – at least when the occasion merited it. The notional, but not actual, presence of the king was the reason for a feast being laid out on a table in the great hall during the visit of a group of French dignitaries in 1671, 'at which none sat, but was only for show after the old English fashion'.[88] When the king and queen were staying at Hampton Court in the summer of 1662, Charles touched for the king's evil in the great hall in the company of the Archbishop of Canterbury and other luminaries, after which he withdrew to the private apartments to dine alone with the queen; however, in 'the great dining hall' (probably the presence chamber) 'according to custom some dishes were served up ceremoniously and immediately taken off again and everything removed'.[89]

While the king did not dine in public every day, he did so frequently. After formal dining in the presence chamber was resumed in 1667 (see below), it was announced that the king and queen would dine in public together on three days a week. Certainly the king dined in public before or after almost all important ceremonial events, among them royal healing ceremonies and the formal reception of new diplomats and royal marriages; he also often did so after attending chapel on Sundays and on the principal religious festivals of the year, such as Candlemas.[90] This pattern continued throughout the reign; even when the king was unwell in May 1680, after an appearance at the chapel royal, 'He dined with the Queen in public', while the Earl of Ailesbury noted in his memoirs that during the king's 'latter years he had no private meals'.[91]

When Charles dined formally in his palaces he either did so alone or with people of the very highest social standing. Members of his immediate family were acceptable co-diners: the king frequently dined with his brother, his wife, his mother and his sisters when they were at court.[92] Otherwise, the king could and did eat in the company of foreign princes: he asked the Grand Duke of Tuscany to dine in state with him on his 39th birthday, and he dined with the Duchess of Modena and her daughter in the queen's presence chamber in 1673 – but, significantly, he would not permit the duchess's brother to join them, who instead 'had a table apart in his own quarter'.[93] He never dined in public with a member of the English nobility; even the most senior duke was an unthinkable dining companion for the king. Those with whom he did dine in public had to follow very specific seating arrangements, which prescribed precisely who was to sit where, and on what, following painstaking negotiations.[94] The king always sat centrally in the middle of the long side of the table, wearing his hat, with the queen beside him on his left if they dined together, and the person to be most honoured on his right hand at the end of the table. A chair with arms and a back was always provided for the king, while some diners sat on chairs with a back only and others on stools, reflecting the hierarchy of status. The long side of the table opposite the king would be left empty, allowing spectators a clear view of their sovereign. It was as much tableau as table.[95]

The household regulations specified who was to be allowed to come into the royal apartments to observe the king dine. The officers of the guard chamber who manned the outer doors were to let into that room 'Persons of good Fashion and good Appearance that have a desire to see Us at Dinner', and specifically turn away 'any Inferior, Mean, or Unknowne People'. However, in order to pass on into the presence chamber, visitors were vetted by a second group of officials, the Gentlemen Ushers Daily Waiters. More details of the qualifications required for access into the presence chamber are given in the household regulations:

> Gentlemen of Quality, and of good Fashion, and the Gentlemen that attend Our Great Officers and Privy Councellors, and Persons of good Quality, are permitted to come and remaine in the said Chamber, And all Wives & Daughters of the Nobility, and their Women that attend them may passe through this Chamber, and all other Ladyes of good Ranck and Quality, but not their servants.[96]

In essence the rules meant that all men and women 'of quality' and appropriately dressed, were allowed into the presence chamber to watch the king dine. 'Quality' was itself fairly broadly conceived: while all servants were specifically excluded, junior government officials could pass into the presence chamber to watch the king dine, a freedom of access that was remarked upon by foreign visitors.[97] So many came to watch the king dine that the staff of the presence chamber sometimes struggled to maintain decorum.[98] When the Grand Duke of Tuscany entertained the king and Duke of York in 1669, the meal culminated in a magnificent course of fruit from all over Europe, 'But scarcely was it set upon the table, when the whole was plundered by the people who came to see the spectacle of the entertainment', and the plunderers were completely undaunted in their 'pillage of these very delicate viands' by the presence of the king and his guard.[99] During the coronation feast itself, having wandered from table to table ogling the distinguished guests, the young Pepys sat down to consume the loaf of bread, four rabbits and a pullet that he had managed to pester and purloin from the diners. He was not alone in this, as, in his own words: 'everybody else did [eat] what they could get'.[100]

It was again the Gentlemen Ushers Daily Waiters who marshalled the spectators at public dinners. Everyone attending in any capacity wanted to be as close as possible to the king. To try and maintain order Charles I had decreed that the onlookers were to 'stay towards the lower end of the chamber, & shall not presse too neare the table whereby the rome may be pestered, & our service hindered'. Charles II abandoned this reliance on the audience's good behaviour by introducing the physical barrier of the rail.[101] In Charles I's reign a few privileged people – privy councillors, bishops, peers, the Dean of the Chapel Royal, and so forth – were to be allowed onto the royal dais when the king dined. The definition was looser in his son's reign: people would be allowed to stand 'near the Table within the Rayle', so long as they were 'generaly none but Persons of good Quality'.[102] To stand behind the king within the rail was an honour that most of those on friendly terms with the king seem to have been allowed. In 1678 the MP Sir John Reresby 'stood behind [the Duke of York] … as he dined with the King', while it was when John Evelyn was 'Standing by his Majestie at dinner in the Presence' in 1668 that he first tasted pineapple, given to him from the royal plate by the king himself. In 1661 Pepys was able to get his wife a place behind Henrietta Maria's chair in the queen's presence chamber at Whitehall to watch the queen dowager and her two surviving daughters dine in public; and so a woman born without money or social standing was able to stand inches away from three of the most important women of seventeenth-century Europe and watch them eat.[103]

Even those who had no experience of the deprivations of exile recognized that one of the hallmarks of a legitimate majesty was that the king should take his meals in the most splendid manner.[104] The state in which a person dined, more than almost any other activity, gave a true reflection of their condition in the world. It was because of the sheer eloquence of the dining table in expressing the quality of the diner that so much attention was lavished on the plate and furniture given to ambassadors to take on their postings – it directly reflected the honour and splendour of the sovereign they represented. One of the grandest embassies to England during the reign was that of the Comte de Soissons, sent from France to congratulate the king on his restoration in 1660. Contemporaries marvelled at the size and appearance of the ambassador's entourage, but the thing which communicated power and magnificence of the French monarchy most clearly was the manner in which the ambassador ate: 'at his table hee was atended with persons of very great quality of his country when hee sate at diner, a rich canopey over his heade and musicke of his owne playinge before him ... He had a most noble cuboard of plate that the like hath not beene [possessed] by any ambassador.'[105]

The mystique of royal dining emanated from both its splendour and from its exclusivity. At the banquets of the Order of the Garter, Charles II did not eat with the knights but sat separately behind a rail and beneath a canopy of state[106] (*see* Figure 22). Other than members of his own family, the only one of his subjects with whom Charles II ever dined in state was the Lord Mayor of London. The ceremonial logic behind this was that the Lord Mayor enjoyed exceptional status within the city of London, to the extent that everyone other than the king himself had to give way to him there; as a result, the king could, and did, dine as his guest on formal occasions.[107]

On those occasions when Charles dined in public with others it was a powerful gesture of his favour and support. After royal weddings the king usually dined with the bride and groom, signifying his acceptance of a new member of the royal dynasty. This was often simply a symbolic statement, but not always: in December 1660 it was discovered that the Duke of York had secretly married the Lord Chancellor's daughter Anne Hyde – news that met with almost universal disapproval. But when, on 2 January 1661, the king dined in public with the couple he gave an unequivocal statement of his acceptance of the marriage – and the week's newspapers eagerly reported it as such.[108] All meals that the king took in the public eye, even if they were not taken 'in state', could carry this message. In the spring of 1680, following a lengthy standoff, there was a brief reconciliation between the king and the Lord Mayor of London; the event was signified by Charles and the Duke of York eating in the city with the mayor. This in itself caused the king's opponents much disquiet, and various 'malcontent lords' swiftly invited themselves to eat with the mayor, 'wch was done a purpose to keepe up theyr credits in ye citty wch has mitily fallen of late, especially since ye King and Dukes supping there'.[109] The king went to great lengths to express his respect and regard for the Grand Duke of Tuscany during his visit in 1669, and when he wanted to 'give a final proof of it by some positive and public demonstration' it was by going to sup at the grand duke's house – supper was always a much less formal occasion than dinner – that the king achieved this. It is in this light, too, that Charles II's campaign of supping with dozens of his senior subjects during the first year or so of his reign should be viewed. By doing so he was demonstrating in the most public way possible the bonds of loyalty and amity between himself and his people, but without diminishing his status by dining with them in the state rooms of the palace.

The king's personal views about royal dining have to be inferred from his actions. At the Restoration, in Edward Hyde's words, Charles 'directed his own table to be more magnificently furnished than it ever had been in any time of his predecessors', casting him as the architect of the form of state dining at the Restoration.[110] The frequency of public meals must at least have had his consent and was probably of his choosing. When it came to settling any question of precedence, it was to the king that the matter was referred. At state meals there was a strict hierarchy of place at the table and of chair type, each expressing in ever finer calibrations the relative status of the diners. Before important dinners, prolonged discussions took place about exactly who should be seated where and on what; the closer a diner was to the king both in physical place and in manner of seating, the more royal he or she was.[111] In August 1663, when the French ambassador took umbrage at his treatment at a dinner at the Guildhall, it was Charles who looked into the matter and apportioned blame: 'the King, who it seems occasioned the invitation, saith my Lord St. Albans only was at fault'.[112] Similarly, when the Prince of Orange was to dine with the Lord Mayor in 1671, the king was consulted and he gave a ruling on the seating plan: that the prince should rank before the mayor. A fifteenth-century precedent was then unearthed, which, showing Henry V's brothers had ceded place to the Lord Mayor, apparently contradicted Charles's decision on the matter. 'Notwithstanding the King kept his first opinion; alleging that forms of Ceremonies were changed in the world since that time; & that those Dukes were the Kings own brothers; yet they were his subjects; which the Prince of Orange was not.'[113]

During the reign the formal rules for public dining were adapted to reflect changing practice since the days of Charles I. The regulations now made reference to the rail around the table, gave a broader definition of who was allowed to stand at the king's side, and delegated the responsibility for access to the Gentleman Usher Daily Waiter, all indicating that this was an event now much better attended than it had been.[114]

When the financial crisis in the royal household reached its peak in the summer of 1663 the king was forced to accept drastic economies in his own dining arrangements, as well as fierce reductions in those of the court as a whole. To cut costs the king and queen were to take all their dinners together, and the number of dishes served to each was reduced.[115] As a result, the king, queen and other members of the royal family now dined at one table, and took their dinner not in the presence chamber but in the principal withdrawing room of the king's apartments, the Vane Room. The arrangement was in place in the autumn, Samuel Pepys noting on 7 December 1663 that 'the King and Duke and Duchesse came to dinner in the Vane roome, where I never saw them before; but it seems since the tables are down he dines there altogether'.[116] With the change of location from a state room to a privy room, the splendour of royal dining was considerably reduced. Though some spectators still attended, meals held in the privy apartments, with no canopy of state, no cupbearers, carvers and sewers and no royal musicians, effectively signalled the suspension of state dining.[117]

This arrangement continued until the summer of 1667. Then, after three consecutive years of national disasters, and only a matter of weeks after the Dutch raid on the English fleet in the Medway, it was suddenly announced that the king was to resume dining in public in the presence chamber and that he would henceforth do so three times a week. Contemporaries made an immediate connection between the decision and the Dutch war, which had ended abruptly when the king signed a peace treaty a few weeks after the Medway incident. It may be that the end of the war itself prompted the resumption of royal dining. However it is more likely that the decision was taken to restore the king's reputation in the wake of a public relations fiasco; rumour had it that while the English fleet burned, the king had spent the evening with his mistress and his bastard son, chasing moths – hardly an impressive image of majesty.[118] By August the spectators were being readmitted to the king's state apartments where he 'againe dine[d] in the Presence in antient State, with Musique & all the Court ceremonies which had been interrupted since the late warr'.[119] The need for regular state dining was never again questioned.

The king managed to sidestep much of the lasting blame for de facto defeat by the Dutch. As the mismanagement of the war was debated at Westminster and Whitehall, Edward Hyde, Earl of Clarendon, the king's closest adviser for over twenty years, was fingered as a scapegoat. After making valiant efforts to save his career, the old Chancellor realized his fate was fixed, and before the year was out fled England never to return. The king, who had happily placed all blame for a bewildering range of government shortcomings at Clarendon's door, must have felt a sense of relief as a year that had brought such troubles ended. But as the spring approached, a much more serious threat was taking shape within the walls of Whitehall itself: a threat which within a decade would bring the country to the brink of civil war once again. James, Duke of York, was doing the one thing that his father, Charles I, had warned his sons would lose them their kingdoms forever: converting to Catholicism.

1. Charles II and his brothers dining in Bruges in the late 1650s. © *Lukas Art in Flanders*

2. *The Coronation Procession of Charles II*, 1661, by Kirk Stoop. © *Museum of London*

3. Charles II enthroned by John Michael Wright. © *The Royal Collection 2007, Her Majesty Queen Elizabeth II*

8

Protestant king, Catholic heir

In the Declaration of Breda of April 1660, which set out the terms on which the Restoration would happen, Charles II stated his attitude to the thorny question of religion. He wanted to give 'liberty to tender consciences' so that 'no man shall be disquieted or called into question for differences of opinion in matter of religion which do not disturb the peace of the kingdom'; in other words, religious toleration to all peaceful Christians. When a group of leading clerics came to Whitehall a few weeks after his return to England, the king expressed his desire for compromise and concord with such fervour that Mr Ash, the oldest member of the group, broke down into tears with joy and relief. With a clear steer from the king, the matter was formally referred to Parliament to discuss and agree. In the event, though, Parliament would pass over the sovereign's desire for toleration to impose a fiercely conservative Anglican settlement on the kingdom. How it would have horrified Charles I and Oliver Cromwell if they had known that after only a decade, their successors could be involved in such an extraordinary reversal of roles.[1]

After the civil war a plethora of religious sects had flourished in England, enjoying a climate of relative religious toleration. As well as the Anglicans and remaining Catholics, a range of other religious affiliations burgeoned, including Presbyterians, more radically puritan 'Independants', Baptists, Quakers and many smaller groupings. The events of the exile convinced Charles II that unless he showed himself to be a committed Anglican he could have no hope of reclaiming his kingdom. But at the same time he took the view that there was little to be gained by hard-line enforcement of religious conformity. With the Catholics he had a natural sympathy: his mother, sister and many cousins were Catholic and it was thanks to the loyalty of a number of Catholic Englishmen that he had escaped after the battle of Worcester – his repeated payments to them from his personal accounts testify to his enduring gratitude.[2] His experiences in Scotland, among other things, gave him good reason to resent extreme low-churchers. However, there had been a political imperative at play in April 1660: to secure the Restoration he needed to win round General Monck, and with so many soldiers of Monck's army members of the various religious sects, Charles believed that the promise of some degree of religious toleration would be essential to secure a restoration. More fundamentally, perhaps, though Charles believed in the importance of religious conformity to political strength and stability, he was in no sense a religious zealot. Whatever the nature of his own faith, he was certainly not seized by a passion for proselytizing and had no innate desire to persecute those who posed no obvious threat.[3]

But Charles's openness to religious toleration in 1660 would go unexploited. As he had promised, the matter of the national religious settlement was referred to Parliament, and after two years of deliberation, the assembly of the Church of England and Parliament agreed a far stricter line on religion than the king, or indeed many others, had either expected or sought. The new Book of Common Prayer and the Act of Uniformity of 1662 effectively excluded a mass of Christians from the established church. While the religious 'settlement' could have defined a broader Anglican church that accommodated presbyterians within its aisles, the legislation required clerics and teachers to conform very tightly to traditional Anglicanism. The news of a non-conformist rebellion in Yorkshire in October 1663 hardened the king's own views and paved the way for further prescriptive legislation in the form of the Conventicle Act of 1664. This banned all non-Anglican church services outright. Just four years after the Restoration, those with 'tender consciences' whom Charles had declared it his desire to include and support, had been criminalized.

Worship could not simply stop while the clerics and politicians deliberated over national religious policy. In the first two years of the reign parishes simply got on with the business of worship according to whatever formula seemed most appropriate.[4] Among these was the Chapel Royal itself. The committee who had made advance arrangements for the arrival of Charles II had understandably hesitated when it came to setting up his chapel. In fact, while much of Whitehall was lavishly decked-out to receive him, the chapel was left completely untouched. On the evening of his entry into London, the king attended a service held in the presence chamber, 'because the Chappel was not in readiness for His Majesties Reception'.[5]

The chapel at Whitehall had been built by Cardinal Wolsey in the 1520s, and had formed the focus of royal worship ever since Henry VIII appropriated the palace a few years later. Like the rest of Whitehall Palace, it had been used by the parliamentarian high command during the 1650s and for that purpose had been altered in ways that made it quite unsuitable for Anglican use. From 1649 the building had been a venue for public sermons, and a series of galleries had been erected to provide extra seating for the audiences. A great pulpit was built, which, in addition to the platform from which the sermon was delivered, housed various supplementary compartments including seats for the many notaries who recorded the words of edification as they were uttered. From 1654 Cromwell himself occupied the royal apartments at Whitehall and used the chapel in a quasi-royal fashion, even taking his seat in the elevated royal closet to hear sermons.[6]

It was clear as soon as the king took up residence at Whitehall that he would have his chapel arranged along traditional Laudian lines. While the king referred the religious settlement to Parliament, he would continue 'with the Exercise of our Religion in our own Chapel according to the constant Practice and Laws established, without enjoying that Practice and the Observation of those Laws in the Churches of the Kingdom'.[7] Within days the royal joiners were hard at work constructing a large altar for the room, made with a raised block along the back edge on which plate and other ornaments could stand.[8] The altar was placed on a raised step and was enclosed by a timber balustrade fixed into the paving.[9] Though a tantalizing account in the Lord Chamberlain's papers refers to the provision of fine linen for 'the communion table *in the Body* of the said Chappell' in December 1660, this was in fact a classic Laudian arrangement, with the communion table set against the liturgical east end of the chapel, surrounded on three sides by 'ye rayles a bout ye Alter'.[10]

Attention was also given to the tribune gallery that housed the king's closet, which seems to have been structurally as well as decoratively unsatisfactory.[11] The floor was completely rebuilt, cantilevered out from the walls, while the screen which formed the back of the two closets was also remade. The resulting rooms, assembled in a matter of weeks, must have been comparatively simple: a mixture of existing and new woodwork stained and varnished by the royal painter Emmanuel de Critz with very little new decorative embellishment. Perhaps as a time-saving measure, a firm partition was not erected between the two closets, but instead a curtain was hung to separate them.[12] Each of the two closets was provided with its own smaller altar, covered with white linen and a cloth of gold pall. The view from them down into the chapel itself was, as in Elizabeth's day, through glazed windows. On 17 June 1660, barely two weeks after the king's arrival in London, he worshipped once more in the Whitehall chapel.[13]

The Chapel Royal was a unique institution. As a 'royal peculiar', it was exempt from any episcopal or archepiscopal authority; its chief officer, the dean, was appointed directly by the king (always from the episcopate, though not yet from any particular diocese) and his staff formed a discrete sub-department of the royal household.[14] However, as a part of the royal household, and operating within the king's state apartments, the institution and the Dean of the Chapel Royal were under the authority of the Lord Chamberlain. The Lord Chamberlain swore the dean into post and it was through the Lord Chamberlain's office that he was appointed or dismissed.[15]

The dean was responsible for all aspects of the liturgical arrangements of the Chapel Royal, though some of the less spiritually sensitive issues – such as which courtiers were entitled to sit where within the chapel – were dealt with by the Lord Chamberlain.[16] Five men filled the position of dean during Charles II's reign. The first was Gilbert Sheldon, the conservative cleric who was the most prominent member of the small group that brought about the 1662 religious settlement. Sheldon was an Oxford man (responsible for the construction of the university theatre that still bears his name), Warden of All Souls' College, and part of a network of prominent Anglican clerics, including the king's old tutor, Brian Duppa, who corresponded avidly during the 1650s. Though he and the king did not know one another until the Restoration, they were introduced by those whom they both trusted, and the result was immediate: in August 1660 Duppa said of his friend's relationship with the king: 'none hath his ear more'. Sheldon's inclinations were broadly Laudian, but he was no fanatic and believed principally in conformity and stability.[17] After just three years running the Chapel Royal he was elevated to the archbishopric of Canterbury and was succeeded as dean by George Morley, Bishop of Winchester since 1662. Morley was of similar stock; he had been a chaplain to Charles I and participated in services at Richard Browne's chapel in Paris during the 1650s. Like Sheldon he was a close associate of Clarendon: when the latter fell from grace; he was removed from the position of dean rather ignominiously. Herbert Croft, Bishop of Hereford, held the post for barely a year until 1669 when Walter Blandford, Bishop of Oxford, was promoted from Clerk of the Closet to Dean of the Chapel Royal. Blandford remained there until his death in 1675, when Henry Compton, Bishop of Oxford and then London (*see* Figure 23), was appointed to succeed him; he would hold the position until after Charles's death. Compton, the son of the Earl of Northampton, was, unlike his predecessors, a man of the age: he was of the king's own generation rather than his father's, had travelled widely and cut his teeth as a soldier before turning to the church in his thirties.[18] His impeccable connections saw him rise through the ranks with dramatic speed, becoming Bishop of Oxford only eight years after his ordination. He was not, though, a mere opportunist. A moderate, almost shy character, he became an impassioned opponent of Catholicism, and his tenure as dean would see the Chapel Royal become a key battleground in the national debate about royal religion.

In reality, the work of running the Chapel Royal was not undertaken by the dean but delegated to the staff he appointed, the most senior of whom was the subdean.[19] Under the authority of the dean and subdean were the three sections of the Chapel Royal: the chapel, the vestry and the closet.[20] The most numerous body of staff appointed by the dean were the 32 'gentlemen' of the Chapel Royal. Twelve were ordained priests, while the remaining 20 were laymen who assisted in the performance of chapel services, though all wore surplices regardless of the distinction.[21] As a group they were also known as the singing-men and formed the choir of the Chapel Royal; supplying the adult voices for both the sung and spoken elements of chapel services, they used their 'voyces in the Psalmodies and Responsalls ... and in yᵉ Hymnes of yᵉ Church in the time of Divine service, and answer the Amen in a loud voice'.[22] In addition to this collective responsibility, the gentlemen individually filled various additional chapel positions. One acted as confessor to the household, responsible for reading the prayers in the morning service held for the staff of the royal household and for otherwise ministering to their spiritual needs.[23] Another held the post of Clerk of the Check, keeping records of the attendance of the gentlemen at chapel and administering the fines for absence.[24]

The musical programme of the Chapel Royal was the responsibility of the Master of Children, so called because he ran the boys choir, a group of 12 'singing boys', 'brought up for the Service of the Chapel'.[25] The post was held by a series of

23. Henry Compton, bishop of Oxford and then London and Dean of the Chapel Royal 1675–85. © *National Portrait Gallery, London*

distinguished musicians and composers: until 1672 by the accomplished singer and composer Henry Cooke and thereafter by two of his former choristers, Pelham Humfrey (also his son-in-law) and John Blow. Among Cooke's protégés was the young Henry Purcell, who would later secure the post of organist of the Chapel Royal and international fame as a composer. The boys were entirely in the care of the master who received an allowance for providing for their food, clothes and lodgings.[26]

Responsibility for the physical rather than spiritual or musical aspects of the chapel royal lay with the staff of the vestry. These men, a sergeant, two yeomen and a groom, were charged with procuring and caring for all the equipment necessary for the operation of the Chapel Royal.[27] This included the copes and surplices worn by the staff, the fine linen cloths for the altar and the towels used at communion, which they stored, with much else, in numerous large trunks in the vestry at Whitehall. Into their hands came the prayer books, musical scores and Bibles for services and supplies from other household offices, including tapers for the altar from the chandry and the communion fare: bread from the bakehouse and claret from the cellar. In addition to acting as receivers for all these goods, the staff of the vestry were also responsible for setting up the chapel for services, including dressing the altar and hanging the room in black during Lent, and for enforcing the Lord Chamberlain's regulations regarding access to the chapel and spaces within it.[28] There were various junior employees of the vestry, including the bellringer and the man who set out the extra seating, helped the gentlemen on with their gowns and performed other minor tasks.[29]

The king watched most Sunday services from the comfort of the tribune gallery at the west end of the building, and this chapel-within-a-chapel also had its own staff.[30] The most senior member was the Clerk of the Closet, who was responsible for the spiritual aspects of the chapel closet. The post-holder was invariably a senior cleric 'extraordinary esteemed by His Majesty' and appointed directly by the king (the post being itself 'a sure track to preferment in the church'). He had the weighty responsibility of acting as the king's personal chaplain, attending 'at the Kings right hand during Divine Service, to resolve all doubts concerning spiritual matters &c', and also for various other duties such as saying grace for the king before meals.[31] At the Restoration, Charles had appointed his exile chaplain, John Earle, to this post, so confirming him in a role that he had effectively played for almost a decade.[32] His successor, John Dolben, was a Clarendonite and – like Morley as Dean of the Chapel Royal – lost his post in 1668, though he would later return to favour as Lord High Almoner in 1675. Nathaniel Crewe, who would be Bishop of Oxford and then Durham, held the position of Clerk of the Closet from 1669 until the king's death. Crewe prospered greatly from the patronage of James, Duke of York. Shortly after James's succession to the throne, he suspended Compton as Bishop of London and Crewe was elevated to the post of Dean of the Chapel Royal; and it is for his part in the turbulent religious politics of James's reign that Crewe is best remembered.[33]

The other notable position attached to the chapel closet was the Closet Keeper. Usually also a Yeoman of the Vestry, the Closet Keeper managed the physical arrangements in the royal closet, including the enforcement of regulations regarding access to it.[34] Perhaps because of the importance of the equipage supplied for the king's own worship, the Clerk of the Closet, rather than the Closet Keeper, was responsible for receiving all the furnishings for the closet from the Master of the Wardrobe.[35] In addition to the royal closet in the chapel itself, the chapel closet officers were also responsible for the king's oratory, or 'private closet of prayers', which lay between the presence and privy chambers.[36]

Outside the direct authority of the Dean of the Chapel Royal were the 48 chaplains, men 'of considerable reputation and Doctors of Divinity', who preached before the king and court in chapel on various occasions throughout the year, while continuing to hold other clerical positions in the church. Appointed by the Lord Chamberlain directly, the chaplains waited in fours for a month at a time, during which period (except in Lent when different arrangements applied) they preached at all the court services – before the royal household every morning, before the king and court on Sundays, and before the king in his private oratory.[37] The appointment of a dozen presbyterians as chaplains in 1660 advertised the king's early desire to encourage a broader church, but in the end only four of them were actually asked to preach and they only once each.[38]

The routine for dressing the Chapel Royal followed that of many larger churches and cathedrals. On Sundays and other holy days the altar was draped with a 'carpet' of red or purple velvet, and with white and gold satin. On it was placed a collection of plate: a large plate or charger, three basins, six flagons (four of the sixteenth-century 'feathered' variety); two candlesticks and the Bible and Book of Common Prayer in handsome multi-volume editions laid on velvet cushions. Chalices and patens were brought out on days when the communion was taken. During these feast periods, it was not simply the altar that was elaborately dressed. Rich red and purple velvet fabrics were hung before the pulpit and covered the reading desk. On all other days the chapel was much more simply dressed: instead of satin and velvet, plain white linen covered the table, and the plate comprised simply a large basin and two candlesticks[39] (see Figure 24).

The chapel was also specially dressed for the fast days of Lent and on the anniversary of the execution of Charles I. On these occasions the whole building was swathed in black: great swags of cloth covered the walls, the organ loft was given a black curtain, and the altar rail and step were also draped in black. Black velvet hung over the altar, pulpit and reading desk, while the cushions on which the chapel books reposed, and even the books themselves, were given black covers. Special arrangements, albeit a little less elaborate, existed from Christmas Eve to Epiphany, when the altar was adorned with hangings featuring images of the nativity.[40]

The chapel pulpit was an oak structure built, like the altar, by the royal joiners in June 1660, and incorporating various cupboards at a lower level; the reading desk is not mentioned in the June works account but certainly one existed (also called the 'great desk'), while the litany desk was probably brought in only occasionally, as it seldom features in the Lord Chamberlain's accounts.[41] The king's seat was also an occasional feature of the chapel furniture; it was used only when the king descended into the chapel to take communion and was probably set out specifically for him on those days. Erected close to the seats on the right-hand side at the front of the chapel, towards the altar, it consisted of an upholstered chair with arms set under a crimson velvet canopy and encircled by a high rail, six foot square, from which hung a curtain that could be drawn around the king between the ceremonies of offering and receiving.[42] At the south end, near the entrance to the building, stood the seat of the Dean of the Chapel Royal

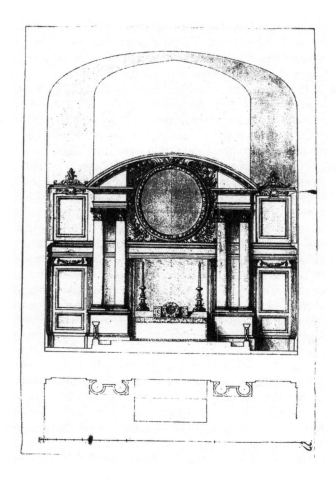

24. The liturgical east end of Whitehall chapel, in a presentation drawing by Sir Christopher Wren, showing the new arrangement of 1676. © *All Souls, Oxford*

with its reading desk, surmounted by a red velvet canopy.[43] Much of the rest of the body of the chapel was taken up by the pews into which the staff of the royal household and officers of state crowded to hear the services; these were of the boxed variety separated from one another by five-foot high wooden partitions with doors, some, at least, fitted with locks for which those who were entitled to use them held the keys.[44]

During the first two years of the reign, before the religious settlement was finalized or a new prayer book issued, some caution was shown in the way the Chapel Royal was run. During this period the Wardrobe accounts include orders for linen for the altar, cushions for kneeling and even a carpet to cover the altar, but not until three months after the Act of Uniformity received royal assent would a great Bible 'Clasped and Bossed' be placed upon the altar, or hangings be set up about it, and not until then were Books of Common Prayer (as opposed to orders of service for particular occasions) again used in the chapel royal.[45] Whatever the subtleties of the arrangements before 1662, the chapel's form and function throughout the rest of the reign remained largely constant, with occasional bouts of activity on the building itself.

In addition to the chapel proper, and the royal closet within it, there was one other dedicated place for the king's worship within Whitehall Palace: his private oratory or 'closet of prayers'.[46] This room, located immediately off the main ceremonial route between the presence and privy chambers, was set up in 1660.[47] Plain matting lay on the floor, while the room was furnished simply with a chair with arms for the king, accompanying stools, and a reading desk for the chaplain whereon was set a 'greate Bible'. The furnishing accounts for the room following its alteration indicate that in the part of the room where the king's chair stood, but only there, the walls were hung with crimson damask, and curtains of the same material were erected in such a way as they could be drawn before the king.[48] The room was probably always rather dark, and the special supply of candles to allow prayers to be read in poor light may still have been necessary after the alterations, despite the sconces that hung on the walls.[49] During the summer of 1682 when the works were taking place, the king heard prayers in the adjoining presence chamber, presumably in an area temporarily partitioned off for that purpose.[50]

There were, of course, chapels in most of the other palaces frequented by the king, though none was used so often as Whitehall and there is no evidence that any had a private oratory used by Charles II. The chapel at Hampton Court was redecorated in 1662 in preparation for the king's honeymoon visit. Here, as at Whitehall, the Tudor chapel was set up for high Anglican worship, a platform was erected for the altar, a rail supplied to separate it from the rest of the room, and a new organ loft erected. The royal closets were also refurbished; while the queen's was simply repaired (a Catholic oratory was set up for Catherine elsewhere in the palace), the king's was supplied with a chair of state and attendant furniture. Beyond this, though, the rest of the reign saw no significant structural alterations to these spaces.[51]

The other palace to which Charles II turned his attention in the 1660s was Greenwich; here a chapel should have formed the focus of the great east range of the king's planned new palace but it was never actually built.[52] In 1668 a Jacobean house was bought for the king in the Suffolk town of Newmarket, then as now famous for its races, and with some additions this was turned into a miniature royal palace. Being small, it was not provided with it own chapel, and the king attended services at the town's parish church instead.[53] Windsor Castle had a substantial medieval chapel, which was similarly adapted for Charles's use, though he only visited the castle very infrequently during the first 15 years of the reign.

The religious calendar of the Chapel Royal was defined by three cycles of celebration: the principal events of Christ's life, the feast days of the Apostles and the Evangelists and English royal anniversaries (*see* Appendix 3). There was a clearly defined hierarchy of celebration, denoted by the scale of the king's active participation: at the bottom of the scale were days when he did not appear at all; then there were those when he simply attended, those he attended wearing the collar of the Order of the Garter, and, at the top, those at which he offered at the altar or received communion.

The greatest ceremonial expression was given to the festivals that commemorated the crucial events associated with the life of Christ: Christmas Day, Easter Sunday and Whitsun. On these occasions the king came down the stairs from the chapel closet and both performed the priestly role of placing the parish alms on the altar and took Holy Communion. The second tier of ceremonial days were those on which other events of Christ's life were celebrated – Circumcision, Epiphany, Candlemas, Annunciation, Ascension, Trinity Sunday, All Hallows – and the feast days of St John the Baptist and St Michael the Archangel. On these occasions the king descended into the chapel royal and offered alms on the altar, but did not receive communion. The third category of ceremonial days comprised the feast days of the Apostles and Evangelists and the commemoration days for the Stuart anniversaries of the Restoration and the king's birthday and of the coronation and St George's day – both conveniently double dates. These were denoted 'collar days', when the king attended the chapel royal wearing the insignia of the Order of the Garter, accompanied by other Garter Knights similarly dressed, but did not descend into the body of the chapel. On all other feast days, including the anniversary of the death of Charles I and all Sundays in the calendar year, the king's attendance at the chapel royal was expected but without his performing any of these special rituals.[54]

During the prolonged fast of Lent, as the draping of the room in black fabric eloquently demonstrated, 'Divine Service and Preaching is performed in a more solemn manner'.[55] From Ash Wednesday to Easter Sunday sermons were preached on every Wednesday, Friday and Sunday by specially appointed senior clerics nominated by the Lord Chamberlain. The first Lent sermon on Ash Wednesday was preached by the Dean of the Chapel Royal and the last, on Easter Sunday, by the Lord Almoner.[56] The celebrated violin music (see below) ceased throughout Lent, and sung anthems after the sermon were omitted from the Sunday services, all adding to the sombre atmosphere.[57]

As well as being a stage for royal worship, the chapel royal was the parish church of the court. Though the king himself attended the chapel only on Sundays and feast days otherwise hearing prayers in his oratory, daily morning and evening prayers, or matins and evensong, were held in the Restoration chapel royal for the royal household at ten o'clock in the morning and four in the afternoon. Regardless of the king's absence from these services the Gentlemen of the Chapel Royal were required to attend.[58]

On Sundays and other sermon days (such as Wednesdays and Fridays during

Lent), the morning service was held an hour earlier at 9 a.m. and the afternoon service at 4 p.m. as usual.[59] On the days when the king attended, the congregation also varied: the morning service was primarily for the household, and the afternoon service for the king and the more senior court officers. Members of the household were in fact allowed to attend both, but could not sit in the pews at the second service and had to 'be contented wth such other Places as they can gett'. The two services were of the same basic form: in both the morning and afternoon, sermons were delivered on Sundays and Holy Communion celebrated monthly and on the appropriate feast days.[60]

The chapel at Whitehall usually functioned regardless of whether or not the king was in residence, though during prolonged absences, including 'such times in y[e] sumer or othertimes when we ar pleasd to spare it', it might cease to operate altogether.[61] One such summer was that of 1682, when the court was absent for almost four months while works were carried out to the royal apartments at Whitehall. On this occasion the Lord Chamberlain was prevailed upon to ask the Bishop of London for the assistance of some of the metropolitan ministers to conduct morning and evening prayers at Whitehall, 'severall persons of quality remaininge in theire Lodgings in Whitehall being very desirous to have prayers & sermons in the kings Chappell'.[62] Perhaps mindful of this, the king was careful to leave a functioning chapel in London on his trip to Newmarket the following spring.[63]

Unfortunately no formal or systematic record exists of how often Charles II was actually present at chapel, but a good impression can be built up from references in contemporary diaries and letters. These show that Charles attended on both feast days and ordinary Sundays throughout his reign.[64] He was often present to hear the sermons given in the chapel royal during Lent; in 1666, for instance, he certainly heard the sermons on Friday 2 March, Friday 16 March and Wednesday 11 April, in addition to the usual Sunday services.[65] There is in contemporary sources firm evidence for the king's attendance at the chapel royal on several separate occasions for almost every year of his reign; his attendance is positively recorded on an average of about six occasions a year for each year after the Restoration (*see* Appendix 4). Making the reasonable assumption that the information on which this is based represents only a portion of the days when the king actually attended chapel, the indication is that he was frequently to be found there and took seriously the traditional royal duty of regular participation in collective court worship. There is no reason to doubt Lorenzo Magalotti's remark that at Charles II's court the king was to be found 'observing with the most exact attention the rites of the Anglican Church'.[66]

Whenever Charles went to chapel he did so in stately fashion. On each occasion this began with a formal procession that bore him from the privy apartments out through the state apartments – the privy chamber, presence and guard chambers – to the first-floor chapel closet (*see* p. xv).[67] On the primary feast days of Easter, Whitsun and Christmas, as well as at New Year, Epiphany, All Hallows and the feast of St George, the heralds and pursuivants of the Office of Arms joined the procession in their technicolour uniforms. The Gentlemen of the Privy Chamber led the procession; after them came the heralds interspersed between various groups of the nobility, in ascending order of status. The Sergeants at Arms, carrying their great maces, processed after the most senior officers of the kingdom, separating out the nobility from the royal party; behind the Sergeants at Arms, directly in front of the king, walked the bearer of the sword of state (always a nobleman) flanked by the Lord Chamberlain and Vice Chamberlain. Behind the king, status progressively decreased, with the principal male members of the royal family directly behind the sovereign, followed – as the procession passed through the presence chamber – by all the members of the band of Gentlemen Pensioners taking up the rear.[68]

Lesser religious festivals and the anniversaries of the Restoration and coronation were known as 'collar days'. On these days the officers of arms did not participate in the procession but members of the nobility did, and the sword of state was borne by a Knight of the Garter.[69] The king dressed in purple and wore the Greater George, the ceremonial collar of the Order of the Garter, around his neck, and the Garter itself on his left leg.[70] On all other days when he attended chapel, mostly Sundays, though the king did not wear special clothing, a procession escorted him there, with four Sergeants at Arms marching at the front and the sword of state carried before him in the hands of a member of nobility.[71]

Onlookers lined the route through the state apartments, waiting to see or speak to the king. Though this was a ceremonial occasion, the Sergeants at Arms and Gentlemen Pensioners still had an active role in standing guard. Only two months after Charles II's return to England, one of the Sergeants at Arms walking in the chapel procession spied 'the glittering of the Sword' among the crowd in the passage between the guard chamber and the chapel closet, and pounced on a would-be terrorist hiding a weapon under his cloak.[72]

As the procession reached the door of the chapel closet, those who walked before the king lined up on either side to allow the king to pass through, which he did, still preceded by the bearer of the sword of state; once the king had gone into the closet, those who were so entitled filed down into the body of the chapel to take their seats for the service.[73] After the chapel closets were altered in 1675, members of the Yeomen of the Guard were sent ahead to keep the closets empty until the procession arrived. Only once the king had taken his seat were the rest of the congregation permitted to take theirs.[74]

With the sovereign settled in the chair of state, the sword was taken out of the closet and held at the door for the duration of the service by one of the Lord Chamberlain's senior officials, usually the Gentleman Usher Daily Waiter. It is clear that, in addition to any members of the royal family, there was normally a number of others in the chapel closet with the king throughout the service. With one or two specific exceptions, only members of the nobility could enter the king's chapel closet.[75] Various members of the Lord Chamberlain's department occasionally remained there during the service; the Lord Chamberlain was entitled to 'turne the Kinges chaire' and then to stand behind it during the service, but in his absence this could be exercised by the Vice Chamberlain or another senior member of the department.[76] Privileged visitors to court were also, periodically, allowed to watch the service from the tribune; but even the Moroccan ambassador, who attended chapel in February 1682, was taken to one of the ancillary rooms rather than the king's own closet to view the proceedings.[77]

The sermon, delivered except in Lent by one of the king's chaplains, was a major feature of all the services attended by the king. That sermons were often boring was a convention of the seventeenth century as well as of more modern times, and in a letter to his sister, Henriette Anne, Charles II sympathized with her complaints about them, remarking that 'We have the same disease of sermons that you complaine of there, but I hope you have the same convenience that the rest of the family has, of sleeping out most of the time.' This jovial remark should not be taken at face value, however: Charles took a close interest in preaching at the chapel royal. He was greatly impressed by the sermon on Catholicism given by the popular London preacher (and future Archbishop of Canterbury) John Tillotson and discussed it at length with the Earl of Anglesey afterwards. That delivered by Nathaniel Crewe during Lent 1668 commanded his attention so much that he stood throughout it to ensure he could hear properly.[78] While there is little evidence that the king had a strong spiritual interest in sermons, there is also no contemporary evidence that – despite his comment to his sister – he ever slept through them; he certainly considered it unquestionable that he, like his sister, had a duty to be there, as one of 'those who are bounde to heare them'.[79] Those sermons which contained a rebuke to the ways of the king and his court were either ignored or derided; when George Morley preached against the form of the Christmas celebrations at court, 'they all laughed in the chapel', while to the sermon by a canon of Christ Church delivered weeks before the king's marriage on the sinfulness of adultery the king made no response.[80] Nonetheless, he regularly heard sermons, took his chaplains with him on his progresses (they delivered their sermons in whichever parish church was appointed for the purpose), and approved the list of those who were to preach.[81]

If occasionally ambivalent about sermons, Charles was always enthusiastic in his enjoyment of chapel music. As happened at cathedrals throughout England after the Restoration, full choral services were sung on weekdays and on Sundays and festivals in the chapel royal; these involved the normal sung parts of the prescribed services, the responses and canticles (sung to fully composed settings), the singing of the psalms of the day and the inclusion of two or more anthems.[82] Music was reintroduced into the chapel royal immediately after the king's return: organs were reinstated in the chapel buildings, while sackbuttists were appointed to accompany them.[83] At first the standard seems to have been patchy – the anthem was so badly sung on 14 October 1660 that the king burst out laughing – but this was not to last. Henry Cooke, appointed Master of the Children in January 1661, drilled the choir intensively and the quality of the singing quickly improved.[84] In August 1662 a new sophistication was introduced when the royal strings (who normally played only during secular ceremonies such as dining in state) were ordered to attend Sunday and feast day services in the chapel royal where they played 'a Symphony' between the verses of the anthem.[85] This struck contemporaries greatly. Some disapproved. John Evelyn recorded in his diary in December of that year: 'instead of the antient grave and solemn wind musique accompanying the *Organ* was introduced a Consort of 24 Violins between every pause, after the *French* fantastical light way, better suiting a Tavern or Play-house than a Church'. Samuel Pepys, less conservative about such matters, thought the effect 'very fine' and before long the music to be heard in the chapel at Whitehall was regarded by many as among the best in the land; one informed commentator, who bemoaned the poor quality of contemporary music in general, conceded just two exceptions: 'I grant in Italy and the Royal Chapel here it hath been extraordinary good.'[86]

The elaboration of the musical part of chapel royal services was probably done at the behest of the king himself. The attendance of the royal musicians at Windsor chapel royal for over three months in the summer of 1674 was required 'by His Maties perticular comand to my Ld Chamberlaine' while with the addition of the strings to the chapel, it was noticed that the king was himself musical, listening attentively and tapping his hand in time to the anthem.[87] The full musical effect was to be heard on Sundays and feast days, when the king attended. During Lent and on 30 January, the violins were absent and some of the solemnity that Evelyn craved returned to the services.[88]

On Sundays the first part of the service was followed by the celebration of the Eucharist. Though the king only took communion in public on a handful of occasions during the year, he performed the priestly function of offering alms at the altar (reintroduced by the 1662 prayer book) on the twelve feast days during the year known as offering days.[89] On these occasions at the appropriate moment during the service the procession reconvened, and the king walked down the small staircase from the closet into the chapel proper with the sword of state carried before him. Passing to the east end of the room he was handed a silver-gilt dish by the Dean of the Chapel Royal containing a quantity of gold (or, if it was Epiphany, gold, frankincense and myrrh); he then knelt down on cushions and carpets specially set out on the steps, and offered it before the altar.[90]

On days when the king took communion (Christmas, Easter and Whitsun) the procedure was slightly different.[91] If the king was just offering, then, having done so, he processed back to the closet for the remainder of the service. On the principal annual feast days, though, he remained in the chancel to receive Holy Communion which happened later in the service.[92] On these occasions a chair of state was set up in the chapel on the right-hand side at the east end, standing within a curtained area, so that he could be hidden from view while the preparations for communion took place and 'till he returne to receive'. This drawing of the curtain had been a ceremonial feature of public royal worship since before the Reformation.[93] The senior clergy, kneeling at the north and south ends of the altar, took communion first. Once they had done so the king emerged. He took his position directly in front of the altar but – in the early part of the reign at least – outside the rail, where 'Carpets & Cushions' were laid out for him and, having bowed eastwards, he knelt. Meanwhile the most senior members of the royal family took up their positions, to the north and south of the altar, where the clergy had received. The Lord Chamberlain and Lord Steward, also kneeling, then took either end of a towel and held it beneath the king's chin as the dean administered the sacrament to him, and then to the royal family. This done, the king returned to his canopied seat near the altar and remained there for the rest of the communion service and blessing. At the end of the service he left the chapel without returning to the closet.[94]

Besides that in the body of the chapel royal, there was also an altar in the chapel closet, though there is no evidence Charles ever took communion there. It is clear, however, that in addition to his weekly attendance at the chapel royal, he also regularly heard prayers in the private oratory. Just as morning and evening prayers were said for the royal household in the chapel, the chaplains conducted similar services for the king.[95] In 1674 the Lord Chamberlain reprimanded the chaplains for their poor attendance 'whereby His Ma[ts] service hath beene neglected and His Ma[tie] hath wanted that service and attendance that is due'; but come the difficult early months of 1679, the king was to be found at prayers every morning without fail.[96]

Like the king in his closet on high, the behaviour of the congregation in the pews below was highly regulated. The seventeenth-century household ordinances set out the seating arrangements. Broadly, the left-hand side of the chapel (facing the altar) was reserved for peers and the most senior officials of the royal household. The right-hand side was divided between the ladies (wives and daughters of the nobility, and the ladies of the royal household) at the back, and mid-ranking household and state officials in waiting, at the front. Thus something of the separation of men and women frequently found in parish churches was reflected in the chapel royal.[97] Procedure in the chapel royal was governed by household regulations – for the first decade or so of the reign those issued by Charles I – a copy of which hung within the chapel itself, where they were regularly consulted by courtiers.[98]

Though there was the occasional complaint about the presence of 'debauched persons', on the whole the seating and access arrangements worked reasonably effectively.[99] People who did not have a seat sometimes viewed the service from obscure corners such as the organ loft, but this was not actually in contradiction of the regulations, which allowed for the presence of such people so long as they did not occupy the main pews.[100] In fact the Subdean of the Chapel specifically permitted the temporary setting out of stools and benches for members of the king's household who did not have a fixed seat, so long as they were not placed too near the pulpit or reading desk and did not obstruct the passage to the altar.[101]

The chapel royal was generally speaking well attended. The king's presence was, understandably, a draw in itself; on Sunday 6 April 1662 when the king was present the chapel was 'crowded' with people, and again on Sunday 22 May 1664 a 'throng of people' appeared at Whitehall to 'attend the King to Chapel'.[102] Feast days when the king took an active role in the proceedings were a particular draw; on the anniversary of the death of Charles I in 1667 'the Chappell was so crowded', wrote Evelyn, 'that I could not possibly approch to heare'. People were equally keen to be present when the king offered and received.[103] In addition to the attraction of observing the monarch, the quality of the preaching in the chapel royal was often high, and people came specially to hear a particular cleric.[104] The chapel royal was at its busiest over Lent and Easter, when the king attended most often and when three times as many sermons were preached. On 3 April 1663, for example, the chapel was so 'monstrous full' that Pepys could not reach his pew and had to squeeze in among the choir.[105] As a result it was often impossible actually to hear much of the proceedings from the body of the chapel; on 28 April 1661 Evelyn could again 'heare nothing' of the sermon, while in 1663 only those who sat right at the front could catch more than the occasional word of William Lewis's sermon.[106]

The gatherings before and after the chapel royal service presented an excellent moment for courtiers to snatch a word with one another, transact a piece of business or share news. In December 1681, for instance, the Earl of Longford was at chapel waiting for the king when the Lord Privy Seal came to complain to him of his treatment by the Duke of Ormond. In the words of Roger North, Sundays at Whitehall were worth attending as 'the great variety of persons coming together always made a diversion'.[107] In addition to casual socializing, Sundays and other feast days provided a good opportunity – if you were able to take it – to speak to the king himself. The Earl of Anglesey was at chapel on 2 July 1671, but was frustrated that he 'got not an oportunity to speak wth the King for iustice about my office'; a week later, when in the procession to the chapel, he seized the moment to speak 'wth him [the king] of my businesse who said he was resolved to be very kind to me, and would speak wth Lord Arlington to dispatch my warrant'.[108] The end of the service, as the king left the chapel, was also an opportune time to intercept him, as, for example, on 8 December 1679, when a crowd of peers stood waiting to waylay the king as he passed through the Vane Room on his return from chapel.[109]

Easter 1672 fell on 7 April and, as usual, the Easter religious cycle was performed in full at the chapel royal. As the swathes of black cloth were torn down to celebrate the miracle of the resurrection, one prominent figure was missing from the usual royal cast: the king's brother and the heir to the throne, James, Duke of York (*see* Figure 25). Among those who felt uneasy at this development was the duke's friend, Nathaniel Crewe, Bishop of Oxford, who had more than a personal interest in the matter being Clerk of the Closet and so spiritual adviser to the king. Crewe knew of the Duke of York's flirtation with Catholicism, but this deliberate absence from the chapel royal on some of the most important days of the religious year suggested matters had become more serious. After the Easter

25. James, Duke of York (the future King James II), as a young man, by John Michael Wright. © *The Government Art Collection*

events were over, Bishop Crewe took himself down to the far end of the Matted Gallery at Whitehall to call on the duke. Here, as Crewe recounted in his memoirs, he told James candidly of his disappointment at his absence from chapel. The duke responded with real passion that 'he could not Dissemble wth God and Man any longer': he was a committed Catholic, and he wished to withdraw completely from the chapel royal and the Church of England. Such was the duke's conviction that Crewe could do nothing to dissuade him. Turning sadly from the room, the bishop could only say that whatever the motives of those who had led him on this path, they were not acting as friends.[110]

In fact the duke's conversion had been in gestation for some years. Having been brought up, like most Englishmen of his age, with wild, satanic images of continental Catholicism, he was deeply struck by the moderate and dignified reality of the faith as he experienced it in exile. This planted a seed in his mind which would germinate many years later. After the Restoration, he and his wife, Anne Hyde, had become interested in the origins of the break from Rome and together became convinced that it was not the Anglican church but the papacy that was the heir to the true Christian church. In April 1668 Samuel Pepys caught a glimpse of the couple's private oratory, where they practised their 'silly devotions', and sometime the following year the duke made contact with the Catholic hierarchy and declared his desire to be received into their communion.[111]

This shattering development came at a highly sensitive political moment. With the end of the Dutch war in 1667, Charles II had started to play an extremely risky international game. On the one hand he had joined Sweden and the United Provinces in a Protestant alliance against France, while on the other, still smarting from the Dutch destruction of the fleet, he engaged in secret negotiations with Louis XIV for an alliance with France against the Dutch. On to the negotiating table with the French, Charles threw down an almost irresistible card: the prospect of his own conversion and the return of England to the Catholic fold. For the ploy to work, it was essential that this was seen as a genuine offer, and that the tiny number who knew of this aspect of the negotiations believed the king to be sincere. Among them was James who, with the eye of faith, was entirely convinced of his brother's desire to convert. In reality, Charles probably never had the slightest intention of doing so, but used it as juicy bait to entice Louis into signing the Secret Treaty of Dover. Under its terms England and France would mount a joint invasion of the United Provinces, and England would receive an annual subsidy of £230,000 with the prospect of a further £150,000 when the king announced his conversion.[112]

Though a public version of the Secret Treaty would soon be signed, the articles relating to Charles II's conversion remained a deadly secret, and the king was determined they should stay that way. While the treaty brought him some immediate advantage and the prospect of much more, he knew it would be political suicide to let news of this devastating clause leak. By the same token, he was anxious to prevent his brother from undertaking any sort of public conversion to Catholicism, fearing the horror to be expected from the public reaction. As Christmas 1672 drew near, Charles became increasingly worried about the consequences of James again being absent from the chapel on a major feast day. His own efforts having failed, he took his brother's friends aside and pressed them to intervene. A series of deputations duly presented themselves at the duke's rooms to try and persuade him to attend chapel with the king on Christmas Day. But the duke's mind was made up and nothing would convince him.[113]

Public feeling against Catholicism had always run fairly high in England, but recent events had seen it climb to new levels. As Charles II and Louis XIV made their treaty public and launched their joint war against the Dutch, Charles had issued a 'Declaration of Indulgence' that alleviated the penal laws against all dissenters, both Catholics and puritans. The principal purpose of the Declaration (which the king had been very reluctant to issue) was to curry favour with English puritans and prevent their forming a fifth column in a war against the Calvinist Dutch. However it was read as precisely the opposite, as a despicable act of favour to English Catholics, and as such provoked almost universal revulsion.

When Parliament met the following spring the king anticipated trouble. Within hours its members tore into the Declaration and insisted that a change to the religious settlement could not be made without an Act of Parliament. Such was their fury that the Test Act was proposed. This piece of legislation required all holders of government offices not only to swear the oaths of Allegiance and Supremacy, but to denounce Catholicism and take Anglican communion at least once a year, thereby making it impossible for any Catholic, however non-practising, to hold any political office. With an irate Parliament on his hands and with its agreement urgently needed if he was to secure the taxes necessary to pay for the war, the king caved in and agreed to the Test Act.[114] Among the prominent Catholics then holding official positions were the King's Lord Treasurer, Thomas Clifford, and – of course – his brother, the Lord High Admiral, James, Duke of York.

The Test Act passed in mid-March 1673 and on Saturday 29 March, Parliament adjourned. The following day was Easter Sunday, one of the three occasions during the year when the king led the kingdom to the altar to receive the sacrament. The eyes of the nation turned to the chapel royal at Whitehall. The crowds who pushed at the doors of the Tudor building that Sunday morning were bigger than ever. Among the curious throng was John Evelyn, who recorded what he saw:

> I staied to see whither (according to custome) the *Duke of York* did Receive the Communion, with the *King*, but he did not, to the amazement of every body; This being the second yeare he had forborn & put it off, & this being within a day of the *Parliaments* sitting, who had Lately made so severe an *Act* against the increase of *Poperie*, gave exceeding griefe & scandal to the whole Nation; That the heyre of it, & the sonn of a Martyr for the *Protestant Religion*, should apostatize: What the Consequence of this will be God onely knows, & Wise men dread.[115]

The scandal was made all the greater as the Duke of York had not been conveniently out of town on naval business, but was actually in the chapel closet during the service; but when the king rose to take communion, he had quietly slipped away.[116]

Three months later, the duke succumbed to the inevitable and resigned his office as Lord High Admiral of the Fleet. Short of making a public statement of his conversion, this was almost as near to an admission of his change of faith as he could go. It was one thing for it to be widely rumoured that he was a crypto-

Catholic, but another altogether if he was prepared to make a de facto statement of his conversion by resigning his offices, so putting his faith before his duty of service to the king.

At this highly charged political moment, Charles II was determined to demonstrate that, notwithstanding rumours to the contrary, the vast majority of those at court were loyal Anglicans. To do so it was essential that his household should be seen to abide by the Act, and suddenly the weekly proceedings at the chapel royal took on new and urgent importance. The following Sunday, a week after Easter, the principal officers of state and almost all members of the Lord Steward's department took communion in the chapel royal. Thomas Lamplugh, Dean of Rochester, wrote to friends in the country that the Duke of Monmouth, the Duke of Ormond, the Lord Steward, the Earl of Bath, the Groom of the Stool, a host of other senior officials, all the officers of the Board of the Greencloth (responsible for the economy of the household below stairs) and the whole of the rest of the below-stairs household celebrated communion.[117] The Sunday after that, 13 April, it was the turn of the household above stairs, and the Earl of St Albans, the Lord Chamberlain, led his department to chapel. This was not simply a case of people who had not been able to take communion at Easter doing so a week or two later. The Lord Chamberlain and many others had already received at Easter but, on the king's instruction, were doing so again in order to demonstrate their Anglican credentials. This was highly unusual, and went way beyond what was actually required by the Test Act – which only prescribed Anglican communion once a year. However, in the light of his brother's conversion, the king clearly considered it crucial that the Protestant allegiance of his court be vividly demonstrated. To this end, various key figures were dispatched to receive communion in parish churches and on 20 April Prince Rupert and a variety of senior lords received communion again, this time at St Martin's in the Fields, which was followed a few days later by Rupert's swearing the oaths required by the Act at the King's Bench bar.[118]

As well as the Duke of York, there was another conspicuous absence from this sacramental frenzy: one of the great office-holders of the kingdom, the capable and committed Lord Treasurer, Thomas, Lord Clifford. Long an advocate of some form of reconciliation between the various branches of Christianity, Clifford began to drift into Catholicism at the end of the 1660s and, like York, was now faced with the necessity of making a decision. He held off for three months, and with each week the speculation mounted. In April Dr Thomas Smith wrote to a friend that 'the Lord Treasurer has not yet received in public', while in June 'All people continue in great expectation to see what my Lord Treasurer and some other great men will doe at Court, in relation to receiving the Sacrament'.[119] Clifford waited until the last possible moment and then, on 19 June, resigned his offices. Three months later the news reached court of his death, and sinister rumours of suicide swirled around the corridors of Whitehall.

Meanwhile the political pressure continued to mount. When Parliament reassembled in the autumn, anti-Catholic feeling ran alarmingly high, fed by the resignations of the previous summer. Sensing that things might escalate still further, the king quickly prorogued the sitting until the new year. In a gesture of conciliation, he issued an order to the Lord Chamberlain and Lord Steward to ban from his presence all courtiers who were known, or even suspected, Catholics. The reason was spelled out clearly: the king wanted 'to let all his subjects see that no Care can be greater then His Owne in ye effectuall suppressing of Popery'.[120]

On 31 March 1671 the Duchess of York (née Anne Hyde) had died an agonizing death, giving the chilling cry, as the life ebbed from her, 'Duke, Duke, death is terrible, death is very terrible.'[121] Since then the question of James's remarriage had been under discussion and in the autumn of 1673 he took as his bride the 15-year-old Mary Beatrice D'Este, daughter of Alfonso IV, Duke of Modena. The arrival of a Catholic princess at such a tense moment could not have been less opportune. The marriage treaty stipulated that Mary should be allowed a public Catholic chapel at St James's Palace, but Charles now claimed that she could not have St James's chapel after all as it belonged to his wife Catherine (who in reality had her own chapel at her palace of Somerset House and didn't need it). Instead she would have to make do with a private chapel in her own apartments.[122]

The Duke of York stuck to his resolution not to take part in Anglican sacraments but, under intense pressure from his brother, agreed to continue to attend the most important services at the chapel royal. This hybrid arrangement struck no one as sustainable, least of all James, and events in the chapel were watched and discussed avidly. At Christmas 1673 Sir Gilbert Talbot, the Master of the Jewel Office, wrote to the Secretary of State, Joseph Williamson, 'The Duke doth not declare himself, but leaveth it much suspected by waiting on the King to the Chappell on Christmas day, and leaving his Majesty when he went down to receive'; he went on to point out that this 'will be the greatest occasion of complaint, because the Government is left in apparent danger whensoever God shall take the King from us'.[123]

There, of course, lay the rub. A decade of marriage had brought the king no legitimate children; his brother remained his actual heir and looked ever more likely to succeed him. The duke's conversion meant that England could at any moment have its first Catholic monarch since the days of Bloody Mary.[124] While he still attended Anglican services, there was the possibility that the duke's religion would remain a personal matter, but the slightest tremor in this fragile arrangement could trigger seismic changes in the national religion and the stability of the realm. In the weeks after the passage of the Test Act Charles ensured his court put on a model performance of Anglican conformity. In the same spirit, with the spotlight trained on the chapel royal for the three years that followed, a series of changes were made to ensure that the performance of Anglican ritual there was exemplary. These changes would also enhance the stateliness and order of the chapel and the king's own role in its liturgy.

In June 1673, the month the Duke of York resigned the Admiralty, the College of Arms was asked to formalize the procession that bore the king to chapel every

Sunday; the officers were to research its history and then to set out the proper form of the occasion, in so doing to 'observe therein as much as may be the practise of former times'.[125] The Closet Keeper and the chaplains, who looked after the king's chapel closet and oratory, were disciplined for neglecting their responsibilities and for allowing disorder in the conduct of religious services.[126] During the following summer a range of repairs and improvements were made to Whitehall chapel: the pulpit was mended, pew doors replaced and a handsome new altar rail supplied.[127] Over the course of 1675 the most significant alteration to any English chapel royal in the century took place at Whitehall: the queen's chapel closet – an essential element of royal chapels since the Middle Ages – was demolished and abolished. In place of the two-cell arrangement the tribune was now formed of a single central closet for the king with an antechamber on either side.[128]

Not since Henry VIII's reign had the two-closet arrangement really worked. With a succession of singleton sovereigns and Catholic queens, the rooms were almost never used as intended. After the Restoration the queen's closet (untouched by Catherine of Braganza) was occupied on an informal footing by prominent female courtiers.[129] The arrangement was fine as far as it went, but without any formal allocation of seats there was always scope for squabbling. This seems to have been tolerated during the 1660s, but was not to last long in the new culture of order and dignity. In March 1674 the Lord Chamberlain wrote a stern memorandum on the subject having received complaints that 'the place on the left hand the Kings Clossett in ye Chappell is ever so thronged & possessed by strangers and servants'.[130] Things were little better in the king's closet.[131] Every Sunday a noisy crowd gathered outside the door to catch the king as he passed; on 29 May 1664 Pepys struggled to hear the sermon from his position 'behind' the royal closet, while at Easter 1666, he took the opportunity with many others to crush into the king's closet itself to watch from above as Charles II received Holy Communion in the chapel below.[132] The disarray which resulted from the arrangements of the first half of the reign would be described in the household ordinances of about 1678, which complained that 'a very great Indecence and Irreverance hath been committed of late by a Throng of Persons that assemble there, and talk alowd, and Walke in time of Divine Service to the great Dishonor: of Religion and the Government of Our House'.[133]

So it was that by the early 1670s access arrangements in the royal chapel closets had become increasingly chaotic, with a mêlée of people clamouring around and within these supposedly orderly spaces. This situation was addressed explicitly in the reconfiguration of the chapel closets of 1675 and in the new regulations regarding access to them that followed later that year. In the spring of 1675 the surveyor of the royal works, Christopher Wren, a member of the ultra-royalist Wren dynasty and head of the royal architectural establishment, was asked to make major alterations to the chapel closets at Whitehall. The importance of these changes were such that he was to present an architectural model for the king's approval before starting work. This done, instructions to proceed were issued in July and, with the court out of London, Wren could set his men to the task at once. The works saw the demolition of the two existing rooms and the creation of a magnificent central closet for the king, with smaller ancillary rooms on either side. While the old royal closets, which had been set up so quickly in June 1660, were very simply decorated, the new king's closet was richly embellished. The glazed windows that had separated the closets from the body of the chapel were removed and instead a great open arch was constructed, surrounded by carved woodwork teeming with gilded and painted heraldic beasts. The new anterooms were to provide seats for various senior members of the royal household and courtiers: with ladies on the king's right and gentlemen on the left, the spaces divided by walls and doors rather than curtains.[134] Written orders naming those entitled to occupy each space were hung up in the body of the chapel to dispel any doubts as to the new arrangement, and the king reissued the long-standing regulation that no one below the status of a baron was to enter his own closet unless he was a privy councillor or Gentleman of the Bedchamber.[135] The new configuration of the Whitehall chapel closet would act as a blueprint that would be faithfully followed when chapels were planned at Windsor Castle and Winchester in the decade that followed.

Other than the creation of a new organ loft in 1663, and the reconstruction of the chapel closets, only one other major alteration was made to the Whitehall chapel during Charles II's reign. Coming over the summer of 1675, it saw the liturgical east end of the chapel reordered with the installation of a new altar and the erection of a new decorative screen, or reredos, behind it.[136] This was a big enough undertaking to necessitate the complete relocation of chapel services for several weeks, first to the chaplains' eating room and then, when the king was out of London, to the privy chamber.[137] The works carried out that autumn involved boarding up the old Tudor window, which had dominated the altar end, and erecting a great Baroque reredos, into which nestled a specially modified altar, and around which the altar rail supplied two years earlier was fitted.[138] The renovations were completed in December 1676, and the arrangement is recorded in a drawing by Christopher Wren (*see* Figure 24).[139] There was nothing dramatically new about the elements of the arrangement or their configuration. Stylistically, though, the work of 1676 was quite different from what went before: it was modern in form, baroque and statuesque in design. Even if only in its great Tudor window, the previous arrangement must still have had tones of sixteenth-century forms of worship. The new work was instead articulated entirely in the architectural language of the Restoration, a language which Wren was busy applying to the burnt-out shells of churches left by the great fire.

In March 1676, the Duke of York finally declared that he would no longer attend chapel. A few days later he was absent from the chapel royal on Easter Sunday, Evelyn noted 'this was the first time the Duke appeared no more in the Chappell' and the French ambassador described it as 'La Profession ouverte' of his conversion.[140] Given that the duke had been pressing the king to allow him to

26. Henry Bennet, first Earl of Arlington, after Sir Peter Lely, late 1660s.
© National Portrait Gallery, London

make this announcement for more than five years, the timing was significant.[141] Just six weeks earlier the duke's two children, Mary and Anne, who had been brought up as Anglicans on the king's insistence, were confirmed as such by Dean Compton within the Whitehall chapel.[142] A matter of days after the announcement the court appeared in full for the Easter service: the king was regally conveyed to chapel in the newly ordered procession, the congregation took their seats in the newly rearranged chapel pews, and at the crucial moment turned to watch the king descend from the new chapel closet – now focused architecturally entirely on the monarch – to lead his family and congregation in the reception of Anglican communion. This orderly and regal sight could hardly compensate for the crushing blow of the duke's conversion, but it must have been a powerful demonstration of the strength and majesty of the Anglican sovereign, who was still head of church and state.

A number of people could have been behind this concerted programme of chapel reform between 1673 and 1676. It may be significant that those years saw important changes in the senior personnel of the royal household. In September 1674 the Lord Chamberlain, the francophile Earl of St Albans, close confidant of Henrietta Maria before her death and widely believed to be Catholic, resigned the position of Lord Chamberlain. His place was taken by Henry Bennet, erstwhile Keeper of the Privy Purse (*see* Figure 26). Raised to the peerage as the Earl of Arlington in 1665, Bennet had been the leading politician of the later 1660s. While his appointment as Lord Chamberlain marked his retirement from the highest level of national politics, he was still relatively young and zealous. Though Arlington had some personal leanings towards Catholicism, he was a fundamentally cautious politician and was among those who persuaded the king to accept the Test Act, and was active in purging Catholics from court thereafter.[143] The following summer when the Dean of the Chapel Royal, Walter Blandford, died, the relatively junior Bishop of Oxford, Henry Compton, was appointed to succeed him (*see* Figure 23). Compton was another staunch Anglican known for his uncompromising opposition to Catholicism, and could hardly have been less associated with popery and the Duke of York – according to Bishop Burnet 'the Duke hated him'.[144] Though very different men, Arlington and Compton both knew how important it was for the king to see off the real or perceived threat of Catholicism, and following their respective appointments royal ceremonial was the principal mechanism at their disposal for doing so. Yet, while recognizing the likelihood that Compton and Arlington played a part in the changes of the early 1670s, it is inescapable that the king himself was a prime mover. He, more than anyone, was pressurizing his brother to continue attending the chapel royal, and many of the specific initiatives of these years were his express instructions. It may well have been at his instigation, too, that this new atmosphere of order and dignity would spread outwards from the chapel to the state rooms of the palace, effecting a change in almost all areas of court life.

9

A court comes of age

With the Duke of York's change of religion – and in part because of it – a gradual shift took place in the king's public life. Much of the custom and practice of exile had continued little changed into the organized court life of the 1660s. But the events of that decade – natural disasters, national disgrace and the conversion of the heir to the throne – had a sobering effect on king and court. The salad days of the Restoration had passed and, behind the rouge and the revelry, court life became a more serious business. While Charles II had always taken great care with the most formal ritual occasions – such as receiving foreign diplomats or touching for the king's evil – the atmosphere of his court in general was jovial, sometimes even decadent. Doors that would once have been closely guarded were often left unattended and courtiers flowed easily around the passages of the palace. But with the second decade of the reign things began to alter. Ceremonial activities that did not speak clearly of the power and majesty of the king no longer seemed appropriate and a feeling that things ought to be more regularized and formalized crept slowly down the corridors of Whitehall. Guards and ushers were reprimanded, locks were changed, rules were enforced and court life moved onto a new footing.

About a fortnight after the Lord Chamberlain issued the order banning Catholic courtiers from Whitehall in 1673, new regulations governing the king's private apartments were issued. These 'Bedchamber Regulations' were based on an earlier set of 1661 but, as the rubric explained, those earlier orders had been 'of late neglected and discontinued' and the time had now come for them to be 'revived and confirmed'.[1] In formulating the new orders the staff of the Bedchamber drew up a paper proposing additional and alternative paragraphs; these were then commented upon through a series of annotations by the Lord Chamberlain, and the resulting debate was put before the king for consideration.[2] The paper proposed that the regulations should contain further explanation of the responsibilities of the Bedchamber staff and a stronger emphasis on the rules of access to the privy lodgings: no one other than the Bedchamber staff, it was suggested, should be admitted without the king's special leave, as 'by such Intrusions his Ma^{ty} doth not only receive disquiet in his Person but disturbance in his most weighty affaires'. The author of the annotations was clearly uneasy about the proposals; as his notes explain, it was right that the privy apartments should be entirely under the control of the Groom of the Stool 'while his Ma^{ty} is private in them', but this could not be the case 'w[he]^n ye King is in publick

& company is admitted' as on those occasions 'yᵉ direction hath ever been in yᵉ L[ord]: Ch[hamberlain]: to w[ho]ᵐ it belongs to bring Amb[assado]ʳˢ & other strangers to yᵉ Audience, w[hi]ᶜʰ he doth frequently in those private Roomes'. Here was the problem: by using private spaces for public functions, the king had thrown into confusion the division of responsibilities between the Groom of the Stool and the Lord Chamberlain. The controversy to which the proposals gave rise meant that, in the event, only one or two of them were adopted. Yet, though the new regulations differed little in substance from those of 1661, when they were introduced in December 1673, they were much more strictly followed. On 2 January 1674 Sir Gilbert Talbot, Master of the Jewel House, a senior officer of the Lord Chamberlain's department, described to Sir Joseph Williamson how a foreign envoy was received that day 'in the bedchamber, whence all men but the Lords of the Bedchamber and the grooms are excluded by new order'.[3]

The other shift in practice in the privy apartments in the mid-1670s was more gradual but just as important. For centuries kings of England had been waited on as they rose and dressed in the morning and disrobed and retired in the evening. The household ordinances issued by Henry VIII in 1526 describe what procedures his servants were to follow on such occasions and similar arrangements existed at courts across Europe. What changed in England come the accession of Charles II, though, was that people who had no role in the proceedings, who held no position in the Bedchamber or Wardrobe of the Robes, were freely admitted to the bedchamber at these times of day.[4] The practice was not the result of any formal policy, and was not explicitly reflected in the Bedchamber regulations, but developed almost organically in the early years of the reign. In 1661, at which time 'no rules or formalities were yet established', the Spanish ambassador, it was observed with some surprise, 'came to the king at all hours, and spake to him when and as long as he would, without any ceremony, or desiring an audience according to the old custom; but came into the bedchamber whilst the king was dressing himself'.[5] This caused eyebrows to be raised among the older English courtiers, but the king was so used to doing business in his bedchamber that he barely noticed, often summoning people himself. In 1665, for example, he called John Evelyn into his bedchamber 'as he was dressing', keen to hear the news Evelyn had recently received from the English fleet.[6]

The mid-1670s saw the gradual formalization of this ad hoc practice and an event began to take form. The king's 'rising' became a noun rather than a verb, the Yorkshire MP John Reresby wrote of being 'at the Kings riseing', and for the first time Englishmen began to use the French terms 'levée' and 'couchée' to describe the occasion.[7] This transition would be spread over several years, but it is clear that changing practice reflected a new desire to control access. A watershed in the use of the private apartments had been reached.

The new Bedchamber regulations of 1673 were one of a series of household orders issued in the immediate aftermath of the Test Act, all of which were designed to make court life more orderly and more regal. In May of that year regulations were issued for the royal healing services. Disagreements between the various officials who oversaw them had caused 'many inconveniencies & disorders'; the new rules were designed, again, to restore dignity and propriety.[8] The effect was soon felt, with the numbers healed by the king exceeding five thousand for the first time since the crowds had flocked to Whitehall in his Restoration year (*see* Appendix 1).[9]

The practice of letting visitors to Whitehall use the privy gallery as a way into the palace was also circumscribed. In May 1673 new rules were issued for the gallery, designed, as the Lord Chamberlain explained to his staff, 'for the effecting of His Ma^{ts} purpose with reducem[en]t of his Privy Gallary into some order'. The locks were to be changed on all the doors leading into the privy gallery and only people officially entitled to be there were to enter the room at all.[10] All other visitors were to be turned back at the doors to the gallery and referred to the proper route into the palace, which was through the king's state apartments. This in itself necessitated change in the outer state apartments: the guard chamber, the first of these state rooms, had been neglected over the previous years and as a result had become rather squalid, with the unsavoury smell of the nightwatch

27. Charles II seated, by an unknown artist, with a guard chamber, staffed by the Yeomen of the Guard, in the background. © *Courtauld Institute of Art*

hanging in the air throughout the day and a thick fug of pipe smoke and beer fumes deterring visitors (*see* Figure 27). All this was to change; tobacco and alcohol were banned, the windows were to be opened, sweet herbs burned in the grate and rules of access strictly enforced.[11]

It was not just the king's contact with his subjects that changed in the early and mid-1670s. How he dealt with his equals, sibling sovereigns and their families from other nations was also subject to revision. During the course of the reign about a dozen foreign princes and senior members of foreign ruling dynasties visited England. These included Cosimo Medici, Grand Duke of Tuscany, Prince Charles of the Palatinate (who succeeded his father as Elector during the visit), Prince George of Hanover (who would become the future King George I), and the future William III (who came to England a total of three times during Charles II's reign).[12] Like much else, visits from these foreign princes were either official undertakings conducted with all consequent pomp, or less formal 'incognito' affairs, which sidestepped the need for many of these formalities.

Visits undertaken for an official purpose were almost always conducted 'in state'. Prominent among them were those made to contract a marriage with a member of the host family: as for example when William of Orange and George of Denmark each came to marry one of the Duke of York's daughters, or when members of the D'Este family accompanied Mary Beatrice on her journey to England to marry the duke himself.[13] As state visits, they followed a well-established formula designed to embody and communicate the mutual respect that, in theory at least, existed between the visitor and the host. From their inception every opportunity was taken to demonstrate solicitous concern, to the extent that the visiting party was not even allowed to cross the sea in their own ship, the king's vessels being dispatched to collect them. With especially grand guests the Duke of York, or even the king himself, travelled some distance towards the coast to meet them.[14] The visitor was then carried to court in the king's coach or barge, and was here met by the Lord Chamberlain and conducted up the great stairs into the state apartments, with the household guards standing to arms as they passed.[15]

Unlike the arrival of diplomats, the arrival of a foreign ruler or members of his family did not involve a state audience in the Banqueting House or presence chamber, the purpose of which was for letters of accreditation to be presented. Instead, introductions normally took place in the privy apartments.[16] If the king and queen were receiving visitors together they usually did so in the queen's withdrawing room; if they received separately the king usually conducted his audience in the bedchamber.[17]

As ever the precise form of the meeting depended entirely on the relative ranking of guest and host. An elaborate choreography of gestures was worked out in advance, prescribing who stood or sat, whether either party was to step forward (and if so by how many steps), and whether kisses or embraces would be exchanged.[18] Visitors of high rank were invited to sit on stools, carefully positioned next to the king's chair, but only another reigning sovereign could claim the right to be seated, like Charles II, on a throne.[19]

After visiting the king and queen, the guests usually called upon other members of the royal family. However, if the visitor was of higher status than the Duke of York or Prince Rupert, he or she would expect to receive a visit first.[20] Naturally this required agreement between the parties on their relative status, which was sometimes hard to reach. As the Duke of York and Prince George of Denmark were both brothers of crowned heads of Europe, each argued that he should honour the other by making the first visit. Eventually Prince George was forced to back down and accept the first visit from his father-in-law.[21] In 1673, the reverse occurred, Prince Rinaldo D'Este, Mary of Modena's uncle, and Prince Rupert each considered that he ought to be the recipient of a visit from the other and, being unprepared to compromise, consequently did not exchange formal visits of any kind.[22]

After a guest had paid the initial visits to those who were of superior status, the guest would receive visits from those of inferior status. These visits were then returned. In exceptional circumstances even the king and queen themselves might return the visits they had received. When Charles of the Palatinate unexpectedly succeeded his father while he was in England, he immediately became a head of state, and in recognition, both Charles II and the Duke of York paid him a visit.[23] In addition, visitors from foreign ruling dynasties would exchange visits with important ambassadors resident in London, and might also dine with the Lord Mayor of London.[24]

A further defining characteristic of state visits was that the visitor was entertained at the king's expense. The guest was transported in the king's coach, lodged in princely houses, sometimes even in the royal palaces themselves, and supplied with every comfort from canopies of state to close stools; even William of Orange's preference for quilts over blankets was catered for.[25] The visitor and his retinue were provided with two full meals a day for the duration of the visit, and were allocated staff from the royal household to serve them in appropriate style.[26] In 1677 the Lord Chamberlain assigned no fewer than fifty members of his own staff to wait on William of Orange, while in 1680 nine members of the Lord Chamberlain's department were assigned solely to present Charles of the Palatinate's food.[27]

Given what a performance state visits were it is not surprising that many princely travellers chose to avoid the cost and inconvenience of the costumes, gifts and retinue with which they were expected to travel by designating their visits 'incognito'.[28] By so doing a visitor chose to travel as a private individual and so decline the hospitality of the head of state of the country being visited.[29] As he was not the king's guest, neither lodgings, household servants, food nor furnishings were provided for him. It also meant that since the visitor took no role in public life, there would be no formal entry, no public appearances at any of the ceremonies conducted in the state apartments, no meetings with the host family outside the private apartments and no exchanges of formal visits.[30]

Though an incognito visit avoided a good deal of the expense and pomp of a state visit, many highly ritualized exchanges still took place within the private apartments of the royal palaces and these were negotiated with as much care as any public meeting. Before the arrival of the Grand Duke of Tuscany on his incognito visit in 1669, for instance, Charles was sent a detailed list of questions on how the duke could expect to be treated in England, to which he gave painstaking consideration – even writing to the queen mother in Paris for advice.[31] Because meetings between the king and incognito visitors took place within the private apartments, they were, in theory, outside the jurisdiction of the Lord Chamberlain and his staff. In reality, though, these officials were almost always involved, with the Lord Chamberlain himself usually leading the visitor up the backstairs into the privy apartments for the meeting.[32] Meetings between incognito visitors and other members of the royal family, senior diplomats and public figures were conducted in a similarly 'private' manner.[33]

There were benefits to incognito visits over and above the degree of effort and expense which they spared. Among other things they provided a sometimes welcome way of avoiding the almost infinite and occasionally intractable complications that sprang from both parties' desire to assert their status.[34] So when the Duke of York offered to call on the visiting Prince George of Denmark in 1669, the Dane declined on the basis that his incognito status prohibited it; in reality, though, it suited him well not to receive the duke, for had he done so he would have been forced to treat the duke with a deference that he preferred not to concede.[35]

Despite their many practical advantages, Charles II himself disliked incognito visits. Having spent 14 years incognito, he may have had personal reservations, but more than this, such visits represented missed opportunities for asserting his place in the international club of kings. When Prince Christian, heir to the Danish crown, visited England in 1662 on 'a tour of the world to study the customs of other Courts and gratify his curiosity', he set off as an incognito traveller with only a modest train.[36] On arrival in England, however, he came up against Charles's determination that the visit should be put on a more formal footing. Despite all efforts to prevent it, Christian was 'obliged to submit to his Majesty's wishes' in the matter. He was immediately deprived of all pretence of travelling in a private capacity, being put up at Exeter House (one-time home of Elizabeth I's chief minister Lord Burghley), conveyed around town in the royal coach and waited on by the great office-holders and diplomats of the kingdom. The ceremonies culminated with his investiture as a Knight of the Garter – with the king personally tying the George and ribbon around his neck.[37]

In 1669 Charles tried similarly to persuade Cosimo de Medici to abandon his incognito status, and repeatedly offered him the royal palace of Somerset House as lodgings. But when the Italian stood firm he did not insist, and other incognito visits followed during the decade.[38] Before long, however, Charles's views on the subject hardened permanently. The matter was brought to a head by news of the visit of the 18-year-old son of the Duke of Pfalz-Neuburg in 1675.

The boy was to come to England with his governor on an educational tour and so travel incognito. Charles remembered well the generosity and honour that the duke had shown him as a friendless exile in Germany, and was determined that his son should be received in England in a way that would 'testify a sense of his father's kindness'.[39] In preparation for the visit, the pale vellum-bound precedent books were pulled down from the shelves of the Lord Chamberlain's office as officials considered how best to fulfil the king's wishes within the rules of past precedent. The trouble was that only very summary records were available to consult, as incognito visits were not recorded in anything like the detail of their state equivalents. The officials eventually reported that they could offer little guidance.[40] At this the king's patience snapped. The assumption of incognito status by his most important visitors was insufferable on two counts, he and the new Lord Chamberlain agreed: first, it denied him the opportunity to demonstrate the splendour of his own court in receiving them; and second, by avoiding the usual ceremonial procedures and supervisions, lapses and inconsistencies in treatment occurred that could prejudice future visits.[41] Something of a stalemate followed, as the prince and his governor were determined to 'make the same use of the word incognito which the Prince of Tuscany had done ... it being indeed an advantage to them, but a manifest inconvenience to the King'. Probably to avoid causing any offence to Pfalz-Neuburg (who he was, after all, trying to flatter), Charles eventually agreed to a compromise whereby the prince maintained 'his Quality of being Incognito', but was attended by the Master of the Ceremonies on all his visits.[42] However, Charles then drew a line under the occasion and from that moment until the end of the reign no 'incognito' visits from members of foreign dynasties were tolerated.

Even very senior visitors were forced to submit to the king's wishes. In 1680 Charles of the Palatinate, son of the Elector Palatine and nephew of Prince Rupert, landed so discreetly and incognito that the king only knew he was in England when he read about it in the morning's newspaper.[43] The Master of the Ceremonies was immediately dispatched to intercept him. Dispensing laden apologies to the prince for his 'not being received according to his Quality, by reason of his sudden coming without notice given', Cotterell bundled him into the royal coach and took him to Windsor, where 'the King was resolved he should be lodged at the Castle & defrayed at his charge'. Faced with the king's determination on the matter, the prince 'took al in good part' and acquiesced.[44]

There were other dimensions to the king's hardening attitude to court ceremonial in the 1670s; in some cases it meant enforcing rules and regulations that had been neglected in previous years, but most notably in respect of the royal maundy, it involved abandoning rituals that did not fit well with the king's idea of his own majesty. Before the Reformation, English monarchs had performed a series of religious rites on feast days, especially during Easter and Lent. These included the taking of ashes on Ash Wednesday, the ceremony of the palms on Palm Sunday, and the adoration of the cross on Good Friday – the last involving the monarch

28. Christ washing the feet of his disciples in a late 15th-century book of hours probably created for the young King Edward V of England. The event merges biblical events with the English royal maundy, with Christ performing the ritual in a northern European great hall. © *The British Library*

in a penitent ritual known as 'creeping to the cross'. All these were swept away in the sixteenth century, with one prominent exception: the ceremony in which the king himself washed the feet of the poor on Maundy Thursday. Indeed, a form of the event (long since stripped of the foot-washing) is still performed by the sovereign today. Before the Reformation the Maundy Thursday rituals had three distinct parts: in the first the king washed the altars in the chapel royal, in the second he washed his subjects' feet (known as the pediluvium) and distributed alms, and in the third he performed the ritual of royal mortification known as 'receiving discipline'.[45] Only the second survived the Reformation, and by the seventeenth century it was largely separated from its wider liturgical context. The washing of feet, a common practice among travellers and pilgrims of antiquity before entering a house, had been given its special religious significance when Jesus had washed the feet of his apostles at the Last Supper, asking them to follow his example. Through the Middle Ages the practice was regularly performed at monasteries and churches, and, from at least the reign of Edward II, English monarchs performed the ceremony, showing that they, too, were Christ's successors (*see* Figure 28).[46]

At the Restoration, therefore, the maundy ceremony involved the pediluvium itself and the distribution of alms to the poor. Because of the importance of the latter, the management of the event was one of the main areas of responsibility of the Lord Almoner. Like the Dean of the Chapel Royal, the Lord Almoner was usually a senior bishop, and he too headed a sub-department of the Lord Chamberlain's department, in his case responsible for all aspects of royal almsgiving.[47] Brian Duppa, the king's old tutor, held the post from 1660, and was succeeded by Humphrey Henchman, Bishop of Salisbury; he in turn was followed by John Dolben, Bishop of Rochester and Archbishop of York (who had been Clerk of the Closet in the 1660s), and Francis Turner, Dean of Windsor and Bishop of Rochester.[48] The other key figure in the organization of the royal maundy was the Subdean of the Chapel Royal who conducted the prayers and anthems with which the ritual was punctuated.

Among the Lord Almoner's responsibilities was the selection of the paupers who were to receive the alms and experience the honour of having their feet washed by their sovereign.[49] By long convention the number of recipients was determined by the king's age, one for every year of his life. The men – and it was always men – who were chosen were frequently aged and for the most part genu-inely impoverished, often as a result of some sort of loyal service. That said, they needed the support of a patron, since the recommendation of a senior courtier was a sure route to gaining a place as a maundy man; the Lord Chamberlain, Lord Treasurer and the bishops were frequently prevailed upon to write to the Lord Almoner recommending deserving candidates.[50]

Though Charles had not practised the royal maundy during his exile, he started to do so as soon as he returned to England, first performing the ceremony on Maundy Thursday 1661.[51] The location for the event in the post-Restoration period was always either the great hall at Whitehall or the Banqueting House; that it was no longer held in the chapel shows how disassociated it had become from the Easter chapel cycle of which it had once been part.[52] The form of the ritual was the same each year: the king entered the hall in a procession similar to that which carried him to chapel on Sundays. Before him walked an official carrying the sword of state and on either side of him the Gentlemen Pensioners, the ceremonial guard of the presence chamber, carrying their weapons. Once the king had taken his seat in the chair of state the subdean then began what was effectively a religious service, reading Psalm 41 ('Blessed is he that considereth the poor and needy ...') and the lesson, St John 13, verses 1–18, describing Christ washing his apostles' feet. At the end of the lesson, the king rose from his seat and, wearing a large linen apron to protect his clothes, began the laborious process of washing the feet of the maundy men.

The poor men sat in a long row, and the king knelt before each one, with the Lord Almoner in close attendance. He then took the feet of each in his hands and, using a sprig of the aromatic hyssop bush, sprinkled them with scented water and wiped them clean with a linen towel. Each gnarled and calloused foot was then pressed to the royal lips for a kiss, before the king shuffled down the line on his knees to the next recipient. Having done the same to all the maundy men, he returned to his chair of state, washed his hands and the service continued. There followed four anthems, after each of which the Lord Almoner distributed alms in kind to the maundy men: shoes and stockings after the first, wool and linen clothes after the second, purses of money after the third, and fish and bread after the fourth. The Gospel was then read, a last anthem sung and the maundy prayer said, following the form of the end of the evening service. Finally, the Lord Almoner called for claret, he and the maundy men drank the king's health, and the occasion drew to a close.[53]

The royal maundy was a well-established part of the royal calendar, and Charles II regularly participated in it during the 1660s.[54] Come the end of the decade, however, his attitude towards the ceremony was clearly undergoing a shift. He asked the Bishop of London to stand in for him, and what was at first an exception turned into the rule, so that the king did not participate in the royal maundy at all during the 1670s.[55] That a ceremony which emphasized royal humility rather than power and authority lost its appeal in the late 1660s is significant. It seems that Charles felt this was no longer the image of kingship that a sovereign of England should project.

Since the execution of his father, Charles had been head of the Order of the Garter. Like Charles I and the other Garter Knights he was never seen without the 'lesser George' (the simpler version of the order's emblem) on a ribbon around his neck, and like other sovereigns before him he made appointments to the order and sometimes participated personally in installations. However, though the order with its officials and annual round of installations and elections was fully operational after the Restoration, Charles does not appear to have had any particular passion for it. The most important and spectacular moment in the Garter calendar was the annual feast day of the order's patron saint, St George, on 23 April. This occasion was traditionally honoured with three days of feasting and celebration at the order's home, Windsor Castle. During his reign, Charles staged a full Garter feast on only five occasions (out of a possible 24), and each of those can be explained by his desire to use the pageantry to make a political point.[56] At the feast of April 1661 the knights created during the exile were installed; in 1663 Prince Christian of Denmark, who had just left England, was installed

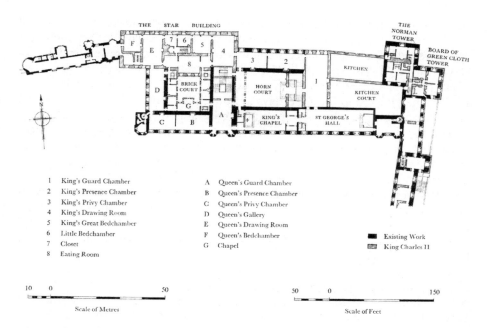

1   King's Guard Chamber   A   Queen's Guard Chamber
2   King's Presence Chamber   B   Queen's Presence Chamber
3   King's Privy Chamber   C   Queen's Privy Chamber
4   King's Drawing Room   D   Queen's Gallery
5   King's Great Bedchamber   E   Queen's Drawing Room
6   Little Bedchamber   F   Queen's Bedchamber
7   Closet   G   Chapel
8   Eating Room

Existing Work
King Charles II

10   0   50   50   0   150

Scale of Metres   Scale of Feet

29. First-floor plan of Windsor Castle showing the royal apartments as reconfigured
by Charles II.

by proxy alongside the king's illegitimate son James.[57] In 1667 the feast was
held in full public view at Whitehall, rather than at Windsor Castle, in order to
impress the Swedish delegation then in England negotiating what would become
the Triple Alliance. Not only was the location changed because of 'the present
Conjuncture of publique affaires', but the knights did not, as usual, remove their
finery immediately after the ceremony but were seen about town in their robes
until nightfall. The Swedes were clearly impressed, and after the Triple Alliance
was signed King Charles XI was himself elected a knight.[58] His installation was
the main purpose of the feast held at Windsor in May 1671, on which occasion
the Duke of Saxony, John George II, was also installed by proxy.[59]

The only occasion during the reign when the full Garter feast was held without
some such explanation was at Windsor Castle in May 1674. There was no foreign
prince or member of the king's family to install, indeed only one knight of any
variety. The rising soldier, John Sheffield, Earl of Mulgrave, was installed but he
was hardly important enough for his installation alone to merit the staging of a
full feast.[60] To understand the significance of the feast of 1674, and the massive
changes at Windsor that followed immediately afterwards, it is necessary to look
beyond the Order of the Garter to the wider court context.

In April 1674 royal officials had been advised that not only was there to be a
feast of the Order of the Garter the following month, but that the court would

be going to Windsor for the entire summer. Sure enough that year the king and royal household was in residence at Windsor for over 100 days.[61] This might not appear remarkable at first glance, but it was a dramatic change given that Charles had hardly used Windsor since the Restoration, spending little more than a few weeks there in a decade and a half. Most recently, in the summers of 1670 and 1671, he had looked in for a few days to hunt in the park, but had soon moved on.[62] Prince Rupert, who was appointed constable of the castle in 1668, had overseen various repairs to the buildings; but though a survey pointed out how much remedial work the castle needed, and though plans for repair were made, very little was actually done.[63] Once the court was in residence in 1674, though, it became clear that the visit was not a one-off: in April the Office of Works opened accounts books for a major building campaign, which would see over a hundred thousand pounds spent at Windsor, and involve, among other things, the almost complete reconstruction of the royal apartments (see Figure 29). Before the summer was out the king announced his intention to take the court to Windsor every year.[64]

The decision to take the court to Windsor was communicated to the officials at the castle on 14 April 1674. This was Tuesday of Holy Week, just two days before Maundy Thursday and the start of the Easter cycle. It was also the first Easter since the Duke of York had resigned his offices.[65] With the proceedings at court under close scrutiny and almost every aspect of public ceremonial undergoing some sort of reform to enforce rules of access and increase order and splendour, the decision to pack up the royal household and move it out of London was highly significant. Here the court was at some remove from the volatile political world of London, and out of the spotlight of public scrutiny. Unlike the modest residence at Newmarket, Windsor was both big enough for the royal household to operate in full and was an unmistakably regal building.[66] It was also a fortress, a building which, if trouble mounted, could be secured against any opponents.[67] Such was the desire to distance the court from the principal mouthpieces of criticism that the privy council was not to meet at the castle, but instead to assemble instead some 15 miles away at Hampton Court Palace, 'where all persons should attend him'.[68]

As Charles II processed down into the chapel at Easter 1676, his court on a new footing, his nieces confirmed as Anglicans and the news of his brother's conversion finally out in the open, he must have felt that the worst was over. He could not know that the real incendiary power of the Duke of York's conversion was, as yet, unrealized; two years later, when the match was lit, a crisis would explode on such a momentous scale that many felt the nation was once again on the brink of civil war.

10

The apotheosis of Charles II

In August 1678 a fanatical cleric called Israel Tongue presented Charles II with a dossier containing details of a Jesuit plot to kill the king and raise the country in a Catholic rebellion. Tongue's information would bring about one of the biggest debacles of the century; ministers would fall, the king's brother and son would be banished and the very institution of hereditary monarchy would be brought to the brink of collapse.

Tongue owed his information to one Titus Oates, who, despite his slightly crazed appearance, was able to give precise details of the supposed conspiracy and name various of the conspirators, among them the Duchess of York's former secretary, Edward Colman. The king was deeply sceptical of tall tales from such a discreditable duo, and gave the story little credence. But news of a Catholic plot spread among his receptive subjects like a plague and a dangerous atmosphere of suspicion and suspense poisoned the early autumn air. Oates had given his testimony under oath to a London JP, Sir Edmund Bury Godfrey. On 17 October Godfrey's lifeless body was pulled from a ditch on Primrose Hill. As news of his murder swept across the capital the story of the plot and of malevolent forces at work acquired instant credibility. The king had a crisis on his hands (*see* Figure 30).

The discovery of the supposed plot had an immediate and direct effect on the public life of the court. With the alleged assassins still at large, the royal household was put on a maximum security alert. Doors and passageways across Whitehall Palace were walled up to make it easier to guard, and sheds and small structures were demolished 'that may harbour & entertaine idle & meane people that are not His Ma[jes]t[ie]s servants, which in this tyme of Danger may lurke about ye Court'.[1] The old Catholic chapel at St James's Palace, the Duke of York's residence, was an obvious target and the doors were swiftly locked and then nailed up, the keys being returned to Christopher Wren himself. Lord Arlington, the Lord Chamberlain, mobilized his staff. He wrote to his senior officials stressing the importance of their vigilance in each of the state rooms day and night, 'Especially at this tyme for the safety of His Ma[jes]ties person'. While he usually left the staff rotas entirely to the Gentlemen Ushers, the weekly lists of those in waiting were now to go through him personally.[2] The king's safety was paramount, and occasions when he was among a crowd were the most dangerous. Before he took his seat in the court theatre, constructed in the old great hall, one of the Lord Chamberlain's staff was to search the voids in the structure below to ensure no

30. A contemporary broadsheet describing the murder of Sir Edmund Bury Godfrey in 1678. © *Trustees of the British Museum*

assassins lay in wait. But even this was not thought enough, and 'an honest person' was to remain beneath the king's seat throughout the performance to fend off any danger.[3] Healing ceremonies were another high-risk occasion, with the king coming into close contact with so many of his poorer subjects. As the large-scale ceremonies had resumed after the summer break the numbers admitted at first remained at their usual autumn levels, but as winter approached and the king himself became convinced of the existence of some sort of conspiracy against him, there was a sudden and dramatic crackdown. In the three months of December, January and February 1678–9, when some five hundred people would normally have been ushered into the Banqueting House to be stroked, the king touched just twelve.[4]

Three weeks after Godfrey's body was discovered, new orders for regulating the king's private apartments were issued. Dated 10 November 1678 they were drawn up by his 'especiall Command' and bear the royal signature and intials on every page.[5] The rubric at the beginning explains that the 1673 orders had been 'very much neglected' and that 'to Our great displeasure', a 'multitude of keyes of Our Bedchamber are made and disposed through the House, and also abroad in the Towne in the hands of Strangers' which 'may be of very dangerous Consequence to the safety of Our Person'.[6] The regulations of 1678 were quite unlike those of 1661 and 1673, which had been very similar to one another in content and form.

The new orders were made up of just eight directives, emphasizing or modifying the previous regulations. Their clear underlying concern was to increase the security of the king's privy lodgings. First, physical security was addressed: new locks and keys were to be provided for all the rooms of the Bedchamber, and while this was being arranged, the old locks were to be altered.[7] Strict procedures for passing the keys between staff as they came into and out of waiting were laid down. Second, the rules for admitting visitors to the privy lodgings were tightened: the criteria for access were re-emphasized, and the Bedchamber staff's duty to enforce these reasserted. Pages were to be more vigilant about access to the room; one was to 'stand constantly at the Doore of Our Bedchamber' to open the door automatically to the king, princes of the blood, and the Bedchamber staff, and to open it only with the Groom of the Stool's permission to the Master of the Robes, the Keeper of the Privy Purse and the first physician, but 'to noe other person or persons whatsoever' without the king's permission, and this was to be 'upon paine of being suspended, and such farther punishment as Wee shall thinke fitt to inflict'. As well as dealing with the admission of an authorized few, the orders laid down stricter rules for those who were allowed to apply for access. A written list was to be provided to the Bedchamber staff of all those who could request access to the privy lodgings. Footmen and the 'meaner sort of people' were to be excluded altogether from the ranks of those allowed to wait in the withdrawing room for the king's coming forth.[8] Two further orders followed. The Bedchamber staff were to concentrate on maintaining security and decorum within the bedchamber itself, rather than in the other rooms, notably the withdrawing room, over which they technically held sway, and an officer of the horse guard was 'allwayes to attend and follow next Our person' when the king walked out from his bedchamber.[9] The orders represent a concerted effort to regulate, restrict and control access to the king in his bedchamber and to ensure the security of that room itself.

Soon after these orders, there came a second set, governing the king's state rooms. In 1660 Charles had declared his intention to set out 'in a booke' a 'forme of goverment ... for the modelling and regulating of this house'.[10] In the event no orders were issued, those of his father presumably being thought sufficient. However, the circumstances of the autumn of 1678 led the king and Lord Chamberlain to revive the scheme and 'articles' governing the king's household above stairs were issued in late 1678 or early 1679.[11] For the most part their stipulations duplicated those of the 1630s but a number of important adjustments were made to increase the security of the king's person, among them changes to the duties and responsibilities of the officers of the guard.[12]

After Godfrey's murder, Parliament took over the evidence for the plot, such as it was, and began a full investigation. In truth, Titus Oates was a conman and a crook, and the plot a complete fiction, but it chimed so well with anti-Catholic paranoia that his lies had been easily construed as truth. When the house of the Duchess of York's former secretary, Edward Colman, was searched various letters to Louis XIV's confessor were unearthed that described a series of schemes to promote Catholicism in England, of which it seems the duke was aware. This was music to the ears of James's enemies and members of both houses of Parliament immediately leapt to their feet in their respective chambers to call for the duke to be banished. A barrage of proposals for anti-Catholic measures, many of which were aimed specifically at emasculating the Duke of York as a political and dynastic player, were now thrust up before the king. Only by calling in every favour was the government able to defeat them and keep the duke in a position of influence. Even then it was a close call. With moves afoot to impeach the king's principal minister, Lord Danby, and anti-Catholic measures still simmering, the king dissolved Parliament (still the assembly elected in 1662) for new elections in February 1679. The ill feeling against the court was such that as the elections drew near it was clear that a house even more hostile than its predecessor would be returned; as Charles himself remarked, a dog would be probably be elected to Parliament if it stood against a court figure.[13]

These fears proved prescient. The new house that assembled in March soon began to debate a piece of legislation which struck at the core of the institution of hereditary monarchy: a bill to change the succession and exclude the Duke of York from the throne. Sensing the real storm clouds were only starting to gather, Charles insisted that James leave England and he very reluctantly did so, heading for Brussels where he was to remain in lugubrious exile for the next six months.

The following two years were to be the most testing of Charles II's reign. The new Parliament, known as the First Exclusion Parliament (there would be two more), pushed forward with its bill, unmoved by conciliatory measures proposed by the government. As the bill was read a second time, a desperate Charles again dissolved Parliament, barely three months after it had first met. General elections were again held and the Second Exclusion Parliament was appointed. The 'exclusion' in question was, of course, that of the Duke of York from the succession, on which matter this Parliament was to be as adamant as the last. In September 1679 the nation held its breath when the king fell dangerously ill. After suffering a seizure and being bedridden at Windsor for several weeks, Charles made a full recovery. Following this brush with his own mortality, the king seems to have resumed the reins of power with relish and started to act with renewed decision and determination. Though the new Parliament had been elected in 1679, he kept it from actually meeting for a year by means of numerous prorogations. His previous policy of trying to ease tensions by including exclusionists within the privy council was abandoned. The Earl of Shaftesbury – the tiny but brilliant nobleman who had become the leading exclusionist, or 'Whig', as they were now known – was dismissed from the council and the Duke of Monmouth, around whom the Whigs increasingly gathered, stripped of his offices and sent to Holland.

The second Exclusion Parliament was finally allowed to meet in October 1680. The bill to exclude the Duke of York from the succession was immediately tabled in the House of Commons and, to the delirious delight of the Whigs, it passed. Only the House of Lords now stood in the way of a constitutional revolution. Charles attended almost every day of the nail-biting debates in the upper chamber; here, with their sovereign watching their every move, the Lords finally rejected the bill by 63 votes to 30. Now with a much stronger hand, the king dissolved Parliament once more, and a third set of elections were held. The body was called to meet in March 1681 away from the volatile capital, in the statuesque surroundings of Oxford. Within a week of Parliament meeting, the king strode into the House of Lords in Oxford Cathedral, dressed in the regalia and full state robes, and announced its dissolution. He was met with gasps of surprise, but the victory was his. He dined in public, then threw off his finery and boarded the royal coach for Windsor; as he did so he remarked with bravado that as of fifteen minutes ago England finally had one king and not five hundred.[14]

After that memorable meeting in Oxford Charles II would never again call Parliament. With the defeat of the exclusion bills he was a leader with a new lease of life. In his dealings with his subjects, both individually and institutionally, he displayed a new authority and stateliness, communicating with word and action the majesty of his position. Without Parliament, the court was the single major focus of national politics and in such circumstances the impact of events there dramatically increased.

During the troubled years of 1678–82, when the nation was in political schism, the question of who supported whom was no longer glorified gossip but the guts of national politics. The act of kissing hands had long been a defining gesture of allegiance to the crown. Symbolizing both a subject's loyalty and a sovereign's acceptance of it and his reciprocal responsibilities, it now took on dramatic new significance.[15] During this period Charles kept his brother away from court as much as possible, judging his presence to be, at best, politically abrasive. James had rushed back from the Low Countries when he heard of the king's illness in September 1679, but was sent away again almost immediately, this time to Scotland where he spent most of the following two years. At the duke's arrival and departure, those loyal to him flocked to demonstrate their regard by kissing his hand, while committed exclusionists were equally anxious to demonstrate their allegiances by not doing so. As a consequence every moment of every court occasion, be it the queen's drawing room or the king's levée, was watched and discussed with avid interest. On the duke's return from Brussels in September 1679, the number who had come to kiss his hand was an important and highly visible indicator of the support that existed for him at court.[16] The same was true of his brief visit in January 1680: at a meeting of Whig lords it was reported that Lord North must 'bee looked on now as a renegade, because he has kissd the Duke's hand'. At the same time the exclusionist William, Lord Cavendish, deliberately attended a whole series of court gatherings in order not to speak to the duke or kiss his hand. The message was clear and the outcome direct: 'The King has commanded him from his presence.'[17] Attempts, omissions and permissions to kiss the king or his brother's hand were headline news, reported in the gazettes, noted in diaries, and their nuances and significance pored over.[18] The Duke of Monmouth, whose hopes had soared with the possibility that, if his uncle was removed from the succession, he could occupy the throne himself, moved ever closer to the opposition. But after the shocking discovery of a genuine plot to assassinate the king in 1683, Monmouth briefly returned to the royal fold in November of that year. A public reconciliation was arranged, at which he knelt in penitence before his father and uncle (something he had previously refused to do). The Duke of York gestured for him to rise to his feet, whereupon Monmouth was allowed to kiss both their hands.[19]

During the last six years of the reign Charles developed a palpable new formality in receiving his subjects. He used meetings with a whole variety of delegations to assert his royal authority, insisting on their being staged in the most correct and conservative fashion to emphasize his own sovereignty. This gave the separation between the monarch and his subjects vivid visual form. In dealing with groups with grievances, he rationed access, reacted with frowns and silence to any complaints, and insisted on elaborate acts of humility and submission. Like a patient parent finally raising his voice, a king known normally for his easy manner amplified his impact by adapting his behaviour in this way.

In January 1680, when three months had passed since the election of the second Exclusion Parliament though it had yet to meet, a troupe of MPs waited on the king at Whitehall with a petition asking for it to be called. Sir Gilbert Gerrard, Whig MP for Northallerton, was spokesman for the occasion, and delivered the paper in the royal apartments at Whitehall. Unusually he was left doing so on his knees. Halfway through his speech the king interrupted, and 'sayd he would have them to know that hee was head in ye government'. When Gerrard attempted to reply to this, 'ye K^g w^d not heare him' rolled up the petition and disappeared into the private apartments.[20] Similar deputations came to court during those years, part of an orchestrated Whig campaign of petitioning for Parliament to be recalled, but most had similar experiences. In June 1681, for instance, a group of apprentices brought a petition with 18,000 signatures, and also in that month a large delegation from Surrey 'presented their Addresses' to the king at Hampton Court.[21]

Charles's newly commanding manner was displayed to the full when it came to dealing with the Lord Mayor of London. The capital has been a principal power-base for the exclusionists in 1679–81, as it had been for Charles I's opponents exactly forty years earlier. After the eye of the crisis passed, Charles II levelled his sights on the city. When a London Grand Jury defied the king by acquitting the Whig ring-leader, Shaftesbury, of treason, charges were rustled up against the city which resulted, ultimately, in the confiscation of its charter, the document that guaranteed the corporation's numerous liberties and privileges. The city had no choice but to negotiate a new charter, which the king would only grant if it included a crown veto on the appointment of executive officers. The success of this audacious ploy gave the king and his government the confidence to try it elsewhere. Something similar happened in towns and cities across the land, so that in just three years, over fifty boroughs had new charters in many of which royal control had been considerably extended. Between 1680 and 1683, therefore, the king and the city of London were locked in a battle of wills that Charles was determined to win. The form of his meetings with their representatives at this time embodied his steely resolve. Rather than waiving various conventions on such things as dress and location, as he had done in earlier years, Charles now conducted these meetings with an icy formality. In July 1681 the Lord Mayor and the principal magistrates of London came, like many others, with a petition again asking for Parliament to be assembled. Approaching the king, the Mayor bowed down. If he was waiting for the king to gesture him to his feet, he waited in vain. Charles left him kneeling throughout the meeting, during which the Lord Mayor read the whole document aloud. When he had finished, the king refused to respond directly, and instead instructed the Lord Chancellor, the Earl of Nottingham, to give the royal reply. Nottingham responded that this 'being matter beyond their province to meddle in, it would become them better to mind their duty in their Places and Calling'. With that, the interview ended. Reports of the king's magisterial conduct spread far and wide. The French ambassador described the event to Louis XIV, musing that 'je ne croit pas que le Roy d'Angleterre respondre a leur requeste d'une ffaçon qui'leur plaise', while a report of the event appeared in the *True Protestant Mercury* giving precise details of the bowing and kneeling of the petitioners and the imperious behaviour of the king.[22]

An equally frosty audience took place in June 1683 when the Lord Mayor, sheriffs and aldermen of London came to Windsor to make their submission to the king after the courts had ruled against them regarding their charter. Here, as in 1681, the deputation delivered its speech kneeling before the sovereign, having been received in the most formal state room in the whole palace, the presence chamber. The king heard the submission from beneath the magnificent gold and crimson canopy of state; overhead soared Antonio Verrio's extravagant baroque ceiling canvas depicting Mercury displaying the king's portrait to the four quarters of the world, and around the walls hung the series of tapestries of the Old Testament king and religious reformer Hezekiah. After the Lord Mayor finished his speech, the king again refused to speak. Francis North, Lord Keeper of the Great Seal, replied in his stead, describing how by their 'dissorderly & royotous behavious in the late Election' they had 'incurr'd upon themselves his Majesties high displeasure', and specifying the form of their submission.[23]

In this area of royal receptions, the king expressed his disapproval of attempts to interfere in matters that he considered his alone to order by observing the utmost formality. By so doing, by using the presence chamber, leaving the visitor on his knees, and declining to reply personally, Charles was emphasizing in the most vivid and visual way his own majesty and the distance between himself as king and his visitors as subjects. When the civic deputation from Leicester had come to congratulate him on his restoration in 1660, they were warmly received in the king's bedchamber. When the representatives of the House of Lords came in March 1668 to lobby the king about precedence within the nobility they were received in the intermediate space of the Vane Room. When the Lord Mayor and aldermen came in 1683 they were received in the formal outer space of the presence chamber.[24] Buildings as well as people could be eloquent.

Healing the sick was precisely the sort of activity that advertised the quasi-divine status of the monarchy, and it appealed profoundly to Charles's sense of his own authority in the 1680s. At the height of the security scare of 1678–80 numbers admitted to healing ceremonies had remained unusually low.[25] The following two years saw numbers increase slightly, but they stayed under four thousand a year. From the dissolution of the Oxford Parliament, though, there was a dramatic recovery. Six thousand people were touched in 1681, more than in any year since 1660, and in 1682 the number was almost eight and a half thousand – by far the largest in any year of the reign and about double the numbers of most years (see Appendix 1). In April 1682 alone the king touched 2471 of his subjects – almost a third more than in any previous April. Unfortunately records of attendance do not survive for the last two years of the reign, but the trend was clear: the king was touching on an unprecedented scale.[26]

The early 1680s saw work begin on the second phase of rebuilding Windsor Castle. The first campaign of works, which started straight after the Garter Feast of 1674, had seen the almost complete reconstruction of the king's and queen's apartments. The new suites of rooms followed the conventional sequences with a couple of exceptions: on the king's side two bedchambers, great and little, were built next to one another for the first time, and on the queen's side a gallery was inserted into the sequence between the privy chamber and the drawing room, presumably to provide extra space for visitors to the ever-popular evening drawing rooms. The rooms were all given allegorical painted ceilings by the Italian artist Antonio Verrio and handsome new sets of furniture were supplied (see Figure 29). An eating room in the private apartments was also built, not for state meals, which were taken in the presence chamber, but for suppers and other private repasts. The works were completed over the summer of 1678, so that king and court were able to take up residence just as Tongue and Oates's horror stories began to circulate round the coffee houses of London.[27]

The second phase of work at Windsor involved the reconstruction of the two largest rooms of the king's state apartments, the chapel royal and the great hall of the castle, known as St George's Hall after its use for the feasts of the Order of the Garter (see Figure 22). The decision to reconstruct these rooms had been taken before 1678; by the summer of 1680 structural work was largely complete and the decoration was being looked to. St George's Hall was given a rampant, wrap-around baroque scheme: on the ceiling was Charles II enthroned, surrounded by insignia of the Garter; on the long north wall Edward III and the Black Prince and on the west end St George and the Dragon (see Figure 31). Interestingly, despite the expense and trouble to which the king went in reconstructing the room, and though two of his illegitimate sons were elected and installed as knights during the 1680s, he never again took part in a Garter feast, and the room remained splendidly empty. That Garter imagery featured large in the room is unsurprising given that it had long been used for Garter feasts. But the room was only in part about the Garter. The most prominent scene, that on the north wall, depicted Edward III not as the founder of the Garter but as the father of the Black Prince, who was shown being carried home in a Roman triumph after annihilating the French (and capturing their king) at the battle of Poitiers.[28] A similar message was conveyed on the ceiling of the king's bedchamber, where the figure of France was shown kneeling at Charles's feet (*see* Figure 32). The Windsor scheme was not, therefore, simply a celebration of the Order of the Garter but an assertion of royal power, and of national supremacy over the ancient foe, France.[29]

The chapel royal at Windsor was also given a magnificent baroque makeover (*see* Figure 33). As well as accommodating the usual chapel ceremonies, the Windsor chapel served an important additional function. It was here that Charles touched for the king's evil when he was at Windsor. As a rule, religious buildings were the preferred location for healing ceremonies, and when outside his palaces

31. St George's Hall, Windsor as remodelled by Charles II in 1680–2, painted by Charles Wild *c.* 1810 for W. H. Pyne's *Royal Residences of England* . *The Royal Collection* © 2007, *Her Majesty Queen Elizabeth II*

32. The king's great bedchamber at Windsor Castle, painted by Charles Wild, *c.* 1810 for W. H. Pyne's *Royal Residences of England*. The baroque ceiling created by Antonio Verrio for Charles II shows the figure of France kneeling at the king's feet. *The Royal Collection © 2007, Her Majesty Queen Elizabeth II*

the king always healed in churches and chapels.[30] The sheer weight of numbers who came to be touched at the principal royal buildings made this impossible, and the largest available room was used instead, at Whitehall the Banqueting House, at Hampton Court the great hall.[31] At Windsor, though, Charles seems always to have used the chapel for healing; the king's surgeon, John Browne, described the first time he attended the king at a healing ceremony, as being 'at his Chappel Royal at Windsor', and there is no indication that any other room was used.[32] The chapel royal at Windsor was the largest of those in any of the palaces regularly used by Charles II and it seems likely he was adopting at Windsor the practice he would have liked to have followed elsewhere. It may also be that it suited him well in the climate of the late 1670s and 1680s to heal the sick in a consecrated space, and so lend a more sacral air to the whole proceedings.[33]

When the Windsor chapel was decorated, the use of the building for touching for the king's evil was reflected in the iconography. Over the altar was the Last

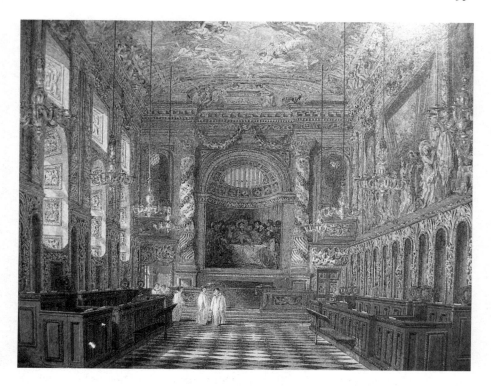

33. The chapel royal at Windsor as remodelled by Charles II in 1680–2, painted by Charles Wild, *c.* 1810 for W. H. Pyne's *Royal Residences of England. The Royal Collection © 2007, Her Majesty Queen Elizabeth II*

Supper, on the ceiling the Resurrection of Christ and on the long north wall Christ healing the sick, seen through a screen of twisted, Solomonic columns[34] (*see* Figure 34). This last scene was based on Raphael's design for a tapestry of 'St Peter Healing the Lame Man at the Beautiful Gate', part of a series in the royal collection depicting the acts of the apostles. Here, though, the subject was changed to show Christ instead of Peter. The impact of a vast image of Christ healing in the room where Charles II himself healed must have been dramatic. The Easter imagery of the Resurrection and Last Supper found elsewhere in the rooms was also appropriate to royal healing. Good Friday was believed to be the best possible day on which to be touched, and March and April were the two months in which the largest number of scrofula-sufferers came to be healed. The vast vivid scenes that soared upwards in the chapel and St George's Hall at Windsor were the embodiment of an exuberant attitude towards royal healing and the institution of monarchy as a whole.

34. Study by Antonio Verrio for the north wall of the Windsor Castle chapel, showing Christ healing the sick. *The Royal Collection © 2007, Her Majesty Queen Elizabeth II*

The fervour with which the king healed in the last years of his reign is also interesting in the light of the Duke of Monmouth's activities. When Monmouth had become increasingly alienated from his father after 1679, he was drawn into plots and schemes with Shaftesbury and his cronies. They tried endlessly to prove that the king had married Monmouth's mother before he was born (which Charles always denied) and so the duke and not his uncle was the true heir to the throne. In the absence of any proof of this, Monmouth sought to assert his claim to the throne in other ways. Fascinatingly, not least given that the exclusionists were prepared to dispense with hereditary monarchy in order to avoid the Duke of York's succession, Monmouth began himself to touch for the king's evil, which, if he could indeed cure, was a sure sign of his right to succeed.[35] Uncomfortable as it must have been to some Whigs to be using the miracle of the royal touch as a means to assert the legitimacy of their leader, it says a great deal about the power of this ritual in contemporary politics.

The gradual process by which morning and evening attendance on the king in his bedchamber evolved from an impromptu occurrence to a court occasion was significantly accelerated by the events of the late 1670s. Though the English levée and couchée never achieved the finely calibrated formality of their French equivalents, by the end of the reign they were almost unrecognizable from the practice of the early 1660s.

Always an early riser, the king now awoke before his servants soon after six in the morning and called out to the Gentleman of the Bedchamber. This official, who was invariably a peer of the realm (or heir to one), slept on a collapsible bed in the royal bedchamber, upholstered in the same fine material as the king's own furniture and with its own canopy.[36] The Gentleman of the Bedchamber rose and unlocked the bedchamber doors, which were fastened from the inside with brass bolts every night and protected on the outside by Yeomen of the Guard.[37] The first into the room were the Pages of the Bedchamber who lit the fire while the gentleman went to the backstairs room to dress. In his absence the Grooms of the Bedchamber waited on the king, who rose and went to his stool room to relieve himself. The Captain of the Guard then came in to receive the watchword (the security code of the day), and on the designated shaving days the barber was admitted and trimmed the royal whiskers as the king sat back, a linen cloth draped over his chest, with his knees pressed against the window seat. Whichever of the king's physician, surgeon or apothecary were required would then be summoned from the withdrawing room where they stood in waiting.[38]

Dressing the king involved two groups of staff. His linen, or undergarments, was the responsibility of the Grooms of the Bedchamber. A groom warmed the king's linen in front of the fire before handing each item in turn to the Groom of the Stool, or Gentleman of the Bedchamber in waiting, who would put it on the body royal. The king's outer garments were the responsibility of the department of the Robes, and it was the duty of a Gentleman of the Robes to come every morning to the bedchamber to dress the king in these.[39] Henry Sidney, who was Master of the Robes to Charles from 1679, recorded in his diary on 24 June 1681, 'I dressed the King', confirming that the officer of the Robes did indeed do as the Bedchamber orders prescribed.[40]

According to the written rules, only the staff of the Bedchamber and Robes and princes of the blood had the right to come into the king's bedchamber; everyone else had to have the king's permission to enter.[41] Those who wished to come in waited in the adjoining withdrawing chamber, and the gallery keepers were instructed not to open the door into this room until after the king had risen and been shaved and the watch had been set.[42] From the withdrawing room, to which access was relatively easily achieved by people of rank or position, admission to the bedchamber was gained by sending a Page of the Bedchamber in to ask the king's leave. After 1678, only those named on the pages' list could even request permission to enter.[43] As well as a stricter admissions policy, the occasion became increasingly ceremonialized in later years; in October 1682 music was introduced to the king's levée, with troops of musicians arriving from various English towns to play, 'all came with their Cloaks and Liveries very formally; which was much liked of by His Majesty'.[44]

The couchée took place in the late evening, at 11 p.m. or so, and those who attended witnessed the king undressing and getting into bed. The event did not take place in solemn silence, but lively conversations were conducted between king and courtiers throughout, sometimes prolonging the occasion for an hour or more. The couchée on Christmas Eve 1680, for instance, went on until 1.30 a.m., such was the discussion as the king undressed. By the late 1670s the king had a couchée several times a week, at which attendance might be as few as four or five or as many as perhaps twenty.[45]

In counselling his son on how to behave at court in 1678, the old Duke of Ormond advised him to 'make your court assiduously, not in the drawing room only, when everybody is there, but at the King's and Duke's rising', going on to explain that 'it is a duty (especially in an officer and person of your station in such a time)'. At this time Ormond's son, the Earl of Arran, did not hold a Bedchamber post, so it was largely his position as a senior soldier and a nobleman that rendered such attendance a duty. As well as English grandees, diplomats were regularly to be found at the king's levée; the French ambassadors' letters are littered with accounts of conversations conducted with the king 'ce matin a son lever'. But it was not only those of the highest social status who were admitted. Some of the best evidence for the levée and couchée of Charles II comes from the Yorkshire MP Sir John Reresby who, though he was one of the king's supporters, held only local offices. As his memoirs record, other 'Parlament men' were also to be found in the king's bedchamber on these occasions.[46]

Like most events that allowed the king's subjects into close personal contact with him, the levée and couchée were times when petitions were made and the king's support sought. Charles II talked easily with those who attended of the political issues about the moment; on going to bed in April 1681 'His discours was generally of the impossibilty of such a thing as the Popish Plot, and the contradictions of which it was framed.' As Ormond explained, at the levée 'opportunities may happen and discourses set on foot wherein you may properly bear a part, or usefully take notice of them'. On 12 April 1677, 'being at the Kings riseing', Reresby was gratified that the king, knowing that a petition against his election as MP for Aldborough was pending, 'gave an order to his servants that were members to attend the committe, and to assist me when it came on'. At a levée later in 1677 the king was careful to reassure the French ambassador on the matter of his discussions with the visiting Prince of Orange.[47] Attendance at such occasions could have less specific goals for courtiers, and might be worthwhile simply to demonstrate that you were allowed to be there. Prominent appearances in the bedchamber were certainly regarded as an indicator of a courtier's position in royal favour.[48] At such gatherings people met and exchanged news and conversation, both with one another and with their sovereign. The Earl of Ailesbury recorded that after his son was born, his father 'went out after the birth to the king's rising, who perceiving he had a more cheerful countenance than usual, his majesty took notice of it ... My father saying he had a grandson born that morning, the king replied, "And my Godson, God's fish!"'.[49]

Despite Charles's numerous and well-charted sexual liaisons, he never received his wife or his mistresses in his own rooms, always visiting them in theirs. In the early part of his reign, he would sometimes spend the night with his wife or mistress in her own lodgings, but by the 1680s he always returned to sleep in his own bedchamber.[50] Because the levée and couchée were real as well as ceremonial occasions, they took place in the rooms where the king actually slept and not, unlike diplomatic receptions, in the ceremonial alcove bedchamber at Whitehall.[51] The construction of two adjacent bedchambers in the state apartments at Windsor reflected this distinction, albeit in a rather restricted space: the great bedchamber could be used for meetings and investitures, the little bedchamber for more private congresses or sleep (*see* Figure 29).[52]

After dramatically tightening up regulations for access to the rooms of the Bedchamber in 1678–9, the king decided to expand and improve the rooms of his privy lodgings at Whitehall. During the summer of 1682 extensive works were carried out to the king's private apartments, and in late October Charles moved into his new rooms.[53] The state apartments were left untouched, but the king now had at his disposal, east of the alcove bedchamber, a new withdrawing room (in addition to the existing Vane Room), ante-room, bedchamber with ancillary closets and eating room (*see* Figure 13).[54]

After the completion of this work the regulations concerning access to the private apartments were reiterated, and on 15 January 1683, the Groom of the Stool issued the list (as the 1678 orders had prescribed) of exactly who could ask permission to enter the region of the bedchamber.[55] The order reminded the Bedchamber staff to make reference to the existing orders, nailed to the wall in the alcove bedchamber, when exercising their responsibilities. Despite the recent expansion in rooms, the alcove bedchamber still defined the beginning of the sequence of rooms under the sway of the Bedchamber staff. The nature of the geography of the new lodgings in Whitehall meant that so long as the status of this room, and the Vane Room that adjoined it, as part of the domain of the Bedchamber, continued to be asserted, all the rooms beyond would by definition also be part of that domain (see p. xv). Thus, having tightened up significantly the rules for access to his privy lodgings in 1678/9, three years later Charles II considerably expanded and improved the rooms that constituted the privy lodgings.

Unsurprisingly, these changes caused some consternation among the staff of the state rooms, who were effectively losing power by the expansion of the domain of the Bedchamber, and it was only a matter of weeks before a serious dispute arose – something that had been in the offing since at least 1673.[56] At some moment in January 1683, the Lord Chamberlain, the Earl of Arlington, presented himself at the door to the bedchamber and asked the page for the king's permission to enter. When the Bedchamber staff refused to go to the king in his closet to request this permission, the Lord Chamberlain finally lost his temper, and there and then began a great quarrel that was to run for the rest of the reign, in which Arlington argued that he should not have to request permission from the king to enter the bedchamber, 'claiming the right by virtue of his office of entering into it without leave first asked'.[57] This was more than a dispute over the privileges that applied to a household post. Arlington repeatedly pointed out the absurdity of a situation in which the officers of his department – responsible for the ceremonial activities of the royal apartments – were involved in arranging ceremonial occasions in rooms to which he himself did not have the right of access. The king's disingenuous response to Arlington's claims was that 'he would have the Bedchamber governed by the rules and practises of the King, his father, and that according to them right should be done to him'; a clear statement to one observer that the 'K^g has determined ye cause agst my Ld Cham: so as that he is not to come in wth out leave'.[58]

Nonetheless, in early March a commission was appointed to investigate the matter. During the following two months Arlington gathered written testimonies from ceremonial officers present and past which he was confident would convince the commission to decide in his favour. The case of the Groom of the Stool, who denied the Lord Chamberlain's claims, depended entirely on the three sets of Bedchamber ordinances, which did not include the Lord Chamberlain on the list of those allowed access to the bedchamber as of right, while the Lord Chamberlain's turned on the actual practice, which, he claimed often required his staff to perform their duties in the rooms of the bedchamber.[59] As the final report of the commission described, the real problem was that these two types of evidence, one comprising the rules and the other the practice, were irreconcilable. The commissioners concluded that the Bedchamber orders clearly excluded 'all persons whatsoever, except princes of the blood, and such as are sworn of the Bedchamber' from automatic right of entry to the bedchamber. However, they added that they were duty-bound to point out that 'the aforementioned Bookes of Orders made in 1661 have been but rarely put into practice … and that they do conteyne severall paragraphs … which wee do find unusuall and not agreeable to constant practice'.[60] It is remarkable that at this moment, when the king could have taken the opportunity to update and clarify the orders governing the use of his privy lodgings, he deliberately avoided doing so. Instead, he flew in the face of his own practice of the last twenty years and declared that his Bedchamber would function exactly according to his father's orders.

Thus, despite the commissioners' attempt to encourage the king to confront this anomalous situation, Charles was determined to leave the anomaly in place. The case was decided in favour of the Groom of the Stool and the king himself continued to exercise personal control over the Bedchamber. By denying the Lord Chamberlain automatic right of access, a situation was perpetuated in which the most senior ceremonial officer in the household could only gain access to perhaps the most important ceremonial space in the palace with the sovereign's specific permission. Unlike in the presence or privy chambers, in the bedchamber there had been little delegation of responsibility for the performance and attendance at ceremonial events to the staff of officers that manned them and all decisions continued to rest with the king. By insisting on the continuance of the rules that had governed his father's Bedchamber and that had given the sovereign complete authority over what was then a genuinely private space, and by refusing formally to recognize the dramatic changes in the use of the royal bedchamber during his own reign, Charles II ensured he continued to exercise direct and complete control over what happened there.

Despite the inherent anomalies in Charles II's use of his apartments, the greater formality and stricter security of the 1680s served to sharpen the distinctions between the various rooms and the reality of their use. By the third decade after the Restoration there were, in effect, three zones to the royal apartments: the state rooms, under the direct control of the Lord Chamberlain; a series of intermediate rooms, principally the withdrawing room and great bedchamber, governed by the Groom of the Stool; and a number of genuinely private rooms beyond the principal bedchamber (including additional smaller and more private bedchambers), under the sole control of the king and his closet keeper (who was one of the Pages of the Bedchamber). Charles II's reign saw much greater, though regulated, access to the middle zone of rooms than had been the case in the past, and a growing emphasis on the strict privacy of the innermost rooms. While the door from the privy chamber to the withdrawing room still marked out the state apartments from the privy apartments, the king's withdrawing room had now become, in effect, the waiting room to the bedchamber, a place where courtiers and visitors gathered ready for admission to this room for the king's coming forth into the public sphere of the state rooms.[61] However, the additional Bedchamber Ordinances of 1678 confirm what had no doubt been the case for some time: that access to the withdrawing room was not hard to gain. 'Persons of Quality', 'Our Servants' and 'others who come to waite on Us' were in fact 'permitted to attend and stay in the Withdrawing Roomes without our Bedchamber' and the only individuals specifically denied this privilege were 'Footmen, or meaner sort of People'. That this degree of access was an innovation of the reign is also made plain, the ordinances stating: 'Wee are pleased that soe many persons more then formerly are admitted to waite in Our Withdrawing Roome.'[62] These stand in direct opposition to the written stipulations that the withdrawing room, as part of the domain of the Bedchamber, was open only to the staff of that department and princes of the blood and no others without the specific authorization of the king.

A locksmiths' account for the new royal apartments at Windsor Castle confirms that by the mid-1670s the area of highly restricted access was beyond the great bedchamber: locks to the doors from the guard chamber through the sequence of rooms to the great bedchamber were all opened with the 'household' key, whereas the door from the great bedchamber to the little bedchamber, from the little bedchamber to the closet and from the closet to the terrace, were opened with a 'housekey with a distinction for the K and Mr Chiffinch'.[63] It is clear from contemporary accounts for the later years of the reign, that while the court elite would generally expect to be granted access to the principal bedchamber, they would not expect access to the king in the closet: even a Gentleman of the Bedchamber dared not enter this area to attend the king.[64] When he came to design a new palace at Winchester in the 1680s (*see* Figure 35), the king expanded the middle zone by inserting between the drawing room and great bedchamber a substantial privy gallery and an anteroom, presumably to accommodate the various visitors and courtiers who would come to wait on, or for, the king.

Though the withdrawing room was now open to a wider spectrum of people than ever, access to the principal royal bedchamber was nonetheless carefully regulated, and (especially in the absence of the Groom of the Stole), the king

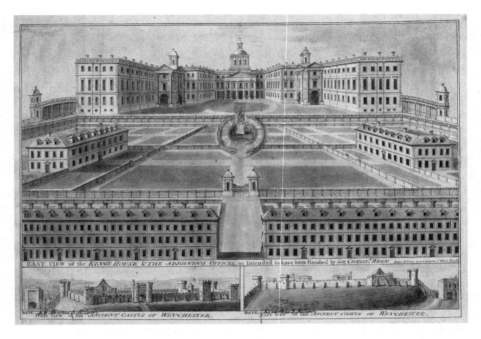

35. View of Winchester Palace as planned. © *Winchester Museum Service*

remained substantially in control of it. John Evelyn mentions in his diary several occasions on which he attended the king there, but he makes it clear that he entered only when the sovereign 'call'd me into his bedchamber'. Similarly at Windsor in 1676 it was only when 'His Matie was pleased to call mee into his bedchamber' that the Earl of Essex went through.[65] When the young Earl of Ailesbury tried to gain access to the king's bedchamber in 1679, he found 'the door … shut against me', the Bedchamber staff not having been told that he 'followed him [the king] *by order* towards his Bedchamber'.[66] When a clutch of peers waited to speak to the king after his return from chapel on 8 December 1679, they 'stood ready in the Faire [Vane] Chamber' and only when 'his Majesty went into his bed-chamber' did they enter that room, following at his heels.[67] Ailesbury recorded a conversation he had with the king on this very subject. The earl remarked that Charles II 'was the first and the last king that could have his bedchamber door open', and then recalled that 'In my hearing one told me that persons would thrust in "I would willingly see that", said the king; and one Thomas Vernon happening to come in soon after, the King's countenance only made him go out faster than he came in, and I never saw a poor gentleman so ashamed.'[68] There was a gulf between the disdain Charles II sometimes voiced for ceremonial procedures and formalities, and the way his personal as well as public activities were actually conducted.[69]

The likelihood is that before the security of the privy lodgings was increased in 1678, some visitors were assumed to have the king's permission to enter the bedchamber without asking for his permission, even though they did not meet the official criteria. When Sir Charles Lyttleton wrote to Lord Hatton of the orders regarding access issued on completion of the new apartments at Whitehall in early 1683, Lyttleton reported 'No body except ye Duke, Ld Ormond, and I think Halifax, the 2 Secretaryes of England, and ye Secretaries of Scotland are to come into the ye bedchamber wthout leave first asked.'[70] Hatton's tone indicates that this would represent a curtailment of access to the privy lodgings, which would mean many more people had been allowed in without official consent in the past. For the favoured, access might be relied upon. When Sir John Reresby waited on the king in the bedchamber in January 1682, Charles expressed his satisfaction with Reresby's conduct, and 'said thes words, that he thanked me for my endeavours in this other perticulers of his service, that whenever I had a mind that I should freely have accesse to him'.[71] Though there might be disputes over who exactly had the right to enter 'without leave first asked' and who should request permission to enter, the principle remained that these were both rare and sought-after privileges.[72]

By not changing the Bedchamber regulations to reflect actual practice – of allowing daily access to watch the king rising and retiring, or staging of formal diplomatic ceremonies and audiences in a royal bedroom – Charles II was deliberately perpetuating an inconsistency between the regulations and the activities which were being regulated. The way in which access to Charles's privy lodgings operated both embodied the king's love of personally granting privileges to those he favoured and of leaving to others the task of withholding privileges from those he did not favour. As Ailesbury explained of Charles's attitude to granting access to his privy lodgings and ceremonies in general: 'when he would, he could keep up majesty to the height of his great countenance, for he could not say a hard word to any one, and if that was of absolute necessity, it was executed by another'.[73] The Bedchamber staff alone would refuse access, while the king alone would overrule them and grant it. The perfect arrangement for a king famous for his disinclination to say 'no'.

Something of the same spirit can also be detected in Charles's long-standing use of the bedchamber for diplomatic receptions. By holding meetings in rooms not originally intended for that purpose, an ambiguous situation was allowed to exist and in the gulf between past practice and current use, greater flexibility in the performance of these events was possible. Lacking the standard chair and canopy of state, the bedchamber allowed for more elasticity, a wider range of configurations of furniture and people. The king could dispense with chairs and stand when he chose to do so, or to make use of the bed as an altogether exceptional piece of furniture from which visitors could be received. When Mary of Modena's mother was in England, for instance, the noblewomen of the court refused to visit her unless they were also allowed to sit on a chair with arms, claiming parity of status with her. The proposed solution, intended to satisfy all parties, was for the event to be held in the bedchamber, where the ladies could indeed sit on armchairs but the duchess could recline on her bed, thereby acknowledging her exceptional status.[74]

The king's own role in devising such solutions is clear from the Master of the Ceremonies' notebooks. When the Elector Palatine had initially demurred to the suggestion that he receive the king and duke lying on his bed, it was the news that it was the king's personal wish that moved him: 'He at first was very unwilling but when I told Him, it was the King's advice He submitted: and their several visits were made accordingly in the afternoon.'[75]

The new climate of monarchy of the 1680s visibly affected form of royal worship, and did so in ways that would acquire greater significance in the light of the dramatic and unexpected events of February 1685. At the height of the Exclusion crisis the king attended daily prayers every morning in the private oratory, and two years later ordered the reconfiguration and redecoration of the room, with handsome new crimson damask hangings, and a curtain to draw around his own chair.[76] He attended the chapel royal on Sundays and other holy days with great regularity, taking communion and offering alms as the calendar prescribed (see Appendix 4).[77] The chapel ritual was also enriched. By 1684 'there was perfume burnt' there, the incense filling the room at the beginning of the service, and the king now actually passed within the rails of the altar to offer alms. On 30 March 1684, Easter day, Charles took three of his illegitimate sons with him past the altar rail; while he kneeled facing the altar, they took their position on the south side, with the officiating bishops on the north.[78]

When the exclusion bill was defeated, the painter Antonio Verrio, who though Catholic was given a special dispensation to allow him to continue to work, was starting to paint the walls of Windsor chapel. The building had been erected for Edward III, remodelled for Elizabeth I in 1570–1 and, like all royal chapels, had raised closets at the west end, separated from the body of room by glazed windows.[79] The alterations made for Charles II in the early 1680s reversed the orientation of the space, saw the closets rebuilt and the creation of the dramatic decorative scheme.[80] The chapel was furnished very much as the Whitehall chapel, having an altar three foot high, with a raised step at the back to support plate, a pulpit and reading desk, numerous pews and a seat for the Dean of the chapel.[81] Almost all the work to the interior was undertaken between October 1680 and October 1682; it was first used in the spring of 1683.[82] The finished chapel with its triumphant technicolour decoration represented a new departure in English church interiors. Though the subject-matter was acceptably Protestant, relating to the events of Christ's life, its execution was highly dramatic. While the Whitehall chapel had had an empty oval frame built over the altar in 1676, at Windsor by 1683 not only was there an image of the Last Supper over the altar, but the great healing scene and Resurrection paintings covered the entire ceiling and north wall. The contrast between this interior with its vivid figurative painting and the London churches of the same period, in which the sober written word formed the decorative focus, is striking. The whole scheme was ornate, exuberant and iconographically rich to a degree that surprised contemporaries, without outraging them. John Evelyn found it 'stupendious, & beyond all description' and Celia Fiennes, visiting some years later, thought it 'exceeding beautiful'.[83]

The new chapel closet at Windsor was in a raised gallery facing the altar and was reached from the body of the chapel by small staircases; the whole structure was given a decorative flourish by the pillars that supported it in the shape of 'four Brass Gyants'.[84] The form of the closet followed the pattern established by Charles at Whitehall in 1675. A single central room replaced the bipartite Tudor arrangement, with an ante-room on 'each side without' the closet itself. The new Windsor closet was separated from the chapel by two velvet curtains hung either side of the opening onto the body of the chapel, which could be 'tyed back or drawne as Occasion shall require'.[85] All the details were decided by Charles himself. He made visits to the castle specifically to inspect the chapel, and even the arid Wardrobe accounts record that the furnishings were to be 'according to His Ma[ts] perticular direction'.[86] After two years' work (during which time St George's Chapel was used for regular services), the new chapel was ready for use; John Evelyn heard a service there for the first time on Sunday 16 June 1683, when one of the royal chaplains preached before the king.[87]

The Windsor chapel was a triumphalist scheme, overseen personally by a king who believed that royal religious practice was fundamentally linked to royal authority. The 'stupendous' result was a chapel interior so glorious and majestic that it stunned visitors. No longer was Charles anxiously corralling his courtiers to conform to Parliament's religious legislation, as in 1673. Now, in boldly confident mood, he was finally creating a setting for royal worship that was truly in keeping with his own conception of majesty.

It was at this time, and in this frame of mind, that Charles set about his last and most ambitious building project. In August 1682 he visited the Hampshire town of Winchester and there and then resolved to build a great new house on the site of the old medieval palace. Feeling instinctively that his time was running out, the king ordered Wren to build at breakneck speed, though in the end only the shell of the building would be complete before his death (see Figure 35).[88] The project was hugely ambitious: the palace was to have extensive courtier lodgings, eight kitchens to feed the household and, unlike Windsor, a council chamber and extensive subsidiary rooms for the administrative machinery of the council. Whereas English palaces had normally been built with a chapel royal accessible from both the king's and queen's apartments, designed (if not always used) for joint royal worship, this was not the case at Winchester. Instead there was no communal chapel, but instead two separate chapels, one in the king's and one in the queen's apartments. No longer was the king apologizing for his wife's Catholicism, he was now recognizing that the king and queen of England worshipped apart as members of equally legitimate churches.[89]

The decision to start building at Winchester took place against an interesting international background. As Wren began work on his preparatory surveys,

Louis XIV moved the headquarters of his court out of Paris, taking it from the Louvre to his great baroque palace of Versailles. It is quite possible Charles II had something similar in mind for Winchester. Rather than being a summer stopping-off point, or even a favoured country house, it may have been designed from the start as a new seat for the English monarchy, conceived and hurried-on by a king who had finally taken charge of his own affairs.[90] The palace was sited in a loyal town where his court could lodge and his council could meet, it was equipped for the business of government, and it was arranged so his family could worship freely. Though it was articulated in the most handsome modern style, its axis was fixed on Winchester cathedral, the resting place of the Anglo-Saxon kings. Its foundations stood on the remains of the castle that had been home to the court of the most ancient and magnificent sovereign of them all, King Arthur. Where better to re-establish glorious monarchy?

Throughout his life Charles had followed the advice of his old governor, the late Duke of Newcastle, on religion: belief in God was essential to the natural hierarchy, and regular attendance at divine worship was an important royal responsibility; but too much faith was not a fitting thing in a king. He had a firm understanding of the political ramifications of changes to his family's religious affiliation. His words to his brother, Henry, Duke of Gloucester, when, during the exile, he heard of his mother's attempts to convert him to Catholicism had been a *cri de coeur*: if Henry abandoned Anglicanism, said Charles, he would both dishonour the memory of their sacred father and utterly destroy any chances they had of ever seeing England again. Though he had dangled the bait of his own conversion for political profit, there is nothing substantial to show that he was anything other than a quintessential Anglican, stronger on conformity than profound spiritual experience. All of which makes the events of the king's final illness deeply puzzling; for, on the last evening of his life, Charles II was received into the Catholic church.[91]

The first signs of the king being unwell came on Sunday 1 February 1685. Charles, now 54, had been troubled for some days by a sore on his leg, which made walking uncomfortable; so instead of taking his usual brisk constitutional in a wintry St James's Park, he went to his laboratory after chapel and spent the afternoon there tinkering with a mercury experiment. By evening his stomach was turning and he struggled to hold down even the mildest food. That night he shifted restlessly in bed and when a Groom of the Bedchamber accompanied him to the lavatory the next morning, he was shocked to discover that the king, his face icy pale, had lost the power of speech. Terrified but carrying on regardless, the Bedchamber staff settled the king in his shaving chair and, just as the barber was shaking out the towel, the king was seized by an apoplectic fit and lurched from his seat, his eyes rolling and shaking violently, caught as he fell by the Gentleman of the Bedchamber, Lord Ailesbury.

Over the next five days the king would suffer excruciating pain, with the symptoms and treatment vying to give him the greater discomfort. The staff of six doctors who attended him on Monday morning had risen to thirteen by Wednesday, and together they prescribed a bewildering cocktail of potients and medication, anxious to avoid any accusation that there was something they had not tried. That first afternoon their efforts concentrated on purging the royal body in the hope of removing whatever had infected him: a needle was inserted in the king's right arm and 16 ounces of blood were drawn. Toxic tonics, one to make him vomit and another to purge his bowels, were repeatedly administered, while tubes were inserted into his anus into which a series of enemas and clysters were forced every hour. Searingly hot cupping glasses were applied to his skin, filling the air with the stench of his burning flesh as they were pressed on. They extracted a further eight ounces of blood. A pungent powder was pushed up the king's nostrils to flush out his sinuses and bring on purgative sneezing fits. His seizures came hard and fast and he lost consciousness completely for several hours. In an attempt to ease his troubled brain the king's head was shaved and agonizing 'blistering agents' applied to his scalp; when these did not seem to be strong enough, the physicians called for the red hot cauterizing irons. Over the following three days these and many other treatments were applied again and again; when they didn't work the doses were doubled and if they did work they were doubled once more. The king bore the pain valiantly, thanking the doctors for their efforts, but in his more lucid periods he spoke softly of being 'burnt up within'. Royal clerics hovered by, reading prayers and urging the king to ask forgiveness for his sins. The king murmured contrition; but when they started trying to administer the sacrament, he waved them away.

On Thursday the Duke of York, who had been constantly on hand, was told that the king, now barely conscious, would not last the night. The duke slipped out and set an extraordinary sequence of events in motion. At about seven that evening the crowds of doctors and divines were ushered out of the bedchamber, and one of the queen's Catholic priests, the same Father Hudleston who had helped the king hide from enemy troops after the battle of Worcester, was brought up the back stairs. Two Protestant noblemen, the head of the Bedchamber the Earl of Bath, and one of the Gentlemen, Lord Feversham, remained to watch as Hudleston gave the king Holy Communion and received him into the Catholic church. It all took less than 45 minutes. In following hours the king rallied briefly. He pleaded with his brother to look after his children, his wife and mistresses. He saved his most heartfelt words for Louise de Kéroualle, of whom he said that 'he had always loved her, and loved now to the last'. His words to James, though simple, summed up his supreme achievement: 'he now delivered all over to him with great joy'. As the sky over Lambeth grew light on Friday morning he asked for the curtains to be drawn so he could see the sun, but he 'sank lower and lower' until, with his brother and five of his children about him, the ebbing tides of tortured breath ceased and the life fell from him.

To most commentators, past and present, Charles II's deathbed conversion was deeply puzzling. Compared to his predecessor and successor on the throne, he had shown little personal religious conviction in life.[92] Though he treated the forms of religion and his own participation in them very seriously, he never seemed to be spiritually affected either in chapel or anywhere else.[93] As his niece Mary would observe when she returned to England as queen four years later, the English chapel royal that her uncle had created was characterized by 'so much formality and so little devotion'.[94] Only a tiny number of people had witnessed Charles's conversion. His brother, who orchestrated it and in whose interests it was to advertise it, gave the most detailed account but the veracity of its detail is hard to confirm. Perhaps Charles II had always harboured a spiritual commitment to Catholicism, hidden deep beneath the husk of disinterest and suppressed for reasons of state. Much more likely, paralysed with pain and with life slipping from him he agreed to do what his brother, his wife and his mistress must all have been urging. Confronted with his own death, it may have been a real epiphany, his one genuinely spiritual experience. Or perhaps, as in exile and then in power, he was simply adjusting to circumstance and readying himself for whatever opportunities this last ritual might offer. We will simply never know.

11

Epilogue: The mist that is cast before us

As he had mumbled to James, Duke of York, on his deathbed, Charles II died happy in the knowledge that he had 'delivered all over to him'. For over half his reign he had struggled, above all, to ensure that his brother would succeed him and that the principle of hereditary monarchy would remain unbroken. He was so successful that, when his death was announced, James, a Catholic, acceded to the throne without a murmur. That James would go on to squander this inheritance in less than four years, and end his reign in ignominious flight, was his own doing and not his brother's.

One of James's first acts on becoming king was to order the reconstruction of the spine of the king's apartments at Whitehall Palace, the privy gallery. Before the army of workmen started the dismantling, an inventory of the paintings there and at a number of the other royal palaces was taken, so capturing the arrangement at the end of Charles II's life. Some works of art at Whitehall had already been moved around, but much of Charles's scheme at Windsor remained. As the recent reconstruction of the royal apartments there had necessitated a complete reorganization of paintings and furniture, the decoration of the king's apartments in 1685 reflected closely Charles's tastes in the last years of his life.

A close look at the picture hang is revealing. In the presence chamber hung a painting of Charles's youngest brother, Henry, Duke of Gloucester, whose death in 1660 had so saddened him.[1] In the withdrawing room was a double portrait of his childhood companions, the sons of the first Duke of Buckingham, painted by Van Dyck in those Richmond days, while an image of their sister, Mary, hung in the adjacent privy chamber. Also in the presence chamber was the portrait of William, Duke of Hamilton, painted in The Hague on his elevation to the Order of the Garter in 1650. He had accompanied Charles to Scotland only months later, and died by his side on the battlefield at Worcester. In the great bedchamber were four paintings. On one wall hung the only contemporary portrait in the rooms, a full-length oil painting of Louise de Kéroualle, Duchess of Portsmouth. Another wall bore the large preparatory cartoon by Antonio Verrio for his wall-painting of Christ healing the sick in the Windsor chapel – a measure of just how significant and personal a commission this was to Charles. Also in the bedchamber was a double portrait of the king's sister Mary and her husband William II of Orange, painted soon after their wedding in 1641. The fourth and final picture was another full-length portrait from this period, this time showing

Charles himself, as a boy of seven in splendid child armour, the pair to one at the home of his old governor, William, then Earl of Newcastle.[2]

These were not paintings of the wits and actresses of Restoration London, nor were they triumphant history pieces celebrating the Stuart dynasty. They reveal, instead, a king who in the last years of his life surrounded himself with images from his first years. As he grew older, and survived at least one near-fatal illness, he had come to reflect on the period before the Restoration and to muse, perhaps, on the friends he had lost and the lessons he had learned.

Throughout his life, but perhaps especially in those first decades and his last years, Charles believed completely in the institution of monarchy and understood that in nothing was it more effectively embodied than royal ceremonial. Newcastle had counselled him carefully, recognizing that ritual was inherently intangible and yet explaining that it was the substance of power: 'even the wisest ... shall shake off his wisdom and shake for fear of it, for this is the mist [that] is cast before us'.[3]

An education in the essence of kingship was nothing out of the ordinary; all princes raised to the throne enjoyed something similar – though in Newcastle Charles had a tutor prepared to be unusually candid with his pupil. What set Charles II's experience apart, however, was exile. A prince whose royal authority had never been challenged might grow careless of its ritual expressions, but one who had had to survive shorn of all the institutions of authority knew just how much ritual not only expressed, but also embodied power.

In considering this period, many have found it hard to see beyond the accounts of court lotteries and love affairs. His friends admitted Charles had a short attention span for things that he did not consider important, and it has been an easy assumption that these must have included the myriad nuances of court etiquette.[4] But we should not take contemporary caricatures at face value and assume that Charles II could not have had the patience to listen to a sermon every Sunday, or put up with ceremonial state dining, or sit still in the Banqueting House for hours on end to receive petitions or heal the sick.

The reality is that for Charles II the rituals of royalty were among those things that *were* important enough to command his attention. When Halifax wrote in the 1690s of Charles II's 'aversion to Formality', he was not referring to ceremonial events, but to his attitude to dealing with matters of administration, where 'aversion to Formality made him dislike a serious Discourse, if very long, except it was mixed with something to entertain him'.[5] Despite his restless nature, he performed his part in royal ceremonial with patience and charisma. He was a stickler for ensuring things took the correct form (never allowing himself, or his representatives, to be dishonoured) and it was he, personally, who decided matters of controversy or debate. Not for nothing are officials' notebooks littered with proposals to be put to the king, with the questions 'whether his Ma[jes]tie will have...' or 'to know his Ma[jes]ties pleasure in'.[6]

Charles also knew that – despite what some of his officials may have wished – royal ceremonial was not an immutable code, but something much more subtle that could be moulded and manipulated to serve his purposes. He would insist on full ceremonial honours in a meeting, only to waive them when the event was underway so delighting his guest without necessitating any alteration to the precedent books. Alternatively he might require the most painstaking observance of ceremonial conventions on relatively informal occasions in order to reinforce his own sovereignty with devastating impact. He certainly frustrated his Master of the Ceremonies by making changes to the form ceremonial occasions had taken under his father, but even Cotterell admitted that he did so to make them suit him better and 'if any should take it as a respect done to them, or insist for it, they would find He only did it in the way of using his own liberty'.[7]

Several of those whom Charles II knew well described him as 'easy of accesse' – more visible to his subjects than princes usually were.[8] This is undoubtedly true, but it should not be taken to imply an antipathy to the conventions of kingship.[9] To some extent his accessibility was a matter of being in evidence in his energetic exercise of normal business, walking in St James's Park or viewing the dockyards at Portsmouth, but it also encompassed his involvement in public ceremonial. People in their thousands were able to watch their king perform the rituals of state, see him receive communion alone at the altar rail or watch him being served his meals on bended knee.[10]

In Charles II's hands the rituals of monarchy flourished – promoted, overseen and shaped by the king himself. Far from being fossilized remains of an old world order, these ceremonial occasions were dynamic events carefully shaped to the king's own advantage. Through them, he asserted the strength of the English monarchy, bound his people to him and projected an often dazzling image of his own sovereignty, and as such they served as powerful weapons in his own political struggles. Charles II succeeded where his father had failed by managing to strike a balance between formality and informality, combining magnificence and stateliness in court ceremonial with exuberance and charm in his personal dealings with his subjects.[11]

When news of Charles's death spread through London on 6 February 1685, it was greeted with almost universal sadness. Even John Evelyn, who had come to disapprove of Charles II, noted in his diary that ''Tis not to be express'd the teares & sorrows of Court, Citty & Country'.[12] When compared to his father's execution and his brother's abdication and exile, Charles's peaceful death in the royal bedchamber at Whitehall was a considerable achievement. That he managed it was thanks, in part, to his care for the advice of his tutor almost fifty years earlier: 'Ceremony' Newcastle had counselled, 'though it is nothing in itself yet it doth everything – for what is a king more than a subject but for ceremony and order'.

Appendix 1

Numbers touched for the king's evil, 1660–82

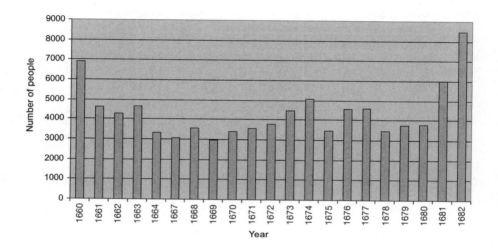

Compiled from John Browne's *Adenochoiradelogia: or An Anatomick-Chirurgical Treatise of Glandules & Strumaes or King's Evil Swellings* (London, 1684), pp. 197–207.

Appendix 2

Numbers healed on recorded occasions in 1668, 1671, 1672, 1679

Year	Date	Month	Day	Number	Suggested status of event	
1668						
1668	10	April	Friday	147	public	
1668	17	April	Friday	88	public	
1668	25	April	Saturday	202	public	
1668	29	April	Wednesday	134	public	
1668	5	May	Tuesday	2		private
1668	8	May	Friday	204	public	
1668	11	May	Monday	196	public	
1668	14	August	Friday	15		private
1668	21	August	Friday	4		private
1668	2	September	Wednesday	48	?	
1668	6	September	Sunday	1		private
1668	14	September	Monday	1		private
1668	16	September	Wednesday	2		private
1668	25	September	Friday	211	public	
1668	12	October	Monday	21	?	
1668	16	October	Friday	16		private
1668	23	October	Friday	103	public	
1668	28	October	Wednesday	51	?	
1668	6	November	Friday	92	public	
1668	13	November	Friday	116	public	
1668	20	November	Friday	54	?	
1671						
1671	25	August	Friday	3		private
1671	27	August	Sunday	7		private
1671	20	September	Wednesday	83	public	
1671	29	September	Friday	22	?	
1671	30	September	Saturday	14		private

Year	Date	Month	Day	Number	Suggested status of event
1671	1	October	Sunday	4	private
1671	13	October	Friday	63	?
1671	3	November	Friday	191	public
1671	17	November	Friday	199	public
1671	1	December	Friday	152	public
1671	8	December	Friday	102	public
1671	15	December	Friday	64	public
1672					
1672	12	January	Friday	10	private
1672	22	January	Monday	4	private
1672	2	February	Friday	15	private
1672	7	February	Wednesday	10	private
1672	23	February	Friday	99	public
1679					
1679	8	June	Sunday	21	private
1679	29	June	Sunday	43	?
1679	12	July	Sunday	5	private
1679	16	July	Wednesday	4	private
1679	19	July	Sunday	7	private
1679	25	July	Friday	35	?
1679	15	August	Friday	9	private
1679	17	August	Sunday	4	private
1679	11	September	Thursday	5	private
1679	14	September	Sunday	78	?
1679	22	September	Monday	5	private
1679	8	October	Wednesday	77	?
1679	9	October	Thursday	2	private
1679	24	October	Friday	4	?
1679	1	November	Saturday	7	private
1679	12	November	Wednesday	154	public
1679	26	November	Wednesday	172	public
1679	9	December	Tuesday	1	private
1679	12	December	Friday	90	public

Compiled from the surviving accounts of the Clerk of the Closet, to be found in F. H. Garrison, 'A relic of the King's Evil' and BL, Egerton MS 806, fos 59r–60r.

Appendix 3

The principal feast days of the Restoration Chapel Royal

'Yes' indicates that there is contemporary evidence for the given day being designated as indicated in the reign of Charles II. When the 'yes' is in **bold**, this indicates there is also a first-hand account of Charles II actually doing so. Not every reference is recorded, as many simply duplicate information in the references cited.

Date	Occasion	King offers	King receives	King wears collar
1 January	Circumcision/New Year's day	yes[1]	–	yes[2]
6 January	Epiphany	**yes**[3]	–	yes[4]
30 January	Anniversary of Charles I's death	–	–	–
2 February	Candlemas	**yes**[5]	–	yes[6]
24 February	St Mathias's day	–	–	yes[7]
25 March	Annunciation	yes[8]	–	yes[9]
–	Easter Sunday	**yes**[10]	**yes**[11]	yes[12]
23 April	St George's day	–	–	yes[13]
25 April	St Mark's day	–	–	yes[14]
1 May	St Philip and St James's days	–	–	**yes**[15]
–	Ascension	yes[16]	–	yes[17]
29 May	Anniversary of Restoration	–	–	yes[18]
–	Whitsun	**yes**[19]	**yes**[20]	yes[21]
–	Trinity Sunday	yes[22]	–	yes[23]
24 June	St John the Baptist's day	yes[24]	–	yes[25]
29 June	St Peter the Apostle's day	[yes][26]	–	yes[27]
25 July	St James the Apostle's day	–	–	yes[28]
24 August	St Bartholomew's day	–	–	yes[29]

Date	Occasion	King offers	King receives	King wears collar
21 September	St Matthew's day	–	–	yes[30]
29 September	St Michael the Archangel's day	yes[31]	–	**yes**[32]
18 October	St Luke's day	–	–	yes[33]
28 October	St Simon and St Judes's days	–	–	yes[34]
1 November	All Hallows' day	**yes**[35]	–	yes[36]
5 November	Gunpowder plot anniversay	–	–	yes[37]
16 November	Queen's birthday	–	–	yes[38]
30 November	St Andrew's day	–	–	yes[39]
21 December	St Thomas's day	–	–	yes[40]
25 December	Christmas day	**yes**[41]	**yes**[42]	yes[43]
31 December	New year's eve	–	–	yes[44]

Appendix 4

Primary records of Charles II attending the chapel royal, 1660–85

Year	Date	Month	Day	Feast	Receiving	Offering	Source
1660	29	May	Tuesday	Restoration			*The Parliamentary Intelligencer*, 23, 29 May 1660
	17	June	Sunday	~			*Diurnal of Thomas Rugg*, p. 93
	28	July	Thursday	[thanksgiving]			*The Parliamentary Intelligencer*, 27, 28 July 1660
	14	Oct	Sunday	~			Pepys, *Diary*, I, p. 266
	25	Dec	Tuesday	Christmas			*Elias Ashmole*, II, p. 807
1662	12	Jan	Sunday	~			Evelyn, *Diary*, III, p. 311
	2	Feb	Sunday	Candlemas		yes	Schellinks, *Journal*, p. 72
	2	March	Sunday	[Lent]			Schellinks, *Journal*, p. 75
	9	March	Sunday	[Lent]			Pepys, *Diary*, III, p. 42
	6	April	Sunday	[Lent]			Pepys, *Diary*, III, p. 60
	30	April	Sunday	Easter	yes		Bod. Lib., Rawl. MS B 58, p. 139
	1	May	Tuesday	St Philip			Schellinks, *Journal*, p. 84
	25	Dec	Thursday	Christmas	yes		Pepys, *Diary*, III, p. 292
1663	2	Feb	Monday	Candlemas			Pepys, *Diary*, IV, p. 31
	22	Nov	Sunday	~			Pepys, *Diary*, IV, p. 394
1664	22	May	Sunday	~			Pepys, *Diary*, V, p. 155
	29	May	Sunday	Whitsun			Pepys, *Diary*, V, p. 161
	16	Oct	Sunday	~			Evelyn, *Diary*, III, p. 381
1665	1	March	Wed	[Lent]			Evelyn, *Diary*, III, p. 401
	22	March	Wed	[Lent]			Evelyn, *Diary*, III, p. 403
	23	April	Sunday	Coronation			Evelyn, *Diary*, III, p. 407
	21	June	Weds	[thanksgiving]			*The Newes*, 48, 21 June 1665
	23	July	Sunday	~			Pepys, *Diary*, VI, p. 166
1666	2	March	Friday	[Lent]			Evelyn, *Diary*, III, p. 432
	16	March	Friday	[Lent]			Evelyn, *Diary*, III, p. 432
	11	April	Weds	[Lent]			Evelyn, *Diary*, III, p. 433
	15	April	Sunday	Easter	yes		Pepys, *Diary*, VII, p. 99
	5	June	Tuesday	[fast]			Evelyn, *Diary*, III, p. 439; Pepys, *Diary*, VII, p. 151
	25	July	Weds	St James			Pepys, *Diary*, VII, p. 217.
	2	Sept	Sunday	~			Pepys, *Diary*, VII, p. 269

Year	Date	Month	Day	Feast	Receiving	Offering	Source
1667	30	Jan	Weds	Regicide			Evelyn, *Diary*, III, p. 474
	1	Nov	Friday	All Souls		yes	Evelyn, *Diary*, III, p. 501
1668	4	Oct	Sunday	~			*CSPD*, 1668–9, pp. 9–10
	27	Dec	Sunday	~			Pepys, *Diary*, IX, p. 400
1669	29	May	Saturday	~			Magalotti, *Travels*, p. 364
1671	18	June	Sunday	~			BL, Add. MS 40860, fol. 8v
	2	July	Sunday	~			BL, Add. MS 40860, fol. 10v
	9	July	Sunday	~			BL, Add. MS 40860, fol. 11r
	8	Oct	Sunday	~			North, *General Preface*, p. 115
1672	21	March	Thursday	[Lent]			BL, Add MS. 40860, fol. 27r
	21	April	Sunday	~			*HMC 12th Report*, Fleming Papers, VII, p. 92
	4	Aug	Sunday	~			BL, Add. MS 40860, fol. 33r
1673	30	March	Sunday	Easter	yes		Evelyn, *Diary*, IV, p. 7; *HMC 7th Rep*, Verney, p. 490
	18	Oct	Saturday	St Luke			BL, Add. MS 40860, fol. 57r
	1	Nov	Saturday	All Saints			BL, Add. MS 40860, fol. 57v
	21	Dec	Sunday	~			Evelyn, *Diary*, IV, p. 29
	24	Dec	Weds	~			BL, Add 40860, fol. 62r
	25	Dec	Thurs	Christmas	yes		BL, Add. MS 40860, fol. 62v
	27	Dec	Saturday	~			BL, Add. MS 40860, fol. 62v
1674	1	Jan	Thurs	New Year			BL, Add. MS 40860, fol. 63r
	17	April	Friday	Good Friday			Evelyn, *Diary*, IV, p. 34
	19	April	Sunday	Easter	yes		BL, Add. MS 40860, fol. 68r
	25	Dec	Friday	Christmas			BL, Add. MS 40860, fol. 80r
	26	Dec	Saturday	~			BL, Add. MS 40860, fol. 80v
	28	Dec	Monday	~			BL, Add. MS 40860, fol. 80v
1675	1	Jan	Friday	New Year			BL, Add. MS 40860, fol. 81r
	2	Feb	Tuesday	Candlemas			BL, Add. MS 40860, fol. 83r
1676	31	Jan	Monday	Regicide			Evelyn, *Diary*, IV, p. 82
	6	Feb	Sunday				Evelyn, *Diary*, IV, p. 83
	18	Feb	Friday	[Lent]			Evelyn, *Diary*, IV, p. 83
	10	March	Friday	[Lent]			Evelyn, *Diary*, IV, p. 85
	12	March	Sunday	[Lent]			Evelyn, *Diary*, IV, pp. 85–6
	24	March	Friday	Good Friday			Evelyn, *Diary*, IV, p. 87.
	14	May	Sunday	Whitsun	yes		BL, Add. MS 18730, fol 10v
	15	May	Monday	~			BL, Add. MS 18730, fol 11r
	4	June	Sunday	~			Evelyn, *Diary*, IV, p. 93
	29	June	Thursday	St Peter			BL, Add 18730, fol. 12v
	16	July	Sunday	~			Evelyn, *Diary*, IV, p. 94
	3	Sept	Sunday	~			Evelyn, *Diary*, IV, p. 97
	22	Oct	Sunday	~			Evelyn, *Diary*, IV, p. 100
	3	Dec	Sunday	~			Evelyn, *Diary*, IV, p. 103
1677	4	Feb	Sunday	~			Evelyn, *Diary*, IV, p. 105

Year	Date	Month	Day	Feast	Receiving	Offering	Source
	25	Feb	Sunday	~			Evelyn, *Diary*, IV, p. 106
	4	March	Sunday	~			Evelyn, *Diary*, IV, p. 106
	18	March	Sunday	~			Evelyn, *Diary*, IV, p. 107
	18	Oct	Thurs	St Luke			BL, Add. MS 18730, fol. 30r.
	1	Nov	Thurs	All Hallows			BL, Add. MS 18730, fol. 31r
	5	Nov	Monday	[Gunpowder]			BL, Add. MS 18730, fol. 31r
	11	Nov	Sunday	~			Evelyn, *Diary*, IV, p. 123
	2	Dec	Sunday	~			Evelyn, *Diary*, IV, p. 125
	23	Dec	Sunday	~			BL, Add. MS 18730, fol. 31r.
	25	Dec	Tuesday	Christmas	yes		BL, Add. MS 18730, fol. 33r.
1678	21	April	Sunday	~			Evelyn, *Diary*, IV, p. 134
	28	April	Sunday	~			Evelyn, *Diary*, IV, p. 134
	12	May	Sunday	~			Evelyn, *Diary*, IV, p. 134
	26	May	Sunday	Trinity Sunday			Evelyn, *Diary*, IV, p. 135
	16	May	Thursday	~			Evelyn, *Diary*, IV, p. 136
	21	July	Sunday	~			Evelyn, *Diary*, IV, p. 138
	4	August	Sunday	~			Evelyn, *Diary*, IV, p. 140
	20	Oct	Sunday	~			Evelyn, *Diary*, IV, p. 155
	10	Nov	Sunday	~			Evelyn, *Diary*, IV, p. 157
	17	Nov	Sunday	~			Evelyn, *Diary*, IV, p. 157
	24	Nov	Sunday	~			Evelyn, *Diary*, IV, p. 158
	1	Dec	Sunday	~			Evelyn, *Diary*, IV, p. 160
	25	Dec	Monday	Christmas	yes		BL, Add 18730, fol 50r
1679	30	Jan	Thurs	Regicide			Evelyn, *Diary*, IV, p. 163
	2	Feb	Sunday	Candlemas			Evelyn, *Diary*, IV, p. 164
	16	Feb	Sunday	~			Evelyn, *Diary*, IV, p. 164
	23	Feb	Sunday	~			Evelyn, *Diary*, IV, p. 164
	16	March	Sunday	~			Evelyn, *Diary*, IV, p. 165
	4	April	Friday	[Lent]			Evelyn, *Diary*, IV, p. 166
	6	April	Sunday	[Lent]			Evelyn, *Diary*, IV, p. 166
	18	April	Friday	Good Friday			Evelyn, *Diary*, IV, p. 167
	20	April	Sunday	Easter	yes		BL, Add MS 18730, fol. 53v
	4	May	Sunday	~			Evelyn, *Diary*, IV, p. 167
	29	June	Sunday	St Peter		yes	Evelyn, *Diary*, IV, p. 171
	14	Sept	Sunday	~			Evelyn, *Diary*, IV, p. 181
	19	Oct	Sunday	~			Evelyn, *Diary*, IV, p. 182
	9	Nov	Sunday	~			Evelyn, *Diary*, IV, p. 185
	16	Nov	Sunday	~			Evelyn, *Diary*, IV, p. 185
	23	Nov	Sunday	~			Evelyn, *Diary*, IV, p. 187
	7	Dec	Sunday	~			Evelyn, *Diary*, IV, pp. 190–1
	21	Dec	Sunday	~			Evelyn, *Diary*, IV, p. 191
	25	Dec	Thurs	Christmas	yes		BL, Add. MS 18730, fol. 64r
1680	25	Jan	Sunday	~			Evelyn, *Diary*, IV, p. 192

Year	Date	Month	Day	Feast	Receiving	Offering	Source
	1	Feb	Sunday	~			Evelyn, *Diary*, IV, p. 193
	25	Feb	Weds	Ash Wed			Evelyn, *Diary*, IV, p. 195
	7	April	Weds	[Lent]			Evelyn, *Diary*, IV, p. 198
	11	April	Sunday	Easter	yes		BL, Add. MS 18730, fol. 69v
	10	Oct	Sunday	~			Evelyn, *Diary*, IV, p. 222
	18	Oct	Monday	St Luke			BL, Add MS 18730, fol. 76v
1681	31	Jan	Monday	Regicide			Evelyn, *Diary*, IV, p. 237
	13	Feb	Sunday	~			Evelyn, *Diary*, IV, p. 238
	9	March	Weds	~			Evelyn, *Diary*, IV, p. 239
	1	April	Friday	Good Friday			Ailesbury, *Mem*, I, p. 54; Evelyn, *Diary*, IV, p. 240
	5	April	Tuesday	~			*True Protestant Mercury*, 29 5 April 1681
	7	April	Thurs	~			*Loyal Protestant*, 10, 7 April 1681
	10	April	Sunday	~			Evelyn, *Diary*, IV, p. 240
	24	April	Sunday				Evelyn, *Diary*, IV, p. 242
	5	Nov	Saturday	[Gunpowder]			Evelyn, *Diary*, IV, p. 260
	6	Nov	Sunday	~			Evelyn, *Diary*, IV, p. 260
	27	Nov	Sunday	~			Evelyn, *Diary*, IV, p. 263
1682	2	Feb	Thursday	Candlemas		yes	*Loyal Protestant*, 113, 2 February 1682
	5	Feb	Sunday	~			Evelyn, *Diary*, IV, p. 271
	12	April	Weds	[Passion wk]			Evelyn, *Diary*, IV, pp. 277–8
	28	May	Sunday	~			*HMC Ormonde*, VI, p. 376
	25	July	Sunday	St James			*Loyal Protestant*, 174, 25 June 1682
	19	Nov	Sunday	~			Evelyn, *Diary*, IV, p. 295
1683	1	Jan	Monday	New Year	yes		NUL, Portland Pw V 95, fol. 44r.
	6	Jan	Saturday	Epiphany		yes	NUL, Portland Pw V 95, fol. 46r
	30	Jan	Tuesday	Regicide			Evelyn, *Diary*, IV, p. 300
	6	April	Friday	Good Friday			Evelyn, *Diary*, IV, p. 309
	17	June	Sunday	~			Evelyn, *Diary*, IV, pp. 317–18
	23	Dec	Sunday	~			Evelyn, *Diary*, IV, p. 357
1684	30	March	Sunday	Easter	yes	yes	Evelyn, *Diary*, IV, pp. 374–5
	7	Dec	Sunday	~			Evelyn, *Diary*, IV, p. 397
1685	25	Jan	Sunday	~			Evelyn, *Diary*, IV, p. 403

Appendix 5

Officers of Charles II's court in exile

May 1649 Chamber staff[1]	June 1649 Court leaving UP[2]	July 1654 Boardwages[3]	August 1654 Board-wages[4]	Oct? 1654 Royal retinue[5]	April 1657 Beer & wine list[6]	c1657 Court list[7]	c1657 Court positions[8]
						Alborrow, Mr Richard	
						Alborrow, Mr Wm	
					Allen, Mr, Tayleur	Allen, Mr John	Tayleur
Amias, Mr, Carver	Amias, B			Amiss, not Bedchamber			
Andover, Lord, Gent of Bedchamber	Andiver, Ld						
Andrewes, John, Groom of the Chamber	Andrews, John						
	Armorer, Wm, Equerry	Armorer	Armorer	Armorer, Mr, Stables	Armourer, Mr, esquier	Armorer, Mr Wm	Esquier du Roy
	Armstrong, Henry						
		Arnott, George	Arnett				
	Austen, Elizabeth						
						Auston, Mr	
	Avery, George, sumpterman	Avert, George	Avery, George				Multier
Ayton, Mr, Gent Ush of Presence	Ayton, Mr John						
(Bacon, Mr, Huntsman)	Bacon, Philip						
		Ball, Lawrence			Ball, Mr, Boulanger	Ball, Mr	
				Bellasis, Lord, not Bedchamber			
						Ballasy, Mr de	
Barker, George, Avenor		Barker	Barker	Barker, Mr, Stables	Barker, Mr	Barker, Mr George	Officier de l'Escuyrie (Stables)
						Barker, Mr Wm	

May 1649 Chamber staff[1]	June 1649 Court leaving UP[2]	July 1654 Boardwages[3]	August 1654 Board-wages[4]	Oct? 1654 Royal retinue[5]	April 1657 Beer & wine list[6]	c1657 Court list[7]	c1657 Court positions[8]
						Barrow, Mr Thomas	
						Beling, Mr	
					Belling, Mr	Beling, Mr Richard	Le Sr Ric Belling
						Bennett, Mr Tho:	
						Berkeley, Mr Charles	
						Berkeley, Sir John	
						Biens, Jacob	Cordonnier
						Binnion, Mr George	
		Blake	Blake				
(Blague, Mr, Groom of the Bedchamber)	Blagge, Mr			Blage, Mr, Bedchamber	Blagge, Mr, de la chambre du lict du Roy	Blagge, Mr Thomas	de la chambre du lict du Roy
	Boane, John						
						Bramhall, Mr Thomas	
	Bosicene, Frederick						
Braye, Mr, Groom of Bedchamber	Bray, Mr Thomas						
Brentford, E of, Lord Chamberlain	Bramnford, Earl of						
						Brett, Mr	
					Bristol, Earl of, Councillor and Sec of State	Bristol, Earl of	Conseiller du Roy
						Broughton, Mr	
		Buton, Thos					
(Burges, Mr, Groom of the Privy Chamber)	Burges, Roger						
						Bultell, Mr John	
						Cannon, Mr	
		Carteret, Mr	Carteret, Mr		Carteret, Mr	Carterett, Mr Edward	Le Sieur Edouard Carteret
						Cartwright, Sir Hugh	
				Cartryght, Dr, not Bedchamber			
Chase, Mr, Apothecary	Chase, Mr J.						

May 1649 Chamber staff[1]	June 1649 Court leaving UP[2]	July 1654 Boardwages[3]	August 1654 Board-wages[4]	Oct? 1654 Royal retinue[5]	April 1657 Beer & wine list[6]	c1657 Court list[7]	c1657 Court positions[8]
Chiffieanch, Mr, Page of Bedchamber	Chiffinch, Thomas	Chiffince, Mr	Chiffinch, Mr	Chinin, Tom, Bedchamber	Chiffinch, Mr, sous officier de la chambre du lict	Chiffinch, Mr Thomas	Page de la Chambre du lict du Roy
(Chiffeanch, Mrs, Seamtress)	Chiffinch, Mrs Dorothy	Chiffince, Mr	?				
Clare, Dr of the Chapel	Claire, Andrew, Dr						
						Clerke, Mr	
	Clarke, Matthew, stables				Clerke, Mr, cocher (coachman)	Clerke, Mr Matt	Cocher
	Clarke, Thomas						
						Cogan, Sir Andrew	
	Cooke, Francis, Footman						
(Cooke, Mr, Groom of the Privy Chamber)	Cook, Thomas					Cooke, Mr Thomas	
						Cooper, Mr John	
	Cordier, Michael	Cordier, Michael					
	Cottington, Lord Treasurer						
						Cottrell, Mr	
					Cottrell, Chevalier, Sec to the D of Glocs	Cottrell, Sir Charles	Secretaire de Duc de Gloucester
	Chreighton, Dean, Robert				Creighton, Dr, chaplain de sa M	Creighton, Dr	Chapelain de sa Maj
						Crispe, Mr	
						Crowther, Mr Joseph	
					Curtisse, Mr, portier de la chambre du conseil	Courtise, Mr	Concierge de la Chambre de Conseil
Culpeper, Ld	Culpeper, Lord	Culpeper, Ld				Culpeper, Lord	Conseiller du Roy
	Dalton, Maurice						
					Darcy, Mr, de la chambre privée	Darcy, Mr	Gentilhomme de la Chambre Privée du Roy
						Davenant, Mr	
						Dorrell, Mr	

May 1649 Chamber staff[1]	June 1649 Court leaving UP[2]	July 1654 Boardwages[3]	August 1654 Board-wages[4]	Oct? 1654 Royal retinue[5]	April 1657 Beer & wine list[6]	c1657 Court list[7]	c1657 Court positions[8]
						Dowthwait, Mr Richard	
Earles, Dr, of the Chapel	Earles, Jo. Dr	Earles, Dr	Earles, Dr	Earles, Dr, not Bed-chamber	Earles, Dr, chaplaine de sa M	Earles, Dr	Chapelain de sa Maj
(Easter, Richard, Porter at Backstairs)	Easter, Richard						
(Eliot, Mr, Groom of the Bedchamber)	Elyott, Thomas	Eliott	Elliott	Eliot, Mr, Bedchamber	Elliot, Mr, de la chambre du lict du Roy	Elliott, Mr Thomas	de la chambre du lict du Roy
Ellis, Edward, Multier							
		Erskin, Mr	Erskin, Mr		Ersken, Mr, 'eschanson'	Erskin, Mr	
		Flemming, Sir William			Fleming, Chevalier, de la chambre privée	Fleming, Sir Wm	Gentilhomme de la chambre privée du Roy
(Floyde, Mr Chaplain)	Floyd, John	Floyd, Mr		Floyd, Dr, not Bed-chamber	Floid, Mr	Floyde, Mr John	
	Floyd, Roger,					Floid, Mr	
					Folliart, Mr, Barbier	Folliart, Mr	Barbier au Roy
		Forbus, John	Forbes, John				
		Fountaine, La	Fontaine, La				
	Fox, John, Closet Keeper						
		Fox, Mr	Fox, Mr		Fox, Mr	Fox, Mr. Stephen	Le Sr Estienne Fox
Fraser, Dr, Physician	Fraiser, Dr	Frazer, Dr	Frayzer, Dr	Fraesarr, Dr, not Bedchamber			
Freeman, Mr, Quarterwaiter	Freeman, Thomas						
(Freeman, Mrs, Laundress)	Freeman, Mrs Mary						
Gerard, Ld Gent of Bedchamber	Jarrett, Lord	Garrett, Lord		Garrard, my lord of, Bedchamber	Gerrard, Ld Gentilhomme de la chambre du Roy	Gerrard, Lord	Gentilhomme de la Chambre du Roy
		Gibbs, Edward	Gibbs, Edward				
						Gilby, Sr Theop:	
						Giles, Mr John	

May 1649 Chamber staff [1]	June 1649 Court leaving UP [2]	July 1654 Boardwages [3]	August 1654 Board-wages [4]	Oct? 1654 Royal retinue [5]	April 1657 Beer & wine list [6]	c1657 Court list [7]	c1657 Court positions [8]
						Golden, Mr John	
	Goldsmith, Henry						
						Grandison, Lord	
				Griffin, Mr, Duke of G's staff	Griffith, Mr, of the D of G's chambre		
		Griffith	Griffith	Griffin, Bedchamber	Griffith, Mr, sous officier de la chambre du lict	Griffith, Mr Hugh	Page de la Chambre du lict du Roy
						Grosse, Mr	
					Halsey, Mr de l'escurie of D. of G.	Halsey, Mr	Le Sieur Halsey
		Hamington, Mrs					
						Hamilton, Sir Alexander	
		Hambleton, George			Hamilton, George, Page of Honour	Hamilton, Mr George	Page d'honneur
						Hamilton, Mr James	
		Harding, Mr Robes					
					Hamilton, Jacques, Chev. gentilhomme de la chambre privée	Hamilton, Sir James	
		Harding, Mr, privy purse					
Harding, Mr, Groom of Bedchamber	Harding, Mr	Harding, Mr, for my robes	Hardinge	Harding, Mr, Bedchamber	Harding, Mr, de la chambre du lict du Roy	Harding, Mr Richard	de la chambre du lict du Roy
						Haselwood, Mr	
				Heath, Mr, not Bed-chamber	Heath, Mr, Insisconsult	Heath, Mr John	
					Hemmington, Mr	Hemington, Mr	
(Henricke, Mr, Trumpeter)							
		Heathwaite	Heathwaite		Hethwaite, sous sommeller	Hethwaite, Mr Thomas	Pannetier
Hewson, John, Page of Bedchamber	Huson, John						
	Highmore, Richard				Highmore, Mr	Highmore, Mr Richard	

May 1649 Chamber staff[1]	June 1649 Court leaving UP[2]	July 1654 Boardwages[3]	August 1654 Board-wages[4]	Oct? 1654 Royal retinue[5]	April 1657 Beer & wine list[6]	c1657 Court list[7]	c1657 Court positions[8]
(Hill, Alexander, Chamber Keeper to the Waiters)	Hill, Alexander, Chamber Keeper to the wayters						
						Holder, Mr Tobias	
						Holmes, Mr	
	Hopton, Ralph Ld						
	Hustler, William						
						Hunt, Mr Phill	
	Edw Hyde, Mr Chancellor	Exchequer, Chancellor of	Exchequer, Chancellor of	Chancellor, Mr, not bedchamber	Hyde, Chevalier, councillor and chancelier de l'Espargne	Lord Chancellor	Chancelier de l'Epergne & Conseiller de sa M
		Hind, Sam	Hinde, Samuel		Hynde, Mr, sous-escuyer	Hynde, Mr Sam	Sous esquier
(Ides, Mr, Falconer)							
Jacks, James, Yeoman of the Bows	Jacks, James & 6 other footmen	Jack, James	Jack, James		Jacke, Jemmy, Portier		Portier ou Huissier
						Jamott, Mr	
						Jane, Mr Joseph	
					Jane, Mr, clerc du conseil d'etat	Jeanes, Mr John	Greffier du Conseil
						Jefferis, Mr	
						Jermyn, Mr Henry	
	Johnson, Thomas						
		Killigrew	Killigrew	Killigrew, Mr, not Bedchamber		Killegrew, Mr Henry	
						Kingman, Mr	
		Knight, Mr			Knight, Mr 'Chirurgion'	Knight, Mr John	Chirurgean a sa Maj
					Lane, Chevalier de, clerc du counseil d'etat	Lane, Sir George	Greffier du Conseil
Laine, Mr, Gent of Privy Chamber	Lane, Mr Richard	Lane, Mr	Lane, Mr	Lany, Mr, not Bedchamber			
						Langdall, Sir Marmaduke	
						Lendall, Mr Robert	

May 1649 Chamber staff[1]	June 1649 Court leaving UP[2]	July 1654 Boardwages[3]	August 1654 Board-wages[4]	Oct? 1654 Royal retinue[5]	April 1657 Beer & wine list[6]	c1657 Court list[7]	c1657 Court positions[8]
	Libbs, Mrs Elizabeth						
		Lict, James	List, James				
						Lidaleton, Mr Con.	
						Liddleton, Mr	
Lightfoote, Mr, Groom of the Robes	Lightfoot, Anthony						
Lisle, Mr, Barber	Lisle, Thomas						
Long, Secretary	Long, Mr [Robert] Secrit						
	Lon?, Richard, Lord Keeper						
			Lloyd, Mr				
					Derry, Bp of	Londonderry, Bp	
				Lovell, Mr, Duke of G's staff	Lovell Mr, chaplain to the D of G		Precepteur de son Altse Royale
						Loving, Mr Wm	
						Maleririer, Sir Richard	
	Mander, George						
						Marlaye, Mr Robert	
Masonett, Clerk to Mr Secretary	Massonet, P	Massonett, Mr	Massonnet, Mr		Massonet, Mr	Massionet, Mr	
					Mennes, Chevalier, gentilhomme de la chambre privée	Mennes, Sir John	
						Mews, Mr Peter	
					Morgan, Mr	Morgan, Mr Wm	
						Morley, Mr John	
						Morris, Mr	
		Murry, Alester	Murry, Alester				
						Munson, Mr John	
	Mushey, John						
						Napier, Lord	
						Nayler, Mr	

May 1649 Chamber staff[1]	June 1649 Court leaving UP[2]	July 1654 Boardwages[3]	August 1654 Boardwages[4]	Oct? 1654 Royal retinue[5]	April 1657 Beer & wine list[6]	c1657 Court list[7]	c1657 Court positions[8]
				Newbrough, Ld, not Bedchamber		Newburgh, Lord	
		Nicholas, Secretary			Nicholas, Chevalier, councillor and sec of state	Nicholas, secretary	Premier Secretaire d'Etat & Conseiller de sa M
		Norwich, Earl of	Norwich, Ld		Norwich, Earl of, Councillor and Sec of State	Norwich, Earl of	Conseiller du Roy
		O'Neal	O'Neale	O'Neile, Mr, Bedchamber	O'Neile, Mr, de la chambre du lict du Roy	O'Neile, Mr Daniel	de la chambre du lict du Roy
						Orfley, Mr Robert	
		Ormond, Marquis of	Ormonde, Mss of	Ormond, my lord of, Bedchamber	Ormonde, Viceroy of Ireland	Ormond, Marquis	Conseiller et Gentilhomme de la chambre du Roy
						Palden, Mr Tho:	
						Palmer, Mr	
	Palmer, Richard						
	Pennicooke, James						
	Penning, Thomas						
Penriddocke, Mr, Gent of Privy Chamber	Penruddock, Mr						
	Percy, Ld			[Percy, Ld] Lord Chamberlain			
				Philips, Mr, Duke of G's staff	Philllips, Col., of the D of G's chambre	Phillips, Mr Robert	Gentilhomme de la chambre du lict du Duc du Gloucester
	Pickering, Thomas						
Poley, Mr, Gent Ush of Privy Chamber	Poley, Gent of Privy Chbr						
					Pranell, Mr, sous officiers of D of G's chambre		
						Preston, Mr	
		Price, Garvis, trumpet	Gervase the Trumpet			Gervis, Mr	
						Price, Mr Herb:	

May 1649 Chamber staff[1]	June 1649 Court leaving UP[2]	July 1654 Boardwages[3]	August 1654 Board-wages[4]	Oct? 1654 Royal retinue[5]	April 1657 Beer & wine list[6]	c1657 Court list[7]	c1657 Court positions[8]
Progers, Mr, Groom of the Bedchamber	Progers, Edward						
		Progers, Harry	Progers	Progers, Mr, Stables	Progers, Mr, esquier	Progers, Mr Henry	Esquier du Roy
						Puis, Mr de	
(Pyle, Mr, Surgeon)	Pile, Mr Richard						
	Rawleigh, Waler						
					Randu, Mr, sous officiers of D of G's chambre		Page de la Chambre de SAR
						Ranscraft, Mr	
Willmott, Lord, Gent of Bedchamber	Wilmitt, Lord	Rochester, Earl of	Rochester, Earl of		Rochester, Earl of, Councillor and Gentilhomme de la chambre du Roy	Rochester, Earl of	Conseiller et Gentilhome de la chambre de Roy
	Rode, Richard, Stables						
(Rogers, Mr, Page of the Bedchamber)	Rogers, Francis						
						Rootes, Mr John	
	Rosse, Giles, Kitchen				Rose, Giles, sous cuysiniere		
						Ross, Mr Thomas	
			Rustat	Rustat, Toby, Bedchamber	Rustat, Mr, sous officier de la garderobe	Rustat, Mr Tobias	de la Garderobe
(Samford, Mr, Trumpeter)	Sawfort, Jan						
						Sanderson, Mr	
						Sanderson, Mr Ralph	
		Saires and his man	Saers and his man	Sayer, Mr	Sayers, Mr, 'Cuysinier'	Sayers, Mr John	
						Scott, Mr John	
Seymor, Mr, Groom of Bedchamber	Seymour, Henry						
						Sheffield, Mr	
	Shepard, Richard						

May 1649 Chamber staff[1]	June 1649 Court leaving UP[2]	July 1654 Boardwages[3]	August 1654 Board-wages[4]	Oct? 1654 Royal retinue[5]	April 1657 Beer & wine list[6]	c1657 Court list[7]	c1657 Court positions[8]
					Skelton, Mr, Page of Honour		
						Smith, Mr Marc:	
						Smith, Mr Paul	
Smyth, Mr Cupbearer	Smith, Vugh						
	Smyth, Williams, messenger	Smith, William, messenger					
	Snape, Richard, farrier						
						Spencer, Mr	
						Stanley, Mr	
					Steephens, Col.		Le Collonel Stevens
						Stevens, Mr John	
Steward, Dean, of the chapel	Stuart, Dean, Richard						
						Stoidale, Mr James	
						Straghan, Mr John	
(Stampe, Mr, chaplain)							
		Swan, Mr			Swan, Mr, sous officier de la chambre du Presence	Swan, Mr	Page de la chambre de presence
						Sydnam, Mr Ralph	
						Sydney, Mr	
						Taff, Lord	
				Taaff, Ld, not bedchamber		Taffe, Mr Thomas	
						Talbott, Mr Gilbert	
						Talbott, Mr Richard	
				Talbot, Sir Gilbert, not Bedchamber	Talbot, Chevalier, de la chambre privée	Talbott, Sir Gilbert	Gentilhomme de la chambre privée du Roy
						Therwaite, Mr	
					Trethewy, Mr, de la garderobe of D of G	Trethewy, Mr Lewis	de la Garderobe
	Thorneburgh, Gilbert						

APPENDICES

May 1649 Chamber staff[1]	June 1649 Court leaving UP[2]	July 1654 Boardwages[3]	August 1654 Board-wages[4]	Oct? 1654 Royal retinue[5]	April 1657 Beer & wine list[6]	c1657 Court list[7]	c1657 Court positions[8]
		Thorne(church), Thomas					
	Tooley, Richard						
		Toby					
		Thwayts, Richard					
						Utbert, Mr	
						Vaghan, Mr Henry	
	Vickors, George			Vitall			
						Wagstaff, Sir Joseph	
		Warren, Harry					
	Wager, Francis, groom			Wa---, Mr, not Bedchamber			
					Walker, Chevalier, clerc du counseil d'etat	Walker, Sir Edward	Greffier du Conseil
						Waytes, Mr George	
						Webb, Mr John	
						Weeks Mr	
						Weeks, Mr	
Lord Wentworth, Gent of Bedchamber	Wentworth, Lord	Wentworth, Lord	Wentworth, Ld		Wentworth, Ld, Councillor and Gentilhomme d l chambre du Roy	Wentworth, Lord	Conseiller et Gentilhome de la chambre de Roy
					Whittaker, Dr, Doctor	Whitaker, Dr	Medecin de la Maison du Roy
						White, Mr	
						White, Mr	
				Whitty, Mr	Whitley, Col, de la chambre privée		Gentilhommes de la chambre privée du Roy
						Whitley, Mr Roger	
						Whorwood, Mr	
	Windham, Mr Thomas				Windham, Mr	Windham, Mr Charles	
						Windham, Mr Edm.	
Wyseman, Mr, Surgeon	Wiseman, Richard						
						Wise, Mr	

May 1649 Chamber staff [1]	June 1649 Court leaving UP [2]	July 1654 Boardwages [3]	August 1654 Board-wages [4]	Oct? 1654 Royal retinue [5]	April 1657 Beer & wine list [6]	c1657 Court list [7]	c1657 Court positions [8]
						Wisher, Mr	
						Withrington, Mr Fra:	

Notes

Notes to Chapter 1: Introduction

1 *The Works of George Savile, Marquis of Halifax,* Mark N. Brown (ed.), 3 vols (Oxford, 1989), III, p. 67.

2 '... for yet they had not banish'd all appearances of respect to the Royall Family. Yet none of them were so ceremonious as to kneel in their performance of that action, excepting only Cromwell who was then Leiftenant General': J. S. Clarke, *The Life of James the Second,* 2 vols (London, 1816), I, p. 29; J. F. Varley, *The Siege of Oxford* (Oxford, 1932), pp. 16, 131–51.

3 Jeroen Duindam, *Myths of Power: Norbert Elias and the Early Modern European Court* (Amsterdam, 1995), p. 103. Though I have touched on civic ceremonial here, my primary focus is the ceremonies which took place within the royal palaces.

4 For an account of the historiography of royal ritual in this context see the introduction to my thesis, Anna Keay, 'The Ceremonies of Charles II's Court', unpublished PhD (London, 2004).

5 Important recent works include Fiona Kisby, '"When the King Goeth a Procession": chapel ceremonies and services, the ritual year and religious reforms at the early Tudor court, 1485–1547', *Journal of British Studies,* 40 (January 2001), pp. 44–75; Jennifer Loach, 'The function of ceremonial in the reign of Henry VIII', *Past and Present* 142 (1994), pp. 43–68; R. O. Bucholz, *The Augustan Court, Queen Anne and the Decline of Court Culture* (Stanford, 1993); idem, '"Nothing but Ceremony": Queen Anne and the limitations of royal ritual', *Journal of British Studies,* 30 (1991), pp. 288–323. A non-English example is Richard Wortman, *Scenarios of Power: Myth and Ceremony in Russian Monarchy* (Princeton, 1995).

6 Ronald Hutton is one of the few historians to take a different view of Charles II's attitude to court ceremonial. In his summing up of the character of the king, he refers to his 'love of purely symbolic functions, such as touching for the King's Evil' and describes him as 'pedantically conscious of the dignity which was due to the monarchy', (Ronald Hutton, *Charles II: King of England Ireland and Scotland* (Oxford, 1989), p. 453).

7 *The Diary of Samuel Pepys,* Robert Latham and William Matthews, eds, 11 vols (London, 1970–6) (hereafter: Pepys, *Diary*), VII, p. 201; C. H. Hartmann, *Charles II and Madame* (London, 1934) (hereafter: Hartmann, *Charles II*), p. 95.

8 Recent works which discuss the court of Charles II include: Alan Marshall, *The Age of Faction: Court Politics, 1660–1702* (Manchester, 1999); essays in John Adamson (ed.), *The Princely Courts of Europe* (London, 1999); Eveline Cruickshanks, *The Stuart Courts* (Stroud, 2000); R. Malcolm Smuts (ed.), *The Stuart Court and Europe: Essays in Politics and Political Culture* (Cambridge, 1996); David Allen, 'The political function of Charles II's Chiffinch', *The Huntington Library Quarterly,* XXXIX, 3 (May, 1976), pp. 277–90; Brian

Weiser, *Charles II and the Politics of Access* (Woodbridge, 2003); Bucholz, *The Augustan Court*, pp. 12–22.

9   This assumption has coloured some recent surveys. John Adamson has Charles II's reign as a period of inevitable decline of the court: its majesty, its rituals, and its centrality to political life all on the wane. He sees a 'change of tone' and a 'qualitative change in attitudes' which meant that while 'for Charles I the rituals of the Court defined the essence of the royal household, its place as the tabernacle of royalty', after the Restoration, people were no longer fooled, instead recognizing that 'the rituals were a public theatre, a choreography to be invented and reinvented at will'. Neil Cuddy has argued along similar lines that at the Restoration, with the exception of the Garter feast, what he calls 'the pre-war round of display' was 'allowed to lapse' (Neil Cuddy, 'Reinventing a monarchy: the changing structure and political function of the Stuart Court, 1603–88', in E. Cruickshanks (ed.), *The Stuart Courts* (Stroud, 2000), pp. 59–8, p. 70). As it happens the Garter is one of the ceremonies about which Charles II was only lukewarm; the 'annual Garter feast' which Cuddy sees as the one exception to the abandonment of court ceremonial, was in fact only held five times in Charles's 25-year reign. It has also been claimed that royal dining after the Restoration was 'much less frequent' than it had been before the civil war, when the evidence actually indicates that for much of his reign Charles II dined in public at the very least once a week: Adamson, *The Princely Courts of Europe*, pp. 104, 116; Cuddy, 'Reinventing a monarchy', p. 74. The count de Grammont, arriving hotfoot from the Louvre, 'was surprised at the politeness and splendor of the court of England' (Anthony Hamilton, *Memoirs of the Count de Grammont, Containing the History of the English Court under Charles II, with Notes by Horace Walpole, Sir Walter Scott and Mrs Jameson* (London, 1899), p. 113).

10   See, e.g., Keith Thomas, *Religion and the Decline of Magic* (London, 1971; Edition London, 1991), p. 244: 'In seventeenth-century England this mystique was diminishing. Patriarchal adoration of the sovereign was challenged by a frank republican scepticism exemplified in the increasingly common assertion that "kings were but as other men".' See also Neil Cuddy's view that the revival of state dining in the 1630s was 'a case of artificial respiration' ('Reinventing a monarchy', p. 69).

11   Pepys, *Diary*, II, pp. 39, 47, 73, 77, 79, 81; *Elias Ashmole (1617–1692) His Autobiographical and Historical Notes, his Correspondence, and Other Contemporary Sources Relating to his Life and Work*, C. H. Josten (ed.), 5 vols (Oxford, 1966), III, p. 820; *The Diurnal of Thomas Rugg 1659–1661*, William L. Sachse (ed.), Camden Society, third series, XCI (London, 1961), p. 152; British Library (hereafter BL), Add. MS 4457, fol. 74r; *Historical Manuscripts Commission. Third Report* (London, 1872) (hereafter *HMC 3rd Report*), 'The Manuscripts of his Grace the Duke of Devonshire at Hardwicke Hall, Co. Derby', p. 90.

12   Pepys, *Diary*, II, p. 86. See below for the ritual arrangements for the king's rising and for the location of his bedchambers at Whitehall. The coronation had originally been set for February, but was postponed just before Christmas 1660, probably because of the death of the king's sister, Mary, Princess of Orange (Lorraine Madway, '"The most conspicuous solemnity": The coronation of Charles II', in Eveline Cruickshanks (ed.), *The Stuart Courts* (Stroud, 2000), pp. 142–3).

13   Clarendon, Edward Hyde, Earl of, *The Life of Edward, Earl of Clarendon, Lord High Chancellor of England, and Chancellor of the University of Oxford in which is included a Continuation of his History of the Grand Rebellion*, 3 vols (Oxford, 1827), II, p. 10; *Elias Ashmole*, Josten (ed.), II, p. 796; Madway, '"The most conspicuous solemnity"', pp. 141–57; BL, Stowe MS 580, fos 1r–17v.

14   BL, Add. MS 30,195, fos 23v–26v; Add. MS 34,217, fols 71v–72v; Pepys, *Diary*, II, pp. 59,

81–3; *The Diurnal of Thomas Rugg 1659–1661*, pp. 173–6; Clarendon, *The Life of Edward, Earl of Clarendon*, II, pp. 10–15; *The Diary of John Evelyn*, E. S. de Beer (ed.), 6 vols (Oxford, 1955) (hereafter: Evelyn, *Diary*), III, pp. 278–81; John Ogilby, *The Relation of His Majestie's Entertainment Passing through the City of London to his Coronation* (London, 1661).

15   *Calendar of the Clarendon State Papers Preserved in the Bodleian Library*, W. Dunn Macray and H. O. Coxe et al., eds, 5 vols (Oxford, 1869–1932), II, p. 203, 243, 346; *Calendar of State Papers, Domestic* (hereafter *CSPD*), 1661–2, p. 350.

16   The National Archives (hereafter TNA), AO3/910/6, pp. 11–16; LC2/8; Anna Keay, '"Toyes and Trifles": The destruction of the English Crown Jewels', *History Today*, 52 (7), July 2002, pp. 31–7; TNA, LC5/107, fols 64v, 72r, 76r, 75v; BL Add. MS 44,915, fol. 3r–4r, 13r–v; The celebrated Parisian tailor, Claude Sourceau, was paid 'For a very riche Suite made in France' and for 'An other riche Suite made in France likewise against his Maties Coronation' TNA, AO3/910/6, pp. 11–13. In June 1666 Sourceau and Allen's bill for the costs of the king's coronation robes was still largely unpaid (TNA, *CSPD*, 1665–6, p. 481).

17   Pepys, *Diary*, II, pp. 81–8; *The Diurnal of Thomas Rugg*, pp. 176–9; *CSPD*, 1660–1, pp. 579, 580, 584–6; *Memoirs of Sir John Reresby*, Andrew Browning (ed.); 2nd edn, Mary K. Geiter and W. A. Speck (eds) (London, 1991), p. 38; Claude Blair (ed.), *The Crown Jewels: The History of the Coronation Regalia in the Jewel House of the Tower of London*, 2 vols (London, 1998); BL, Add. MS 30,195, fol. 11r–43v Sir Edward Walker, *A Circumstantial Account of the Preparations for the Coronation of his Majesty King Charles the Second* (London, 1820); P. E. Schramm, *A History of the English Coronation* (Oxford, 1937); D. J. Sturdy, '"Continuity" versus "change": historians and English coronations of the medieval and early modern periods', in Janos M. Bak (ed.), *Coronations: Medieval and Early Modern Monarchic Ritual* (San Francisco, 1990), pp. 228–42; Gerald Reedy, 'Mystical politics: the imagery of Charles II's coronation', in *Studies in Change and Revolution: Aspects of English Intellectual History 1640–1800*, Paul Korshin (ed.) (Menston, 1972), pp. 19–42; Roy Strong, *Coronation: A History of Kingship and the British Monarchy* (London, 2005), chapter 7.

18   BL, Add. MS 30,195, fol. 26v.

19   Pepys, *Diary*, II, p. 88.

20   TNA, LC5/60, p. 101; *Elias Ashmole*, Josten (ed.), III, pp. 818–21.

21   *The Diurnal of Thomas Rugg*, p. 165.

22   Evelyn, *Diary*, III, pp. 290–1; Pepys, *Diary*, II, pp. 128–9; *The Journal of William Schellinks' Travels in England 1661–1663*, Maurice Exwood and H. L. Lehmann (eds), Camden Society, Fifth Series, I (London, 1993), pp. 60–1; John Browne *Charisma Basilicon, or The Royal Gift of Healing Strumaes or King's Evil*, the 3rd book of *Adenochoiradelogia: or An Anatomick-Chirurgical Treatise of Glandules & Strumaes or King's Evil Swellings* (London, 1684), appendix.

Notes to Chapter 2: Son and heir

1   *Calendar of State Papers and Manuscripts Relating to English Affairs Exisiting in the Archives and Collections of Venice and in other Libraries of Northern Italy*, Allen B. Hinds (ed.) (London, 1916–35) (hereafter: *CSPVen*), 1629–31, pp. 228, 272, 277, 281, 332, 338.

2   The Venetian ambassador described Charles I at 34 in the following terms: 'more disposed to melancholy than joviality', he 'takes great delight in sculpture and painting, and he professes and indeed posseses a skilled and thorough knowledge of both. He enjoys hunting above all other pleasures ... He loves his wife with remarkable affection'

(*CSPVen*, 1632–6, p. 363). See Kevin Sharpe, *The Personal Rule of Charles I* (New Haven and London, 1992) and Mark Kishlansky, 'Charles I: a case of mistaken identity', *Past and Present*, 189 (November 2005), pp. 41–80 for recent reappraisals of the character of the king.

3   BL, Egerton MS 1818, fos 78r–v: 'The K (as the manner is) sent for the nobilitie & chiefe officers to attend him. Stayd all the while of her Labour they attending his Matie in the same roome wheresoe travelled a traverse being drawn across the roome separating the Queenes Ladies & Women from his Matie & the Lords'; see also the list of screens ordered for the queen for her lying in during 1635 (TNA, LC5/134, p. 83).

4   *Letters of Queen Henrietta Maria*, Mary Anne Everett Green (ed.) (London, 1857), p. 23; *Memoirs of Madame de Motteville on Anne of Austria and her Court*, introduction by C.-A. Sainte-Beuve, Katharine Prescott Wormeley, transl., 3 vols (London, 1902), II, p. 116; *CSPD*, 1629–31, p. 278; *CSPVen*, 1629–31, pp. 344–51, 354–5; Francis Peck, *Desiderata Curiosa*, 2 vols (London, 1736), II, bk xii, p. 36.

5   *CSPVen*, 1629–31, p. 70; Peck, *Desiderata Curiosa*, II, xiv, p. 13; *The Works of Archbishop Laud*, 6 vols (Oxford, 1847–57), III, pp. 211, 212; Peter Heylyn, *Cyprianus Anglicus, or the History of the Life and Death of William Lord Archbishop of Canterbury* (London, 1671), pp. 197–8.

6   *Ceremonies of Charles I: the Notebooks of John Finet Master of Ceremonies, 1628–41*, Albert J. Loomie (ed.) (New York, 1987), p. 79; *CSPVen*, 1629–31, p. 351.

7   *CSPVen*, 1629–31, pp. 68, 70, 351.

8   *CSPVen*, 1625–6, p. 21; Lucy Hutchinson, *Memoirs of the Life of Colonel Hutchinson* (London, 1973), pp. 46–7; Clarendon, Edward Hyde, Earl of, *The History of the Rebellion and Civil Wars in England Begun in the Year 1641*, edited by W. Dunn Macray, 6 vols (Oxford, 1888), IV, pp. 489–90; Sharpe, *The Personal Rule of Charles I*, pp. 207ff.

9   *CSPD*, 1629–31, pp. 269, 355; BL, Egerton MS 1818, fols 78r.

10   *CSPD*, 1629–31, p. 277.

11   Evelyn remembered well the 'jubilie which was universaly express'd for the happy birth', Evelyn, *Diary*, II, p. 10.

12   *CSPVen*, 1629–31, pp. 355, 364.

13   *CSPVen*, 1629–31, p. 349; TNA, LC5/132, pp. 196, 201.

14   *CSPD*, 1629–31, p. 282; TNA, SP16/168, nos 57, 58, 59; BL, Egerton MS 2553 (Nicholas Papers), fol. 34r.

15   *CSPVen*, 1629–32, pp. 349, 355, 361, 369, 372.

16   *The Court and Times of Charles the First … including the memoirs of the Mission in England of the Capuchin Friars … by Father Cyprien de Gamache*, 2 vols (London, 1848), II, pp. 306–7; *CSPVen*, 1629–32, p. 372.

17   BL, Egerton MS 2553 (Nicholas Papers), fol. 34r, Order to Earl Marshal to summon guests to the christening, his job being 'to order and direct all o[u]r Ceremonies of State in suche behalfe'.

18   TNA, SP16/168, nos 64 and 65; E351/3632; *Ceremonies of Charles I*, pp. 88–9; BL, Egerton MS 1818, fols 78r–v; TNA, LC5/132, pp. 201, 196. For accounts of previous royal christenings (gathered together when the arrangements were made for christening one of the Duke of York's short-lived sons), see BL, Add. MS 38,141, W. Dudgale, Heraldic Collections, fols 209rff.

19   BL, Harleian MS 791, fol. 40r. *Historical Manuscripts Commission*, Fourteenth Report, Appendix, Part II (London, 1894), Manuscripts of the Earl of Portland at Welbeck Abbey, III, p. 27.

20 TNA, SP16/168, no. 64. The Lord Mayor of London and aldermen were asked to attend in their velvet and scarlet gowns.

21 '... more glorious attyred and adorned wth Jewells then her selfe would have been in p[er]son': BL, Egerton MS 1818, fols 78r–v; Bod. Lib., Eng. Hist. E 28, fol. 8v; TNA, LC5/132, p. 196; Donald W. Foster, 'Stuart, Frances, duchess of Lennox and Richmond (1578–1639)', *Oxford Dictionary of National Biography*, 2004.

22 *The Works of Archbishop Laud*, III, p. 212.

23 'the Bishop of London his hand trembled when he held the bab to the water', BL, Egerton MS 1818, fols 78r–v.

24 'his majesties expresse pleasure is hear to have ye thanksgiving for the Prince wch was sett bye Mr Cranford *to be sunge*', the last words being annotations to the order of service made in Laud's own hand, TNA, SP16/168, no. 65.

25 'the bab was set in ane great basin standing on the hegh alter', BL, Egerton MS 1818, fols 78r–v.

26 Bod. Lib., Wood MS 33, fols 56r–57v; TNA, SP16/168, no. 64.

27 Laud crossed out all references to the king's attendance in a draft of the proceedings made about two weeks before the event, but Finet is clear that 'the window of the closet above on the kings side was possest by his majesty as spectator all the tyme of the christening', *Ceremonies of Charles I*, p. 82. Henry VIII took no part in the christening of Edward VI, which was an occasion very similar in form to that of Charles II. See, e.g., John Strype, *Ecclesiastical Memorials, Relating Chiefly to Religion* (Oxford, 1822), I, pp. 3ff.

28 The burgeoning trade in luxury goods is discussed fully in Linda Levy Peck, *Consuming Splendor* (Cambridge, 2005).

29 TNA, SP16/1721, no. 81; LC5/51, p. 320; LC5/132, p. 202.

30 *Twelfth Report of the Historical Manuscripts Commission*, Appendix II (London, 1890), Coke Manuscripts, pp. 11, 12, 15, 16, 17; *CSPD*, 1633–4, p. 85. Others of the king's physicians, including Dr Mayerne, were called on to assist Dr Chambers from time to time.

31 TNA, E351/3265.

32 Howard Colvin (ed.), *The History of the King's Works*, 6 vols (London, 1963–82), IV, part II, pp. 222–34; John Cloake, *Palaces and Parks of Richmond and Kew*, 2 vols (Chichester, 1995); Timothy Wilks, '"Forbear the heat and haste of building": rivalries among the designers at Prince Henry's court, 1610–12', *The Court Historian*; 6, 1 (May, 2001), pp. 49–67.

33 *Letters of Queen Henrietta Maria*, pp. 17–18.

34 *HMC Coke MSS*, p. 18; *Letters of Queen Henrietta Maria*, p. 18.

35 TNA, LC5/134, p. 8; *CSPD*, 1633–4, 10 October 1663; *HMC Coke MSS*, p. 26.

36 TNA, SP16/1721, no. 18; LC5/51, pp. 101, 320; *Ceremonies of Charles I*, p. 88.

37 *CSPD*, 1635, p. 80; TNA, E351/3267 and 3265.

38 BL, Add. MS 51,324, fol. 36r; TNA, LC5/134, p. 55; *Letters and Dispatches of Thomas, Earl of Strafford*, 2 volumes (London, 1739), I, p. 410.

39 Ian Green, 'Brian Duppa (1588–1662)', *Oxford Dictionary of National Biography*, 2004; BL, Lansdowne 986, fol. 11r.

40 BL, Lansdowne 986, fol. 11r; *CSPD*, 1661–2, p. 349.

41 *CSPD*, 1633–4, p. 375; *CSPD*, 1638–9, p. 182; TNA, LC5/136A, p. 57; Clarendon, *The History of the Rebellion*, V, pp. 324–5.

42 *CSPD*, 1635, p. 457.

43 BL, Harleian MS 7623, fol. 9v; TNA, LC5/134, p. 260.

44 TNA, LC5/134, pp. 56, 84 (payment to 'ye Princes Comedians'), 88 (the prince's 'Players'), 266.

45   TNA, E351/3269; E351/3271; BL, Harleian MS 6988, fol. 99r.

46   TNA, E351/3271.

47   *CSPVen*, 1636–9, p. 150; TNA, LC5/134, p. 87.

48   *CSPVen*, 1636–9, p. 404; *Ceremonies of Charles I*, p. 251; *Letters and Dispatches of Thomas, Earl of Strafford*, I, p. 167.

49   BL, Harleian MS 7623, *passim*; *CSPVen*, 1636–9, p. 404; *CSPD*, 1636–7, p. 361; *Letters and Dispatches of Thomas, Earl of Strafford*, I, p. 167.

50   BL, Add. MS 34,729, fol. 103r.

51   Margaret Cavendish, Duchess of Newcastle, *The Life of William Cavendish, Duke of Newcastle*, C. H. Firth, ed. (London, 1886), p. 183.

52   Cavendish, *Memoirs of William Cavendish*, p. 4; TNA, E351/3271; *CSPD*, 1636–7, p. 361; *CSPVen*, 1636–9, p. 418.

53   Hyde, *The History of the Rebellion*, III, p. 381; *Ideology and Politics on the Eve of the Restoration: Newcastle's Advice to Charles II*, Thomas. P. Slaughter (ed.) (Philadelphia, 1984); Lynn Hulse, 'Cavendish, William, first duke of Newcastle upon Tyne', *Oxford Dictionary of National Biography*, 2004; S. Arthur Strong (ed.), *A Catalogue of Letters and Other Historical Documents*, pp. 53–64.

54   TNA, LC5/134, p. 341; TNA, LC5/135, 28 December 1641, unpaginated.

55   *Correspondence of Sir Robert Kerr, first Earl of Ancram and his son William, Third Earl of Lothian* 2 vols (Edinburgh, 1875), II, p. 346; Charles Avery, 'The Collector Earl and his Modern Marbles: Thomas Howard and Francois Dieussart', *Apollo*, June 2006, pp. 46–53.

56   *CSPD*, 1641–3, p. 11.

57   *A Catalogue of Letters*, S. Arthur Strong (ed), pp. 54, 210; *Ideology and Politics on the Eve of the Restoration, Passim*.

58   BL, Harl. MS 6988, fol. 111r–12r; *Ideology and Politics on the Eve of the Restoration*, pp. 12, 45, 68–9; Hyde, *The History of the Rebellion*, III, p. 381.

59   I have added very slightly to the punctuation to make the sense clearer, BL, Harl. MS 6988, fol. 111v.

60   BL, Harl. MS 6988, fol. 112r; *Ideology and Politics on the Eve of the Restoration*, p. 59.

61   *Ceremonies of Charles I*, p. 251.

62   *Ceremonies of Charles I*, pp. 261, 264, 268. (TNA, LC5/134, p. 341).

63   TNA, SP16/168, no. 64; E351/3267.

64   TNA, LC5/51, p. 321.

65   TNA, LC5/51, p. 320.

66   *Ceremonies of Charles I*, pp. 120, 154.

67   *Ceremonies of Charles I*, pp. 128, 197.

68   Dr Claire is called the prince's 'confessor' in the 1638 establishment list, and elsewhere his chaplain; he seems to have acted as the head of all aspects of the prince's chapel (BL, Harleian MS 7623, fol. 10r).

69   TNA, E351/3269; LC5/134, pp. 50, 185, 223, 224; E351/3270.

70   *Ceremonies of Charles I*, p. 188.

71   BL, Harleian MS 7623, fol. 16r.

72   BL, Harleian MS 642, Household Book of Henry Prince of Wales, 1610; TNA, LC5/179, Household Regulations for Prince Charles, undated; TNA, SP16/375, no. 2, Household Ordinances of King Charles I, undated, p. 16; also TNA, LC5/135, unfoliated.

73   P. de la Serre, *Histoire de l'entree de la Reyne Mere du Roy Tres-Chrestien dans la Grande-Bretagne* (London, 1639); *Ceremonies of Charles I*, p. 253.

74   D. J. D. Boulton, *Knights of the Crown* (Bury St Edmunds, 1987), pp. 110–66; Elias Ashmole, *The Institution, Laws & Ceremonies of the most Noble Order of the Garter* (London, 1672).

75   In 1637 he was noted to 'desire it exceedingly', *CSPVen*, 1636–9, p. 288.

76   Ashmole, *The Institution, Laws & Ceremonies of the most Noble Order of the Garter*, pp. 341–2; *CSPD*, 1637–8, p. 486; *Letters and Dispatches of Thomas, Earl of Strafford*, I, p. 167.

77   TNA, SP16/391, no. 131; BL Add. MS 32,476, fol. 17r; TNA, LC5/134, pp. 249, 250, 252. Jardine, *On a Grander Scale: the Outstanding Career of Sir Christopher Wren* (London, 2002), pp. 31–3.

78   *CSPVen*, 1636–9, p. 188.

79   *CSPVen*, 1640–2, p. 63; *CSPD*, 1640–2, p. 63; TNA, LC5/134, p. 410.

80   *Ceremonies of Charles I*, p. 313.

81   Mark Kishlansky has pointed out that, contrary to what most historians have implied, Charles I travelled widely as king, and that he participated in a number of public processions, citing several examples from the first decade of the reign, Kishlansky, 'Charles I: a case of mistaken identity', pp. 41–80. However, summer tours of royal houses and courtier residences did not necessarily involve the king in much public ceremonial, and there is clear evidence that as the 1630s wore on the king drew back from a number of aspects of public ceremonial. Peter Heylyn (*Cyprianus Anglicus*, p. 228) contrasts both Charles I and James I unfavourably with Elizabeth I in this respect, commenting that because of their neglect of public ceremonial 'there followed first a neglect of their Persons which Majesty would have made more sacred, and afterwards a mislike of their Government, which a little popularity would have made more grateful'.

82   James F Larkin (ed.), *Stuart Royal Proclamations. Volume II: Royal Proclamations of King Charles I, 1625–1646* (Oxford, 1983), II, p. 665; see Kishlansky, 'Charles I: a case of mistaken identity', pp. 41–80 for an alternative view of the king's dealings with Scotland in the 1630s.

83   *CSPD*, 1638–9, p. 575; *CSPD*, 1640, p. 167.

84   TNA, LC5/134, pp. 321, 368; *Ceremonies of Charles I*, p. 261.

85   *CSPD*, 1639, pp. 283, 350; TNA, SP16/428, no. 104.

86   *Ceremonies of Charles I*, p. 262.

87   *CSPVen*, 1640–2, p. 151; *Journal of the House of Lords*, IV, 1628–42, p. 245.

88   TNA, LC5/134, p. 76.

89   TNA, LC5/134, pp. 87, 89, 222; 136A, p. 1.

90   TNA, LC5/134, p. 204; LC5/136A, pp. 2–4, 35; Thomas Richardson, 'H. R. Robinson's "Dutch armour of the 17th century"', *The Journal of the Arms and Armour Society* XIII, 4 (March, 1991), pp. 256–78.

91   TNA, LC5/136A, pp. 2–4, 34, 36, 40–1, 54; 'Life of Nicholas Ferrar by his Brother John', in *Nicholas Ferrar: Two Lives by His Brother John and by Doctor Jebb*, J. E. B. Mayor (ed.) (Cambridge, 1855), p. 154.

92   BL, Harl. MS 6988, fol. 97r; TNA, LC5/136A, p. 2.

93   *CSPVen*, 1640–2, p. 172.

94   *CSPVen*, 1640–2, p. 172; *CSPD*, 1641–3, p. 63; TNA, LC5/135, 6 September 1641.

95   TNA, LC5/135, 6 September 1641.

96   TNA, LC5/136A, p. 4; *CSPD*, 1641–3, p. 147.

97   'Octavia Carolina', printed in John Somers, *A Collection of Scarce and Valuable Tracts*, 2nd edn, Walter Scott (ed.), IV (London, 1810), p. 139.

98   *CSPD*, 1641–3(1), p. 159; TNA, LC5/135, 6 December 1641.

99   Evelyn, *Diary*, II, p. 77; Donald Nicholas, *Mr Secretary Nicholas 1593–1669: His Life and*

Letters (London, 1955); *Memoirs Illustrative of the Life and Writings of John Evelyn*, William Bray (ed.), 2 vols (London, 1818), 'The Private Correspondence between Charles I and his Secretary of State', pp. 35, 58, 60, 61, 78, 79. One contemporary said of the entry that there was 'a policy in it to see if they [the king and queen] can gain the city' (*Historical Manuscripts Commission. Fifteenth Report, Appendix VIII: Calendar of the Manuscripts of the Duke of Buccleuch at Montagu House*, 3 vols [London, 1899–1926], I, p. 286).

100   *CSPD*, 1641–3 (1), p. 124, 128, 167, 168, 169, 171, 177, 180.
101   Somers, *A Collection of Scarce and Valuable Tracts*, p. 142.
102   R. Malcolm Smuts, 'Public ceremony and royal charisma: the English royal entry in London, 1484–1642', in Beier, Cannadine and Rosenheim, *The First Modern Society*, pp. 65–93. Evelyn, *Diary*, II, p. 77.
103   Somers, *A Collection of Scarce and Valuable Tracts*, pp. 140–51; *England's Comfort and London's Joy* (London, 1641), pp. 1–6.
104   *CSPVen*, 1640–2, p. 254; *CSPD*, 1641–3(1), p. 180.
105   *CSPVen*, 1640–2, pp. 281–2.

Notes to Chapter 3: War

1   *CSPVen*, 1640–2, pp. 281–2; *CSPD*, 1641–3 (1), p. 252.
2   Michelle Anne White, *Henrietta Maria and the English Civil Wars* (Aldershot, 2006), pp. 55–7.
3   *Journal of the House of Commons*, II, 14 January 1641/2, p. 379.
4   *Journal of the House of Commons*, II, 14 January 1641/2, pp. 379; 24 February 1641/2, p. 450; 25 February 1641/2, p. 456; 26 February 1641/2, p. 457; 28 February 1641/2, p. 458; Hyde, *History of the Rebellion*, I, pp. 575–6; *Journal of the House of Lords*, IV, p. 608, 24 February 1641/2.
5   Hyde, *Life*, I, pp. 122.
6   *A True and Exact Relation of the manner of his Majesties setting up of His Standard at Nottingham on Munday the 22 of August 1642* (London, 1642); *CSPVen*, 1642–3, pp. 145, 148.
7   Clarendon, *History of the Rebellion*, II, pp. 353–4; III, p. 366; *CSPVen*, 1642–3, p. 191; *Monarchy Revived in the most Illustrious Charles the Second whose Life and Reign is described in the ensuing Discourse* (London, 1661), p. 12.
8   Brian Robinson, *Silver Pennies and Linen Towels: The Story of the Royal Maundy* (London, 1992), pp. 37–9.
9   TNA, LC5/135, 2 April 1642.
10   *CSPD*, 1641–3 (1), p. 304.
11   *CSPD*, 1641–3 (1), p. 308.
12   G. F. Beltz, *Memorials of the Most Noble Order of the Garter* (London, 1841), p. clxxxviii; *A True and Exact Relation*.
13   Clarendon, *The History of the Rebellion*, II, pp. 375, 388–9; *Oxford Council Acts*, M. G. Hobson and H. E. Salter (eds) (Oxford, 1933), p. 111; BL, Harley MS 6,851, fol. 156r; Add. MS 15,750, fols 16r–v; Varley, *The Siege of Oxford*, pp. 3, 4, 5, 6, 10, 12; *Oxford Books. A bibliography of printed works relating to the University and City of Oxford*, Falconer Madan (ed.),3 vols (Oxford, 1895–1931), II, pp. 234, 243; *Henrietta Maria and the English Civil Wars*, pp. 122–51.
14   TNA, LC5/136A, p. 61; Bod. Lib., Clarendon State Papers 26, no. 2066, fol. 127v.
15   TNA, LC5/136A, p. 58; SP16/498, no. 8, pp. 1, 3.

16 *Monarchy Revived in the most Illustrious Charles the Second*, p. 13; J. R. Phillips, *Memoirs of the Civil War in Wales*, 2 vols (London, 1874), II, pp. 26–9.

17 David L. Smith, 'Seymour, William, first marquess of Hertford and second duke of Somerset (1587–1660)', *Oxford Dictionary of National Biography*, 2004.

18 *Monarchy Revived in the most Illustrious Charles the Second*, p. 12.

19 He was elevated to the peerage, as Viscount Andover in 1622, and as Earl of Berkshire in 1626, and in 1625 he was created a Knight of the Garter; a good summary of his career can be found in James Anderson Winn, *John Dryden and his World* (New Haven and London, 1989), p. 121.

20 Clarendon, *The History of the Rebellion*, III, p. 449, to 'less consider what governor or servants he put about him, resolving to form his manners by his own model'.

21 *CSPVen*, 1636–9, p. 188.

22 Clarendon, *The History of the Rebellion*, III, p. 449; *CSPVen*, 1642–3, p. 172.

23 'Life of Nicholas Ferrar by his Brother John', p. 151.

24 Varley, *The Siege of Oxford*, p. 45; *Oxford Books*, Madan (ed.), II, p. 262.

25 Edward Walker, *Historical Discourses upon Several Subjects* (London, 1705), p. 45; Diary of Dr. Edward Lake', G. P. Elliot (ed.), *The Camden Miscellany*, I, 1847, pp. 26–7. Clarendon, *The History of the Rebellion*, IV, p. 490.

26 Clarendon, *The History of the Rebellion*, III, pp. 449, 502–3.

27 'Diary of Dr. Edward Lake', G. P. Elliot (ed.), *The Camden Miscellany*, I, 1847, p. 27.

28 *The Journal of Thomas Juxon, 1644–1647*, Keith Lindley and David Scott (eds), Camden Society Fifth Series, 13 (Cambridge, 1999), p. 69.

29 *The Kings Cabinet opened: or Certain Packets of Secret Letters & Papers Written with the Kings Own Hand and taken in his Cabinet at Naseby-Field June 14 1645 by Victorious Sir Thomas Fairfax* (London, 1645); *The Memoirs of Ann Lady Fanshawe, wife of the Right Honb*ble *Sir Richard Fanshawe, Bart., 1600–72* (London, 1907), p. 39.

30 Clarendon, *The History of the Rebellion*, IV, p. 93.

31 *CSPVen*, 1643–7, p. 223.

32 *Calendar of Clarendon State Papers*, I, p. 279; *The Memoirs of Ann Lady Fanshawe*, p. 39.

33 *Journal de Jean Chevalier*, J. A. Messervy (ed.), Société Jersiaise (St Helier, 1906), I, pp. 286–8; S. Elliott Hoskins, *Charles the Second in the Channel Islands*, 2 vols (London 1854), I, pp. 352ff.

34 *Journal de Jean Chevalier*, pp. 289–90; *Charles the Second in the Channel Islands*, p. 366. I am grateful to Dr Florian Reinaud for his help with translating Chevalier's esoteric French.

35 BL, Harl MS 6988, fols 185r, 211r; Bod, Clarendon State Papers 27, no. 2131; Clarendon, *The History of the Rebellion*, IV, p. 78.

36 *Journal de Jean Chevalier*, I, pp. 299–30, 305, 317.

Notes to Chapter 4: The shadow of a king

1 *CSPVen*, 1643–7, pp. 267–8.

2 For Charles II in exile see esp. Eva Scott, *The King in Exile: The Wanderings of Charles II from June 1646 to July 1654* (London, 1905) and *The Travels of the King: King Charles II in Germany and Flanders 1654–1660* (London, 1907); Hutton, *Charles II*; Hester W. Chapman, *The Tragedy of Charles II in the Years 1630–1660* (London, 1964).

3 Henry Ellis, *Original Letters Illustrative of English History*, second series, III (London, 1827), p. 347.

4   *CSPVen*, 1652–3, p. 235.
5   *Journal de Jean Chevalier*, II, p. 713; *Memoirs of Madame de Motteville*, Wormeley trans., I, pp. 211–12; *Memoirs of Madamoiselle de Montpensier* (London, 1848), I, p. 93; II, p. 77; *Memoirs of La Grande Mademoiselle Duchess de Montpensier 1627–1693*, translated by Grace Hart Seeley (London, 1928) p. 72; Anthony Harvey and Richard Mortimer, *The Funeral Effigies of Westminster Abbey* (Woodbridge, 1994), p. 80.
6   Bod. Lib., Clarendon MS 54, fol. 162; *Journal de Jean Chevalier*, II, p. 711; Bod. Lib., Clarendon MS 45, fol. 503r.
7   BL, Add. MS 38,854, fols 31v, 33r.
8   *Calendar of the Clarendon State Papers*, II, pp. 386–7.
9   *The Letters, Speeches and Declarations of King Charles II*, Arthur Bryant (ed.) (London, 1935), pp. 14, 39, 50, 52.
10 DRO, D/FSI, Box 268, General Household Accounts, 1658–9, unpaginated, December 1658.
11 *The Letters, Speeches and Declarations of King Charles II*, pp. 50, 51, 52.
12 BL, Add. MS 38,854, fol. 31v; *Journal de Jean Chevalier*, II, p. 713.
13 *The Nicholas Papers*, IV, p. 5; *Calendar of Clarendon State Papers*, III, p. 290.
14 Geoffrey Smith, *The Cavaliers in Exile 1640–60* (Basingstoke, 2003) is the most recent publication on the subject of the courtiers in exile.
15 *Journal de Jean Chevalier*, II, p. 713.
16 City Archives of Bruges, Oud Archief nr 101, Politieke Oorkonden, 1st reeks no. 621.
17 Bod. Lib., Clarendon MS 54, fols 162rff.; a list of 1657 people names just over 70 officials paid by the king, while a list of 1649 names about 75. About 50 Chamber staff accompanied the king to Scotland, so the whole household probably numbered around 70 or 80 (*The Historical Works of Sir James Balfour*, 4 vols [London, 1825], IV, pp. 83–4; Bod. Lib., Clarendon MS 49, fol. 107r).
18 Patrick Morrah, *Prince Rupert of the Rhine* (London, 1976), p. 282.
19 *Calendar of the Clarendon State Papers*, II, pp. 212–13; III, p. 330; Clarendon, *The History of the Rebellion*, V, pp. 337–8; *HMC Pepys*, p. 249; *CSPD*, 1652–3, p. 340; BL Add. MS 51,324, fol. 37v.
20 Bod. Lib., Clar. MS 54, fol. 162; *HMC Pepys*, p. 249.
21 Clarendon, *The History of the Rebellion*, IV, pp. 341–2.
22 City Archives of Bruges, Oud Archief nr 101, Politieke Oorkonden, 1st reeks no. 621; BL Stowe MS 677, fols 80r–v; Bod. Lib., Clarendon MS 49, fol. 107r; Clarendon MS 54, fols 162ff.
23 TNA, LC5/134, p. 50; LC5/136A, pp. 2, 54; BL, Harleian MS 7623, fol. 9v; *CSPD*, 1641–3, p. 63; *HMC Pepys*, p. 249.
24 Allen, 'The political function of Charles II's Chiffinch', pp. 277–90.
25 *The Nicholas Papers*, IV, p. 5. For the Duke of Buckingham complaining that he did not get paid when he was not in waiting, see Reynolds, 'The Stuart Court and Courtiers in Exile', p. 123.
26 *A Collection of the State Papers of John Thurloe, Esq: Secretary, First to the Council of State and afterwards to the two Protectors, Oliver and Richard Cromwell*, Thomas Birch, ed., 7 vols (London, 1742), I, p. 682; DRO, D/FSI, Box 268, General Household Accounts, 1658–9, unpaginated: May 1658 account for altering livery suits; June 1659 account for black cloth for liveries.
27 Clarendon, *The History of the Rebellion*, VI, pp. 13–14.
28 *Memoirs of Madamoiselle de Montpensier*, I, pp. 91–2, 115; *CSPVen*, 1643–7, pp. 266, 276. See N. A. C. Reynolds, 'The Stuart Court and Courtiers in Exile, 1644–1654', unpublished

PhD thesis, Cambridge, 1996, p. 90 for some thoughts on where Charles's apartments were at St Germain en Laye.

29 Clarendon, *The History of the Rebellion*, IV, p. 372; *CSPVen*, 1647–52, p. 75.

30 *CSPVen*, 1647–52, p. 87.

31 Clarendon, *The History of the Rebellion*, V, p. 49; *CSPVen*, 1647–52, p. 109. There was no official royal palace in Antwerp, so it is likely the 'palace' referred to was St Michael's Abbey, which was used regularly by the Hapsburgs when they stayed in the city, and of which a wing was consequently known as the 'prinsenhof' (Luc Duerloo, *pers. comm.*, 2007). The palace in Brussels was the Coudenburg, which was almost completely destroyed by fire in the early eighteenth century.

32 'A Short Journal of Several Actions Performed in the Kingdom of Scotland', in Edward Walker, *Historical Discourses upon Several Occasions* (London, 1705), pp. 160ff.

33 *Calendar of Clarendon State Papers*, II, p. 26; *The Nicholas Papers*, II, p. 63.

34 BL, Harleian MS 7623; BL, Add. MS 51,324, fol. 26v; Christopher Clay, *Public Finance and Private Wealth: The Career of Sir Stephen Fox, 1627–1716* (Oxford, 1978).

35 BL, Add. MS 32,093, fol. 338; *The Nicholas Papers*, II, p. 102; BL, Egerton MS 2542, Nicholas Papers, fol. 233r; BL, Stowe MS 677, fols 80r–v; *Calendar of Clarendon State Papers*, II, pp. 386–7; DRO, D/FSI, Box 268, Household Accounts, 1654–5, pp. 41–2; Clarendon, *The History of the Rebellion*, V, p. 337.

36 DRO, D/FSI, Box 268, General Household Accounts, 1658–9, payments in January 1659 and October 1659; *State Papers of Sir John Thurloe*, V, p. 47. See *State Papers of John Thurloe*, V, p. 471 for the enlargement of the king's quarters in October 1656. The household accounts do not state whether these houses were in Brussels or Bruges; I have assumed the former, though it is possible they were actually in Bruges. I am grateful to Dr Andre Vandewalle, archivist of the city of Bruges, for his generous assistance in relation to Charles II's court in Flanders.

37 Clarendon, *The History of the Rebellion*, V, p. 355; *Journal de Jean Chevalier*, II, p. 708.

38 *The Nicholas Papers*, II, p. 417; III, pp. 276, 278; Clarendon, *The History of the Rebellion*, VI, p. 15; Armaud de Behault de Dornon, *Bruges séjour d'exil d'Edouard IV et de Charles II rois d'Angleterre* (Brussels, 1931), pp. 155ff.

39 DRO, D/FSI, Box 268, Kitchen Accounts of Charles II in exile, 1656–9, pp. 16, 45, 80; S. R. Gardiner, *Letters and Papers Illustrating the Relations between Charles II and Scotland in 1650*, p. 61.

40 BL, Add. MS 51,318, Household Expenses, October 1654–December 1655, fols 1v, 11r, 19v, 37v, 62v, 71r.

41 DRO, D/FSI, Box 268, General Household Accounts, 1658–9, January 1659.

42 For instance, DRO, D/FSI, Box 268, General Household Accounts, 1658–9, June 1659.

43 *Journal de Jean Vallier, Maître d'Hôtel du Roi (1648–1657)*, Henri Courteault and Pierre de Vaissière (eds), 4 vols (Paris, 1902), IV, pp. 100, 105.

44 DRO, D/FSI, Box 268, Household Accounts, 1654–5, p. 52; Kitchen Accounts of Charles II in exile, 1656–9, p. 99; *Memoirs of Tobias Rustat, Esq Yeoman of the Robes to King Charles II*, William Hewett (ed.) (London, 1849).

45 *Letters, Speeches and Declarations of King Charles II*, p. 60.

46 DRO, D/FSI, Box 268, General Household Accounts, 1658–9, January 1659; *The Nicholas Papers*, III, pp. 278–9.

47 DRO, D/FSI, General Household Accounts, 1658–9, June 1658; BL, Add. MS 51,318, fol. 1r; *Letters, Speeches and Declarations of King Charles II*, p. 48.

48 S. R. Gardiner, *Letters and Papers Illustrating the Relations between Charles II and Scotland*

in 1650 (Edinburgh, 1894), pp. 39–41. *The Nicholas Papers*, II, p. 17; Wicquefort, *A Relation in form of Journal*, p. 45.

49   Sir Edward Walker, *Historical Discourses upon Several Occasions* (London, 1705), p. 160.

50   John Nicoll, *A Diary of Public Transactions and other Occurrences Chiefly in Scotland from January 1650 to June 1667* (Edinburgh, 1836), pp. 16–17, 20.

51   Nicoll, *A Diary of Public Transactions*, p. 20; *The Historical Works of Sir James Balfour*, 4 vols (London, 1825), IV, pp. 90–1.

52   Clarendon, *The History of the Rebellion*, V, p. 135; *Calendar of Clarendon State Papers*, II, p. 84; *The Historical Works of Sir James Balfour*, IV, pp. 62, 71, 81; Walker, *Historical Discourses*, p. 105.

53   Walker, *Historical Discourses*, p. 195; Clarendon, *The History of the Rebellion*, V, pp. 134–5.

54   Hyde, *The History of the Rebellion*, V, pp. 134–5; *Burnet's History of my Own Time*, Osmund Airy (ed.), 2 vols (Oxford, 1897–1900), I, p. 93.

55   BL, Add. MS 37,047, fols 5r–14v; *The Historical Works of Sir James Balfour*, IV, pp. 83–4.

56   *The Nicholas Papers*, I, pp. 185–6; Gardiner, *Letters and Papers Illustrating the Relations between Charles II and Scotland*, p. 119.

57   Clarendon, *The History of the Rebellion*, V, p. 133; *The Historical Works of Sir James Balfour*, IV, pp. 71, 78.

58   *The Diplomatic Correspondence of Jean de Montereul and the Brothers de Bellièvre, French Ambassadors in England and Scotland 1645–48*, J. G. Fotheringham (ed.), 2 vols (Edinburgh, 1898), I, p. 350; John Willcock, *The Great Marquess: The Life and Times of Archibald 8th Earl and 1st (and only) Marquess of Argyll* (Edinburgh and London, 1903), pp. 235–75; David Stevenson, 'Campbell, Archibald, marquess of Argyll (1605x7–1661), *Oxford Dictionary of National Biography*, 2004.

59   Walker, *Historical Discourses*, p. 161; *The Autobiography of Anne Lady Halkett*, John Gough Nichols (ed.), Camden Society (London, 1875), pp. 58–61.

60   The concise household regulations of 9 January 1651 are printed in *Correspondence of Sir Robert Kerr; first Earl of Ancram and his son William, third Earl of Lothian 1616*, 2 vols (Edinburgh, 1875), II, pp. 331–2.

61   On 27 March 1649, for instance, the Scottish delegation had presented their credentials in the king's bedchamber at The Hague, and a year later in Breda they did the same. *The Letters and Journals of Robert Baillie*, 3 vols (Edinburgh, 1842), III, p. 84; Gardiner, *Letters and Papers Illustrating the Relations between Charles II and Scotland in 1650*, p. 41.

62   Walker, *Historical Discourses*, p. 196; *The Historical Works of Sir James Balfour*, IV, pp. 127–8; Gardiner, *Letters and Papers Illustrating the Relations between Charles II and Scotland in 1650*, p. 144.

63   *The Nicholas Papers*, I, pp. 207–8; *Correspondence of Sir Robert Kerr*, II, p. 283; Walker, *Historical Discourses*, p. 177.

64   *The Historical Works of Sir James Balfour*, IV, pp. 128–9.

65   *The Historical Works of Sir James Balfour*, IV, pp. 112, 116, 233.

66   *Correspondence of Sir Robert Kerr*, II, pp. 290, 303; *The Historical Works of Sir James Balfour*, IV, pp. 84–5.

67   John Nicoll, *A Diary of Public Transactions*, pp. 23, 37; *The Historical Works of Sir James Balfour*, IV, pp. 123–4; John Stuart, Marquis of Bute, *Scottish Coronations* (London, 1902), pp. 143ff.; Clarendon, *The History of the Rebellion*, V, pp. 171–2.

68   Stuart, *Scottish Coronations*, p. 143ff.; Dougal Shaw, 'The Coronation and Monarchical Culture in Stuart Britain and Ireland 1603–1661', unpublished PhD (Cambridge, 2002), pp. 166ff.

69   Charles McKean, *The Scottish Chateau: Country Houses of Renaissance Scotland* (Stroud, 2001), pp. 209–10; *CSPVen*, 1647–52, p. 168.

70   Sir James Balfour, *The Forme and Order of the Coronation of Charles the Second King of Scotland, England, France and Ireland. As it was acted and done at Scone, the first day of January 1651* (Aberdeen, 1651), *passim*.

71   *Calendar of Clarendon State Papers*, II, p. 71; *Correspondence of Sir Robert Kerr*, II, p. 341.

72   Balfour, *The Forme and Order of the Coronation of Charles the Second*, p. 24.

73   Walker, *Historical Discourses*, p. 187; *The Historical Works of Sir James Balfour*, IV, pp. 90–1.

74   *Charles II's Escape from Worcester: A Collection of Narratives Assembled by Samuel Pepys*, William Matthews (ed.) (London, 1967).

75   *Memoirs of Madamoiselle de Montpensier*, I, p. 170; *Journal de Jean Vallier*, III, pp. 42–3.

76   The king's Master of the Ceremonies, Sir John Finet, had died in 1641, and the role remained unfilled throughout the exile, *Ceremonies of Charles I*, pp. 10–11.

77   *CSPVen*, 1643–7, pp. 267–8, 272; *The Journal of Thomas Juxon*, p. 132.

78   *CSPVen*, 1643–7, pp. 267–8, 270; *Mémoires de Madame de Motteville sur Anna D'Austriche et sa Cour*, M. Sainte-Beuve (ed.), 3 vols (Paris, 1855), I, p. 284.

79   *Memoirs of La Grande Madamoiselle Duchess de Montpensier*, Seeley (ed.), p. 58; *Mémoires de Madame de Motteville*, M. Sainte-Beuve (ed.), I, pp. 284, 314, 389.

80   *Mémoires de Madame de Motteville*, M. Sainte-Beuve (ed.), I, p. 284.

81   Clarendon, *The History of the Rebellion*, IV, pp. 206–7.

82   *Mémoires de Madame de Motteville*, M. Sainte-Beuve (ed.), I, p. 284, which describes the arrangements as 'avois été concerté entre les deux reines'.

83   Similarly, when Charles II came to France in 1650, again travelling there from Jersey, he dispatched the Duke of Buckingham in advance to ensure all arrangements were in place for a dignified and regal reception (*Journal de Jean Chevalier*, II, pp. 761–2).

84   *CSPVen*, 1647–52, pp. 103, 105, 109; Clarendon, *The History of the Rebellion*, V, p. 49; *The Nicholas Papers*, I, pp. 125–6, 133–4; Add. MS 51,324, fols 33v, 38r.

85   *Memoirs of Madame de Motteville*, Wormeley trans., II, p. 132; *CSPVen*, 1647–52, p. 109; *Journal de Jean Vallier, Maître d'Hôtel du Roi*, I, pp. 367–8.

86   Guizot, *History of Oliver Cromwell*, 2 vols (London, 1854), II, pp. 383–4, 387, 399; *CSPVen*, 1647–52, pp. 87, 89; *The Nicholas Papers*, I, pp. 116–17; *Memoirs of Madame de Motteville*, Wormeley trans., II, p. 87.

87   M. Guizot, *History of Oliver Cromwell*, II, pp. 387–8, 392, 396, 403, 418.

88   BL, Add. MS 37,047, fol. 15r; Guizot, *History of Oliver Cromwell*, II, pp. 396, 400.

89   Guizot, *History of Oliver Cromwell*, II, pp. 401, 403.

90   BL, Add. MS 37,047, fol. 15r.

91   Clarendon, *The History of the Rebellion*, V, p. 355; *CSPVen*, 1656–7, p. 229; *Calendar of the Clarendon State Papers*, III, p. 131.

92   Clarendon, *The History of the Rebellion*, V, pp. 357–8; *Calendar of Clarendon State Papers*, II, p. 411.

93   Gardiner, *Letters and Papers Illustrating the Relations between Charles II and Scotland*, pp. 33–4.

94   *Calendar of the Clarendon State Papers*, III, p. 124; Bod. Lib., Clarendon MS 51, fol. 242r.

95   Hutton, *Charles II*, p. 117; *Calendar of Clarendon State Papers*, II, pp. 212–13; IV, pp. 416, 418; F. J. Routledge, *England and the Treaty of the Pyrenees* (Liverpool, 1953), pp. 70ff.; *Charles II to Lord Taaffe: Letters in Exile*, Timothy Crist (ed.), (London, 1974), p. 37.

96   *CSPVen*, 1643–7, p. 293; 1647–52, pp. 110, 220.

 97 *Memoirs of Madamoiselle de Montpensier*, I, p. 94; *Memoirs of La Grande Madamoiselle Duchess de Montpensier*, Seeley (ed.), p. 57; *The Nicholas Papers*, I, p. 136.

 98 *Calendar of the Clarendon State Papers*, IV, pp. 418, 421.

 99 *CSPVen*, 1647–52, p. 89; *Mémoires de Madame de Motteville*, M. Sainte-Beuve (ed.), I, p. 454; *Memoires of Madamoiselle de Montpensier*, I, p. 133.

100 *State Papers of John Thurloe*, V, pp. 55, 160, 250, 690; *CSPVen*, 1656–7, p. 229.

101 *CSPVen*, 1656–7, pp. 196, 211; *Calendar of the Clarendon State Papers*, III, pp. 131, 216; Clarendon, *The History of the Rebellion*, VI, p. 13; *The Nicholas Papers*, IV, p. 5.

102 *Calendar of the Clarendon State Papers*, IV, p. 46; *CSPVen*, 1643–7, pp. 276, 269; *The Nicholas Papers*, IV, p. 3.

103 *Calendar of Clarendon State Papers*, I, p. 329.

104 *Calendar of the Clarendon State Papers*, II, p. 420; see also his comments to Richard Belling in *State Papers of John Thurloe*, I, p. 744.

105 This is consistent with the view expressed for the earliest years of Charles II's exile by N. A. C. Reynolds, 'The Stuart Court and Courtiers in Exile 1644–1654', unpublished PhD thesis, Cambridge, 1996, p. 103.

106 *The Correspondence of John Cosin D.D.*, George Ornsby (ed.), 2 vols (Edinburgh, 1869, 1872), I, esp. p. 286; Evelyn, *Diary*, III, pp. 20, 633–4; *Calendar of Clarendon State Papers*, II, p. 113; *The Cheque Books of the Chapel Royal with Additional Material from the Manuscripts of William Lovegrove and Marmaduke Alford*, Andrew Ashbee and John Harley (eds), 2 vols (Aldershot, 2000), I, p. 34; DRO, D/FSI, Box 268, Household Accounts, 1654–5, pp. 58, 98; General Household Accounts of the King in exile, 1658–9, unfoliated, April 1658, May 1658, September 1659; J. Sainty and R. Bucholz (eds), *Officials of the Royal Household 1660–1837, Part I: Department of the Lord Chamberlain and Associated Offices* (London, 1997), p. 56; *CSPD*, 1661–2, p. 113.

107 David Baldwin, *The Chapel Royal Ancient and Modern* (London, 1990), p. 423; *The Cheque Book of the Chapel Royal*, I, pp. 120, 126; II, pp. 204, 284; DRO, D/FSI, Box 268, *passim*, see, e.g., Kitchen Accounts of Charles II in exile, 1656–9, pp. 73, 98; General Household Accounts of the King in exile, 1658–9, entries for June 1658 and September 1659'; *Calendar of the Clarendon State Papers*, IV, p. 97.

108 Evelyn, *Diary*, III, pp. 51, 53, 633; *Calendar of the Clarendon State Papers*, II, p. 110; *The Nicholas Papers*, I, p. 159; Clarendon, *The History of the Rebellion*, V, p. 166; *Correspondence of John Cosin*, I, p. 286.

109 A 'Prayer Roome' is referred to in March 1656 (which must have been either in the king's lodgings at Cologne, or in his new residence in Bruges) and again in May 1658 (which was certainly in Brussels), DRO, D/FSI, Box 268, Kitchen Accounts of Charles II in exile, 1656–9, p. 45; General Household Accounts of the King in exile, 1658–9, unfoliated, May 1658. See also Wicquefort, *A Relation in form of Journal*, p. 74.

110 Evelyn, *Diary*, III, p. 633; Robert S. Bosher, *The Making of the Restoration Settlement: The Influence of the Laudians 1649–1662* (London, 1951), p. 59.

111 Clarendon, *The History of the Rebellion*, V, p. 166.

112 BL, Add. MS 51,318, '1st Booke off Houshold Expence from October 1654 to the end of December 1655', fols 17r, 19v, 73r.

113 BL, Add. MS 51,318, '1st Booke off Houshold Expence from October 1654 to the end of December 1655', fols 11r, 17r, 58v; DRO, D/FSI, Box 268, Household Accounts, 1658–9, May 1658.

114 DRO, D/FSI, Box 268, Household Accounts, 1654–5, pp. 49, 98; General Household Accounts of the king in exile, 1658–9, unfoliated, May 1658, September 1659; Clarendon,

The History of the Rebellion, V, p. 166; VI, p. 232; *A Brief Historical Relation of the Life of Mr John Livingstone*, Thomas Houston (ed.) (Edinburgh, 1848), p. 120; Nicholas Pocock, *Life of Richard Steward, Dean Designate of St Paul's* (London, 1908), p. 110.

115 DRO, D/FSI, Box 268, General Household Accounts, 1658–9, May 1658; Clarendon, *The History of the Rebellion*, VI, p. 232.

116 *A Brief Historical Relation of the Life of Mr John Livingstone*, pp. 124–5.

117 Evelyn, *Diary*, III, pp. 51, 53; DRO, D/FSI, Box 268, General Household Accounts of the King in exile, 1658–9, unfoliated, April 1658, June 1658, January 1659, April 1659.

118 *State Papers of John Thurloe*, V, pp. 673–4; *Journal de Jean Chevalier*, II, pp. 717–18; Evelyn, *Diary*, III, pp. 51, 53; 'Walking this morning in the court at the King's house, before prayers', *CSPD*, 1657–8, p. 292'; *Charles II to Lord Taaffe*, p. 1; *Calendar of Clarendon State Papers*, III, p. 157. See also Hutton, 'The religion of Charles II', p. 237.

119 *The Letters and Journals of Robert Baillie*, III, p. 86.

120 DRO, FSI, Box 268, Kitchen Accounts of Charles II in exile, 1656–9, p. 29; *The Nicholas Papers*, I, p. 275; *Charles II to Lord Taaffe*, p. 15; *Calendar of Clarendon State Papers*, III, p. 157.

121 *Calendar of Clarendon State Papers*, II, p. 215.

122 *Calendar of Clarendon State Papers*, III, p. 117; *State Papers of John Thurloe*, I, p. 647; V, p. 447.

123 *State Papers of John Thurloe*, II, p. 567, 662.

124 *The Nicholas Papers*, III, p. 61; *State Papers of John Thurloe*, IV, pp. 88–9; II, p. 567.

125 *The Nicholas Papers*, IV, p. 71.

126 Evelyn, *Diary*, III, pp. 53, 128; DRO, D/FSI, Box 268, Household Accounts, 1654–5, p. 98; *Calendar of Clarendon State Papers*, II, p. 62.

127 BL, Egerton MS 2542, fol. 233r.

128 *Calendar of Clarendon State Papers*, III, p. 111.

129 *Diary of Alexander Jaffray, Provost of Aberdeen*, John Barclay (ed.) (Aberdeen, 1856), p. 55.

130 *A Brief Historical Relation of the Life of Mr John Livingstone*, Thomas Houston (ed.), pp. 120–5.

131 *Calendar of Clarendon State Papers*, II, p. 110.

132 *Journal de Jean Chevalier*, II, pp. 744–5, 764; Wicquefort, *A Relation in form of Journal*, pp. 74–6.

133 Wicquefort, *A Relation in form of Journal*, p. 78.

134 Wiseman, *Severall Chirurgical Treatises*, p. 245.

135 DRO, D/FSI, Box 268, General Household Accounts, 1658–9, October 1659; Box 273, Daily Receipts and Payments, 1660–2, May 1660.

136 Richard Wiseman, *Severall Chirurgical Treastises* (London, 1686), p. 247; *Memoirs of the Verney Family during the Civil War*, Frances Parthenope Verney (ed.), 4 vols (London, 1892–9), III, p. 78.

137 Browne, *Adenochoiradelogia*, III, pp. 153–4, 159–60.

138 Browne, *Adenochoiradelogia*, III, p. 156.

139 Wicquefort, *A Relation in form of Journal*, pp. 75–6; Browne, *Adenochoiradelogia*, III, pp. 156–7. Browne even refers to tickets being distributed for healings during the king's exile; *Journal de Jean Chevalier*, II, pp. 744–5.

140 *Journal de Jean Chevalier*, II, p. 760.

141 *The Nicholas Papers*, I, p. 222; *Calendar of Clarendon State Papers*, IV, p. 134.

142 In 1657 payments were made for an 'extraordinary supper upon his Ma[ties] Birthday', DRO,

D/FSI, Box 268, Kitchen Accounts of Charles II in exile, 1656–9, p. 109 and in June 1658 extra wages to grooms and footmen for attending 'upon the occation of his ma[ties] Birthday', *ibid.*; *Journal de Jean Chevalier*, II, pp. 722, 731.

143   *Journal de Jean Chevalier*, II, p. 713.

144   Beltz, *Memorials of the Most Noble Order of the Garter*, pp. clxxxix–cxci; *Calendar of Clarendon State Papers*, II, pp. 173, 175; III, p. 330; BL, Add. MS 37,998, Sir Edward Walker's Garter Papers, fols 69r–75r, 99r.

145   Hutton, *Charles II*, p. 105; *CSPVen*, 1657–60, p. 180; DRO, D/FSI, Box 268, General Household Accounts, 1658–9, unpaginated (March).

146   For the carefully planned ceremonies followed at the election of various other Garter Knights during the exile see BL, Add. MS 37,998, fols 69r, 70r, 74r–75r.

147   *CSPD*, 1657–8, pp. 296, 297, 298, 311, 313.

148   See, e.g., *Letters, Speeches and Declarations of King Charles II*, pp. 12–13.

149   *Memoirs of Madame de Motteville*, Wormeley trans, II, p. 132; *Journal de Jean Vallier*, I, pp. 367–8.

150   Clarendon, *The History of the Rebellion*, IV, p. 372; *CPSVen*, 1647–52, p. 87.

151   *Calendar of the Clarendon State Papers*, II, p. 411; Clarendon, *The History of the Rebellion*, V, pp. 357–9.

152   Clarendon, *The History of the Rebellion*, V, p. 135.

153   Wicquefort, *A Relation in form of Journal*, pp. 79–81.

154   DRO, D/FSI, Box 268, Household Accounts, 1654–5, p. 43; General Household Accounts, 1658–9, May 1658.

155   DRO, D/FSI, Box 268, Kitchen Accounts of Charles II in exile, 1656–9, p. 104.

156   *Calendar of Clarendon State Papers*, II, p. 261; III, p. 360. *Letters, Speeches and Declarations of King Charles II*, pp. 45–6.

157   Bod. Lib., Clarendon State Papers 37, fol. 193r; BL, Add. MS 51,318, fols 1v, 40v, 56r, 62v.

158   BL, Add. MS 51,318, fol. 17v.

159   BL, Add. MS 51,318, fol. 10v; DRO, D/FSI Box 268, General Household Accounts, 1658–9, August 1658.

160   *Calendar of Clarendon State Papers*, III, p. 199.

161   *Memoirs of Madamoiselle de Montpensier*, I, p. 93; II, p. 77; *Journal de Jean Chevalier*, II, p. 713; *Memoirs of Madame de Motteville*, Wormeley trans., I, pp. 211–12; *Memoirs of La Grande Madamoiselle Duchess de Montpensier*, Seeley (ed.), p. 72; Anthony Harvey and Richard Mortimer, *The Funeral Effigies of Westminster Abbey* (Woodbridge, 1994), p. 80.

162   *Journal de Jean Chevalier*, II, p. 713.

163   BL, Egerton MS 2542, fol. 90r.

164   *Memoirs of Madamoiselle de Montpensier*, I, p. 93; *Journal de Jean Chevalier*, II, pp. 708ff., 742; *Memoirs of La Grande Madamoiselle Duchess de Montpensier*, Seeley (ed.), p. 72.

165   BL, Add. MS 38,854, fol. 50r; DRO, D/FSI, Box 268, General Household Accounts, 1658–9, June 1658.

166   BL, Add. MS 38,854, fol. 33r; *Correspondence of Sir Robert Kerr, first Earl of Ancram*, II, p. 332; *CSPD*, 1657–8, p. 277.

167   DRO, D/FSI, Box 268, General Household Accounts, 1658–9, unpaginated, June 1658, December 1658.

168   *Letters, Speeches and Declarations of King Charles II*, pp. 30, 34, 40.

169   TNA, LC5/132, p. 193; SP16/428, no. 104; Clarendon, *The History of the Rebellion*, IV, pp. 22–3.

170   Hartmann, *Charles II, passim*; Hutton, *Charles II*, pp. 271–2.

171 See Tim Harris, 'Scott, James, duke of Monmouth and first duke of Buccleuch (1649–1685)', *Oxford Dictionary of National Biography*, 2004.

172 *Calendar of Clarendon State Papers*, II, pp. 218, 220–1, 228; III, p. 341, 392–3; *The Nicholas Papers*, III, p. 92; *State Papers of John Thurloe*, II, p. 502; V, p. 645.

173 *CSPD*, 1657–8, pp. 267–9, 311.

Notes to Chapter 5: England reclaimed

1 *The Journal of Edward Montagu, First Earl of Sandwich and General at Sea*, R. C. Anderson (ed.), Navy Records Society, 1929, pp. 75–8; BL, Add. MS 30,195, 'Manner of the Return and Coronation of Charles II', fols 3r–8v; *The Diaries of Anne Clifford*, D. J. H. Clifford, ed. (Stroud, 1990), p. 144; Fleming Papers, *HMC 12th Report*, VII, pp. 25–6; *The Memoirs of Ann Lady Fanshawe*, pp. 94–5; *Mercurius Publicus*, 24–31 May 1660, pp. 341–2.

2 *The Diurnal of Thomas Rugg*, pp. 79–80; *CSPVen*, 1659–61, pp. 145–6.

3 *HMC Ormonde*, III, p. 1; *CSPVen*, 1659–61, pp. 142–3; BL, Add. MS 37,998, fols 91v–92v.

4 Pepys, *Diary*, I, p. 160; *CSPVen*, 1659–61, pp. 148, 151.

5 *The Diurnal of Thomas Rugg*, pp. 85, 86; *Mercurius Publicus*, 24–31 May 1660, p. 339; *CSPD*, 1660–1, p. 115.

6 *Mercurius Publicus*, 24–31 May 1660, pp. 341–2; BL, Add. MS 37,998, fols 90r–92v.

7 DRO, D/FSI, Box 273, Daily Receipts and Accounts 1660–2, May 1660; Walker, *A Circumstantial Account*, pp. 11–15.

8 Clarendon, *The Life of Edward, Earl of Clarendon*, I, pp. 326–7; *The Diurnal of Thomas Rugg*, p. 88; *Mercurius Publicus*, 24–31 May 1660, pp. 349–52; Clarendon, *The History of the Rebellion*, VI, p. 234; *The Parliamentary Intelligencer*, 23, 29 May 1660.

9 For Whitehall Palace see Simon Thurley's extensive work in the following publications: *Whitehall Palace: An Architectural History of the Royal Apartments, 1240–1690* (New Haven and London, 1999); *The Lost Palace of Whitehall*, catalogue of an exhibition at the RIBA Heinz Gallery, 10 September–24 October 1998; *The Whitehall Palace Plan of 1670*, London Topographical Society Publication 153 (London, 1998).

10 *CSPD*, 1660–1, p. 215; *CSPVen*, 1659–61, pp. 156–7, 159.

11 Sainty and Bucholz, *Officials of the Royal Household 1660–1837*, *passim*, cf. *HMC Pepys*, pp. 255–6; BL, Add. MS 37,047, fols 5r–14v; BL, Stowe 677, fol. 80r–v; *Calendar of Clarendon State Papers*, II, pp. 386–7; Bod. Lib, Clar. MS 49, fol. 107r; Bod. Lib., Clar. MS 54, fol. 162; City Archives of Bruges, Oud Archief nr 101, Politieke Oorkonden, 1st reeks no. 621.

12 TNA, LC5/201, p. 1.

13 TNA, LC5/201, p. 2; Victor Stater, 'Grenville, John, first earl of Bath (1628–1701)', *Oxford Dictionary of National Biography*, 2004; *Burnet's History of My Own Time*, I, pp. 178–9; Aylmer, *The Crown's Servants*, p. 23; Ronald Hutton, *The Restoration* (Oxford, 1985), pp. 106–8; *HMC Fleming*, p. 67. When an argument over access arose between the Groom of the Stool and the Lord Chamberlain in the 1680s, it was one of the Gentlemen of the Bedchamber (and not Lord Bath), who first disputed the Lord Chamberlain's right to enter the room: *Correspondence of the Family of Hatton being Chiefly Addressed to Christopher, Viscount Hatton AD 1601–1704*, Edward Maude Thompson (ed.), 2 vols, Camden Society, NS XXII, XXIII (London, 1878), II, pp. 21–2; Thurley, *The Whitehall Palace Plan of 1670*, pp. 32–3; Bucholz and Sainty, *Officials of the Royal Household*, XI, p. 7.

14 Bucholz and Sainty, *Officials of the Royal Household*, XI, p. 8.

15   Nottingham University Library, Manuscripts Collection (hereafter NUL), Portland MSS,
     Pw V 92, fols 4v–6r; Edward Chamberlayne, *Angliae Notitia or the Present State of England,
     Together with Divers Reflections upon the Ancient State Thereof* (London, 1669) (hereafter:
     Angliae Notitia, 1669), pp. 262–3; *The Present State of the British Court or, An Account of the
     Civil and Military Establishment of England* (London, 1720), p. 22, *The Memoirs of Thomas,
     Earl of Ailesbury written by Himself*, W. E. Buckley, ed., 2 vols (London, 1890), I, p. 86; Count
     Lorenzo Magalotti, *Travels of Cosimo the Third, Grand Duke of Tuscany through England
     during the reign of King Charles the Second (1669)* (London, 1821), p. 383.

16   *Angliae Notitia*, 1669, pp. 265–6; NUL, Portland MSS, Pw V 92, fols 6r–v; TNA, SP29/230,
     no. 84; British Library, Egerton MS 3350, fol. 7r; Magalotti, *Travels*, p. 384.

17   *The Historical Works of Sir James Balfour*, IV, pp. 82, 112.

18   NUL, Portland MSS, Pw V 92, fol. 7r; Pw V 93, fol. 20r; TNA, SP29/230, no. 84;
     Correspondence of the Family of Hatton, II, pp. 21–2; *The Present State of The British Court*,
     p. 25; Evelyn, *Diary*, III, pp. 299–300; TNA, LC5/138, p. 362, Ailesbury, *Memoirs*, I, p. 87;
     Journal des Voyages de Monsieur de Monconys, 2 vols (Lyon, 1666), II, p. 57.

19   Sainty and Bucholz, *Officials of the Royal Household*, pp. 16–17; Aylmer, *The Crown's
     Servants*, pp. 23–5; Cuddy, 'The revival of the entourage', p. 187; Allen, 'The political
     function of Charles II's Chiffinch', pp. 277–90; only the king and Mr Chiffinch had keys
     to the king's most private spaces, TNA, LC5/142, p. 51.

20   Allen, 'The political function of Charles II's Chiffinch', p. 287.

21   Clarendon, *The Life of Edward, Earl of Clarendon*, I, pp. 367–8; Ian J. Gentles, 'Montagu,
     Edward, second earl of Manchester (1602–1671)', *Oxford Dictionary of National Biography*,
     2004; *Burnet's History of My Own Time*, I, p. 175.

22   C. H. Firth, 'Carteret, Sir George, first baronet (1610?–1680)', rev. C. S. Knighton, *Oxford
     Dictionary of National Biography*.

23   *Angliae Notitia*, 1669, p. 247; Sainty and Bucholz, *Officials of the Royal Household*,
     pp. xx–xxx.

24   *Angliae Notitia*, 1669, p. 290; BL, Stowe MS 562, fols 2v–4r.

25   'They wait in the Presence-Chamber next to the King's Person, and order all Affairs, next
     to the Lord Chamberlain and Vice-Chamberlain, and all under Officers above Stairs
     are to obey them' (*The Present State of The British Court*, p. 27); *Angliae Notitia*, 1669,
     p. 269.

26   TNA, SP16/1721, no. 81; LC5/134, pp. 50–2.

27   *Angliae Notitia*, 1669, pp. 269–70; *The Present State of The British Court*, p. 28; BL, Stowe
     MS 562, fols 4r–7r.

28   *The Present State of The British Court*, pp. 35–6, 61–2; *Angliae Notitia*, 1669, p. 289.

29   BL, Stowe MS 562, fol. 9v–13r; *The Present State of The British Court*, p. 26; *Angliae Notitia*,
     1669, p. 268; LC5/140, fol. 248v–249v.

30   *Burnet's History of My Own Time*, I, p. 453, n. 2; Victor D. Sutch, *Gilbert Sheldon, Architect
     of Anglican Survival, 1640–1675* (The Hague, 1973).

Notes to Chapter 6: The clamour of kingship

1   *The Letters, Speeches and Declarations of King Charles II*, pp. 92–3.

2   *The Diurnal of Thomas Rugg*, pp. 93, 94, 97; *HMC Sutherland*, pp. 151, 154; *CSPVen*,
     1659–61, pp. 170–1; *The Parliamentary Intelligencer*, 23, May 1660; *Mercurius Publicus*,
     24–31 May, pp. 349–352; 28 June–5 July 1660, pp. 430–1.

3   College of Arms, MS M 3, Ceremonial, fols 20r–21r; *The Diurnal of Thomas Rugg*, pp. 98–9; *CSPVen*, 1659–61, pp. 170–1.

4   *CSPVen*, 1659–61, pp. 170–1; David Stevenson, 'Campbell, Archibald, marquess of Argyll (1605x7–1661), *Oxford Dictionary of National Biography*, 2004.

5   *The Diary of John Evelyn*, III, p. 247; *CSPVen*, 1659–61, pp. 154–6.

6   See chapter one for Charles II's 1661 coronation.

7   *The Diurnal of Thomas Rugg*, pp. 111–12; *The Parliamentary Intelligencer*, 38, 15 September 1660.

8   Thurley, *Whitehall Palace: An Architectural History of the Royal Apartments*, pp. 63, 106.

9   TNA, LC5/134, pp. 321, 368; *Ceremonies of Charles I*, p. 261.

10 TNA, WORK 5/1, fols 163r–v, 196v; WORK5/2, fol. 40v.

11 Louis Hautecoeur, *L'histoire des Chateaux du Louvre et des Tuileries* (Paris, 1927), pp. 7–22; *Journal de Jean Vallier*, IV, pp. 100, 105; TNA, WORK5/1, fols 163r–v. Thurley, *Whitehall Palace*, p. 106; Simon Thurley established this relationship, in preparation for a paper we both gave at the 'Tudor and Stuart Interior' conference at the Victoria and Albert Museum, February 2002. A drawing of the French royal alcove is among a collection of drawings brought to England at some point in the mid-seventeenth century and now in the Ashmolean Museum. It is worth noting that the French *chambre de parade*, roughly equivalent in function to the alcove bedchamber at Whitehall, did not have an alcove, while the *chambre à coucher*, which did, was closer in function to Charles II's new bedchamber(s) of 1662, 1666–8 and 1682, which did not have alcoves.

12 Edward Croft Murray, *Decorative Painting in England 1537–1837. Volume One: Early Tudor to Sir James Thornhill* (London, 1962), pp. 228–9; Evelyn, *Diary*, III, p. 337 (with the creation of a new bedchamber in the summer of 1662, it would understandably have been referred to as the 'old' bedchamber in October of that year); Thurley, *Whitehall Palace*, p. 106.

13 '... of such Colour as the said ffrancis Rogers shall informe yor Lord^{PP} to be his Ma:^{ties} Choyse & directions', TNA, LC5/39, pp. 55, 61; LC5/137, pp. 27, 31.

14 Most of the fabric of the west range was completed; this is now part of the Old Royal Naval Hospital and is known as the 'King Charles Block'. John Webb's sketch for 'the Alcove in his Ma^{ts} Bedchamber Greenwich 1665' is in the collection of the RIBA (John Harris, *Catalogue of the Drawing Collection of the Royal Institute of British Architects, Volume One: Inigo Jones and John Webb* [Farnborough, 1972], p. 24, cat. 130 and fig. 129). For the story of the scheme and its abandonment see Simon Thurley, 'A country seat fit for a king: Charles II, Greenwich and Winchester', in Cruickshanks (ed.), *The Stuart Courts*, pp. 214–40.

15 For example, in August 1670 the mourning hangings of this bedchamber were taken down, which had included '4 yds of Cloth the [sic] cover ye rayle of ye Alcove' (TNA, LC5/201, p. 454); while in August 1682 new hangings, stools and a chair were provided for 'the Room betweene the old Bedchamber and Closset on the Garden side' – which must refer to the bedchamber set up in 1661, which (unlike the others set up later) looked out over the privy garden; see also Worcestershire Record Office (hereafter: WRO), Caspar Frederic Henning Papers, BA 2252/5 (705:366), unfoliated, order signed by the Earl of Bath, 15 January 1682/3.

16 See, for instance, Sir John Finet, *Finetti Philoxenis: som choice Observations of Sr John Finett Knight and Master of the Ceremonies to the two last Kings Touching the Reception and Precedence and Treatment and Audience, the Punctillios and Contests of Forren Ambassadors in England* (London, 1656), *passim*. Only when James I was so ill as to be bed-bound did he receive visits in his bedchamber.

17 *The Parliamentary Intelligencer*, 23, 20 May 1660; *Mercurius Publicus*, 31 May–7 June 1660, p. 368; *Mercurius Publicus*, 14–21 June 1660, p. 400.

18 TNA, LC5/140, pp. 248, 249; Pepys, *Diary*, V, p. 254.

19 *Mercurius Publicus*, 14 June–21 June 1660, p. 395.

20 Pepys, *Diary*, II, pp. 239, 287; IV, p. 360; *The Diary of Robert Hooke 1672–1680*, H.W. Robinson and W. Adams, eds. (London, 1935), pp. 162, 185.

21 Evelyn, *Diary*, III, p. 407. *HMC Ormonde*, V, p. 467.

22 *London Gazette*, 936, Thursday 5 November 1674; *HMC Verney*, p. 466, William Fall to Ralph Verney, 7 October 1675; *London Gazette*, 1254, Friday 23 November 1677; 1699, Saturday 25 February 1682.

23 *London Gazette*, 1643, Sunday 14 August 1681.

24 *Calendar of the Clarendon State Papers*, III, pp. 392–3; *The Rawdon Papers*, Edward Berwick (ed.) (London, 1819), pp. 175–7; *The King My Brother*, p. 67; Pepys, *Diary*, IV, p. 107; William and Mary married in the princess's bedchamber at St James's Palace, 'Diary of Dr. Edward Lake, chaplain and tutor to the Princesses Mary and Anne, 1677–1678', George Percy Elliot (ed.), *The Camden Miscellany*, I (1847), p. 6.

25 TNA, LC5/201, p. 490.

26 TNA, LC5/2, pp. 124–5; *The Loyal Protestant*, no. 26, Sunday 29 May 1681.

27 Clarendon, *The Life of Edward, Earl of Clarendon*, I, pp. 503–4; Evelyn, *Diary*, III, p. 247; Colbert's account of life at Newmarket in 1669 describes the king as constantly surrounded by people, from dawn until 'son coucher' (TNA, PRO31/3/122, fol. 7r).

28 For the new bedchamber of 1662, in the 'Turks Gallery', see TNA, WORK5/3, fol. 139r.

29 Thurley, *Whitehall Palace: An Architectural History*, pp. 108–9.

30 NUL, Portland MS Pw V 93, fol. 2v; Thurley, *Whitehall Palace: An Architectural History*, p. 109.

31 TNA, LC5/201, pp. 451–5; LC5/62, fols 73r–74v. Charles II's bedchamber ordinances, NUL, Portland MS Pw V 92, fols 1r–9v: 'A Booke conteyning his Majesty's Orders for the Government of the Bedchamber and Privy Lodgings', are the earliest set of regulations to survive for the government of the bedchamber of any Stuart king of England. They assert, though, that they were not new but merely 'a confirmation of the auncient Orders for the Government of Our Bedchamber and Privy Lodgings made by Our Royall ffather and Grandfather' (fol. 9v). The claims made in the 1661 orders for their own antiquity should be treated with some caution, not least as the Lord Chamberlain was to cast serious doubt on aspects of this claim in the 1680s. Neil Cuddy uses the 1661 ordinances as evidence of how James I's Bedchamber operated (Cuddy, 'The revival of the entourage', p. 186, n. 34). Kevin Sharpe uses the bedchamber ordinances issued by William III as a guide to the practice of the reign of Charles I without reference to the Charles II orders (Sharpe, 'The image of virtue', p. 231).

32 *CSPVen*, 1659–61, pp. 166–7.

33 TNA, LC5/2, p. 3; A. J. Loomie, 'The conducteur des ambassadeurs of seventeenth century France and Spain', in *Revue Belge de Philologie et d'Histoire*, LIII 1975 (II), pp. 333–57; Finet, *Finetti Philoxenis, passim*; *Ceremonies of Charles I*, pp. 22–3; Sainty and Bucholz, *Officials of the Royal Household*, pp. 37–8; John M. Beattie, *The English Court in the Reign of George I* (Cambridge, 1967), p. 48.

34 *CSPD*, 1660–1, pp. 415, 455, 522. Cotterell (1615–1701) was also MP for Cardigan, 1663–78, briefly serving as ambassador to Brussels in 1663 and as master of Requests from 1667.

35 TNA, LC5/2, pp. 1, 37.

36 TNA, LC5/201, pp. 71–2; LC5/2, pp. 13, 110–11; *CSPVen*, 1664–6, p. 238. See also, for example, TNA, LC5/2, p. 17.

37 Indeed, the notes of the Master of the Ceremonies in the reign of Charles II (transcripts of the original manuscripts at Rousham Park are in TNA, LC5/2, and a calendar in *Historical Manuscripts Commission. Second Report* [London, 1871], 'The manuscripts of C. Cottrell Dormer, Esq., Rousham, near Oxford', pp. 82–4), though a treasure trove, are a poor shadow of the almost comprehensive record of audiences and presentations maintained by Sir John Finet (Finet, *Finetti Philoxenis* and *Ceremonies of Charles I*).

38 '"Embajada Espanola": an anonymous contemporary Spanish guide to diplomatic procedure in the last quarter of the seventeenth century', H. J. Chaytor (ed.), *Camden Miscellany*, XIV (London, 1926), p. 29.

39 In 1666 Pepys remarked on the King of France's symbolic riposte to Charles II's declaration against the wearing of French clothes, that it was 'an ingenious kind of affront; but yet makes me angry to see that the king of England is become so little as to have that affront offered him' (Pepys, *Diary*, V, pp. 59; VII, pp. 380–1).

40 Garrett Mattingly, *Renaissance Diplomacy* (London, 1955), pp. 36–9, citing Bernard du Rosier's 'Short Treatise about Ambassadors' of 1436; Phyllis S.Lachs, *The Diplomatic Corps under Charles II and James II* (New York, 1965), pp. 96–8; M. S. Anderson, *The Rise of Modern Diplomacy 1450–1919* (London and New York, 1993), pp. 56–64.

41 TNA, LC5/2, p. 37.

42 TNA, LC5/2, pp. 38–9; see, e.g., *Une Ambassade du Prince de Ligne en Angleterre, 1660*, Félicien Leuridant (ed.) (Brussels, 1923), p. 4. In some cases, extraordinary ambassadors might be brought over in English boats (TNA, LC5/2, p. 39). See *A French Ambassador at the Court of Charles II: Le Comte de Cominges from his Unpublished Correspondence*, J. J. Jusserand (ed.) (London, 1892), pp. 72–4, 207–9, *passim*, for all aspects of the entry of the ambassador of a crowned head. Until 1626 it had been quite normal for ambassadors to be met at Dover, but in that year it was ruled that they would be met no further than Gravesend (TNA, LC5/2, p. 21); Finet, *Finetti Philoxenis*, p. 181.

43 *The First Triple Alliance: The Letters of Christopher Lindenov Danish Envoy to London 1668–1672*, Waldemar Westergaard (trans. and ed.) (New Haven, 1947), pp. 7–8, 20, 164; *CSPVen*, 1661–4, p. 192; 1666–8, p. 252; TNA, LC5/2, p. 39; *Une Ambassade du Prince de Ligne*, p. 18.

44 *The Diurnal of Thomas Rugg*, p. 158; TNA, LC5/2, pp. 39–40; *Une Ambassade du Prince de Ligne*, p. 20. After October 1661 no foreign diplomats resident in London were permitted to send their coaches to the entry of an ambassador; *CSPD*, 1661–2, p. 104.

45 *Une Ambassade du Prince de Ligne*, pp. 20–1; TNA, LC5/2, p. 40; *CSPVen*, 1664–6, p. 125.

46 *CSPVen*, 1666–8, p. 252; TNA, LC5/2, p. 40.

47 *CSPVen*, 1661–4, p. 23; TNA, LC5/2, p. 41; *Journal des Voyages de Monsieur de Monconys*, II, pp. 9–10; the house belonged to Rebecca Williams: *London Gazette*, 1700, 2 March 1681/2; TNA, LC5/64, fol. 92v; Lachs, *The Diplomatic Corps under Charles II and James II*, p. 98.

48 Reresby, *Memoirs*, p. 18; *The First Triple Alliance*, p. 155. See also the comte de Soissons's 'great preparations to surpass the prince de Ligne in everything', *CSPVen*, 1659–61, pp. 207–8.

49 Lemaire, 'L'ambassade du comte D'Estrades à Londres en 1661: l'affaire "du pas"', pp. 181–226; *A French Ambassador at the Court of Charles the Second*, pp. 24–30; *CSPD*, 1661–2, pp. 100, 104, 105; Evelyn, *Diary*, III, pp. 299–300; Pepys, *Diary*, II, pp. 187–9; *CSPVen*, 1661–4, pp. 61–2; François de Callières, *The Art of Diplomacy*, p. 124.

50 Clarendon, *The History of the Rebellion*, VI, p. 228.

51 TNA, LC5/2, p. 39; Schellinks, *Journal*, pp. 173–4.

52 There were occasional exceptions to these rules about the defraying of foreign ambassadors' expenses for only three days, such as the extra allowances given to the Portuguese representative at the time of Charles II's marriage. A long-standing exception were ambassadors from Russia. Historically, the Muscovy Company, which was effectively responsible for so much of Anglo-Russian relations, covered the costs of accommodating the Russian ambassadors in London. By the Restoration, the Muscovy Company was refusing to finance visits that were not principally about trade; nonetheless there was clearly an expectation from the Russians, 'whose Nation stands so much on Ceremony', that they would continue to be entertained. Ignoring Clarendon's attempts to dissuade him from accepting embassies from Russia on the basis of their cost, several came to England during the reign and Charles II was landed with a bill for tens of thousands of pounds for putting them up. It was also accepted that the entry of the Russian ambassadors should be particularly fine, with a troop of the king's horse guards and trumpets preceding the royal coach, an 'honour not shown to any foreign minister': *Ceremonies of Charles I*, p. 48; Finet, *Finetti Philoxenis*, pp. 46, 55; *CSPD*, 1663–4. pp. 126, 127, 358; TNA, PC2/56, fol. 14r; *The Letters, Speeches and Declarations of King Charles II*, p. 136; *HMC Portland*, III, p. 270; *A French Ambassador at the Court of Charles the Second*, pp. 23, 189–90. By 1676 it had been officially accepted that diplomats from Russia 'are allwayes entertayned at His Ma^tes charge': TNA, LC5/201, pp. 346–7, 352; *A French Ambassador at the Court of Charles the Second*, pp. 67, 194; *CSPVen*, 1661–4, p. 219. Ordinary ambassadors, envoys and residents were responsible for arranging and paying for their own accommodation in London: TNA, LC5/2, p. 21

53 In Cotterell's words 'the place whereof is more convenient that the house itself, which is no ways suitable to the magnificence of such entries' (TNA, LC5/2, pp. 40, 120); the house was furnished at the king's expense by the Great Wardrobe, see, e.g., LC5/64, fol. 92v. *Journal des Voyages de Monsieur de Monconys*, II, pp. 1–10.

54 TNA, LC5/39, pp. 13–23, *passim*, 47–8, 69, 70; LC5/60, pp. 10, 14, 42–3; LC5/61, pp. 220, 232; *Une Ambassade du Prince de Ligne*, p. 21.

55 *Elias Ashmole*, C. H. Josten (ed.), II, pp. 788, 801, 813.

56 For example, *London Gazette* 288, 17 August 1668; 887, 19 June 1674; *Une Ambassade du Prince de Ligne*, p. 23.

57 Evelyn, *Diary*, III, p. 256; Pepys, *Diary*, I, p. 275; *The First Triple Alliance*, pp. 8–9; *CSPVen*, 1661–4, p. 23; 1666–8, p. 252.

58 *The First Triple Alliance*, pp. 8–9; *London Gazette*, 1685, 11 January 1681/2; *Une Ambassade du Prince de Ligne*, p. 24. On the few exceptional occasions when the banqueting house could not be used for these receptions, the king's presence chamber would be used instead. In 1682 the Bantam ambassadors had their first public audience in the king's presence at Windsor; the obvious alternative, St George's Hall, was being renovated at the time. In these exceptional cases, the queen would participate in ceremonial occasions in the king's state apartments: *London Gazette*, 1721, 14 May 1682.

59 The set showing the life of Abraham woven for Henry VIII was generally brought up from Hampton Court and hung with another from the collection to cover the walls of the great room: TNA, LC5/137, pp. 65, 358; LC5/6, fols 66v, 71v.

60 Evelyn, *Diary*, III, p. 412; *CSPVen*, 1666–8, pp. 252, 280; *Oxford Gazette*, 66, 30 June 1666; *Une Ambassade du Prince de Ligne*, p. 25.

61 'HM's Royall Band of Pensioners being placed along the Raules': *The Parliamentary*

Intelligencer, 36, August 1660; TNA, LC5/39, p. 15; *Loyal Protestant*, 104, 16 January 1681/2, when the Moroccan ambassador was 'conducted within the rails to Their Majesties'.

62 'Wind musick playing all the while in the Galleries' (Evelyn, *Diary*, III. p. 349); *CSPVen*, 1661–4, p. 23; 1666–8, p. 280; *London Gazette*, 1685, 11 January 1681/2; *The Parliamentary Intelligencer*, 36, August 1660; *Une Ambassade du Prince de Ligne*, p. 25.

63 *London Gazette*, 1685, 11 January 1681/2; *Une Ambassade du Prince de Ligne*, p. 24; Evelyn, *Diary*, III, p. 349.

64 *CSPVen*, 1666–8, pp. 280–1, 317; *Une Ambassade du Prince de Ligne*, p. 25.

65 'Embajada Espanola' p. 27; *CSPVen*, 1666–8, p. 280.

66 *The Diurnal of Thomas Rugg*, p. 126; Evelyn, *Diary*, IV, pp. 262–3, 265–6; *The Parliamentary Intelligencer*, 47, 2 November 1660; *CSPVen*, 1661–4, p. 45; Reresby, *Memoirs*, p. 245; Denis Mahon, 'Notes on the "Dutch Gift" to Charles II', *The Burlington Magazine*, XCI, 1949, pp. 303–5, 349–50; XCII, 1950, pp. 12–29.

67 Evelyn, *Diary*, IV, p. 262; Pepys, *Diary*, III, p. 297; *CSPVen*, 1661–4, p. 219.

68 *London Gazette*, 1721, 14 May 1682; *Loyal Protestant*, 111, 29.

69 Pepys, *Diary*, III, p. 297; *The Parliamentary Intelligencer*, 36, August 1660.

70 *CSPVen*, 1661–4, p. 23.

71 *CSPVen*, 1666–8, pp. 281–2.

72 *Une Ambassade du Prince de Ligne*, p. 25; *CSPVen*, 1666–8, pp. 252, 281–2; *London Gazette*, 669, 13 April 1672; 727, 5 November 1672.

73 *Une Ambassade du Prince de Ligne*, pp. 32–3; *London Gazette*, 151, 26 April 1667; 1738, 14 July 1682; *True Protestant Mercury*, 1685, 11 January 1681/2.

74 *CSPVen*, 1666–8, p. 280; Evelyn, *Diary*, IV, p. 266.

75 Pepys, *Diary*, III, p. 297.

76 *Une Ambassade du Prince de Ligne*, p. 25; Pepys, *Diary*, III, p. 297.

77 '"Embajada Espanola"', p. 27; *A French Ambassador at the Court of Charles II*, pp. 75, 208–9; *The First Triple Alliance*, p. 240; *London Gazette*, 1649, 5 September 1681. The allowance of the king's coach for envoys was a novelty of Charles II's reign; he permitted it following the 'example of France where that honour was first done to my Lord Crofts who was send thither immediately after his Majesty's restoration' (TNA, LC5/2, pp. 37–8). Christopher Lindenov, Danish Resident in London, tried to secure the royal coach for his first audience, but was told 'that it has always been customary here at court for the royal envoys and residents to be taken to the audience in the Lord Chamberlain's carriage' (*The First Triple Alliance*, p. 233). There was some scope for increasing the honour of the entry of residents and envoys, as in 1674 when the Duke of Monmouth's coach was sent to the prince of Brabanson as 'a particular favour shown this young prince for his great quality' (*HMC Fleming*, p. 109).

78 *A French Ambassador at the Court of Charles II*, pp. 75, 208–9.

79 TNA, LC5/2, pp. 38, 135.

80 Evelyn, *Diary*, III, p. 494; TNA, LC5/2, p. 135.

81 TNA, LC5/2, p. 38; *London Gazette*, 403, 24 September 1669. Lindenov was told by the Master of the Ceremonies that he would be met at the door by the Lord Chamberlain, but 'as he was not at hand, a gentleman of the chamber met me and accompanied me back again' (*The First Triple Alliance*, p. 234); see *CSPVen*, 1661–4, p. 217 for the Hanse ambassadors being received in the king's drawing room.

82 TNA, LC5/2, p. 38.

83 TNA, LC5/2, p. 38; Lindenov noted: 'At the door to the queen's anteroom I met the vice-chamberlain, Killegray' (*The First Triple Alliance*, p. 234).

84 Evelyn, *Diary*, III, p. 494; TNA, LC5/2, p. 135.
85 Hartmann, *Charles II*, p. 106; *CSPVen*, 1659–61, p. 211; '"Embajada Espanola"', p. 23; Pepys, *Diary*, VI, p. 76.
86 For informal meetings between the king and diplomats see, e.g., Reresby, *Memoirs*, p. 238.
87 *CSPVen*, 1666–8, pp. 252, 255–7, 284–5; TNA, LC5/201, p. 70; *Une Ambassade du Prince de Ligne*, p. 26.
88 TNA, LC5/2, pp. 13, 110–11; *Loyal Protestant*, 105, 16 January 1682; *CSPVen*, 1666–8, pp. 256, 284–5; *Une Ambassade du Prince de Ligne*, p. 26.
89 *CSPVen*, 1659–61, pp. 145–6, 153, 154–6, 157, 164, 168.
90 *CSPVen*, 1659–61, p. 174; *The Diurnal of Thomas Rugg*, p. 94; *Mercurius Publicus*, 21–28 June 1660.
91 TNA, LC5/2, p. 37: this account is undated, but is datable by the identification of Coventry and Arlington as the secretaries of state at the time. See also p. 141.
92 *CSPVen*, 1661–4, p. 89.
93 *CSPVen*, 1659–61, pp. 165–6.
94 Evelyn, *Diary*, III, p. 344; *CSPVen*, 1659–61, pp. 154–6.
95 Rousham MC 5, 53–4, quoted in R. Clayton, 'Diplomats and Diplomacy in London 1667–72' Unpublished PhD, Oxford University, 1995, pp. 192–3.
96 Hartmann, *Charles II*, p. 145; C. H. Hartmann, *The King My Brother* (London, 1954), p. 145.
97 Cotterell himself noted that the manner of the reception of foreign ministers was dictated by two principal concerns: 'what is done to our Amb[assado]rs & Envoyes, &c, in other courts' and 'the latest precedents of what hath been practiced here': TNA, LC5/2, pp. 37–42, 46–8; SP29/256, no. 92, fols 14r–15r; 93, fols 16r–17r; 94, fols 18r–v; Bodleian Library, Rawl. MS A 477, fols 108r–20v. This way of setting out a ceremonial matter under consideration, so that the left-hand side of the document could be marked up with rulings and remarks, is also followed in the undated bedchamber orders in the state papers, suggesting that the annotations on these were the king's own views: TNA, SP29/230, no. 84; LC5/2, p. 32.
98 TNA, LC5/2, pp. 115, 125.
99 Beyond the scope of this study, but clearly relevant, is the king's firmness on maintaining the rule that his ships would be saluted at sea by foreign ships, on which subject he is said to have declared that he would rather lose his crown than abandon the salute at sea: Hartmann, *Charles II*, p. 36; *CSPD*, 1668–9, p. 117; *HMC Fleming*, pp. 71, 80, 82; *Letters, Speeches and Declarations of Charles II*, p. 246; *Correspondence of the Family of Hatton*, I, p. 106; Pepys, *Diary*, II, p. 12; *CSPVen*, 1661–4, pp. 69, 96–7, 101, 105.
100 Hartmann, *Charles II*, pp. 149, 207. For an example of this being the case, see Bod. Lib., Rawl. MS A. 477, fol. 117r.
101 *HMC Ormonde*, IV, p. 388.
102 TNA, LC5/133, p. 1.
103 Pepys, *Diary*, I, p. 182; *Mercurius Publicus*, 28 June–5 July 1660, pp. 430–1; *The Diurnal of Thomas Rugg*, p. 93.
104 *Mercurius Publicus*, 28 June–5 July 1660, pp. 430–1.
105 Larkin, *Stuart Royal Proclamations*, 17 (18 June 1625); 201 (28 July 1635); 267 (15 July 1638). Crawford, *The King's Evil*, Appendix. See also Judith Richards, '"His Nowe Majestie" and the English Monarchy', pp. 70–96; Sharpe, *The Personal Rule of Charles I*, pp. 217, 630–1; *A Proclamation for Suspending the Time of Healing the Disease called The King's Evill untill Easter Next* (London, 1638); Helen Farquhar, 'Royal charities. Part 1: Angels

as healing pieces for the King's Evil', *British Numismatic Journal*, XII, 2nd series, II, 1916; *Oxford Books*, Madan (ed.), II, p. 243. Only one Jacobean proclamation regarding the king's evil survives, dated 25 March 1616, which declares that the king would not be touching in the summer months between Easter and Michaelmas; James F. Larkin and Paul L. Hughes (eds), *Stuart Royal Proclamations. Volume I: Royal Proclamations of King James I 1603–1625* (Oxford, 1973), p. 159 (25 March 1616).

106 TNA, SP45/11, p. 123; PC2/70, pp. 97–8; *The Kingdom's Intelligencer*, 28, 14 July 1662. In the orders to the royal surgeons for the conduct of the healings of the mid-1670s, it was again emphasized that 'all persons that shall come to be healed shall bring a Certificate und^r the hands of the Minister & Churchwardens of the parish where they lived that they were never touched by his Ma^{te} for the Evill': TNA, LC5/140, pp. 493–4 (4); LC/144, p. 195; SP29/379, 1 (4).

107 *The Flemings in Oxford being Documents Selected from the Rydal Papers in illustration of the Lives and Ways of Oxford Men 1650–1700*, John Richard Magrath (ed.), 3 vols (Oxford, 1904), I, p. 453, n. When healing was suspended during the summer months, the parish clergy were sometimes asked to stop issuing certificates to prevent people from flocking to court regardless; see, e.g., *London Gazette*, 1828, 24 May 1683; *The Letters of Sir Thomas Browne*, Geoffrey Keynes (ed.) (London, 1931), p. 151.

108 Browne, *Adenochoiradelogia*, III, p. 85.

109 *The Letters of Sir Thomas Browne*, p. 222; William Vickers, *An Easie and Safe Method for Curing the King's Evil* (5th edn, London, 1711), p. 5.

110 Harold Weber, *Paper Bullets: Print and Kingship under Charles II* (Kentucky, 1996); Bloch, *The Royal Touch*.

111 *The Present State of Great Britain*, p. 49; Sainty and Bucholz, *Officials of the Royal Household*, pp. 48–9, 56–7.

112 TNA, LC5/141, p. 33; LC5/140, pp. 493–4; SP29/379, no. 1.

113 As the Lord Chamberlain put it in a memorandum to the sergeant surgeon, Richard Pyle, in February 1682, no one was to be allowed admission 'but those person themselves that you shall examine and find they have the disease of the Evill or bring a Certificate that they have been viewed and examined by one of his Ma^{ts} Physitians in ordinary to His person or Houshold': TNA, LC5/144, p. 195; LC5/140, pp. 493–4. So it was, in April 1675, that Dr William Denton, one of the physicians in ordinary to the royal household, wrote to his kinsman Ralph Verney that he had put several people forward for the touch, one of whom 'returned and gave me most wonderful thanks, and would have given me a quart of sack' (*HMC Verney*, p. 492).

114 Browne, *Adenochoiradelogia*, III, p. 84. Helen Farquhar suggested that the base-metal coin or token known as the 'Soli Deo Gloria Halfpenny', which bears a ship on one side and a George and dragon on the other, was one of the specially made admission tickets to Restoration healings (Farquhar, 'Royal charities: Part II', p. 123).

115 *CSPD*, 1661–2, p. 428; *Mercurius Publicus*, 28 June–5 July 1660, pp. 430–1; *The Parliamentary Intelligencer*, 28, 27 June 1660.

116 TNA, LC5/140, pp. 493–4 (7); SP12/379 no. 1 (7).

117 TNA, SP29/57, no. 16; LC5/140, pp. 493–4 (5); SP29/379 no. 1 (5).

118 *Mercurius Publicus*, 28 June–5 July 1660, pp. 430–1; *The Parliamentary Intelligencer*, 28, 27 June 1660. In reality, according to John Browne, writing towards the end of the reign, 'as the case is now, it is harder to approach the Chirurgeon, than obtain a Touch' (Browne, *Adenochoiradelogia*, III, p. 89).

119 Evelyn, *Diary*, IV, p. 374.

120   The Lord Chamberlain ordered Richard Pyle 'not to deliver any Ticketts whatsoever but unto persons themselves': TNA, LC5/144, p. 195; SP29/57, no. 16.

121   *Mercurius Publicus*, 28 June–5 July 1660, p. 431.

122   Stephens's help in securing a ticket for a healing was also enlisted by a gunsmith from Winchester: Browne, *Adenochoiradelogia*, III, pp. 172, 174; Bod. Lib., Rawl. MS A 194, fols 247v–8r.

123   *CSPD*, 1668–9, p. 239; TNA, SP29/152, no. 10. When one ailing visitor to Charles II's exiled court was refused a ticket to the touching on the basis that he was suffering not from scrofula but smallpox, his friend – one of the officers of the chapel royal – spoke to the Clerk of the Closet and persuaded him to arrange for the unfortunate visitor be touched, Browne (*Adenochoiradelogia*, III, pp. 156–7, 171, 172). Samuel Pepys wrote to the royal surgeon, James Pearce, in pursuit of 'a touch' for his friends on more than one occasion in the early 1680s: Bod. Lib., Rawl. MS 194, fols 247v–248r.

124   TNA, LC5/140, pp. 493–4 (8).

125   Bloch, *The Royal Touch*, pp. 184–5; Wicquefort, *A Relation in form of Journal*, p. 74; Browne, *Adenochoiradelogia*, III, pp. 95, 106; *The Loyal Protestant*, 142, 14 April 1682; Magalotti, *Travels*, p. 214.

126   *The Kingdom's Intelligencer*, 28, 14 July 1662; TNA, SP45/11, p. 123; BL, Egerton MS 806, fols 59r–60r; Fielding H. Garrison, 'A relic of the King's Evil in the Surgeon General's Library (Washington DC), *Proceedings of the Royal Society of Medicine*, 7, 1914, pp. 227–34.

127   A slightly more realistic note of healing times is in the Lord Chamberlain's orders for the surgeons, which puts the autumn season as starting on 1 September and running to the end of November, and the spring season as starting on Ash Wednesday and finishing at the end of May. Notices were frequently issued in April or May declaring that there would be no more touching until the autumn. For declarations of the cessation of public healing during the summer in 1660, 1661, 1664, 1665, 1670, 1676, 1679, 1682 and 1683 see *The Parliamentary Intelligencer*, 28; *The Kingdom's Intelligencer*, 18; *The Newes*, 38; *The Intelligencer*, 32; *London Gazette*, 461, 1091, 1403, 1723, 1828; Browne, *Adenochoiradelogia*, III, Appendix.

128   As was acknowledged by the Lord Chamberlain's note that any changes to the times 'by His Ma^ts Especiall Comand' would be publicized; the timings of the healings were actually decided by the sovereign, who touched as 'frequently as He pleaseth', though the Lord Chamberlain might 'move His Matie for Healing': Browne, *Adenochoiradelogia*, III, p. 83; TNA, LC5/141, p. 33.

129   *CSPD*, 1668–9, p. 285.

130   *HMC Verney*, 1675; p. 493.

131   *CSPD*, December 1671–May 1672, p. 58; Browne, *Adenochoiradelogia*, III, p. 31; *HMC Verney*, p. 493.

132   *Mercurius Publicus*, 28 June–5 July 1660, p. 431.

133   The Clerk of the Closet's figures for healings do not distinguish between private and public occasions (see Appendix 2). However, the numbers themselves make it pretty clear whether they were private or public. BL, Egerton MS 806, fol. 59r; Browne, *Adenochoiradelogia*, III, pp. 177–8; Garrison, 'A relic of the King's Evil', pp. 229–30; *True Protestant Mercury*, 88, 6 November 1681; *HMC Verney*, p. 494. See, e.g., BL, Egerton MS 806, fol. 59r, which shows that a lone person was touched on the 6th and another on the 14th of September 1668.

134   *CSPD*, 1671–2, p. 58; 1675–6, p. 411; *HMC Verney*, p. 493; Browne, *Adenochoiradelogia*, III, pp. 170, 172, 174, 176.

135   *CSPD*, 1668–9, p. 239; Browne, *Adenochoiradelogia*, III, pp. 165, 166–7, 168, 179; *The Diary of Thomas Isham of Lamport (1658–81)*, Norman Marlow and Sir Gyles Isham (eds) (Farnborough, 1971), p. 167.

136   Browne, *Adenochoiradelogia*, III, pp. 84, 103–4.

137   Pepys, *Diary*, I, p. 182.; Bloch, *The Royal Touch*, p. 188; Wicquefort, *A Relation in form of Journal*, pp. 74–5; *The Life and Times of Anthony Wood, Antiquary, of Oxford, 1632–1695, Described by Himself*, Andrew Clark (ed.), 5 vols (Oxford, 1891–1900), I, p. 496.

138   TNA, LC5/200, unfoliated.

139   Browne, *Adenochoiradelogia*, III, p. 96.

140   The chair was that which normally stood on the dais beneath the canopy of state if within one of the royal palaces, or one specially placed in the choir if being performed in a church. The best accounts of procedure at Charles II's healing are the following sources, from which this account is largely taken (other sources are mentioned in the following notes where relevant): Evelyn, *Diary*, III, pp. 250–1; Schellinks, *Journal*, p. 73; Magalotti, *Travels*, pp. 214–16; Browne, *Adenochoiradelogia*, III, pp. 95–101; Wicquefort, *A Relation in form of Journal*, pp. 74–8.

141   George MacDonald Ross, 'The royal rouch and the Book of Common Prayer', *Notes and Queries*, October, 1983, pp. 433–5.

142   *CSPD*, 1661–2, p. 428; TNA, SP29/57, no. 16.

143   Browne, *Adenochoiradelogia*, III, pp. 165–6, 168.

144   TNA, LC4/140, p. 493.

145   From Mark 16.14. W. Sparrow Simpson, 'On the forms of prayer recited "at the healing" or touching for the King's Evil', *Journal of the British Archaeological Association*, XXVII, 1871, pp. 282–307; Hamon L'Estrange, *Alliance of Divine Offices, exhibiting all the Liturgies of the Church of England since the Reformation, as also the late Scotch Service-Book, with all their respective variations, and upon them all Annotations vindicating the Book of Common Prayer from the objections of its adversaries, etc* (Oxford, 1846), pp. 559–61.

146   *Anglia Notitia* (1671), pp. 107–8.

147   *The Kingdom's Intelligencer*, 13, 27 March 1662; 'I held yᵉ bason after at healing', BL, Add. MS 40,860, fols 15v, 34v; LC5/200, unfoliated.

148   Browne, *Adenochoiradelogia*, III, p. 96; TNA, LC5/141, p. 33.

149   TNA, LC5/2, p. 55; *Letters Addressed from London to Sir Joseph Williamson*, II, pp. 103–4.

150   Magalotti, *Travels*, pp. 214–16.

151   *The Loyal Protestant*, 111, 29 January 1681/2.

152   Pepys attended again in 1667 with Sir George Carteret, while William Schellinks watched three healings in the course of his visit in 1662: two at Whitehall and another at Hampton Court, Pepys, *Diary*, I, p. 182; VIII, p. 161; Schellinks, *Journal*, pp. 73, 91, 177.

153   TNA, LC4/140, p. 493; Browne, *Adenochoiradelogia*, III, pp. 94, 177–8.

154   *HMC Verney*, p. 488.

155   TNA, SP29/152, no. 10.

156   Wiseman, *Severall Chirurgical Treastises*, p. 247.

157   E. A. Wrigley and R. Schofield, *The Population History of England 1541–1871: A Reconstruction* (London, 1981). That is not to say Charles touched 2 per cent of all his subjects; the numbers of those touched represent a total for an almost 25-year period. I am grateful to Dan Wolfe for his advice on this point.

158   *Loyal Protestant*, 111, 29 January 1681/2.

Notes to Chapter 7: Reform and retrenchment

1   Pepys, *Diary*, III, p. 82; TNA, LC5/40, p. 89; LC5/41, fols 12v–13r, 74r; LC5/67, fol. 27r; LC5/63, pp. 97–101; LC5/119, 22 October 1669; Hartmann, *Charles II*, p. 68; TNA, LC5/39, p. 242; Evelyn, *Diary*, III, pp. 347–8; BL, Harley MS 4180.

2   Charles II to Henriette Anne, 10 December 1663, Hartmann, *Charles II*, p. 89.

3   '... most of the gallantry for apparel [for the coronation] will be from France, which the city resents ill', The Manuscripts of his Grace the Duke of Devonshire at Hardwicke Hall, Co. Derby, *Historical Manuscripts Commission. Third Report* (London, 1872), p. 90; Evelyn, *Diary*, III, pp. 464–5; E. S. de Beer, 'King Charles II's own fashion: an episode in Anglo-French relations 1666–1670', *Journal of the Warburg Institute*, II (1938–9), pp. 105–15; Aileen Ribeiro, *Fashion and Fiction: Dress in Art and Literature in Stuart England* (London and New Haven, 2005), pp. 230–9. See, for example, the newsletter of 14 March 1677/8: 'The Council is considering how to discourage the wearing of French stuffs and druggets to the neglect of English. The King and Court will set an example ...' (Fleming Papers, *HMC 12th Report, VII*, p. 143).

4   For Monmouth's election to the Order of the Garter on 28 March 1663 see BL, Add. MS 37,998, fols 132r–v, 146r.

5   Pepys, *Diary*, VI, p. 191.

6   See Hutton, *The Restoration*, pp. 185ff.

7   Pepys, *Diary*, III, p. 71.

8   TNA, LC5/137, p. 297.

9   *CSPVen*, 1661–4, pp. 143, 146, 150; Schellinks, *Journal*, pp. 85–6; *The Journal of Edward Montagu, First Earl of Sandwich*, pp. 138–9.

10 Bryant, *Letters*, p. 126; *The Memoirs of Ann Lady Fanshawe*, pp. 98–9; Pepys, *Diary*, III, p. 71; Evelyn, *Diary*, III, p. 320; *The Diaries of Anne Clifford*, p. 157; *The Journal of Edward Montagu, First Earl of Sandwich*, pp. 139–40; Clarke, *Life of James the Second*, I, p. 394.

11 Hartmann, *The King My Brother*, p. 39; *The Letters, Speeches and Declarations of King Charles II*, pp. 126–7; *The Journal of Edward Montagu, First Earl of Sandwich*, p. 140.

12 Schellinks, *Journal*, p. 90.

13 Pepys, *Diary*, III, pp. 97, 100; Evelyn, *Diary*, III, pp. 320–1; Hartmann, *Charles II*, p. 43; *The Letters, Speeches and Declarations of King Charles II*, pp. 126–8; *CSPD*, 1661–2, p. 396.

14 S. M. Wynne, 'Catherine (1638–1705)', *Oxford Dictionary of National Biography*, 2004; Edward Corp, 'Catherine of Braganza and cultural politics', in Clarissa Campbell Orr (ed.), *Queenship in Britain 1660–1837: Royal Patronage, Court Culture and Dynastic Politics* (Manchester, 2002), pp. 53–74; BL, Add. MS 36,916, fols 95r, 96r; Lillias Campbell Davidson, *Catherine of Bragança, Infanta of Portugal & Queen-Consort of England* (London, 1908); Pepys, *Diary*, pp. 348, 352; Hamilton, *Memoirs of the Count de Grammont*, pp. 122–4, 168–9.

15 Evelyn, *Diary*, III, p. 333; Pepys, *Diary*, III, p. 175.

16 Pepys, *Diary*, III, pp. 190–1.

17 Pepys, *Diary*, III, p. 299; IV, pp. 48–9; Magalotti, *Travels*, p. 372; *Correspondence of the Family of Hatton*, I, p. 240.

18 Colvin, *King's Works*, V, pp. 255–6. It was in the presence chamber at Greenwich that Henrietta Maria first received her daughter-in-law, Queen Catherine, in July 1662, 'Historia Genealogica, Casa Real, Portuguesa' quoted in Strickland, *Lives of the Queens of England*, pp. 325–6. De la Serre, *Histoire de l'entree de la Reyne Mere*, unpaginated.

19 *Journal des Voyages de Monsieur de Monconys*, II, pp. 19–20, Monconys stayed in the

presence chamber for some time, though he found the tapestries only 'passablement belle' and the firedogs ugly and badly polished.

20 Pepys, *Diary*, III, p. 299; IV, p. 230. In January 1663/4 the grooms of the queen's privy chamber complained that the usual allowance of coal was 'to[o] Little to mentayne the two fyres in the presence & wth drawing Chamber', especially as 'her Matie is a great parte of ye Evening in the wthdrawing Chamber' (TNA, LS13/170, fol. 145r). Catherine later abolished the position of Lady of the Bedchamber, though she retained the post of Mistress of the Robes; see Edward Corp, 'Catherine of Braganza and cultural politics', pp. 57–8.

21 See, e.g., Pepys, *Diary*, VII, pp. 159, 297–8; IX, pp. 290–3; 322–3; Evelyn, *Diary*, III, p. 568; *CSPD*, 1673–5, p. 43; Hamilton, *Memoirs of the Count de Grammont*, p. 141.

22 TNA, PRO31/3/113, fol. 53r; Evelyn, *Diary*, III, p. 334.

23 *HMC Fleming*, p. 47; Pepys, *Diary*, VIII, p. 590; IX, pp. 11, 276, 294–5, 320, 382, 418; Ailesbury, *Memoirs*, I, pp. 83, 93; Magalotti, *Travels*, pp. 177–9ff., esp. pp. 177–9; *The First Triple Alliance*, p. 35.

24 Pepys, *Diary*, IX, p. 322.

25 TNA, LC5/62, pp. 25, 29; LC5/144, p. 115; LS13/170, fols 145r, 151r.

26 Special glass hoods for the candles were made to prevent the flames damaging the ceiling of the queen's withdrawing room at Windsor. As at Whitehall, the room was not furnished with a canopy of state, but provided with two armchairs and ten stools: Croft Murray, *Decorative Painting in England*, p. 240; TNA, LC5/143, pp. 50–1, 121. The king's withdrawing room was never the location for the evening 'circles': that room was used exclusively by men (like the whole of the king's apartments) both as a waiting room to the privy lodgings beyond and, on occasions, for meetings and audiences between the king and his visitors; this had also been the case under Charles I, who held numerous 'private' audiences in his withdrawing room at Whitehall (Finet, *Finetti Philoxenis, passim*).

27 Magalotti, *Travels*, p. 178; Evelyn, *Diary*, III, p. 568. Magalotti describes the queen's evening assemblies as taking place in a room adjoining the queen's bedchamber, with sky blue upholstered furniture and lit with a chandelier, all of which accords with the withdrawing room, which was provided with sky blue furnishings the previous year. Both the room and event that he is describing would be known in England as the withdrawing room and that the word 'closet' is a mistake by either Magalotti or his translator; Magalotti, *Travels*, pp. 177–8. I very am grateful to Dr Rod Clayton for his confirmation of this interpretation and his advice on Magalotti's use of the word 'gabinetto'. On the very rare occasions when the queen was pregnant, as in 1669, she received on a sofa rather than a chair of state for reasons of comfort, but the principle remained that she was seated while those who attended stood (Magalotti, *Travels*, pp. 314–16).

28 TNA, LC5/2, p. 51; Magalotti, *Travels*, p. 178; *CSPD*, 1673–5, p. 43.

29 TNA, LC5/2, p. 51; BL, Stowe MS 203, fol. 209r.

30 *The First Triple Alliance*, p. 35; one visitor describes 120 people attending the occasion in the late 1660s, W. E. Knowles Middleton, 'Marchese Francesco Riccardi and Alessandro Segni in England 1668–69 (Segni's Diary', *Studi Secenteschi*, 21 (1980), pp. 187–279; p. 213). I am grateful to Dr Rod Clayton for bringing this source to my attention and for his translation of this section.

31 It was towards the end of the evening in May 1669, as Cosimo III was bowing to the queen, that 'the king and duke made their appearance', while in June 1666 gossip and card-playing were well underway in the queen's withdrawing room when 'the King then coming in' overheard his mistress tell his wife of his inconstancy to them both: Magalotti, *Travels*, pp. 290, 372; *HMC Ormonde*, IV, p. 312.

32 Pepys, *Diary*, VII, pp. 49, 159; *HMC Fleming*, p. 47; *Memoirs of Lady Warwick also her Diary, from 1666 to 1672, now First Published: to which are added, Extracts from her Other Writings*, Anthony Walker (ed.) (London, 1847), pp. 116–17; John Evelyn, *The Life of Mrs Godololphin* (Oxford, 1939), pp. 28–34, 50.

33 Pepys, *Diary*, VIII, p. 71; IX, p. 493; *CSPD*, 1673–5, p. 43.

34 TNA, PRO31/3/137, fols 4r, 27r; Magalotti, *Travels*, p. 178; *Memoirs of Lady Warwick*, p. 132; *Journal des Voyages de Monsieur de Monconys*, II, pp. 19–20.

35 Written regulations for the circle from before the civil war confirm that the gentlemen ushers had permission to admit more-or-less anyone who looked reasonably respectable and was appropriately dressed (TNA, LC5/201, p. 494).

36 Pepys, *Diary*, IV, p. 230; VII, pp. 159, 297–8; VIII, p. 71; Evelyn, *Diary*, III, pp. 334, 361; IV, p. 89.

37 Pepys, *Diary*, IV, p. 230; *Memoirs of Lady Warwick*, p. 132; *The Secret History of Francelia*, pp. 48–9; Magalotti, *Travels*, pp. 290–1. The frenzy over clothes worn on the queen's birthday was simply an exaggerated version of the great interest in clothes worn at the daily drawing rooms, cf., e.g., *HMC Rutland*, II, p. 21.

38 Pepys, *Diary*, VIII, p. 464; IX, p. 382; *HMC Rutland*, II, p. 37; Hamilton, *Memoirs of the Count de Grammont*, p. 141.

39 Magalotti, *Travels*, p. 192; Pepys, *Diary*, IX, p. 320.

40 Here Pepys asked Lord Peterborough and Lord Sandwich to dine with him, while it was in the queen's withdrawing room that courtiers and diplomats were able to present their compliments to the Grand Duke of Tuscany: Pepys, *Diary*, IX, p. 419; Magalotti, *Travels*, p. 290.

41 Magalotti, *Travels*, p. 178.

42 The king 'me mena dans l'embrasure d'une fenêtre, et me dit qu'il avid sceu de M. le Duc d'York que j'avais pris quelque allarme du voyage que M le Prince d'Orange devoit faire en Angleterre mais qu'il n'en arriverait aucun mal ...' (TNA, PRO31/3/137, fol. 27r).

43 TNA, PRO31/3/137, fols 4r–5r. It was again, in 'the withdrawing room, wher the Queen was at cards' that Sir John Reresby saw the king who 'tould me in my ear that he expected some further account from the king of Denmarke before he intended to send to that Prince; but whenever he sent he had pitched upon me for that service' (Reresby, *Memoirs*, p. 242).

44 Pepys, *Diary*, IX, pp. 294–5, 445. See also *The Correspondence of the Earl of Essex*, pp. 23–4 for politicians taking political discussions 'into [the] Queen her very drawing room'.

45 Magalotti, *Travels*, p. 195.

46 *HMC Ormonde*, IV, p. 53; *Correspondence of the Family of Hatton*, I, pp. 191–2.

47 TNA, LC5/2, p. 51.

48 Ailesbury, *Memoirs*, I, pp. 82–3; *HMC 7th Report*, Manuscripts of Sir Frederick Graham of Netherby Hall, p. 375.

49 TNA, LC5/2, p. 51; BL, Stowe MS 203, fol. 209r.

50 Evelyn, *Diary*, III, p. 463.

51 Pepys, *Diary*, V, p. 40; IX, pp. 557–8.

52 Glasgow University Library, Hunter MS 238, fol. 100, 'In the Kings Greate Bed Chamber ... The Dutchess of Portsmouth at length'. This inventory is from the reign of James II, but I believe much of it records Charles II's picture arrangement. This is suggested for several reasons. First it contains discrete lists of pictures that were *not* part of Charles II's collection; second much of it dates to before the rebuilding of the privy gallery at Whitehall, so a time before many changes were made at Whitehall, and third – perhaps most convincingly – the subject matters preferred by James and Charles are very different. James's bedchambers

were hung with devotional pictures, and it is more-or-less unthinkable he would have had a painting of Charles II's principal mistress, and mother to potential challengers to the throne, in his bedchamber.

53 Miller, *Charles II*, p. 207; Hutton, *Charles II*, pp. 279–80; Nancy Klein Maguire, 'The duchess of Portsmouth: English royal consort and French politician, 1670–85', in Smuts (ed.), *The Stuart Court and Europe*, pp. 247–73.

54 In the 18 months that followed, Reresby found himself 'waiting upon the King at the Duchess of Portsmouth's' at the end of the stone gallery at Whitehall on several occasions (Reresby, *Memoirs*, pp. 115, 133, 135).

55 In the spring months of 1678 the king and the French and Dutch ambassadors were to be found 'ofton very merry and intimate at the Duchesse of Portsmouth's lodgeings', while on 3 August 1679 Barillon wrote to Louis XIV that the king had given him 'a long audience in Lady Portsmouth's apartment at Windsor', Sir John Dalrymple, *Memoirs of Great Britain and Ireland from the Dissolution of the last Parliament of Charles II till the Capture of the French and Spanish Fleets at Vigo*, 3 vols (London, 1790), I, p. 316; Reresby, *Memoirs*, pp. 141, 149.

56 *CSPD*, 1682, p. 43. The king was to some extent exercising control over who attended him there; when the Earl of Halifax was reconciled to the Duchess of Portsmouth in 1681, it was indicated by the fact that he would 'visit her and attend ye king in her lodgings wch formerly he never would, and this too, they say, by ye King's possitive demand' (*The Correspondence of the Family of Hatton*, II, p. 11).

57 Although it is not clear from the evidence, it seems likely that the formal part of the occasion happened first, and the card-playing thereafter: Reresby, *Memoirs*, p. 248; Pepys, *Diary*, VII, p. 49, VIII, p. 71; TNA, LC5/201, p. 494; *Diary of the Times of Charles the Second by Henry Sidney*, II, pp. 141–2; Ailesbury, *Memoirs*, I, p. 82.

58 Magalotti, *Travels*, p. 178.

59 BL, Add. MS 36,916, fol. 103r.

60 Hutton, *The Restoration*, pp. 225–6; Pepys, *Diary*, VI, pp. 141–2.

61 Pepys, *Diary*, VII, p. 269; Adrian Tinniswood, *By Permission of Heaven: The True Story of the Great Fire of London* (New York, 2004), pp. 53ff.

62 Burnet, *History of My Own Time*, II, p. 471; N. A. M. Rodger, *The Command of the Ocean: A Naval History of Britain, 1649–1815* (London, 2004), pp. 76–7; Hutton, *Restoration*, pp. 269–70.

63 Hutton, *Charles II*, p. 155.

64 This account of the reduction of the bouche of court is based largely on Andrew Barclay's important article 'Charles II's failed restoration: administrative reform belowstairs 1660–4', in Cruickshanks (ed.), *The Stuart Courts*, pp. 158–70. See also Evelyn, *Diary*, III, pp. 261, 352; Clarendon, *The Life of Edward, Earl of Clarendon*, I, p. 367; *Elias Ashmole*, p. 785; *The Court and Times of Charles the First … Including the Memoirs of the Mission in England of the Capuchin Friars in the service of Henrietta Maria by Father Cyprien de Gamache* 2 vols (London, 1848), II, pp. 416–17.

65 *Angliae Notitia*, 1669, pp. 298–9.

66 By 13 October 1663 it could be stated categorically that 'The tables at Court are now absolutely gone': *CSPD*, 1663–4, p. 264; *HMC Ormonde*, III, p. 91; *HMC 3rd Report*, The Manuscripts of his Grace the Duke of Devonshire, p. 92.

67 *The Diurnal of Thomas Rugg*, p. 122; Clarendon, *The Life of Edward, Earl of Clarendon*, I, p. 367. A further wave of cuts to household dining, though again sparing the king, queen and maids of honours' tables, came in 1679; this saw Prince Rupert's meals converted

to board wages, the end of the Waiters' table and the cessation of the provision of meals to privy councillors when they met at Hampton Court: TNA, LS1/21 Lord Steward's Accounts, 1678–9, unfoliated, 30 January 1679.

68   *CSPVen*, X, 1603–7, p. 46; *The Letters of John Chamberlain*, E. McClure (ed.), 2 vols (Philadelphia, 1939), I, pp. 250–1; David Stephenson, 'The English devil of keeping state', pp. 126–44.

69   *Historical Manuscripts Commission. Report on the Manuscripts of the Earl of Denbigh preserved at Newnham Paddox, Warwickshire. Part V 1622–1787* (London, 1911) (hereafter: *HMC Denbigh*, V), p. 18; *CSPD*, 1631–3, p. 207; Smuts, 'George Wentworth goes to court, March 1634', *The Court Historian*, 6, 3 (December, 2001), pp. 213–25; BL, Stowe MS 561, fols 4v–5r, 6r, 8v, 9v: references to 'King Hen: 8: tyme' *passim*. See also Cuddy, 'Reinventing a monarchy', pp. 68–9; Sharpe, *The Personal Rule of Charles I*, pp. 216–18. For the service of a meal to an absent sovereign in the presence chamber at Greenwich in the late 1590s, see Paul Hentzner, *Travels in England during the Reign of Queen Elizabeth with Fragmenta Regalia; Or, Observations on Queen Elizabeth's Times and Favourites* (London, 1899), pp. 49–51.

70   *The Parliamentary Intelligencer*, 23, May 1660; *Elias Ashmole*, III, p. 810.

71   Schellinks, *Journal*, pp. 60–1; *Journal des Voyages de Monconys*, II, pp. 23–4, 28, 45; the same arrangement applied when the king ate with his mother (Hartmann, *Charles II*, p. 102); see also *London Gazette*, 573, 21 June 1671.

72   Pepys, *Diary*, III, p. 202; in 1663 Balthazar de Monconys went to Whitehall 'd'où le Roy sortoit pour aller disner avec les Reynes': *Journal des Voyages de Monsieur de Monconys*, II, p. 28; *CSPD*, January–November 1671, p. 317.

73   Magalotti, *Travels*, p. 364.

74   Evelyn, *Diary*, III, pp. 479–80; *Memoirs of Lady Warwick*, pp. 109–10; *Elias Ashmole*, III, pp. 1085–91.

75   Unfortunately, the decorative iconography of Charles II's presence chambers is largely lost to us. The Banqueting House at Whitehall bore, as it has done since they were installed for Charles I, Peter Paul Rubens's great 'Triumph of Peace' canvases celebrating the union of the crowns and the Solomonic virtues of James I. The only one of the king's presence chambers for which detailed information concerning the decorative painting survives is that built in the 1670s at Windsor Castle. There Antonio Verrio's ceiling painting (obliterated in the nineteenth century) depicted Mercury, as messenger of the gods, showing a portrait of Charles II 'with transport, as it were' to the four corners of the Earth: W. H. St John Hope, *Windsor Castle: An Architectural History*, 2 vols (London, 1913), I, p. 339; Croft Murray, *Decorative Painting in England*, p. 240.

76   TNA, LC5/62, fols 73r–74v; LC5/66, fols 52r–v; '… their royal highnesses came to dine in publick seated under a State': LC5/2, p. 50; LC5/41, fol. 92r, 102r, 106v; LC5/210, p. 451; St John Hope, *Windsor Castle*, I, p. 339; 'ils disnent dans une grande sale sous un dais de broderie' (*Journal des Voyages de Monsieur de Monconys*), II, p. 24; 'when Wee are to dine no man shall presume to tread upon the Carpet or Half Pace …' (BL, Stowe MS 562, fol. 5v).

77   TNA, LC5/201, p. 373; Stephen B. Baxter, *William III* (London, 1966), pp. 54–7.

78   Magalotti, *Travels*, p. 364. The use of a dining table rail was not confined to meals in the Banqueting House – there were rails in both the king's and queen's presence chambers at Hampton Court in the early 1660s and by the 1670s the rail about the royal dining table in the presence chamber was a standard feature of that room. TNA, LC5/39, p. 308; LC5/60, p. 314; BL, Stowe MS 562, fol. 5v: 'Presence Chamber'. It was behind the rail in the

presence chamber at Portsmouth that Charles II and Catherine of Braganza were married (*The Memoirs of Ann Lady Fanshawe*, pp. 98–9). Katharine Gibson, 'The decoration of St George's Hall, Windsor, for Charles II: "Too resplendent bright for subjects' eyes"', *Apollo*, May 1998, pp. 30–40, p. 36; see also *Historical Manuscripts Commission. Fifth Report, Part One* (London, 1876), 'Manuscripts of His Grace the Duke of Sutherland at Trentham, Co. Stafford' (hereafter *HMC Sutherland*), p. 154. For the crush in the room when the royal family dined, see *The Court and Times of Charles the First*, II, p. 420.

79 TNA, WORK5/23, fol. 68r; LC5/201, pp. 451–2, 'A Breviate taken of the Blacks in the King and Queenes Lodgeings att Whitehall the 22ᵈ of August 1670'.

80 TNA, LC5/62, fols 73r–74v; LC5/64, fol. 145r; LC5/201, p. 65; LC5/141, p. 304.

81 *The Diary and Correspondence of Dr. John Worthington*, James Crossley (ed.), Chetham Society, XIII, 1847, p. 195; Ailesbury, *Memoirs*, I, p. 57; *Burnet's History of My Own Time*, II, p. 247. BL, Stowe MS 561, fol. 5r; Evelyn, *Diary*, III, pp. 290–1; Schellinks, *Journal*, p. 90; Magalotti, *Travels*, p. 364; Pepys, *Diary*, VIII, p. 404. See also Peter Holman, *Four and Twenty Fiddlers: The Violin at the English Court 1540–1690* (Oxford, 1993), pp. 306–7. Charles I had enjoyed wind instruments being played both when he dined and in the chapel royal; see, e.g., the list of the musicians 'for yᵉ winde Instruments for wayting in the Chappell and at his Maᵗˢ Table', which includes Andrea and William Lanier, Henry and Alfonso 'Frabosco' (TNA, LC5/134, p. 221).

82 BL, Stowe MS 562, fol. 5v.

83 BL, Stowe MS 562, fol. 5r; *Angliae Notitia*, 1669, pp. 267–70; TNA, LC5/201, pp. 259–60; unfortunately the order is undated, and it is just possible it is an early seventeenth-century precedent; however, the fact that it was written out in the Lord Chamberlain's notes in the second half of the century strongly suggests it was still relevant and that this type of formal dining was still taking place.

84 Beattie, *The English Court*, p. 35.

85 TNA, LS13/170, fol. 28r; Pepys, *Diary*, II, p. 84; *Angliae Notitia*, 1669, p. 109.

86 Pepys, *Diary*, VIII, p. 428.

87 'Memoirs of Nathaniel, Lord Crewe', Andrew Clark (ed.), *The Camden Miscellany*, X (London, 1895), p. 20; *The Court and Times of Charles the First*, II, p. 420.

88 *HMC Fleming*, p. 78; for this ritual in the sixteenth century see Strong, *Feast*, pp. 204–9.

89 Schellinks, *Journal*, p. 91. BL, Stowe MS 562, fol. 4v; cf. TNA, LC5/180, fol. 9r (Charles I's household orders, which do not include the injunction to perform the usual ceremony to the state).

90 *HMC Fleming*, p. 52; Evelyn, *Diary*, III, p. 434; *CSPD*, 1667, p. 388. John Adamson's claim that, while Henry VIII and Charles I sometimes dined in state as frequently as once a week, this gave way 'to much less frequent observance under the later Stuarts' does not hold true for the court of Charles II (Adamson, *The Princely Courts*, p. 104). *The Parliamentary Intelligencer*, 23, May 1660; Evelyn, *Diary*, III, p. 513; TNA, LC5/2, pp. 50, 144; *Elias Ashmole*, III, p. 810; *HMC Verney*, p. 474. Schellinks, *Journal*, pp. 60–1, 72, 91, 177; Pepys, *Diary*, II, p. 60; viii, p. 161; *True Domestic Intelligencer*, 51, December 1678.

91 *Diary of the Times of Charles the Second by Henry Sidney*, II, pp. 64–5; Ailesbury, *Memoirs*, I, p. 85.

92 *The Works of George Savile, Marquis of Halifax*, III, p. 492; Schellinks, *Journal*, p. 61. The king never normally dined formally with his mistresses or illegitimate children, though he did so as an exception on the occasion of the marriage of his daughter, Anne Fitzroy, in 1674 (G. S. Steinman, *Addenda to a Memoir of Barbara, Duchess of Cleveland including Corrections* (London, 1874), pp. 6–7).

93   *HMC Fleming*, p. 64; TNA, LC5/2, p. 50. *Letters Addressed from London to Sir Joseph Williamson*, I, p. 86.

94   See, for example, the endless discussion about the seating arrangements during the visit of the Duchess of Modena in 1673: TNA, LC25/2, pp. 47, 50, 54; SP29/256/92, fol. 114v.

95   So, for example, in 1663 a French visitor to court recorded the immediate members of the royal family at dinner, with the Duke of York, heir to the throne, in pole position: 'Nous vismes disner le Roy avec la Rayne proche l'un de l'autre assis au costé de la table, & le Duc d'York assis au bout de la table', while in 1673 the seating was designed to honour the new Duchess of York so: 'The Duke and Duchess of York; at the end of the table, on the right hand; the Duchess next the King & the Duchess of Modena, at the other end, on the left hand of the Queen' (TNA, LC5/2, pp. 54, 143). The French Master of the Ceremonies, who was present, considered this seating arrangement to be incorrect, being 'of the opinion, that it had been better if the Duke of York had been alone, at the end, on the right hand' (*HMC Sutherland*, p. 154); 'le Roy, lequel estoit couvert' (*Journal des Voyages de Monsieur de Monconys*, II, p. 45).

96   'Persons shall be permitted into Our Presence Chamber at the Discretion of the Gentleman Usher daily Wayter, or in his absence the Gentleman Usher Quarter Wayter', BL, Stowe MS 562, fols 3r, 5r.

97   Pepys, *Diary*, III, pp. 60, 202; in 1663 M de Monconys remarked on the ease with which people were given access to the dinner of the king and queen, here 'tout le monde entre & les voit avec liberté, car toutes les portes sont tousjours ouvertes pour tout le monde, & les personnes de quelque condition qu'ils soient, entrent dans les chambres d'audience' (*Journal des Voyages de Monsieur de Monconys*, II, pp. 23–4).

98   Schellinks, *Journal*, p. 90.

99   Magalotti, *Travels*, p. 378.

100   Pepys, *Diary*, II, pp. 85–6.

101   TNA, LC5/180, fol. 10v, cf. BL, Stowe MS 562, fol. 5v.

102   BL, Stowe MS 562, fol. 5v.

103   Reresby, *Memoirs*, p. 135; Evelyn, *Diary*, III, p. 513; Pepys, *Diary*, I, p. 299.

104   See, e.g., Strong, *Feast, passim*; Adamson, *Princely Courts*, pp. 30, 46, 241, 269, 280.

105   *The Diurnal of Thomas Rugg*, p. 122. At the beginning of Charles II's reign, in the anarchic period between Christmas and Epiphany, Lincoln's Inn appointed a student to be a 'prince' until twelfth night. In order to define his status as such, the 'prince' made appointments, had an expensively dressed retinue and sent an ambassador to Whitehall to request the loan of two maces. Significantly, too, he 'entertain[ed] the King with many important persons and his entire college at a royal banquet'. This little oddity of an event touches on two important aspects of dining and kingship: first, further indicating that dining grandly was a defining characteristic of kingship, and, second, that to dine in the company of another was to recognize and reinforce relative parity of status. For the 'prince' to invite the king to dine, and for the king to accept immediately demonstrated that they endorsed one another's royal-ness, Schellinks, *Journal*, pp. 70–1.

106   The only people with whom he ever sat down at a state dinner were other members of his own immediate family or members of other royal families (though not even all of those were acceptable), or on rare occasions with the most prestigious ambassadors as proxies for their royal masters – such as in 1661 when the marriage with Catherine of Braganza was being agreed (Evelyn, *Diary*, III, pp. 290–1). This had also been the case when James I was contracting the Spanish match for his son.

107 *HMC Fleming*, p. 83; TNA, LC5/141, pp. 20, 468; *CSPD*, 1672–3, p. 628; *Diary of the Times of Charles the Second by Henry Sidney*, I, pp. 301–3; *HMC Verney*, p. 497; *HMC Ormonde*, VI, pp. 210–12; Reresby, *Memoirs*, p. 236. TNA, LC5/201, pp. 263–4, 373; *Correspondence of the Family of Hatton*, II, p. 4. Only after long discussion and the king's own intervention was the Lord Mayor persuaded to yield precedence to the Prince of Orange when he came to dine at the Guildhall (TNA, LC5/2, pp. 29–31).

108 *Elias Ashmole*, III, p. 810; *Kingdomes Intelligencer*, 1, 1 January 1660/1.

109 *Correspondence of the Family of Hatton*, I, p. 224; *Diary of the Times of Charles the Second by Henry Sidney*, I, pp. 301–3.

110 Clarendon, *The Life of Edward, Earl of Clarendon*, I, p. 367.

111 TNA, LC5/2, p. 54; *Letters Addressed from London to Sir Joseph Williamson*, I, p. 86.

112 *HMC Ormonde*, III, pp. 101–2.

113 TNA, LC5/2, pp. 29–31.

114 Compare TNA, LC5/180 with BL, Stowe MS 562.

115 *CSPD*, 1661–2, p. 611'; 1663–4, pp. 223, 255; *Letters, Speeches and Declarations of King Charles II*, p. 146; Evelyn, *Diary*, III, pp. 360–1; *HMC Third Report*, 'The Manuscripts of his Grace the Duke of Devonshire at Hardwicke Hall, Co. Derby', p. 92; *HMC Ormonde*, III, pp. 78–9.

116 Pepys, *Diary*, IV, p. 407.

117 The Vane Room had a chair of estate and stools, but not a canopy of state, as is indicated (for example) in the accounts for covering the furniture there with mourning hangings (TNA, LC5/201, p. 453). As mentioned above, to sit beneath a canopy of state when dining was the highest possible indicator of the status of the diner: LC5/201, p. 373; Evelyn, *Diary*, pp. 490–1; TNA, LC5/201, p. 453. As the Vane Room was part of the Bedchamber department's domain, it must be assumed that the royal family were served not by the carvers and cupbearers of the presence chamber, but by the staff of the Bedchamber – as was normally the case for private dinners. NUL, Portland MS Pw V 92, fol. 3v; Pw V 93, fol. 2v: 'the great with-drawing Roome next our old-Bedchamber comonly called the Fane Roome' (*Angliae Notitia*, 1671, p. 172).

118 Pepys, *Diary*, VIII, p. 282.

119 Evelyn, *Diary*, III, pp. 490–1; *HMC Fleming*, p. 52; *CSPD*, 1667, p. 388. Contemporary accounts make it clear that the suspension of public dining involved the reduction of the ritual sophistication and magnificence of formal meals rather than the exclusion of spectators.

Notes to Chapter 8: Protestant king, Catholic heir

1 See Miller, *Charles II*, pp. 50ff.; Hutton, *Restoration*, pp. 174ff.; Hutton, 'The religion of Charles II', in Smuts (ed.), *The Stuart Courts and Europe* (Cambridge, 1996), pp. 241–2; I. M. Green *The Re-Establishment of the Church of England 1660–1663* (Oxford, 1978); *Reliquiae Baxterianae*, p. 231.

2 *Moneys Received and Paid for Secret Services of Charles II and James II 1679–1688*, John Yonge Akerman (ed.), Camden Society (London, 1851), pp. 29, 45, 71. *Reliquiae Baxterianae*, p. 259.

3 See Hutton, 'The religion of Charles II', pp. 228–47.

4 See, for instance, Suzanne Eward, *No Fine but a Glass of Wine: Cathedral Life at Gloucester in Stuart Times* (Lymington, 1985), pp. 118ff. and *The Life and Times of Anthony Wood*,

I, pp. 131, 347. Some, like Nathaniel Crewe, fast adopted Laudian clothes and practices, anticipating that this was the way the settlement was bound to go. 'In 1660 he was ye 1st who appear'd at Chappel in his Surplice & hood, before any order relat^g to ye Habits & Ceremonies came out. The Rector, Dr Hood, questioned him about it; Mr Crew answ'd, he thought every Body understood his Duty in so plain a case, & therefore there seem'd no Necessity for a Meeting of ye Society to settle it' ('Memoirs of Nathaniel, Lord Crewe', p. 6).

5   *The Parliamentary Intelligencer*, 23, 30 May 1660.

6   Thurley, 'The Stuart kings, Oliver Cromwell and the Chapel Royal 1618–1685', *Architectural History*, 45 (2002), pp. 250–5.

7   *Reliquiae Baxterianae*, pp. 260, 264.

8   *The Diurnal of Thomas Rugg*, p. 93; BL, Add. MS 10,116, fol. 103r.

9   TNA, WORK5/1, fols 17v, 22r, 41v, 48r, 140r; WORK5/2, fol. 54v. See Figure 43 and, e.g., G. W. O. Addleshaw and Frederick Etchells, *The Architectural Setting of Anglican Worship: An Inquiry into the Arrangements for Public Worship in the Church of England from the Reformation to the Present Day* (London, 1948), plate IX.

10 My italics. TNA, LC5/39, p. 5; WORK5/1, fol. 140r; Bod. Lib., Rawl. MS B 58, pp. 139–41; see Kenneth Fincham, '"According to ancient custom": the return of altars in the Restoration church of England', *Transactions of the Royal Historical Society*, 13 (2002), pp. 26–54, for Charles II insisting on a traditional 'Laudian' arrangement of furniture (p. 48).

11 Thurley, 'The Stuart Kings, Oliver Cromwell and the Chapel Royal', pp. 254–5.

12 When the closet was altered 15 years later it was noted that it had 'before had onely had loose hangings … the closet haveing not beene made up, as in other of His Ma^es Houses which in the late Warre had not been changed': Pepys, *Diary*, I, p. 266; TNA, LC5/201, p. 53; WORK5/1, fol. 22r.

13 *The Diurnal of Thomas Rugg*, p. 93; TNA, WORK 5/1, fol. 23v. For additional crimson velvet furniture supplied some years later see TNA, LC5/64, fols 64r, 79r; LC5/140, p. 347.

14 'Chapel Royal' is used to describe the institution and 'chapel royal' the room(s): Baldwin, *The Chapel* Royal, pp. 225–47; *Angliae Notitia*, 1669, pp. 234–5; Magalotti, *Travels*, p. 365; *The Present State of the British Court*, p. 48; Peter McCullough, *Sermons at Court: Politics and Religion in Elizabethan and Jacobean Preaching* (Cambridge, 1998), pp. 1–10.

15 TNA, LC5/201, pp. 52, 57.

16 '… ye Deane of the Chappell hath Authority onely to order & direct the Service' (TNA, LC5/201, p. 57); see also *The Cheque Books of the Chapel Royal*, I, p. 123.

17 *Burnet's History of My Own Time*, I, p. 453, n. 2; Sutch, *Gilbert Sheldon*; John Spurr, 'Sheldon, Gilbert (1598–1677)', *Oxford Dictionary of National Biography*, 2004.

18 Andrew M. Coleby, 'Compton, Henry (1631/2–1713)', *Oxford Dictionary of National Biography*, 2004.

19 *The Cheque Books of the Chapel Royal*, I, pp. 34–5; Baldwin, *The Chapel Royal*, pp. 248–59.

20 TNA, LC5/201, pp. 165–6.

21 *The Present State of the British Court*, pp. 50–1; *Angliae Notitia*, 1669, p. 234; *The Cheque Books of the Chapel Royal*, I, p. 124. A proposal to reduce their number to 25 in 1663 seems not to have been acted upon, though a substantial increase in their wages was effected: CSPD, 1663–4, pp. 278, 304, 384; *The Cheque Books of the Chapel Royal*, I, p. 127; Magalotti, *Travels*, p. 365; Evelyn, *Diary*, III, p. 347. They were also sometimes called clerks of the chapel.

22 Pepys, *Diary*, I, p. 195; *The Cheque Books of the Chapel Royal*, I, pp. 124–5; the importance of the choral element of the Gentlemen of the Chapel's duties is indicated by the great

concern to ensure that before taking up post they would 'first quit all Interest in other Quires' (*ibid.*, p. 123).

23 The confessor of the household was to 'read Prayers every Morning to the Family, to visit the Sick, to examine and prepare Communicants, to inform such as desire advice in any Case of Conscience or Point of Religion, &c.', *Angliae Notitia*, 1669, p. 235; *The Cheque Books of the Chapel Royal*, I, p. 34; II, p. 285; Magalotti, *Travels*, p. 365.

24 In addition Gentlemen acted as epistler, and gospeller and performed various senior roles relating to the music of the chapel royal (*The Cheque Books of the Chapel Royal*, I, pp. 34, 120, 124–6).

25 Other specific musical positions included organist and lutenist: TNA, LC5/201, p. 165; *The Present State of the British Court*, pp. 50–1; *CSPD*, 1660–1, p. 25; *The Cheque Books of the Chapel Royal*, I, p. 121; the post of Master of the Children was sometimes combined with that of first organist, and there were frequently several other organists. There were also a fixed number of different vocal parts: basses, tenors, counter-tenors etc., *ibid.*, I, pp. 35–6. Henry Purcell was a Gentleman of the Chapel Royal. *The Present State of the British Court*, p. 52; *CSPD*, 1660–1, p. 560; 1663–4, pp. 278, 304.

26 The Master of the Children advised the dean or subdean on the anthems to be performed during chapel services: TNA, LC5/120, no. 51; LC5/201, p. 165; *The Cheque Books of the Chapel Royal*, I, pp. 36, 124; *CSPD*, 1660–1, p. 497; 1665–6, p. 143; 1670, p. 306.

27 *The Cheque Books of the Chapel Royal*, I, pp. 121, 125–6; TNA, LC5/201, p. 165.

28 TNA, LC5/39, p. 5; LC5/137, pp. 30, 43; LC5/201, pp. 165–6; LC5/120, no. 63; *CSPD*, 1661–2, p. 113; LC5/141, p. 297; *The Cheque Books of the Chapel Royal*, I, pp. 134–5; II, 'Marmaduke Alford's Notes', pp. 277–94, *passim*, esp. pp. 281, 282; a pair of altar candles was delivered every week during the winter and every month in the summer.

29 *The Cheque Books of the Chapel Royal*, I, pp. 134, 136.

30 This had been known as the 'holy day closet' in the early sixteenth century but was generally known in the seventeenth century as the king's chapel closet.

31 *Angliae Notitia*, 1669, p. 242; *The Present State of the British Court*, p. 49; *The Lives of the Norths*, II, pp. 300–1; see also note to R. North, *General Preface & Life of Dr John North*, pp. 123–4; TNA, LC5/120, no. 51; 'Memoirs of Nathaniel, Lord Crewe', p. 20.

32 *Burnet's History of My Own Time*, I, p. 401.

33 BL, Add. MS 36,916, fols 51v, 54v, 56r, 135r; 'Memoirs of Nathaniel, Lord Crewe', *passim*.

34 TNA, LC5/201, pp. 165–6; LC5/140, p. 452; LC5/141, p. 296; LC5/144, p. 567; *The Cheque Books of the Chapel Royal*, I, pp. 122, 123.

35 TNA, LC5/39, p. 2; LC5/137, pp. 174, 180; LC5/61, pp. 108, 243; LC5/138, p. 72; LC5/64, fol. 64r; LC5/201, p. 53. The post of keeper of the chapel closet should not to be confused with that of keeper of the king's cabinet closet, the latter post being responsible for the secular closet in the king's privy lodgings and held by one of the grooms of the king's bedchamber.

36 TNA, LC5/201, p. 53; LC5/66, fol. 69r; Thurley, *Whitehall Palace*, p. 113, fig. 119; *The Present State of the British Court*, p. 49.

37 Magalotti, *Travels*, p. 365; *The Present State of the British Court*, p. 49; *Angliae Notitia*, 1669, pp. 238–9; Evelyn, *Diary*, III, pp. 347–8; IV, p. 5; *HMC Fleming*, p. 114; Pepys, *Diary*, IV, p. 636; VI, p. 87; VII, pp. 382–3; *HMC Ormonde*, VII, p. 198; *CSPD*, 1668–9, pp. 4, 9–10; TNA, LC5/143, pp. 27, 69; LC5/66, fol. 69r. The dean was explicitly excluded from having 'anything to doe with, or comand the Chaplaines who are onely under ye Lord Chamberlaines Nomination & Direction', though they or their episcopal colleagues might be allowed to offer advice on appointments (LC5/201, pp. 52, 57). The Lord Chamberlain's

authority over the appointment of chaplains had been much weaker in Charles I's reign; see Milton, '"That Sacred Oratory": religion and the Chapel Royal during the personal rule of Charles I', pp. 78–9 and Fincham, 'William Laud and the exercise of Caroline ecclesiastical patronage', pp. 73ff. A dispute about the appointment of preachers arose in 1678, see *CSPD*, March–December 1678, p. 612.

38   *Reliquiae Baxterianae*, p. 229; Sutch, *Gilbert Sheldon*, pp. 64–6. Sutch suggests that it was Sheldon's decision to prevent these presbyterians from preaching, but this may not have been the cases as the Lord Chamberlain, not the dean, was responsible for their role in chapel services.

39   *The Cheque Books of the Chapel Royal*, II, p. 282; TNA, LC5/137, p. 30; LC5/120, no. 118; LC5/61, p. 250; LC5/141, p. 501. Arrangements in the chapel royal were essentially those of major cathedrals of the period; for example, the high altar at Salisbury Cathedral was dressed in very much the same way, see R. Beddard, 'Cathedral furnishings of the Restoration period: a Salisbury Inventory of 1685', *The Wiltshire Archaeological and Natural History Magazine*, 66 (1971), part B, pp. 147–55.

40   TNA, LC5/39, pp. 106, 116, 228, 242; LC5/40, p. 59; LC5/60, p. 408; LC5/61, p. 335; LC5/137, p. 184; LC5/141, p. 529; *The Cheque Books of the Chapel Royal*, II, p. 282.

41   TNA, WORK5/1, fol. 44r; WORK5/23, fol. 68r; LC5/137, pp. 30, 43; LC5/66, fol. 44r–v; LC5/120, no. 118; Pepys, *Diary*, III, p. 67.

42   TNA, LC5/62, fol. 77; LC5/41, fol. 123r; LC5/39, p. 2; LC5/64, fol. 64r; WORK5/2, fol. 54v; Bod. Lib., Rawl. MS B 58, p. 139; WORK5/2, fol. 54v. A similar curtain could be drawn around the royal chair in the chapels in France and Spain; I am grateful to Dr Nicole Reinhardt for information on this point.

43   Bod. Lib., Rawl. MS B 58, p. 140; BL, Stowe MS 562, fol. 8r; TNA, LC5/137, pp. 30, 184; LC5/60, p. 408; LC5/120, no. 118; the dean's seat was similarly grandly treated at Sir Richard Browne's chapel in Paris during the Interregnum (Evelyn, *Diary*, III, p. 633).

44   TNA, WORK5/1, fol. 44v; WORK5/2, fol. 54v; WORK5/28, fols 98r, 115v; Nigel Yates, 'Unity in diversity: attitudes to the liturgical arrangement of church buildings between the late seventeenth and early nineteenth centuries', in W. M. Jacob and Nigel Yates, *Crown and Mitre: Religion and Society in Northern Europe since the Reformation* (Woodbridge, 1993), pp. 45–63; pp. 54–9.

45   TNA, LC5/137, pp. 30, 165; black hangings were always erected for Lent, but compare the account for ordering these of February 1661 with that of February 1663 for an indication of how much more elaborate the normal dressings of the chapel had become in the intervening years: LC5/137, p. 43; LC5/60, p. 408.

46   McCullough, *Sermons at Court*, p. 16; for other oratories of the period see L. J. Wickham Legg, *English Church Life from the Restoration to the Tractarian Movement* (London, 1914), pp. 156–9.

47   At the time of the rebuilding of part of the privy lodgings in 1682, the king's private oratory was also altered, though it is not clear precisely what was done: Thurley, *Whitehall Palace*, figs 72, 114; TNA, WORK5/1, fol. 23v.

48   TNA, LC5/40, p. 55; LC5/66, fol. 67r; LC5/144, p. 295; LC5/121, no. 15; Evelyn, *Diary*, IV, pp. 129–30.

49   TNA, LS13/171, p. 97; LC5/144, p. 514.

50   *Loyal Protestant*, 174, 25 June 1682.

51   Colvin, *King's Works*, V, p. 153; Simon Thurley, *Hampton Court: A Social and Architectural History* (New Haven and London, 2003), p. 132.

52   Thurley, 'A country seat fit for a King', pp. 214–39.

53　Colvin, *King's Works*, IV, pp. 214–17; TNA, WORK 5/27, fol. 344; WORK5/28, fol. 320; North, *The Lives of the Norths*, II, pp. 292–3.

54　Bod. Lib., Carte MS 60, fol. 67r–68r; TNA, LC5/139, p. 23b.

55　*Angliae Notitia*, 1669, p. 239.

56　TNA, LC5/63, pp. 340, 341; LC5/41, p. 101; LC5/137, p. 359; LC5/138, pp. 454, 455, 456; LC5/140, pp. 161, 403; LC5/143, pp. 249, 433; *CSPD*, 1668–9, p. 243; Magalotti, *Travels*, p. 366.

57　An order of 1675 declared that two anthems were to be sung after the sermons on weekdays in Lent: *The Cheque Books of the Chapel Royal*, II, p. 284; Pepys, *Diary*, IV, p. 69.

58　Schellinks, *Journal*, p. 61; Evelyn, *Diary*, IV, p. 208; Magalotti, *Travels*, p. 365. During the winter the afternoon prayers were sometimes brought forward to 3.30 p.m., presumably to catch the last hour or so of winter daylight: *The Cheque Books of the Chapel Royal*, I, p. 124; II, p. 284.

59　*The Cheque Books of the Chapel Royal*, I, p. 124.

60　TNA, LC5/137, p. 165; Evelyn, *Diary*, IV, pp. 29, 192; *The Cheque Books of the Chapel Royal*, I, p. 124; II, p. 281; LC5/201, p. 51; Pepys, *Diary*, III, pp. 292–3.

61　*The Cheque Books of the Chapel Royal*, II, pp. 280, 283.

62　TNA, LC5/44, p. 246.

63　*HMC Ormonde*, VII, p. 198; NUL, Portland MS, Pw V 95, fol. 68r.

64　In 1677, for example, there is firm evidence of the king attendance at the chapel royal on six Sundays, none of which was also otherwise a holy day: Evelyn, *Diary*, IV, pp. 105, 106, 107, 123, 125.

65　Evelyn, *Diary*, III, pp. 401, 403, 432, 434; LC5/63, p. 340; Dalrymple, *Memoirs of Great Britain and Ireland*, I, p. 88.

66　Magalotti, *Travels*, p. 456.

67　*The Parliamentary Intelligencer*, 27, Thursday 28 July; in the passage between the guard chamber and the chapel was the cupboard where the maces of the sergeants at arms were stored (*CSPD*, 1677–8, p. 256).

68　College of Arms, MS I 25, Earl Marshal's Book, fol. 127v; Bod. Lib., Rawl. MS B 58, pp. 139–40; TNA, LC5/201, pp. 355–62, 363, 366, 370; BL, Stowe MS 562, fol. 6v; Add. MS 40,860, fol. 8v; *Elias Ashmole*, II, pp. 806–7; Pepys, *Diary*, V, pp. 161; *The Parliamentary Intelligencer*, 27, Thursday 28 July.

69　Bod. Lib., Carte MS 60, fol. 67r; LC5/139, p. 23b; College of Arms, MS I 25, Earl Marshal's Book, fol. 127v; Maglotti, *Travels*, pp. 365–6; BL, Add. MS 40,860, fol. 8v; *Angliae Notitia*, 1669, pp. 237, 289; Schellinks, *Journal*, p. 72; Pepys, *Diary*, III, pp. 207–8; IV, p. 401. On days when the king offered the alms at the altar, the participation was expected of all the peers resident at court.

70　Schellinks, *Journal*, p. 84; BL, Add. MS 37,998, fol. 244r. The remnants of the crown wearings of the Middle Ages can be seen in these processions: in the presence of the Treasurer of the Chamber and Master of the Jewel House (the holder of which office had, since the Middle Ages, been responsible for overseeing the regalia worn on these occasions) and the colour of the king's clothing, a survivor from the days of 'wearing the purple'; see Kisby, '"When the King Goeth a Procession"', pp. 44–75. The other Knights of the Garter present also wore the insignia of the Garter on collar days.

71　BL, Stowe MS 562, fol. 6v; Add. MS 40,860, fols 18r, 21v, 33r, 35r.

72　*The Parliamentary Intelligencer*, 27, Thursday 28 July.

73　Bod. Lib., Rawl. MS B 58, pp. 138–9.

74　BL, Stowe MS 562, fol. 7v–8r; *Cheque Books of the Chapel Royal*, II, p. 279.

75 The Master of the Requests claimed and was granted this right because chapel services were traditionally a time when he would 'procure the King's hand to bills'. Privy councillors and Gentlemen of the Bedchamber were also excepted but were usually members of the nobility anyway: *CSPD*, 1661–2, p. 453; TNA, LC5/201, p. 53; LC5/180, fols 16v–21r; see also LC5/135.

76 TNA, LC5/201, p. 53.

77 *Loyal Protestant*, 113, 2 February 1682.

78 Though he refused to authorize its publication for fear 'it would occasion heats and disputes': BL, Add. MS 40,860, fol. 27r, see also fols 61r, 82v; BL, Add. MS 18,730, fol. 69r; *HMC Fleming*, p. 92; 'Memoirs of Nathaniel, Lord Crewe', pp. 9–10.

79 Hartmann, *Charles II*, p. 95.

80 Pepys, *Diary*, III, pp. 60, 292–3; 'Memoirs of Nathaniel, Lord Crewe', p. 8.

81 TNA, LC5/201, p. 48; *CSPD*, 1668–9, p. 9; *The Life and Times of Anthony Wood*, I, p. 445; II, pp. 531, 532.

82 Horton Davies, *Worship and Theology in England*, 3 vols, combined edition (Michigan, 1996), II (*From Andrewes to Baxter and Fox 1603–1690*), pp. 258–64.

83 *CSPD*, 1660–1, p. 598; LC5/137, pp. 64, 88; Holman, *Four and Twenty Fiddlers*, pp. 394–5; *Angliae Notitia*, 1669, p. 236.

84 Pepys, *Diary*, I, p. 266; II, pp. 41, 84–5; IV, p. 428.

85 'Robert Strong and Edward Strong to attend with their double Curtolls in his Maties Chappell Royall at Whitehall and Thomas Bates and William Gregory with their violls very Sunday and Holyday and all the rest to wayte in their Turnes', TNA, LC5/137, p. 352; Henry Carte de Lafontaine, *The King's Music: A Transcript of Records Relating to Music and Musicians (1460–1700)* (London, 1909), pp. 118, 114; Holman, *Four and Twenty Fiddlers*, pp. 395–400.

86 Evelyn, *Diary*, III, pp. 347–8; Pepys, *Diary*, III, pp. 191, 197, 293; *The Lives of the Norths*, III, p. 69; Schellinks, *Journal*, pp. 84, 89.

87 Pepys, *Diary*, IV, p. 394; Holman, *Four and Twenty Fiddlers*, p. 281; TNA, LC5/141, p. 124.

88 *The Cheque Books of the Chapel Royal*, II, pp. 282, 284.

89 Francis Proctor and Walter Howard Frere, *A New History of the Book of Common Prayer with a Rationale of its Offices* (London, 1902), p. 197; Davies, *Worship and Theology in England*, II, p. 381. In the revised prayer book the deacons and churchwardens were to collect the alms from the congregation and then to pass it 'reverently' to the priest, who then 'humbly' placed it on the altar. For examples of the king offering on these feast days see Evelyn, *Diary*, III, p. 53 (Epiphany 1652); Schellinks, *Journal*, p. 72 (Candlemas 1662); Evelyn, *Diary*, III, p. 501 (All Souls 1667); Evelyn, *Diary*, IV, p. 171 (feast of St Peter the Apostle 1679).

90 Schellinks, *Journal*, p. 72; Pepys, *Diary*, III, p. 84; TNA, LC5/137, p. 90; *Angliae Notitia*, 1669, p. 236; see Ashmole, *The Institutions, Laws and Ceremonies of the Most Noble Order of the Garter*, pp. 580–2, for a detailed description of offering at the Garter feast, at which time the 'Ceremony is one and the same, having not anything peculiarly local to Windesor'.

91 Most notably in that on these principal feast days the alms dish was passed to the king by the Lord Steward or one of the other most senior household officers.

92 TNA, LC5/139, p. 23b; *Angliae Notitia*, 1669, pp. 236–8; Bod. Lib., Rawl. MS B 58, pp. 139–40.

93 Bod. Lib., Rawl. MS B 58, p. 139; TNA, LC5/62, fol. 77r; LC5/66, fol. 26r; LC5/144, p. 126. For the traverse before the Reformation see, e.g., BL, Add. MS 71,009, fol. 22r.

94   *HMC Verney*, p. 490; Bod. Lib., Rawl. MS B 58, p. 139; Evelyn, *Diary*, III, p. 53; IV, pp. 374–5; *Memoirs of Mary, Queen of England (1689–1693) together with her Letters and those of James II and William III to the Electress Sophia of Hanover*, R. Doebner (ed.), (Leipzig, 1886), pp. 13, 19; Pepys, *Diary*, III, p. 84; 'Diary of Dr. Edward Lake', p. 29. The king would only receive communion with his immediate relations; generally speaking this meant his siblings and Prince Rupert (whose brother had received communion with Charles I on Christmas Day 1635: *The Works of the most Reverend Father in God, William Laud, D. D., Sometime Lord Archbishop of Canterbury*, James Bliss (ed.), 7 vols (Oxford, 1853), III, p. 225). Interestingly, come the 1680s, the king received with his illegitimate children, Evelyn, *Diary*, IV, p. 374.

95   They were 'to read Divine Service before the King out of the Chapel daily twice in the Kings Private Oratory': Magalotti, *Travels*, p. 366; *Angliae Notitia*, 1669, p. 239.

96   Ailesbury, *Memoirs*, I, pp. 93–4; Evelyn, *Diary*, IV, pp. 129–30; 'Memoirs of Nathaniel, Lord Crewe', p. 20; TNA, LC5/140, p. 495; BL, Add. MS 29,577, fol. 180r.

97   Nigel Yates, *Buildings, Faith and Worship: The Liturgical Arrangement of Anglican Churches 1600–1900* (Oxford, 2000), p. 37.

98   The wording of Charles I's regulations are repeated in the notebook of his son's Yeoman of the Vestry, Marmaduke Alford, as 'Orders for his Maj^ties Chapell Royall'; Pepys, *Diary*, V, p. 96 '… so they turned to the orders of the chapel which hung behind upon the wall'; *The Cheque Books of the Chapel Royal*, II, pp. 278–80. See also TNA, LC5/141, p. 297 for a 1670s reference to the 'orders of his Maj^ts Chappell Royal under his Ma^ts Royall signature now hanging up in the Chappell'.

99   Pepys, *Diary*, V, pp. 96, 155.

100   TNA, LC5/180, fol. 19r; LC5/141, p. 297; Pepys, *Diary*, VI, p. 87.

101   *The Cheque Books of the Chapel Royal*, I, pp. 134–5.

102   *Memoirs of Mary, Queen of England*, pp. 11–12; Pepys, *Diary*, I, p. 266; II, p. 60; V, p. 155.

103   Evelyn, *Diary*, III, p. 474; IV, pp. 374–5; Pepys, *Diary*, VII, p. 99.

104   In January 1662 John Evelyn accompanied a great number of senior courtiers to hear a renowned French Protestant preacher at St James's; later that year Pepys was anxious to get to court in time to hear Dr South, 'the famous preacher and Orator of Oxford', while in 1664 he had almost to fight his way into chapel which was 'most infinite full to hear Dr. Critton': Pepys, *Diary*, III, p. 67; V, p. 96; Evelyn, *Diary*, III, p. 311; Dr 'Critton' is probably Robert Creighton, later Bishop of Bath and Wells.

105   Schellinks, *Journal*, p. 76; Pepys, *Diary*, IV, p. 93.

106   Evelyn, *Diary*, III, p. 285; Pepys, *Diary*, IV, p. 63.

107   *HMC Ormonde*, VI, pp. 258–9; *The Lives of the Norths*, III, p. 170; Pepys, *Diary*, VIII, p. 32; Evelyn, *Diary*, IV, p. 208; BL, Add. MS 40,860, fol. 15r.

108   BL, Add. MS 40,860, fols 10v, 11r; *A Catalogue of Letters*, Strong (ed.), p. 223.

109   *HMC Verney*, p. 496; Evelyn, *Diary*, III, p. 434.

110   'Memoirs of Nathaniel, Lord Crewe', pp. 12–13.

111   John Miller, *James II* (New Haven and London, 1978; 2nd edn, 2000) pp. 58–64; John Callow, *The Making of James II: The Formative Years of a Fallen King* (Stroud, 2000), pp. 125–59; Pepys, *Diary*, IX, pp. 163–4; 'Memoirs of Nathaniel, Lord Crewe', pp. 12–13.

112   See Hutton, *Charles II*, pp. 263–71; Miller, *Charles II*, p. 162ff.

113   Clarke, *The Life of James the Second*, I, pp. 482–3.

114   Andrew Browning, *Thomas Osborne, Earl of Danby and Duke of Leeds, 1632–1712*, 3 vols (Glasgow, 1944), I, pp. 96–102.

115   Evelyn, *Diary*, IV, p. 7.

116 TNA, PRO31/3/128, fol. 58v; *HMC Verney*, p. 490.

117 In so doing they 'came up all decently to the rails before the Communion Table' (*HMC Fleming*, pp. 100–1).

118 '... though he had himself received there on Easter Sunday, resolved to receive againe, with all the Privy-chamber men and officers above staires; so carefull the King is that all the court observe the late Act of Parliament to that purpose' (*HMC Fleming*, pp. 100, 101).

119 *Letters Addressed from London to Sir Joseph Williamson*, I, p. 21; *HMC Fleming*, p. 100; TNA, PRO31/3/127, fol. 62v.

120 'That no Person who is a Roman Catholique or is reputed to be of ye Roman Catholique Religion do presume after the 18th day of this instant November to come into his Mats Royall Presence or to his Palace or to the Place where his Court shall be': TNA, PC2/64, p. 132; *London Gazette*, 834, Friday 14 November 1673.

121 *HMC Verney*, p. 489, entry for 6 April 1671.

122 Clarke, *The Life of James the Second*, I, pp. 486–7.

123 *Letters Addressed from London to Sir Joseph Williamson*, I, p. 106; this is also recorded by the Earl of Anglesey: 'The morning and afternoon I was at Whitehall Chappell the King & pr. Rupert received the comunion but ye Duke of Yorke went away as soone as the Bishop of Chester had done his sermon': BL, Add. MS 40,860, fol. 62v. Browning, *Thomas Osborne, Earl of Danby*, I, p. 102.

124 Miller, *James II*, pp. 66–7.

125 College of Arms, MS I 25, Earl Marshal's Book, fol. 127. When the household regulations were reissued in 1678 they included the new stipulation that 'all Men keepe their Rankes orderley and distinctly, and not break them with pretence of Speaking one with another, or for any other occasion whatsoever': BL, Stowe MS 562, fol. 8r; *CSPD*, 1661–2, p. 453. The officers of arms had tried before, in 1665, to make the procession 'more regular'. BL, Add. MS 38,140, fol. 107r; College of Arms, MS I 25, Earl Marshal's Book, fol. 127v; TNA, LC5/201, pp. 355–62, 363, 366, 370.

126 TNA, LC5/140, p. 452; LC5/140, p. 495.

127 TNA, WORK5/23, fols 67r, 68r, 73r.

128 TNA, LC5/141, pp. 245, 296, 297, 317.

129 It was certainly being used well before the arrival of Catherine of Braganza, by – among others – the king's mistress, Lady Castlemaine, indicating that access was not restricted to those who held specific court positions: Pepys, *Diary*, I, p. 266; TNA, LC5/137, p. 180. That the arrangement was to some extent official is indicated by the issuing of warrants for the provision of books of Common Prayer for the use of 'the Ladyes' in the closet (TNA, LC5/137, p. 180).

130 TNA, LC5/140, p. 452.

131 TNA, LC5/40, pp. 122–3; LC5/201, p. 53. *HMC Verney*, p. 490; *Letters Addressed from London to Sir Joseph Williamson*, I, p. 106.

132 Pepys, *Diary*, V, p. 96; VII, pp. 99, 409. It was also from the crowd gathered outside the king's closet that Pepys's news of the great fire of London was taken into the king on 2 September 1666 (*ibid.*, VII, p. 269).

133 BL, Stowe MS 562, fol. 7v. Though these household regulations were based on Charles I's ordinances, the section covering disorder in the chapel is an addition of the Charles II version; cf. LC5/180.

134 Wren's task was to 'alter His Maties Closett in the Chappell & make both sides of it Open': TNA, LC5/141, p. 229; LC5/201, p. 53; Thurley, *Whitehall Palace*, p. 117; TNA, LC5/141,

p. 245; LC5/41, fol. 123r; WORK5/26, fols 58v, 60r; LC5/201, p. 53. A complicated series of changes to the seating arrangements within the ladies' ante-room followed, which are discussed in full in my PhD thesis: Keay, 'Ceremonies of Charles II's Court', pp. 162ff.; TNA, LC5/141, pp. 317, 362, 363, 366, 471; LC5/64, fol. 148v.

135 The 'orders of his Maj^{ts} Chappell Royal under his Ma^{ts} Royall signature now hanging up in the Chappell': TNA, LC5/141, p. 297.Overseeing the enforcement of the access rules on the ground was the job, in the body of the chapel, of the Yeomen of the Vestry and in the tribune of the Closet Keeper. Ultimately the Lord Chamberlain was responsible for all matters of access, but the vestry and closet staff usually referred to the Gentlemen Ushers Daily Waiters on matters of dispute: *Cheque Books of the Chapel Royal*, II, p. 280, 281; BL, Stowe MS 562, fol. 9r; TNA, LC5/140, p. 452; LC5/141, p. 296; LC5/201, p. 57.

136 TNA, LC5/137, p. 292; WORK5/5, fols 43r, 53r, 54r.

137 *The Cheque Books of the Chapel Royal*, II, p. 283.

138 '… new wanescotting ye East End of ye Kings Chappell and ye Walls of Each Side of ye Alter': TNA, WORK5/28, fols 82r, 93r, 103r–107v, 112r, 308r–309v; Thurley, 'The Stuart Kings, Oliver Cromwell and the Chapel Royal', p. 263; idem, *Whitehall Palace*, p. 117. The altar rail, measuring 47 foot with 46 balusters, carved by Henry Phillips just two years previously, was adapted for the new arrangement and reused.

139 Alterations were then required to the furnishings 'as ye Chappell is now new waynscoted' in the winter months, including to the frontals which were taken away 'to be made fitt for ye Alter as it now is': Thurley, 'The Stuart Kings, Oliver Cromwell and the Chapel Royal', pp. 263–5; *The Cheque Books of the Chapel Royal*, II, p. 283; TNA, WORK5/27, fols 103r–107v, 112r–116v, 308r–309v. See also, Kenneth Fincham, '"According to ancient custom": the return of altars in the Restoration church of England', pp. 26–54; TNA, LC5/141, p. 490, 529; LC5/62, fol. 123v; WORK5/23, fols 67r, 73r; WORK5/28, fols 308r–309v, 112r.

140 Evelyn, *Diary*, IV, pp. 34, 87; *HMC Verney*, p. 467; TNA, PRO31/3/132, fol. 137r.

141 Marquise de Campana de Cavelli, *Les Derniers Stuarts à Saint-Germain en Laye: Documents Inédits et Authentiques Puisés aux Archives Publiques et Privées par la Marquise Campana de Cavelli*, 2 vols (Paris, 1871), I, 'Documents', p. 166; TNA, PRO31/3/132, fol. 137r.

142 *London Gazette*, 1065, 23 January 1676; Clarke, *The Life of James the Second*, p. 502.

143 Barbour, *Henry Bennet, Earl of Arlington*, pp. 242–3; Miller, *Charles II*, p. 212; John Kenyon, *The Popish Plot* (London, 1972), pp. 310–11; Alan Marshall, 'Bennet, Henry, first Earl of Arlington (*bap.* 1618, d. 1685)', *Oxford Dictionary of National Biography*, 2004.

144 *Burnet's History of My Own Time*, II, pp. 99–100. See also Andrew Barclay, 'The rise of Edward Colman', *Historical Journal*, 41, I (1999), pp. 127–8. Compton was also, significantly, tutor to Princesses Anne and Mary.

Notes to Chapter 9: A court comes of age

1 NUL, Portland MS, Pw V 93.

2 Though the author of neither the proposals nor the annotations that were made to them is identified, the nature of the content makes it highly likely that the paper was written by the Groom of the Stool and annotated by the Lord Chamberlain (TNA, SP29/239, no. 84). The document is undated, but internal evidence strongly suggests it was written after 1661 and before 1673: the paper refers to only one set of previous bedchamber ordinances, indicating that it predates the 1673 orders, while several of the paragraphs make suggestions that are

taken up in the 1673 ordinances; the requirement for the Bedchamber staff to wait without their cloaks (para. 5), was set aside by the 1678 orders.

3   *Letters Addressed from London to Sir Joseph Williamson*, I, p. 106.
4   For English practice in the early sixteenth century (as expressed in the Eltham ordinances of 1526) see *A Collection of Ordinances and Regulations for the Government of the Royal Household, made in divers reigns, from King Edward III to King William and Queen Mary. Also Receipts in Ancient Cookery* (London, 1790), pp. 155–6. For French practice, in which spectators had formed an integral part of royal rising since at least the reign of Henri II, see Nicolas Le Roux, 'La cour dans l'espace du palais: l'exemple du Henri III', in Marie-France Auzepy *et al.*, *Palais et Pouvoir: de Constantinople à Versailles* (Vincennes, 2003), pp. 229–67, esp. p. 246; D. Potter and P. R. Roberts, 'An Englishman's view of the court of Henri III, 1584–5: Richard Cook's "Description of the Court of France"', *French History*, 2: 3 (1988), pp. 323–4, 339; David Buisseret, *Henry IV* (London, 1984), pp. 101–5; J. Levron, *Daily Life at Versailles in the Seventeenth and Eighteenth Centuries*, transl. C. E. Engel (London, 1968), pp. 36–53; B. Saule, *Versailles Triomphant: Une Journée de Louis XIV* (Paris, 1996), pp. 30–45, 175–83. For the Spanish and other Hapsburg courts, where there was no question of broad access to the royal bedchamber to witness the sovereign dressing, see Yves Bottineau, 'Aspects de la cour d'Espagne au XVIIe siècle: l'étiquette de le chambre du roi', *Bulletin Hispanique*, LXXIV (1972), 1–2, pp. 138–58; Christina Hofmann, *Das Spanische Hofzeremoniell von 1500–1700* (Frankfurt, 1980), pp. 66–7. At the *ankleiden* and *abziehen* of the Imperial court in Vienna and the Bavarian Wittelsbach court, there were present 'only a very small number of courtiers who assisted the prince according to a strict etiquette': S. J. Klingensmith, *The Utility of Splendor* (Chicago and London, 1993), pp. 156–7; Adamson (ed.), *The Princely Courts of Europe*, pp. 174, 200.
5   Clarendon, *The Life of Edward, Earl of Clarendon*, I, pp. 503–4.
6   Evelyn, *Diary*, III, p. 406; in 1667 the 'Quaking' Earl of Pembroke dashed into the royal bedchamber to tell the king of the imminent end of the world, which he did on his knees at the king's bedside: *Historical Manuscripts Commission: Report on the Manuscripts of the late Reginald Rawdon Hastings Esq. of the Manor House, Ashby-de-la-Zouch*, 4 vols (London, 1928–47) (hereafter, *HMC Hastings*), II, pp. 150–1.
7   Reresby, *Memoirs*, pp. 116, 134; *HMC Ormonde*, IV, pp. 92–3; see also Ailesbury, *Memoirs*, I, p. 93. Brian Weiser's assertion (*Charles II and the Politics of Access*, p. 34) that 'In fact, English contemporaries do not refer to their king's rising as ceremonial, or term it a "*levée*"' is incorrect.
8   TNA, LC5/140, pp. 493–4.
9   NUL, Portland MS, Pw V 93, fols 1–13; TNA, LC5/140, pp. 493–4.
10 TNA, LC5/140, pp. 248, 249.
11 TNA, LC5/140, p. 249.
12 Magalotti, *Travels*, pp. 161–80; Ragnhild Hatton, *George I: Elector and King* (London, 1978), pp. 41–2; TNA, LC5/201, p. 378; LC5/2, pp. 120–6; *London Gazette*, 1546, 12 September 1680.
13 TNA, LC5/2, pp. 58–70, 101–3, 143–5; *London Gazette*, 1844, 19 July 1683; *HMC Fleming*, VII, pp. 140–1, 163; *HMC Ormonde*, IV, p. 53; Baxter, *William III*, p. 149; BL, Stowe MS 203, fol. 209r.
14 See, for, example, Baxter, *William III*, p. 55; TNA, LC5/2, pp. 25, 100 (William of Orange in 1670–1 and 1677) and 143 (George of Denmark in 1683); PRO31/3/155, fols 35r, 47v. The visitors would then be met on the coast by the Master of the Ceremonies with a member of the English nobility, usually an earl, to welcome them For example, in 1677 William of

Orange was met at Harwich (*HMC Fleming*, p. 140), while the D'Este family were met at Dover (LC5/2, pp. 48–9).

15   They travelled in the king's barge or coach, with, in the former case, a pause at the Tower of London for the firing of a salute: TNA, LC5/2, pp. 25–6, 49–50, 95, 121, 143; LC5/201, p. 373; *The Diaries of Anne Clifford*, p. 207.

16   Although the Earl of Essex records that Mary of Modena was introduced to Catherine of Braganza in 'the Queens Presence Chamber', Cotterell is clear in his record that the meeting took place in the queen's withdrawing room. Given that details of this sort were of great consequence to the officers of the Ceremonies, and that he was there, it is likely that Cotterell's account is the more reliable: TNA, LC5/2, p. 50; BL, Stowe MS 203, fol. 209r.

17   TNA, LC5/201, p. 373; LC5/2, pp. 27, 50. So in 1683 Prince George of Denmark was received by the king and queen separately in their respective bedchambers (TNA, LC5/2, p. 143), as it seems was Charles of the Palatinate, once he had been relieved of his incognito status (*ibid.*, p. 121).

18   In his first audience with his nephew, the Prince of Orange, in the autumn of 1670, Charles II 'came 3 or 4 steps forward', while two years later he received Prince Rinaldo, Mary of Modena's uncle, 'standing still without stepping forward at all' (TNA, LC5/2, pp. 27, 51); for kissing, see, for example, LC5/2 p. 121.

19   So the queen invited Prince George of Denmark to sit on a stool in their meeting in the queen's bedchamber (TNA, LC5/2, p. 143); while when Mary of Modena and her mother visited the queen in 1673, they were invited to sit 'on stools, Her Royal Highness on the right hand of the queen, side ways; her Mother below them' (*ibid.*, p. 50).

20   So William of Orange recognized the Duke of York's superior status by visiting him before receiving a visit from him; see, e.g., *The Diaries of Anne Clifford*, p. 207; TNA, LC5/2, p. 27.

21   Straight after Prince George's audience with the king and queen, the Duke of York sent the Earl of Peterborough to find out when he might pay his visit to the prince, to which 'he answered that he begged for to wait on him' but as Peterborough would not open discussion on this subject, 'the Prince was forced to yield & the Duke came immediately' (TNA, LC5/2, p. 143).

22   TNA, LC5/2, p. 53.

23   *London Gazette*, 1546, 12 September 1680; TNA, LC5/2, pp. 51, 124. To avoid the problem of how the various signs of honour should be deployed in their meeting, the elector received the king reclining on his bed. Both the king and queen also returned the visits of Mary's mother, the Duchess of Modena, although this was not because her own status required it, but rather to be consistent with the honour with which the new Duchess of York treated her mother. TNA, LC5/2, p. 46.

24   For ambassadorial visits, see, for example, TNA, LC5/2, pp. 28, 53–4, 115, 144; for dining with the Lord Mayor of London, see LC5/201, p. 373; LC5/2, pp. 29, 116. See also BL, Add. MS 40,860, fol. 61r.

25   TNA, LC5/82, fol. 117r; LC5/41, fols 57r–v; LC5/2, pp. 117, 121. On all of his three visits to the English court during Charles II's reign, William of Orange was lodged at court, usually in the Cockpit at Whitehall, or in the apartments of members of the royal family or prominent courtiers at Windsor and Newmarket: *Correspondence of the Family of Hatton*, I, p. 59; *The Diaries of Anne Clifford*, p. 207; *HMC Ormonde*, IV, p. 53; TNA, LC5/65, fol. 52v; LC5/2, pp. 100–1, 115; *Loyal Protestant*, 40, 23 July 1681. Charles, son of the Elector Palatine, was lodged in the Cockpit at Whitehall and the keep at Windsor Castle in 1680; the Duchess of Modena in St James's Palace in 1673 and Prince George of Denmark in his father-in-law's rooms at Whitehall in 1683: TNA, LC5/144, p. 25; LC5/2, pp. 121, 143;

London Gazette, 1546, 12 September 1680; Campana de Cavelli, Les Derniers Stuarts, I, 'Documents', pp. 113–14. The Duke of York gave up his rooms at Whitehall to each of his sons-in-law on their visits to England to marry his daughters: TNA, LC5/41, fols 92v–93r, 130r; LC5/62, fol. 115r; LC5/201, p. 373; LC5/2, p. 100; 'one Indian downe quilt Covered with White Satten to be presently sent to Windsor Castle for the service of the prince of Orange, the quilt is to be laid upon the Bed instead of blanquets': TNA, LC5/66, fol. 20r.

26 When William of Orange came in 1677, he and his entourage had 'for their diet four tables served twice a day at the Prince's lodgings at Whitehall', and this seems to have been true of all such visitors who were not travelling incognito: HMC Fleming, pp. 140–1; TNA, LC5/2, pp. 27–8, 100–1, 116, 118, 121.

27 '… a Quarter waiter, a server, two Grooms of the Chamber & 5 Yeomen of the Guard to carry up the Dishes': TNA, LC5/2, p. 121; LC5/201, p. 374.

28 For a discussion of what was meant by 'incognito' travel in the mid-eighteenth century, see Ulrik Langen, 'The meaning of "Incognito"', The Court Historian, 7: 2 (December, 2002), pp. 145–55. The reasons cited for doing so were usually money and convenience: as Pepys put it of the visit of Cosimo III in 1669, the duke intended to 'remain Incognito' throughout his visit 'for avoiding trouble to the King and himself, and expence also to both'; or, as was expressed regarding the visit of the Duchess of Modena and her train in 1673, the assumption of incognito status would mean 'the avoiding of many troublesome and chargeable ceremonies': Pepys, Diary, IX, p. 526; Cavelli, Les Derniers Stuarts, I, 'Documents', pp. 9–10.

29 One contemporary summarized incognito visits as 'omitting all exterior hospitality' (Magalotti, Travels, p. 373).

30 Reresby, Memoirs, p. 76; Magalotti, Travels, pp. 161–2, 178, 349, 351, 373; TNA, LC5/2, pp. 16–19.

31 TNA, SP29/256/92, fols 14r–15r; 93, fols 16r–17r; 94, fols 18r–v.

32 When Cosimo had his audience with the king at Whitehall on 9 April 1669, the meeting was arranged with the Lord Chamberlain, and at the appointed time the grand duke travelled to Whitehall attended by two of his own gentlemen. The Lord Chamberlain met the duke in the privy garden and, circumventing both the outer state apartments and the privy gallery, led him 'up a small and secret staircase' (presumably the king's backstairs) into the king's presence in a closet. Here, as Magalotti proudly recorded, Charles II greeted the grand duke with 'a most courteous embrace, a reception demonstrative of cordiality and especial regard', which most visitors could not expect 'others being only admitted to kiss his hand' (Magalotti, Travels, pp. 166–8, pp. 171–3).

33 See, for example, TNA, LC5/2, pp. 78–9; Hartmann, Charles II, p. 249; TNA, PRO31/3/122, fols 5r–6r, 11r, 14r.

34 TNA, LC5/2, p. 76.

35 The Master of the Ceremonies thought it likely that 'he was unwilling to meet his Royal Highness, at the stair head; & conduct him to his coach, which would have been insisted upon, had he accepted it' (TNA, LC5/2, p. 18).

36 CSPVen, 1661–4, pp. 192–3, 200.

37 CSPVen, 1661–5, pp. 192–3, 200. The Kingdomes Intelligencer, 46, 6 November 1662; TNA, LC5/60, p. 355.

38 Magalotti, Travels, pp. 161–2.

39 Clarendon, The History of the Rebellion, V, pp. 357–9; TNA, LC5/2, pp. 76–81.

40 The Lord Chamberlain asked the Master of the Ceremonies to report on what had happened at the incognito visit of Cosimo de Medici six years earlier. Cotterell, however,

was unable to oblige. As he explained, the grand duke had maintained incognito status throughout his visit, consequently the Office of Ceremonies had 'been excluded from that service' and could offer no advice on the procedure that had been followed.

41   '... whereby the King & his Lordship, being in the dark, were both convinced that the word Incognito, affected by any stranger Prince, or other Person of great quality ought not to make the King to be so here, in his own Court; but that unless such Persons will be so really incognito, as not to be taken notice of at all, there is a kind of necessity (where that word is made use of only, to excuse their appearing in an Equippage not equal to, their Quality which they can hardly do out of their own country;) that the respect which is shewed them by the King should be performed, by his proper Officers; & Especially by the Master of the Ceremonies; to the end that, all remarkable passages in such receptions; being observed, & Registered by him; may serve as presidents, to guide the proceedings of his Majesty for the future upon the like occasions' (TNA, LC5/2, p. 76).

42   The *London Gazette* noted for 15 May 1675 that the king received the prince 'with very particular demonstrations of kindness and esteem, for the sake of the Duke his father': TNA, LC5/2, pp. 76–9; *London Gazette*, 982, 15 May 1675; a play was performed in his honour on 7 June 1675, *HMC Beaufort*, p. 65.

43   '... the first certainty we had of his arrival was from this days Gazette' (TNA, LC5/2, p. 120).

44   TNA, LC5/2, pp. 120–1; *London Gazette*, 1546, 12 September 1680; 1547, 15 September 1680.

45   Kisby, 'When the King Goeth a Procession', *passim*; BL, Add. MS 71,009, fol. 23r; Robinson, *Silver Pennies and Linen Towels*, pp. 26–7.

46   Robinson, *Silver Pennies and Linen Towels*, pp. 18ff.

47   *Angliae Notitia*, 1669, pp. 241–2; Lawrence E. Tanner, 'Lord High Almoners and Sub-Almoners 1100–1957', *Journal of the British Archaeological Association*, third series, XX (1957–8), pp. 72–83; *The Present State of The British Court*, pp. 47–8.

48   Tanner, 'Lord High Almoners and Sub-Almoners 1100–1957', pp. 78–9.

49   The money for the alms was allocated to the Almoner by the treasurer of the chamber: *CSPD*, 1660–1, p. 560; 1668–9, pp. 222, 223; *Calendar of Treasury Books*, 1660–7, p. 594; 1667–8, pp. 256, 257, 604; TNA, LC5/141, p. 128; *The Cheque Book of the Chapel Royal*, I, p. 164.

50   *Calendar of Treasury Books*, 1672–5, p. 648; 1680–5, p. 552; TNA, LC5/141, p. 128; LC5/140, p. 142; *CSPD*, 1673, p. 561; *True Protestant Mercury*, 133, 13 April 1682.

51   *The Diurnal of Thomas Rugg*, p. 165.

52   *The Diurnal of Thomas Rugg*, p. 165; *The Kingdom's Intelligencer*, 27 March 1662; BL, Harl. MS 829, fol. 174r; *The Rawdon Papers*, pp. 175–7. In the following reign James II would have an altar erected beneath the canopy of state in the Banqueting House for the maundy ceremony (TNA, LC5/201, pp. 94–5).

53   TNA, LC5/201, p. 93; *The Cheque Books of the Chapel Royal*, I, p. 165; II, p. 287; BL, Harl. MS, fol. 174r; *The Diurnal of Thomas Rugg*, p. 165; *Angliae Notitia*, 1669, pp. 297–8; Henri de Valbourg, *Memoires et Observations faites par un Voyager en Angleterre*, François Misson (ed.) (The Hague, 1698), pp. 343–4. The annual accounts for supplying the fabrics for the maundy are to be found in the Lord Chamberlain's papers for almost every year of the reign: see, e.g., TNA, LC5/39, p. 193, LC5/139, p. 3.

54   He certainly performed the maundy himself in 1661, 1662, 1663 and 1665 and very probably on other years as well: *The Diurnal of Thomas Rugg*, p. 165; *The Kingdom's Intelligencer*, 13, 27 March 1662; BL, Harl. MS, fol. 174r; *The Rawdon Papers*, pp. 175–7.

55   The Bishop of London performed the ritual in 1667 and 1671, see Fleming Papers, *HMC 12th Report, VII*, p. 77; Pepys, *Diary*, VIII, p. 150.

56   In 1669 Sir Edward Walker, the chief herald, responsible for the Order, compiled a list of how often previous sovereigns had held the Garter feast at Windsor, as if by way of justification for Charles II's failure to celebrate the feast for the previous six years (BL, Add. MS 37,998, fol. 163).

57   TNA, LC5/60, pp. 143, 153–4; LC5/107, fol. 75r; LC5/193, p. 3; *Elias Ashmole*, III, pp. 818–21; Beltz, *Memorials of the Most Noble Order of the Garter*, pp. cxci–cxcii. Knights could be, and were, installed outside the feasts, but these were the most splendid occasions on which installations could take place: TNA, LC5/193, pp. 6–8; LC5/137, pp. 295–6; LC5/61, pp. 3–4; LC5/107, fol. 97r; Pepys, *Diary*, IV, pp. 108, 112, 113–14; *CSPD*, 1663–4, pp. 103, 119; *Elias Ashmole*, Josten (ed.), III, pp. 914ff.

58   Pepys, *Diary*, VIII, pp. 177, 184–5; TNA, LC5/201, pp. 399ff.; LC5/193, pp. 5ff.; *The First Triple Alliance*, pp. xxviii, 33, 47.

59   TNA, LC5/193, pp. 16–21, 27; Beltz, *Memorials*, p. cxcii. The appointment of a European sovereign to the Order brought about a rearrangement of the seating plan in the stalls at St George's Chapel. Until 1669 the 'Prince's stall', in which the sovereign's son would sit, was kept empty, following an order by Charles II in 1662. With the prospect of a legitimate heir very faint in 1669, this was overturned and the King of Sweden was given the Prince's stall: BL, Add. MS 37,998, fols 197v–198r, 224r; TNA, LC5/201, pp. 412–13.

60   The Lord Chamberlain, St Albans, went to some lengths to ensure the event was well attended: his own department and that of the Lord Steward were to be out in force, while members of the nobility were written to and told 'that his Ma[jes]tie doth desire & expect yo[u]r Lo[rdshi]pp to be there': TNA, LC5/193, pp. 41, 42, 45; LS1/16, unfoliated.

61   'His Ma^te intending with His whole Court to be at Windsor Castle great part of the Sumer, and to keepe the Feast of St George there': LC5/193, p39; LC5/141, p. 124; Evelyn, *Diary*, IV, p. 42; *London Gazette*, 887, Wednesday 20 May. The difficulty of allocating lodgings is clear from the Lord Chamberlain's notebooks, see especially the full lodgings list (crossed out) of June 1674, LC5/193, pp. 157–61.

62   *Correspondence of the Family of Hatton*, I, p. 69; Colvin, *King's Works*, V, pp. 315ff.; Evelyn, *Diary*, III, pp. 558–9.

63   Evelyn, *Diary*, III, pp. 558–9, 571–3.

64   The account book for the works opens in April 1674. Though the Garter notebooks for that year refer to '*the new lodgings being not yet fitt to lodge in*' this is in a marginal note and I do not think it can be taken as evidence that the works were yet underway: TNA, LC5/193, p. 39; Fleming Papers, *HMC 12th Report, VII*, pp. 111–12; Colvin, *King's Works*, V, pp. 316ff.

65   The duke attended chapel at Whitehall during the Easter festivities (Evelyn, *Diary*, IV, p. 34).

66   The newspapers described Windsor as 'that Princely seat': *London Gazette*, 579, Saturday 3 June 1671.

67   Among the few works that had been done over the preceding few years was the repair of the gun platforms and the creation of new artillery stores (St John Hope, *Windsor Castle*, I, p. 308).

68   Fleming Papers, *HMC 12th Report, VII*, pp. 111–12.

Notes to Chapter 10: The apotheosis of Charles II

1   *CSPD*, 1678, p. 499; LC5/143, p. 191; Kenyon, *The Popish Plot, passim*; Barclay, 'The rise of Edward Colman', pp. 109–31.

2   TNA, LC5/143, pp. 174–6; LC5/143, p. 191. The Gentlemen Ushers were to direct separate orders to the Esquires of the Body, the Gentlemen of the Privy Chamber and the Gentlemen Ushers Quarter Waiters.

3   TNA, LC5/143, pp. 193, 194.

4   Browne, *Adenochoiradelogia*, appendix, pp. 197–207.

5   Ordinances were also issued for the state apartments; the Lord Chamberlain's order of 8 March 1678/9 refers to 'New Orders for the Better regulateing the resort of persons unto' both 'his Palace & Privy Lodgings', LC5/143, p. 282; this is discussed below.

6   NUL, Portland MS, Pw V 93, 'Additional Orders' for the Bedchamber of Charles II, fols 20r– 21r.

7   Concerns about the security of the king as he slept had been raised in February 1676/7 when a gang of drunken courtiers went on the rampage at Windsor and smashed up Prince Rupert's laboratory; in the ensuing chaos 'about 2 or 3 aclock one of Henry Killigrew's men was stabbed in the company in the next chamber to the King ... the Duke ran speedily to His Majesty's bed and drew the curtaine and said "Sir will you lie in bed till you have your throat cut?" where upon His Majesty got up at 3 aclock in the night and came immediately away to Whitehall', *HMC Rutland*, II, pp. 37–8; see also Reresby, *Memoirs*, p. 155.

8   The Groom of the Stool was to give the pages 'a List under his hand' of those who could ask for permission to enter: NUL, Pw V 93, fol. 20v. See also WRO, Caspar Frederic Henning Papers, BA 2252/5 (705:366), unfoliated, order signed by Bath dated 15 January 1682/3.

9   The Groom of the Stool vigorously objected to this order, viewing it as a diminution of his own right of walking 'next immediately to our person', and complaining that such an alteration 'at this time when the safety of his royal person is so much concerned' would cause his and his staff's 'fidelity or courage' to be 'much suspected' (*CSPD*, 1678, pp. 503–5).

10   TNA, LC5/135, unfoliated; LC5/180, fols 1r–30v; BL, Stowe MS 561, fols 2r–10r; *The Diurnal of Thomas Rugg*, p. 122.

11   BL, Stowe MS 562, fols 1r–21r; SP29/421, no. 180. They must have been issued before March 1679 when they are refererred to: LC5/143, p. 282. Weiser, 'A call for order', pp. 151–6.

12   TNA, LC5/180, fols 1r– 30v; cf. BL, Stowe MS 562, fols 1r–21r. A small number of adjustments were also made to reflect changed practice since Charles I's day, including amendments to the rules on formal dining and changes to the access and seating rules for the chapel royal.

13   '... the K. saith the contry would choose a dog if he stood against a courtier' (*The Diary of Ralph Josselin 1616–1683*, p. 619).

14   Ailesbury, *Memoirs*, I, p. 57; see also, I, p. 22 and *HMC Ormonde*, VI, pp. 143–4.

15   For a fuller explanation of the meaning of kissing the king's hand see Keay, 'The Ceremonies of Charles II's Court', pp. 83–6.

16   Cavelli, *Les Derniers Stuarts*, I, 'Documents', pp. 299–300; Evelyn, *Diary*, IV, p. 18; *Correspondence of the Family of Hatton*, I, p. 193; Miller, *Charles II*, p. 316.

17   *Correspondence of the Family of Hatton*, I, p. 224; *HMC Ormonde*, V, p. 291.

18   As Lord Chesterfield told the Mayor of Derby, not all who performed this act could be regarded in the same light, and distinction should be drawn between 'the new kissers of his

majesties hand, and those loyal gentlemen who had ever been faithfull to the crown' (*Letters of Philip, Second Earl of Chesterfield to Several Celebrated Individuals of the time of Charles II, James II, William III and Queen Anne with some of their Replies* (London, 1829), p. 246).

19   Reresby, *Memoirs*, p. 320; Ailesbury, *Memoirs*, I, pp. 82–3; *London Gazette*, 1880, 25 November 1683; *HMC: Second Report*, p. 82; TNA, PRO31/3/156, fols 63v–67r, 68r.

20   *Correspondence of the Family of Hatton*, I, p. 215; Mark Knights, 'London's 'monster' petition of 1680', *The Historical Journal*, 36: 1 (1993), pp. 39–67. Gerrard had been a Gentleman of the Privy Chamber earlier in the reign and it may be he was nominated to present the petition because of this court experience. I am grateful to Andrew Barclay for pointing this out.

21   Evelyn, *Diary*, IV, p. 248; one of the apprentices read the petition aloud, after which the king made his reply 'very graciously', but does not appear to have proffered his hand for them to kiss (*HMC Ormonde*, VI, p. 91).

22   *True Protestant Mercury*, 53, 8 July 1681; TNA, PRO31/3/149, fols 23r–v.

23   TNA, PRO31/3/155, fol. 46v; Evelyn, *Diary*, IV, p. 319; *London Gazette*, 1835, 18 June 1683. The elements of the room's decoration installed in the late 1670s, are described in TNA, LC5/143, pp. 50–1, 121.

24   *London Gazette*, 38, 15 September 1660; Pepys, *Diary*, IX, pp. 106–7; *London Gazette*, 1835, 18 June 1683.

25   In 1676 and 1677 around 4500 people per year had been touched; in 1678 the numbers for the year dropped suddenly by around a thousand, and in December 1678 and February 1679 neither public nor private healings were held.

26   Browne, *Adenochoiradelogia*, appendix; NUL, Portland Pw V 95, fol. 17v; pressure of numbers caused the Lord Chamberlain to write to the sergeant surgeon, Richard Pyle, in February 1682 emphasizing that no one was to be allowed admission 'but those person themselves that you shall examine and find they have the disease of the Evill or bring a Certificate that they have been viewed and examined by one of his Ma^ts Physitians in ordinary to His person or Houshold': TNA, LC5/144, p. 195; LC5/140, pp. 493–4.

27   Evelyn, *Diary*, IV, p. 142; See St John Hope, *Windsor Castle*, I; Colvin, *King's Works*, V, pp. 316–29; Croft Murray, *Decorative Painting in England*, pp. 53–5, 240–2.

28   George Bickham describes the scene as 'Triumph of the Black Prince, the Eldest Son of … Edward III on account of his entire Defeat of the French, at the Battle of Poictiers in which their Royal commander King John [and others] … were taken Prisoner', St John Hope, *Windsor Castle*, I, pp. 337ff.

29   For the traditional interpretation of the scheme in St George's Hall, see Gibson, 'The decoration of St George's Hall, Windsor, for Charles II', pp. 30–40.

30   In the words of his surgeon, healing was done in 'places appointed for Divine Worship, and in the Holy Sanctuary' (Browne, *Adenochoiradelogia*, III, p. 103); when at The Hague in 1660 preparing for his voyage back to England, the king touched after attending chapel on Sunday 30 May, and conducted the ceremony in his sister's chapel there (Wicquefort, *A Relation in form of Journal*, p. 75); when visiting Oxford in September 1663, Charles similarly healed after having attended chapel, performing the cure in the choir of Christ Church chapel; while during his stay at Winchester in September 1682, the king healed around sixty Hampshire residents 'in the Church of that place', *The Life and Times of Anthony Wood*, I, pp. 496, 497; *True Protestant Mercury*, 174, 2 September 1682; *Historical Manuscripts Commission. Seventh Report* (London, 1879), 'Manuscripts of the House of Lords', pp. 1–182, p. 493.

31   Pepys, *Diary*, I, p. 182; Browne, *Adenochoiradelogia*, III, pp. 168–9; *Mercurius Publicus*, 28

June–5 July, p. 431; Schellinks, *Journal*, pp. 91, 177; TNA, LC5/2, p. 55; Magalotti, *Travels*, p. 214.

32 For touching at Windsor see: *True Protestant Mercury*, 1723, 2 May 1682; *London Gazette*, 1828, 24 May 1683; Browne, *Adenochoiradelogia*, III, pp. 165–6, 176. Browne entered royal service as a surgeon in 1677, just as the reconstructed royal apartments at Windsor were nearing completion, but three years before work was to begin on the second phase of reconstruction, which included the chapel and St George's Hall; the king and queen occupied the new rooms for the first time when the court came to Windsor in the summer of 1678.

33 The internal dimensions were around 75 feet by 35 feet, larger than both the Whitehall chapel (about 65 feet long and 33 feet broad) and Hampton Court chapel.

34 Colvin, *King's Works*, V, pp. 316–22; Croft Murray, *Decorative Painting in England*, p. 241; Gibson, 'The decoration of St George's Hall, Windsor, for Charles II', pp. 30–40; Simon Thurley, 'The Stuart Kings, Oliver Cromwell and the Chapel Royal 1618–1685', *Architectural History*, 45, 2002, pp. 238–74.

35 'Some confidently report that James D. of Monmouth did it; quaere', John Aubrey, *Remaines of Gentilisme and Judaisme*, James Britten (ed.) (London, 1881), p. 241; *The Gentlemens Magazine*, 81 (1811), p. 125; *An Answere to a Scoffing and Lying Lybell put forth and Privately Dispersed under the Title of a Wonderful Account of the Cureing the Kings-Evil by Madam Fanshaw the Duke of Monmouth's Sister* (London, 1681). The duke was reported to have touched for the king's evil at Crewkerne in 1680 and at Wallasey in 1682: R. Clifton, *The Last Popular Rebellion* (London, 1984), pp. 127, 136; J. N. P. Watson, *Captain-General and Rebel Chief: The Life of James, Duke of Monmouth* (London, 1979), pp. 132, 144.

36 See, for instance, the bed provided for the Gentlemen of the Bedchamber in 1669: TNA, LC5/62, fols 73r–74v; LC5/119, warrant for 29 December 1669. It was the privilege of the Gentleman of the Bedchamber in waiting to raise any issues he wanted to with the king when the door was bolted. The Earl of Ossory did so, in December 1678, when he discussed with Charles II his plans for better organizing the army 'when we were both in bed, it being my turn to wait in the bed-chamber': *HMC Ormonde*, IV, p. 277; Ailesbury, *Memoirs*, I, pp. 86ff.

37 See, e.g., provision of candles for 'The yeoman of ye Gard that watches at ye Kings bedchambr: doore at night are to have for that service' (TNA, LS13/171, p. 97).

38 Ailesbury, *Memoirs*, I, pp. 88–9; see also Clarke, *The Life of James the Second*, I, p. 566, for the Duke of York entering the king's presence at seven o'clock in the morning as he was being shaved. NUL, Portland MS, Pw V 92, fol. 7v; SP 29/230, no. 84, para. 3.

39 '… the Gentleman of Our Roabes be permitted to come to Us every morning into Our Bedchamber to put on Our Doublett, and to stay in Our Bedchamber untill Wee shall be Apparrelled and drest'; NUL, Portland MS, Pw V 92, fol. 4r, 6r, 7v; Portland MS Pw V 93, fol. 3v, 7r; *CSPD*, 1661–2, p. 350; TNA, SP 29/230, no. 84, para. 2; Edward Chamberlayne, *Angliae Notitia or the Present State of England* (London, 1671), p. 172.

40 *Diary of the Times of Charles the Second by the Honourable Henry Sidney, afterwards Earl of Romney; including his correspondence with the Countess of Sunderland and other distinguished persons at the English Court; to which are added letters illustrative of the times of James II and William III*, R. W. Blencowe (ed.), 2 vols (London, 1843), II, p. 208.

41 '… noe person of what Condition soever doe at any time presume, or be admitted to come to Us in Our Bedchamber but such as now are, or hereafter shall be, sworne of it, without Our speciall Lycense, Except the Princes of Our Blood': NUL, Portland MS Pw V 92, fol. 7v; Portland MS Pw V 93, fol. 20r–v.

42   The Bedchamber ordinances of 1678 stipulate that footmen should not be allowed among those 'who come to waite on Us, [and] are permitted to attend and stay in the Withdrawing Roomes without Our Bedchamber', and that this was 'not only in the morning while Wee are dressing, but the whole day'. In 1683 the keepers of the privy gallery were reminded that they were not to open the gallery doors until the king had risen and the guard had been set. When the Duke of York returned from the Low Countries in September 1679, by coming to the king at seven o'clock in the morning, he was able to be the first to tell the king of his return: Reresby, *Memoirs, passim; Diary of the Times of Charles II by Henry Sidney*, II, p. 77; Clarke, *The Life of James the Second*, I, p. 566; TNA, LC5/144, p. 641.

43   NUL, Portland MS Pw V 93, fol. 20v; WRO, Caspar Frederic Henning Papers, BA 2252/5 (705:366), unfoliated, order signed by Bath 15 January 1682/3.

44   *Loyal Protestant*, no. 226.

45   An indication of attendance is given by Reresby's particular observation in his memoirs of the poor attendance at the coucher on 24 December 1680: 'Ther was but four present' (Reresby, *Memoirs*, p. 208). The upper level of 20 or so is my guess. 'I was at the Kings going to bed (as I was three times in one week)' (Reresby, *Memoirs*, pp. 208, 224).

46   TNA, PRO31/3/137, fols 46r–v; *HMC Ormonde*, IV, pp. 92–3; Reresby, *Memoirs*, p. 134.

47   *Correspondence of the Earl of Essex*, pp. 33–4; Reresby, *Memoirs*, pp. 116, 224; TNA, PRO31/3/137, fols 46r–v; *HMC Ormonde*, IV, pp. 92–3.

48   *HMC Ormonde*, IV, p. 53.

49   Ailesbury, *Memoirs*, I, p. 71. See also *HMC Ormonde*, VI, p. 324. 'I met my Lord of Essex in the King's bedchamber and went with him to the Treasury', *Diary of the Times of Charles the Second by Henry Sidney*, I, p. 186. It was not appropriate to discuss all matters there; as Samuel Pepys reported to Lord Dartmouth in the spring of 1684, he only had a superficial discussion with the king and duke about Dartmouth's recent expedition, 'being in the King's bedd-chamber it was not proper there to enter into any more perticuler discourse with him relateing to nearer matters': *Historic Manuscripts Commission. Eleventh Report, Appendix, Part V: The Manuscripts of the Earl of Dartmouth* (London, 1887) (hereafter: *HMC Dartmouth*), p. 113.

50   The king always visited the queen in her lodgings (Hartmann, *Charles II*, p. 43), and in the early days of their marriage, before the rituals of rising and retiring had fully developed, and when the possibility of his wife conceiving still seemed real, the king usually slept with the queen in her bedchamber: Clarendon, *The Life of Edward, Earl of Clarendon*, II, pp. 184–5, 193–4; Pepys, *Diary*, IV, pp. 1, 30; *The Life, Amours, and Secret History of Francelia, late D[uche]ss of P[ortsmou]th Favourite Mistress of King Charles II* (London, 1734), p. 38. As the reign wore on the king seems to have increasingly slept in his own bedchamber; Ailesbury, *Memoirs*, I, p. 87: 'The King always lying in his own bedchamber'. Reresby's description of the king's routine at Newmarket in 1684 makes it clear that though the king might sup and spend the evening with the Duchess of Portsmouth, he slept in his own bedchamber: 'about three he went to the hors-races, at six to the cockpitt for an hour, then to the play … and soe to supper, next to the Duchess of Portsmouth's till bed time, and then to his own apartment to bed' (Reresby, *Memoirs*, p. 333).

51   '… out of the king's bedchamber windows we saw a waterman in the middle of the river in his boat', Ailesbury, *Memoirs*, I, pp. 84–5.

52   There was at least one other bedchamber at Windsor, on the ground floor below the state apartments; Glasgow University, Hunter MS 238, fols 82–4, 108.

53   See the *Loyal Protestant*, 224, Tuesday 24 October 1682, which states that Charles II 'lies in his new Lodgings'. Thurley, *Whitehall Palace*, p. 112.

54 Thurley, *Whitehall Palace*, pp. 112–13. In May 1684 the Groom of the Stool called for the staff of the Bedchamber attending in these rooms to be more conscientious in their service, 'His Majesty taking notice that the Gentlemen & Groomes of his Bedchamber doe not soe duly attend upon his Royall person as they ought' (Orders for better attendance of the Bedchamber Staff, 17 May 1684, BL, Egerton MS, 3350).

55 WRO, Caspar Frederic Henning Papers, BA 2252/5 (705:366), unfoliated, order signed by Bath dated 15 January 1683. On the list were: members of the privy council, peers of the realm, chief officers of the household, the Duke of York's secretary and the colonels of the king's guards. The completion of the new lodgings was the reason given by Sir Charles Lyttleton for the reiteration of the regulations in January 1683, which he described as 'the new orders ab^t ye bedchamber, since the K^g is come into these new lodgings' (*Correspondence of the Family of Hatton*, II, pp. 21–2). In May 1684 the Groom of the Stool called for the staff of the Bedchamber to be more conscientious in their service in these rooms, 'His Majesty taking notice that the Gentlemen & Groomes of his Bedchamber doe not soe duly attend upon his Royall person as they ought', Orders for better attendance of the Bedchamber Staff, 17 May 1684, BL, Egerton MS, 3350.

56 Aylmer, *The Crown's Servants*, pp. 23–4.

57 *HMC Ormonde*, VII, pp. 29–32; TNA, LC5/201, pp. 9–45, 71–2; *CSPD*, January–June 1683, pp. 90–2, 134, 144, 146, 147, 154, 163, 155, 245, 254, 289, 319; *Correspondence of the Family of Hatton*, II, pp. 21–2.

58 *HMC Ormonde*, VII, p. 28; *Correspondence of the Family of Hatton*, II, pp. 21–2.

59 The locksmith's list of 1665 indicates clearly that the Duke of York, Lord Chamberlain and Lord Steward were to be issued with the 'treble' keys that gave access to the bedchamber (TNA, LC5/137, unpaginated reverse section at end of volume).

60 *HMC Ormonde*, VII, pp. 28–31; TNA, LC5/201, p. 74, 'The Lords Report upon the whole matter'. It was expected that the commission would decide the case in the favour of the Lord Chamberlain; but as one observer sagely remarked, this could not be counted upon as 'perhaps his Majesty may afterwards take different resolutions' on the matter (*CPSD*, January–June 1683, p. 163).

61 The household ordinances of *c.* 1678 and the Bedchamber Ordinances of 1661 and 1673 make clear that the withdrawing room was still officially part of the privy lodgings under the control of the Groom of the Stool: NUL, Portland MS Pw V 92; NUL, Portland MS, Pw V 93; BL, Stowe MS 562.

62 NUL, Portland MS, Pw V 93, fol. 20v.

63 TNA, LC5/142, p. 51; on the queen's side the doors from the drawing room into the bedchamber was on a key exclusive to the queen.

64 Ailesbury, *Memoirs*, I, pp. 86, 88; *Correspondence of the Family of Hatton*, II, pp. 21–2.

65 Evelyn, *Diary*, III, pp. 407, 430; *Correspondence of the Earl of Essex*, p. 74.

66 Ailesbury, *Memoirs*, I, p. 37, my italics.

67 *HMC Verney*, p. 496.

68 Ailesbury, *Memoirs*, I, pp. 93–4.

69 As mentioned above, the contemporary account of Charles II's disdain at the King of Spain's inability to 'piss but another must hold the chamber-pot' is made much more interesting when it is remembered that Charles II relieved himself in the morning attended by a Gentleman and Groom of the Bedchamber, the first holding the candle and the second the paper. 'As soon as he put on his night-gown, he went to ease himself, and often more out of custom than by necessity, by reason nobody could come in there but the gentlemen and groom in waiting; and there he laughed and was more merry and diverting: I holding

the candle and the groom of the bedchamber, Mr. Henry Killigrew ... held some paper'
(Ailesbury, *Memoirs*, p. 93).

70   *Correspondence of the Family of Hatton*, II, pp. 21–2.

71   Reresby, *Memoirs*, p. 247.

72   This was in substantial part the core of the great dispute between the Lord Chamberlain
and the Groom of the Stool in the early 1680s.

73   Ailesbury, *Memoirs*, I, p. 94.

74   TNA, LC5/2, pp. 38, 53, 124.

75   TNA, LC5/2, p. 124.

76   TNA, LC5/66, fols 67r, 69r; LC5/144, pp. 295, 514; LC5/121, no. 15.

77   *CSPD*, 1679–80, pp. 25–6; BL, Add. MS 29,577, fol. 180r.

78   Evelyn, *Diary*, IV, pp. 374–5; this is the only reference I have so far found to the king
receiving within the rails, so I am not clear about the frequency with which it happened.

79   Colvin, *King's Works*, IV, p. 322.

80   St. John Hope, *Windsor Castle*, I, pp. 318–22. Verrio had been excluded from the terms of
the second Test Act in 1678, along with various of his assistants, as he was in the middle
of painting the royal apartments at Windsor; see Kenyon, *The Popish Plot*, p. 120.

81   TNA, LC5/66, fol. 44r–v; LC5/66, fol. 45r.

82   TNA, LC5/66, fols 45r–v; LC5/144, p. 213, 220, 225; Evelyn, *Diary*, IV, pp. 216–17; St John
Hope, *Windsor Castle*, I, pp. 318–22.

83   Evelyn, *Diary*, IV, pp. 316–17; *The Journeys of Celia Fiennes*, Christopher Morris (ed.)
(London, 1947), pp. 278–9; Colvin, *King's Works*, V, p. 326; Croft Murray, *Decorative
Painting in England*, p. 241; Thurley, 'The Stuart kings, Oliver Cromwell and the Chapel
Royal', pp. 265–8; Oliver Millar, *The Tudor, Stuart and Early Georgian Pictures in the
Collection of Her Majesty the Queen*, 2 vols (London, 1977), I, p. 133, II, plate 122.

84   *The Journeys of Celia Fiennes*, p. 278; TNA, LC5/144, p. 567.

85   These curtains may have been what Fiennes saw in 1702, which she described as the 'cloth
which hung before over it all' (*ibid.*).

86   TNA, LC5/144, p. 213; LC5/66, fol. 45v; *HMC Ormonde*, VI, p. 207.

87   *HMC Ormonde*, VI, p. 376; Evelyn, *Diary*, IV, p. 317; *The London Gazette*, 1792, Thursday
18 January 1682/3.

88   Daniel Defoe, *A Tour Through the whole Island of Great Britain*, Pat Rogers (ed.), (London,
1971), p. 188; Colvin, *King's Works*, V, pp. 304–13. The king was anxious that Wren should
build the palace with all imaginable speed, remarking 'if it be possible to be done in one
year, I will have it so; for a year is a great deal in my life' (*Lives of the Norths*, II, p. 207). As
the Earl of Ailesbury waited in the bedchamber in January 1685, he sat a while listening
to Charles talk excitedly about his project, 'that noble Castle and his favourite one that
he was building at Winchester', in Ailesbury's words: '"I shall be most happy this week"
remarked the king, "for my building will be covered with lead". This was Sunday night, and
the Saturday following he was embalmed' (Ailesbury, *Memoirs*, I, p. 22–3).

89   Rooms had of course been constructed or set aside for Henrietta Maria and Catherine of
Braganza to worship in, but Catholic chapels had never before received the sort of parity
of status with the Anglican chapel that the Winchester plan allowed for; compare it, for
example, with the new lodgings at Windsor of the 1670s (Thurley, 'A country seat fit for a
King', p. 234).

90   Until recently it was generally considered to have been intended as an elaborate autumn
retreat, but Simon Thurley showed that it was in fact to have been a 'standing house' to
which the whole court could move, and has characterized his intention as to have an

alternative standing suburban residence to Hampton Court and Greenwich (Thurley, 'A country seat fit for a king', pp. 226–35). See also Miller, *Charles II*, p. 351; Fraser, *Charles II*, pp. 431–2; Hutton, *Charles II*, p. 441; Colvin, *King's Works*, V, p. 305.

91 This and the account that follows come from a wide range of sources that describe the king's death in great detail, including one written by a member of the king's medical staff; see Raymond Crawfurd, *The Last Days of Charles II* (Oxford, 1909); Ailesbury, *Memoirs*, I, pp. 85–90; Burnet, *History of My Own Time*, II, pp. 456ff.; Clarke, *James II*. Some of their merits as sources are discussed thoughtfully in Hutton, 'The religion of Charles II', *passim*.

92 Most recently, Ronald Hutton, 'The religion of Charles II', pp. 228–46; Hutton, *Charles II*, pp. 455–7; Miller, *Charles II*, pp. 56–7, 161–3, 381–3; Jones, *Charles II*, p. 189.

93 Indeed he was more likely to be moved to laughter than to tears by the experience of divine service: Pepys, *Diary*, I, p. 266; II, pp. 292–3.

94 *Memoirs of Mary, Queen of England*, p. 12.

Notes to Chapter 11: Epilogue

1 BL, Harley MS 1890, Glasgow University, Hunter MS 238; 'Few things ever went near his heart. The duke of Gloucester's death seemed to touch him much' (*Burnet's History of My Own Time*, II, p. 470).

2 Miller, *Pictures in the Royal Collection*, I, catalogue no. 153, plate 77.

3 *A Catalogue of Letters*, Strong (ed.), pp. 54, 210; Slaughter, *Ideology and Politics on the Eve of the Restoration*. I have, in this quotation, modernized the spelling and punctuation for clarity.

4 Anthony Hamilton remarking, for example, that the king 'showed great abilities in urgent affairs, but was incapable of application to any that were not so' (Hamilton, *Memoirs of the Count de Grammont*, p. 113).

5 *The Works of George Savile, Marquis of Halifax*, II, pp. 493, 494.

6 See BL, Add. MS 37,998, fols 143r, 155r. I take a different view to those who see the king and those who were trying to rebuild the monarchy as two separate forces. See, e.g., Paul Hammond, 'The king's two bodies: representations of Charles II', in Jeremy Black and Jeremy Gregory (eds), *Culture, Politics and Society in Britain 1660–1800* (Manchester and New York, 1991), p. 17: 'It was the actual character and public behaviour of the king which did much to undermine the reconstructed edifice of Stuart monarchy which his propagandists were building.'

7 TNA, LC5/2, p. 37.

8 Evelyn, *Diary*, IV, p. 409; *The Works of George Savile, Marquis of Halifax*, II, p. 497.

9 Brian Weiser discussed the rise and fall of the king's 'accessibility' at length; he sees changes in the accessibility of the king as a series of deliberate strategies: first, there was his great accessiblity at the Restoration ('Clarendon's policy of open access'), then 'a general policy of restricting access in 1663', then another 'policy of open access' in 1668, and then, from 1673, following 'Danby's policy of closed access', 'he slowly moved away from his adherence to open access' (Weiser, *The Politics of Access*, pp. 30–53, 60, 77). While I would agree that there was a new focus on order from the early 1670s, I am sceptical of his characterization of the decade before then as being made up of such a specific series of initiatives, of his description of these as deliberate 'policies' and of his view of Clarendon's role in promoting accessibility. See Clarendon, *The Life of Edward, Earl of Clarendon*, I, pp. 503–4

for one instance of Clarendon's disapproval of the king's accessibility, by which 'many inconveniencies and mischiefs broke in, which could never after be shut out'.

10   As one recent commentator has noted, the court's openness and the king's accessibility mean that 'almost anyone of gentle birth and appearance could turn up' to witness these occasions (Bucholz, *The Augustan Court*, p. 15).

11   '… in all Triumphs whatsoever or publick shewing yourselfe you cannot put upon you too much King, yet even there sometimes a hat or a smile in the right place will advantage you' (BL, Harleian MS 6988, fol. 112r). The Earl of Ailesbury, who knew the king intimately, remarked that 'although by the king's connivance many men of assurance and of a buffooning humour made the king wink often at their forwardness because they made him laugh for the present, yet, when he would, he could keep up majesty to the height of his great countenance' (Ailesbury, *Memoirs*, I, pp. 93–4).

12   Evelyn, *Diary*, IV, p. 408.

Notes to Appendix 3: The principal feast days of the Restoration Chapel Royal

1   TNA, LC5/139, p. 23b; *Angliae Notitia*, 1669, p. 106; Bod. Lib., Carte MS 60, fol. 68r.

2   TNA, LC5/139, p. 23b; Bod. Lib., Carte MS 60, fol. 67r.

3   Magalotti, *Travels*, pp. 366–7; TNA, LC5/139, p. 23b; Evelyn, *Diary*, III, p. 53; *Angliae Notitia*, 1669, p. 106; Bod. Lib., Carte MS 60, fol. 68r.

4   TNA, LC5/139, p. 23b; Bod. Lib., Carte MS 60, fol. 67r.

5   Schellinks, *Journal*, p. 72; TNA, LC5/139, p. 23b; *The Loyal Protestant*, 113, 2 February 1682; *Angliae Notitia*, 1669, p. 106; Bod. Lib., Carte MS 60, fol. 68r.

6   TNA, LC5/139, p. 23b; Pepys, *Diary*, IV, p. 31; Bod. Lib., Carte MS 60, fol. 67r.

7   TNA, LC5/139, p. 23b; Bod. Lib., Carte MS 60, fol. 67r.

8   TNA, LC5/139, p. 23b; *Angliae Notitia*, 1669, p. 106; Bod. Lib., Carte MS 60, fol. 68r.

9   TNA, LC5/139, p. 23b; Bod. Lib., Carte MS 60, fol. 67r.

10   *Angliae Notitia*, 1669, p. 106; Bod. Lib., Rawl. MS B 58, p. 139; Pepys, *Diary*, VII, p. 241; Magalotti, *Travels*, pp. 365–6; Bod. Lib., Carte MS 60, fol. 68r.

11   Magalotti, *Travels*, p. 366; Bod. Lib., Rawl. MS B 58, p. 139; Pepys, *Diary*, VII, p. 241.

12   TNA, LC5/139, p. 23b; Bod. Lib., Carte MS 60, fol. 67r.

13   TNA, LC5/139, p. 23b; Bod. Lib., Carte MS 60, fol. 67r.

14   TNA, LC5/139, p. 23b; Bod. Lib., Carte MS 60, fol. 67r.

15   Schellinks, *Travels*, p. 84; TNA, LC5/139, p. 23b; Bod. Lib., Carte MS 60, fol. 67r.

16   TNA, LC5/139, p. 23b; Magalotti, *Travels*, pp. 365–6; Bod. Lib., Carte MS 60, fol. 68r.

17   TNA, LC5/139, p. 23b; Bod. Lib., Carte MS 60, fol. 67r.

18   TNA, LC5/139, p. 23b.

19   Pepys, *Diary*, III, pp. 84–5; Magalotti, *Travels*, pp. 365–66; TNA, LC5/139, p. 23b; Bod. Lib., Carte MS 60, fol. 68r.

20   Pepys, *Diary*, III, pp. 84–5; Magalotti, *Travels*, pp. 365–6.

21   TNA, LC5/139, p. 23b; Bod. Lib., Carte MS 60, fol. 67r.

22   TNA, LC5/139, p. 23b; Bod. Lib., Carte MS 60, fol. 68r.

23   TNA, LC5/139, p. 23b; Bod. Lib., Carte MS 60, fol. 67r.

24   TNA, LC5/139, p. 23b; Magalotti, *Travels*, pp. 365–6; Bod. Lib., Carte MS 60, fol. 68r.

25   TNA, LC5/139, p. 23b; Bod. Lib., Carte MS 60, fol. 67r.

26   Evelyn, *Diary*, IV, p. 171; this reference is to the king offering on this day in 1679, this seems to have been an exception, as this was not normally an offering day. De Beer suggests

the ceremony may have been transferred from St John the Baptist's day. TNA, LC5/139, p. 23b.

27 TNA, LC5/139, p. 23b; Bod. Lib., Carte MS 60, fol. 67r.
28 TNA, LC5/139, p. 23b; see also Pepys, *Diary*, VII, p. 217; Bod. Lib., Carte MS 60, fol. 67r.
29 TNA, LC5/139, p. 23b; Bod. Lib., Carte MS 60, fol. 67r.
30 TNA, LC5/139, p. 23b; Bod. Lib., Carte MS 60, fol. 67r.
31 TNA, LC5/139, p. 23b; Magalotti, *Travels*, pp. 365–6; Bod. Lib., Carte MS 60, fol. 68r.
32 TNA, LC5/139, p. 23b; Pepys, *Diary*, III, p. 207; Bod. Lib., Carte MS 60, fol. 67r.
33 TNA, LC5/139, p. 23b; Bod. Lib., Carte MS 60, fol. 67r.
34 TNA, LC5/139, p. 23b; Bod. Lib., Carte MS 60, fol. 67r.
35 Magalotti, *Travels*, p. 365–6; Evelyn, *Diary*, III, p. 501.
36 Magalotti, *Travels*, p. 365–6; Bod. Lib., Carte MS 60, fol. 67r.
37 TNA, LC5/139, p. 23b; Bod. Lib., Carte MS 60, fol. 67r.
38 Bod. Lib., Carte MS 60, fol. 67r. This does not appear in TNA, LC5/139, p. 23b.
39 Pepys, *Diary*, IV, p. 401; TNA, LC5/139, p. 23b; Bod. Lib., Carte MS 60, fol. 67r (which has it on 29 November).
40 TNA, LC5/139, p. 23b; Bod. Lib., Carte MS 60, fol. 67r.
41 TNA, LC5/139, p. 23b; Magalotti, *Travels*, pp. 365–6; Bod. Lib., Carte MS 60, fol. 68r.
42 Evelyn, *Diary*, III, p. 51.
43 TNA, LC5/139, p. 23b; Magalotti, *Travels*, pp. 365–6; Bod. Lib., Carte MS 60, fol. 67r.
44 TNA, LC5/139, p. 23b.

Notes to Appendix 5: Officers of Charles II's court in exile

1 *Historical Manuscripts Commission. Report on the Pepys Manuscripts at Magdalene College, Cambridge* (London, 1911), p. 255–6. 'A list of his Maj[es]tie his servants belonging to the Chamber according to the last reduction in Feb. 1648[/9]', 24 May 1649. The names in brackets are those listed as 'others that are come since and some that were dismissed and remain here'.
2 BL, Add. MS 37047, fols 5r–10v. Payments relating to the court's move from the United Provinces. June 1649.
3 BL, Stowe MS 677, fols. 80r–v. Boardwages to be paid monthly by Stephen Fox. 28 July 1654.
4 *Calendar of Clarendon State Papers*, II, pp. 386–7. Estimates for boardwages. 1 August 1654.
5 Bod. Lib., Clarendon MS 49, fol. 107r. List of the king's retinue. October? 1654.
6 Bod. Lib., Clarendon MS 54, fol. 162r. Beer and wine allowances for the court. 26 April 1657.
7 City of Bruges, Oud Archief, nr. 101. Politieke Oorkonden, 1st reeks no 621. List of Charles II's court. *c.* 1657.
8 City of Bruges, Oud Archief, nr. 101. Politeke Oorkonden, 1st reeks, no 602. List of members of Charles II's court and their court positions. *c.* 1657.

Bibliography of printed works

PRIMARY SOURCES

Allen, Thomas, ΧΕΙΡΕΞΟΚΗ: *The Excellency or Handy-Work of the Royal Hand* (London, 1665).

Une Ambassade du Prince de Ligne en Angleterre, 1660, Félicien Leuridant (ed.) (Brussels, 1923).

An Answere to a Scoffing and Lying Lybell put forth and Privately Dispersed under the Title of a Wonderful Account of the Cureing the Kings-Evil by Madam Fanshaw the Duke of Monmouth's Sister (London, 1681).

Ashmole, Elias, *The Institution, Laws & Ceremonies of the most Noble Order of the Garter* (London, 1672).

Aubrey, John, *Remaines of Gentilisme and Judaisme*, James Britten (ed.) (London, 1881).

D'Aulnoy, Marie Catherine, Baronne, *Memoirs of the Court of England in 1675*, Lucretia Arthur and G. D. Gilbert (eds) (London, 1908).

The Autobiography of Anne Lady Halkett, John Gough Nichols (ed.), Camden Society (London, 1875).

The Autobiography of the Hon. Roger North, Augutus Jessopp (ed.) (London, 1887).

Balfour, Sir James, *The forme and order of the Coronation of Charles the Second King of Scotland, England, France and Ireland. As it was acted and done at Scone, the first day of January 1651* (Aberdeen, 1651).

Bird, John, *Ostenta Carolina, or the Late Calamities of England with the Authors of them. The Greatest Happiness and Happy Government of K. Charles II Ensuing, Miraculously Foreshewn by the Finger of God in two Wonderful Diseases, the Rekets and King's Evil* (London, 1661).

The Boscobel Tracts, relating to the Escape of Charles the Second after the Battle of Worcester, J. Hughes (ed.) (London, 1857).

Browne, John, *Adenochoiradelogia: or An Anatomick-Chirurgical Treatise of Glandules & Strumaes or King's Evil Swellings*, 3 vols (London, 1684).

Burnet's History of my Own Time, Osmund Airy (ed.), 2 vols (Oxford: Clarendon Press, 1897–1900).

Calendar of the Clarendon State Papers Preserved in the Bodleian Library, W. Dunn Macray and H. O. Coxe, *et al.* (eds), 5 vols (Oxford, 1869–1932).

Calendar of State Papers, Domestic Series.

Calendar of Treasury Books preserved in the Public Record Office, 1660–85, 7 vols, William A. Shaw (ed.) (London, 1904).

Calendar of State Papers and Manuscripts Relating to English Affairs in the Archives and Collections of Venice and in other Libraries of Northern Italy, Allen B. Hinds (ed.) (London, 1916–35).

Calendar of Treasury Papers 1556/7–1696, Joseph Redington (ed.) (London, 1868).

Callières, François de, *The Art of Diplomacy*, M. A. Keens-Soper and Karl W. Schweizer (eds) (Leicester: Leicester University Press, 1983).

Campana de Cavelli, Marquise, de, *Les Derniers Stuarts à Saint-Germain en Laye: Documents Inédits et Authentiques Puisés aux Archives Publiques et Privées par la Marquise Campana de Cavelli*, 2 vols (Paris, 1871).

A Catalogue of Letters and other Historical Documents exhibited in the Library at Welbeck, S. Arthur Strong (ed.) (London, 1903).

Cavendish Margaret, Duchess of Newcastle, *The Life of William Cavendish, Duke of Newcastle*, C. H. Firth (ed.) (London, 1886).

Ceremonies of Charles I: The Notebooks of John Finet 1628–1641, Albert J. Loomie (ed.) (Fordham: Fordham University Press, 1987).

Chamberlayne, Edward, *Angliae Notitia or the Present State of England* (London, 1669).

Chamberlayne, Edward, *Anglia Notitia or the Present State of England* (London, 1671).

Charles II to Lord Taaffe: Letters in Exile, Timothy Crist (ed.) (Cambridge: Rampant Lions Press, 1974).

Charles II's Escape from Worcester: A Collection of Narratives Assembled by Samuel Pepys, William Matthews (ed.) (London: G. Bell & Sons, 1967).

The Cheque Books of the Chapel Royal with Additional Material from the Manuscripts of William Lovegrove and Marmaduke Alford, Andrew Ashbee and John Harley (eds), 2 vols (Aldershot: Ashgate, 2000).

Clarendon, Edward Hyde, Earl of, *The Life of Edward, Earl of Clarendon, Lord High Chancellor of England, and Chancellor of the University of Oxford in which is included a Continuation of his History of the Grand Rebellion*, 3 vols (Oxford, 1827).

Clarendon, Edward Hyde, Earl of, *The History of the Rebellion and Civil Wars in England Begun in the Year 1641*, edited by W. Dunn Macray, 6 vols (Oxford, 1888).

A Collection of Ordinances and Regulations for the Government of the Royal Household, made in divers reigns, from King Edward III to King William and Queen Mary. Also Receipts in Ancient Cookery (London, 1790).

A Collection of Scarce and Valuable Tracts, John, Baron Somers (ed.), 2nd edn, Walter Scott (ed.), IV (London, 1810).

A Collection of the State Papers of John Thurloe, Esq: Secretary, First to the Council of State and afterwards to the two Protectors, Oliver and Richard Cromwell, Thomas Birch (ed.), 7 vols (London, 1742).

Correspondence of the Family of Hatton being Chiefly Addressed to Christopher, Viscount Hatton AD 1601–1704, Edward Maude Thompson (ed.), 2 vols, Camden Society NS XXII, XXIII (London, 1878).

The Correspondence of John Cosin D. D., George Ornsby (ed.), 2 vols (Edinburgh, 1869, 1872).

Correspondence of Sir Robert Kerr, first Earl of Ancram and his son William, Third Earl of Lothian, 2 vols (Edinburgh, 1875).

The Court and Times of Charles the First ... Including the Memoirs of the Mission in England of the Capuchin Friars in the service of Henrietta Maria by Father Cyprien de Gamache, 2 vols (London, 1848).

Crofton, Zachary, *Altar Worship, or Bowing to the Communion Table Considered* (London, 1661).

Dalrymple, Sir John, *Memoirs of Great Britain and Ireland from the Dissolution of the last Parliament of Charles II till the Capture of the French and Spanish Fleets at Vigo*, 3 vols (London, 1790).

Defoe, Daniel, *A Tour Through the whole Island of Great Britain*, Pat Rogers (ed.) (Harmondsworth: Penguin Books, 1971).

The Despatches of William Perwich, English Agent in Paris 1669–1677, M. Beryl Curran (ed.) (London, 1903).

Diary of Alexander Jaffray, Provost of Aberdeen, John Barclay (ed.) (Aberdeen, 1856).

The Diaries of Anne Clifford, D. J. H. Clifford (ed.) (Stroud: Sutton, 1990).

The Diary and Correspondence of Dr. John Worthington, James Crossley (ed.), Chetham Society, XIII, 1847.

'Diary of Dr. Edward Lake, chaplain and tutor to the Princesses Mary and Anne, 1677–1678', George Percy Elliott (ed.), *The Camden Miscellany*, I (1847), no. 6.

The Diary of John Evelyn, E. S. de Beer (ed.), 6 vols (Oxford: Clarendon Press, 1955).

The Diary of Ralph Josselin 1616–1683, Alan Macfarlane (ed.) (London: Oxford University Press for the British Academy, 1967).

The Diary of Robert Hooke 1672–1680, H.W. Robinson and W. Adams (eds) (London: Taylor and Francis, 1935).

The Diary of Samuel Pepys, Robert Latham and William Matthews (eds), 11 vols (London: G. Bell and Sons, 1970–83).

The Diary of Thomas Isham of Lamport (1658–81), Norman Marlow and Sir Gyles Isham (eds) (Farnborough: Gregg, 1971).

Diary of the Times of Charles the Second by the Honourable Henry Sidney, afterwards Earl of Romney; including his correspondence with the Countess of Sunderland and other distinguished persons at the English Court; to which are added letters illustrative of the times of James II and William III, R. W. Blencowe (ed.), 2 vols (London, 1843).

The Diplomatic Correspondence of Jean de Montereul and the Brothers de Bellièvre, French Ambassadors in England and Scotland 1645–48, J. G. Fotheringham ed., 2 vols (Edinburgh, 1898).

The Diurnal of Thomas Rugg 1659–1661, William L. Sachse (ed.), Camden Society, third series, XCI (London: The Royal Historical Society, 1961).

Elias Ashmole (1617–1692) His Autobiographical and Historical Notes, his Correspondence, and Other Contemporary Sources Relating to his Life and Work, C. H. Josten (ed.), 5 vols (Oxford: Clarendon Press, 1966).

Ellis, Henry, *Original Letters Illustrative of English History*, second series, III (London, 1827).

'"Embajada Espanola": an anonymous contemporary Spanish guide to diplomatic procedure in the last quarter of the seventeenth century', H. J. Chaytor (ed.), *Camden Miscellany* XIV (London: The Royal Historical Society 1926), no. 2.

England's Comfort and London's Joy (London, 1641).

Evelyn, John, *The Life of Mrs Godololphin* (London: Oxford University Press, 1939).

The First Triple Alliance: The Letters of Christopher Lindenov Danish Envoy to London 1668–1672, trans. and ed. Waldemar Westergaard (New Haven: Yale University Press, 1947).

Finet, John, *Finetti Philoxenis: som choice Observations of Sr John Finett Knight and Master of the Ceremonies to the two last Kings Touching the Reception and Precedence and Treatment and Audience, the Punctillios and Contests of Forren Ambassadors in England* (London, 1656).

The Flemings in Oxford being Documents Selected from the Rydal Papers in illustration of the Lives and Ways of Oxford Men 1650–1700, John Richard Magrath (ed.), 3 vols (Oxford: Oxford Historical Society, 1904).

The Form of His Majesties Coronation Feast to be Solemnized and Kept at Westminster-Hall upon the 23 of April 1661 (London, 1661).

A French Ambassador at the Court of Charles the Second: Le Comte de Cominges From his Unpublished Correspondence, J. J. Jusserand (ed.) (London, 1892).

Gloria Britannica; or a Panegyrick on his Majesties Passage through London to his Coronation (London, 1661).

Hamilton, Anthony, *Memoirs of the Count de Grammont, Containing the History of the English Court under Charles II, with notes by Horace Walpole, Sir Walter Scott and Mrs Jameson* (London, 1890).

Hartmann, C. H., *Charles II and Madame* (London: Heinemann, 1934).

Hartmann, C. H., *The King my Brother* (London: Heinemann, 1954).

Hentzner, Paul, *Travels in England during the Reign of Queen Elizabeth with Fragmenta Reglia; Or, Observations on Queen Elizabeth's Times and Favourites* (London, 1899).

Heylyn, Peter, *Cyprianus Anglicus, or the History of the Life and Death of William Lord Archbishop of Canterbury* (London, 1671).

Hickeringill, Edmund, *The Ceremony Monger* (London, 1689).

Historical Manuscripts Commission. Second Report (London, 1871), 'The Manuscripts of C. Cottrell Dormer, Esq., Rousham, Near Oxford'.

Historical Manuscripts Commission. Third Report (London, 1872), 'The Manuscripts of the Rev. Francis Hopkinson, LLD, Malvern Wells, Co. Worcester' and 'The Manuscripts of his Grace the Duke of Devonshire at Hardwicke Hall, Co. Derby'.

Historical Manuscripts Commission. Fifth Report, Part 1: Report and Appendix (London, 1876), 'Manuscripts of His Grace the Duke of Sutherland, at Trentham, Co. Stafford'.

Historical Manuscripts Commission. Seventh Report (London, 1879), 'Manuscripts of the House of Lords', pp. 1–182 and 'The Manuscripts of Sir Harry Verney, Bart., at Claydon House, Co. Bucks.', pp. 433–509.

Historical Manuscripts Commission. Twelfth Report, Appendix, Part I: The Manuscripts of the Earl Cowper (Coke MSS) ... preserved at Melbourne Hall, Derbyshire (London, 1888).

Historical Manuscripts Commission. Eleventh Report, Appendix, Part V: The Manuscripts of the Earl of Dartmouth (London, 1887).

Historical Manuscripts Commission. Twelfth Report, Appendix, Part V: The Manuscripts of his Grace the Duke of Rutland KG, Preserved at Belvoir Castle, 2 vols (London, 1888–9), volume II.

Historical Manuscripts Commission. Twelfth Report, Appendix, Part VII: The Manuscripts of S. H. Le Fleming Esq of Rydal Hall (London, 1890).

Historical Manuscripts Commission. Twelfth Report, Appendix, Part IX: The Manuscripts of the Duke of Beaufort, K.G., the Earl of Donoughmore, and others (London, 1891).

Historical Maunscripts Commission: Thirteenth Report, Appendix, part VI: The Manuscripts of Sir William Fitzherbert Bart. and Others (London, 1893), 'A manuscript belonging to Lieutenant-General Lyttelton Annesley'.

Historical Manuscripts Commission. Fourteenth Report, Appendix, Part II: The Manuscripts of his Grace the Duke of Portland Preserved at Welbeck Abbey, 10 vols (London, 1891–1931), volume III.

Historical Manuscripts Commission. Report on the Manuscripts of the late Reginald Rawdon Hastings Esq. of the Manor House, Ashby-de-la-Zouche, 4 vols, Francis Bickley (ed.) (London, 1928–47) volume II.

Historical Manuscripts Commission. Report on the Laing Manuscripts preserved in the University of Edinburgh, 2 vols (London, 1914–25), volume II.

Historical Manuscripts Commission. Fourteenth Report, Appendix, Part VII: Calendar of the Manuscripts of the Marquess of Ormonde, K. P. preserved at Kilkenny Castle, 7 vols (London, 1895–1920).

Historical Manuscripts Commission. *Fifteenth Report, Appendix VIII: Calendar of the Manuscripts of the Duke of Buccleuch at Montagu House*, 3 vols (London, 1899–1926), vol. II, part one.

Historical Manuscripts Commission. *Report on the Manuscripts of the Earl of Denbigh preserved at Newnham Paddox, Warwickshire. Part V, 1622–1787* (London, 1911).

Historical Manuscripts Commissions. *Report in the Pepys Manuscripts at Magdalene College, Cambrige* (London, 1911).

The Historical Works of Sir James Balfour, 4 vols (London, 1825).

Hutchinson, Lucy, *Memoirs of the Life of Colonel Hutchinson*, James Sutherland (ed.) (London: Oxford University Press, 1973).

Journal de Jean Chevalier, J. A. Messervy (ed.), (St Helier: Société Jersiaise, 1906).

Journal de Jean Vallier, Maitre d'Hôtel du Roi (1648–1657), Henri Courteault and Pierre de Vaissière (eds), 4 vols (Paris, 1902).

Journal des Voyages de Monsieur de Monconys, 2 vols (Lyon, 1666).

The Journal of Edward Montagu, First Earl of Sandwich and General at Sea, R. C. Anderson (ed.), Navy Records Society, 64, 1929.

The Journal of Thomas Juxon, 1644–1647, Keith Lindley and David Scott (eds), Camden Society Fifth Series, 13 (Cambridge: Cambridge University Press, 1999).

Journal des Voyages de Monsieur de Monconys, 2 vols (Lyon, 1666).

The Journal of William Schellinks' Travels in England 1661–1663, Maurice Exwood and H. L. Lehmann (eds), Camden Society, Fifth Series, I (London: Royal Historical Society, 1993).

The Journeys of Celia Fiennes, Christopher Morris (ed.) (London: Cresset Press, 1947).

The Kingdomes Intelligencer.

The Kings Cabinet opened: or Certain Packets of Secret Letters & Papers Written with the Kings Own Hand and taken in his Cabinet at Naseby-Field June 14 1645 by Victorious Sir Thomas Fairfax (London, 1645).

Lafontaine, Henry Carte, de, *The King's Music: a Transcript of Records Relating to Music and Musicians (1460–1700)* (London: Novello & Co., 1909).

Larkin, James F. and Hughes, Paul L. (eds), *Stuart Royal Proclamations. Volume I: Royal Proclamations of King James I, 1603–1625* (Oxford: Clarendon Press, 1973).

Larkin, James F. (ed.), *Stuart Royal Proclamations. Volume II: Royal Proclamations of King Charles I, 1625–1646* (Oxford: Clarendon Press, 1983).

L'Estrange, Hamon, *The Alliance of Divine Offices, exhibiting all the Liturgies of the Church of England since the Reformation, as also the late Scotch Service-Book, with all their respective variations, and upon them all Annotations vindicating the Book of Common Prayer from the objections of its adversaries, etc* (Oxford, 1846).

Letters Addressed from London to Sir Joseph Williamson while Plenipotentiary at the Congress of Cologne, W. D. Christie (ed.), 2 vols, Camden Society NS, VIII, XI (London, 1874).

Letters and Dispatches of Thomas, Earl of Strafford, 2 volumes (London, 1739).

The Letters and Journals of Robert Baillie, David Laing (ed.), 3 vols (Edinburgh, 1842).

Letters and Papers Illustrating the Relations between Charles II and Scotland in 1650 S. R. Gardiner (ed.) (Edinburgh, 1894).

The Letters of John Chamberlain, E. McClure (ed.), 2 vols (Philadelphia: American Philosophical Society, 1939).

Letters of Queen Henrietta Maria including her Private Correspondence with Charles the First, Mary Anne Everett Green (ed.) (London, 1857).

The Letters of Sir Thomas Browne, Geoffrey Keynes (ed.) (London: Faber and Faber, 1931).

Letters of Philip, Second Earl of Chesterfield to several Celebrated Individuals of the time of Charles II, James II, William III and Queen Anne with some of their Replies (London, 1829).

The Letters of Humphrey Prideaux sometime Dean of Norwich to John Ellis sometime Under-Secretary of State 1674–1722, Edward Maunde Thompson (ed.), Camden Society NS XV (London, 1875).

The Letters, Speeches and Declarations of King Charles II, Arthur Bryant (ed.) (London: Cassell, 1935).

Letters to and from Henry Savile, Envoy at Paris and Vice-Chamberlain to Charles II and James II, William Durrant Cooper (ed.), Camden Society, LXXI (London, 1858).

The Life, Amours, and Secret History of Francelia, late D[uche]ss of P[ortsmou]th Favourite Mistress of King Charles II (London, 1734).

The Life and Times of Anthony Wood, Antiquary, of Oxford, 1632–1695, Described by Himself, Andrew Clark (ed.), 5 vols (Oxford: Oxford University Press, 1891–1900).

The Lives of the Right Hon. Francis North, Baron Guildford; The Hon. Sir Dudley North; and the Hon. and Rev. Dr. John North by the Hon. Roger North together with the Autobiography of the Author, Augustus Jessop (ed.), 3 vols (London, 1890).

The London Gazette.

The Loyal Protestant.

Magalotti, Count Lorenzo, *Travels of Cosmo the Third Grand Duke of Tuscany through England during the Reign King Charles the Second (1669)* (London, 1821).

Memoir of Lady Warwick: also her Diary, from 1666 to 1672, now first Published: to which are Added, Extracts from her other Writings, Anthony Walker (ed.) (London, 1847).

Mémoires de Madame de Motteville sur Anna D'Austriche et sa Cour, M. Sainte-Beuve (ed.), 3 vols (Paris, 1855).

Memoirs Illustrative of the Life and Writings of John Evelyn, William Bray (ed.), 2 vols (London, 1818), 'The Private Correspondence between Charles I and his Secretary of State'.

The Memoirs of Ann Lady Fanshawe, wife of the Right Hon. Sir Richard Fanshawe, Bart., 1600–72 (London, 1907).

Memoirs of La Grande Mademoiselle Duchess de Montpensier 1627–1693, translated by Grace Hart Seeley (London: E. Nash and Grayson, 1928).

Memoirs of Madame de Motteville on Anne of Austria and her Court, Katharine Prescott Wormeley, transl., 3 vols (London: Heinemann, 1902).

Memoirs of Mademoiselle de Montpensier written by herself, 3 vols (London, 1848).

Memoirs of Mary, Queen of England (1689–1693) together with her Letters and those of James II and William III to the Electress Sophia of Hanover, R. Doebner (ed.) (Leipzig, 1886).

'Memoirs of Nathaniel, Lord Crewe', Andrew Clark (ed.), *The Camden Miscellany*, IX (London, 1895), no. 6.

Memoirs of Sir John Reresby, Andrew Browning (ed.), second edition Mary K. Geiter and W.A. Speck (eds) (London: Royal Historical Society, 1991).

Memoirs of Tobias Rustat, Esq Yeoman of the Robes to King Charles II, William Hewett (ed.) (London, 1849).

Memoirs of the Verney Family during the Civil War, Frances Parthenope Verney (ed.), 4 vols (London, 1892–9).

The Memoirs of Thomas, Earl of Ailesbury written by Himself, W. E. Buckley (ed.), 2 vols (London, 1890).

Mercurius Publicus.

Miscellanea Aulica: or a Collection of State Treatises never before Published, T. Brown (ed.) (London, 1702).

Monarchy Revived in the most Illustrious Charles the Second whose Life and Reign is described in the ensuing Discourse (London, 1661).

Newdigate-Newdegate, Lady, *Cavalier and Puritan in the days of the Stuarts, Compiled from the Private Papers and Diary of Sir Richard Newdigate, Second Baronet with Extracts from MS News-letters Addressed to him between 1675 and 1689* (London: Smith, Elder & Company, 1901).

The Newes.

Nicholas Ferrar: Two Lives by His Brother John and by Doctor Jebb, J. E. B. Mayor (ed.) (Cambridge, 1855).

Nichols, J., *The Progresses and Public Processions of Queen Elizabeth*, 4 vols (London, 1823).

Nichols, J., *The Progresses, Processions and Magnificent Festivities during the Reign of King James*, 4 vols (London, 1828).

Nicholas, J., *London Pageants: I: Accounts of Fifty-Five Royal Processions and Entertainments in the City of London. II: A Bibilographical List of Lord Mayor's Pageants* (London, 1831).

Nicoll, John, *A Diary of Public Transactions and other Occurences Chiefly in Scotland from January 1650 to June 1667* (Edinburgh, 1836).

North, Roger, *General Preface & Life of Dr John North*, Peter Millard (ed.) (Toronto: University of Toronto Press, 1984).

Ogilby, John, *The Relation of His Majestie's Entertainment Passing through the City of London to his Coronation with a Description of the Triumphal Arches and Solemnity* (London, 1661).

Oxford Council Acts 1626–1665, M. G. Hobson and H. E. Salter (eds) (Oxford: Oxford University Press, 1933).

The Oxford Gazette.

The Parliamentary Intelligencer.

Peck, Francis, *Desiderata Curiosa*, 2 vols (London, 1736).

Pegge, Samuel, *Curalia; or an Historical Account of some Branches of the Royal Household* (London, 1791).

The Present State of the British Court or, An Account of the Civil and Military Establishment of England (London, 1720).

A Proclamation appointing the times for His Majesties healing of the Disease called the King's Evil (London, 1639).

A Proclamation Suspending the times of Healing the Disease called, the King's Evill untill Easter next (London, 1638).

The Rawdon Papers, consisting of Letters on Various Subjects, Literary, Political and Ecclesiastical to and from Dr. John Bramhall, Primate of Ireland, Edward Berwick (ed.) (London, 1819).

Reliquiae Baxterianae: or Mr. Richard Baxters Narrative of the most Memorable Passages of his Life and Times, Mathew Sylvester (ed.) (London, 1696).

The Remains of Denis Granville, D.D., Dean and Archdeacon of Durham, Surtees Society, 47 (Edinburgh, 1865).

Selections from the Correspondence of Arthur Capel, Earl of Essex, 1675–1677 Clement Edwards Pike (ed.), Camden Third Series, XXIV (London: Royal Historical Society, 1913).

Serre, P. de la, *Histoire de l'entree de la Reyne Mere du Roy Tres-Chrestien dans la Grande-Bretagne* (London, 1639).

Sorbière, Samuel de, *Relation d'un voyage en Angleterre, où sont touché es plusieurs choses, qui regardent l'estat des sciences, et de la religion* (Cologne, 1667).

Stuart Papers relating chiefly to Queen Mary of Modena and the Exiled Court of King James II, Falconer Madan (ed.), Roxburghe Club (London, 1889).

A True and Exact Relation of the manner of his Majesties setting up of His Standard at Nottingham on Munday the 22 of August 1642 (London, 1642).

True Protestant Mercury.

Valbourg, Henri de, *Memoires et Observations faites par un Voyager en Angleterre*, François Maximilien Misson (ed.) (The Hague, 1698).

Vickers, William, *An Easie and Safe Method for Curing the King's Evil* (London, 5th edn, 1711).

Walker, Edward, *A Circumstantial Account of the Preparations for the Coronation of his Majesty King Charles the Second ... to which is Prefixed an Account of the Landing, Reception and Journey of His Majesty from Dover to London* (London, 1820).

Walker, Edward, *Historical Discourses upon Several Subjects* (London, 1705).

Wicquefort, Abraham van, *A Relation in form of Journal, of the Voiage and Residence which the most Excellent and most Mighty Prince Charles the II King of Great Britain, &c. Hath made in Holland, from the 25 of May, to the 2 of June, 1660*, Sir William Lower, transl. (The Hague, 1660).

Wiseman, Richard, *Severall Chirurgical Treastises* (London, 1686).

The Works of George Savile, Marquis of Halifax, Mark N. Brown (ed.), 3 vols (Oxford: Clarendon Press, 1989).

The Works of John Sheffield, Earl of Mulgrave, Marquis of Normanby and Duke of Buckingham, 2 vols (London, 1729).

The Works of the most Reverend Father in God, William Laud D.D., Sometime Lord Archbishop of Canterbury, James Bliss (ed.), 7 vols (Oxford, 1853).

The Works of Sir William Temple, Bart ... To which is prefixed the Life and Character of Sir William Temple. Written by a particular Friend, 4 vols (Edinburgh, 1754).

SECONDARY SOURCES

Adamson, John (ed.), *The Princely Courts of Europe* (London: Weidenfeld and Nicholson, 1999).

Addleshaw, G. W. O. and Frederick Etchells, *The Architectural Setting of Anglican Worship: an Inquiry into the Arrangements for Public Worship in the Church of England from the Reformation to the Present Day* (London: Faber, 1948).

Airy, Osmund, *Charles II* (London: Longman, 1904).

Allen, D., 'The political function of Charles II's Chiffinch', *The Huntington Library Quarterly*, XXXIX, 3 (May, 1976), pp. 277–90.

Anderson, M. S. *The Rise of Modern Diplomacy 1450–1919* (London and New York: Longman, 1993).

Anglo, S, *Spectacle, Pageantry and Early Tudor Policy* (Oxford: Clarendon Press, 1969).

Asch, Ronald G., and Adolf M. Birke (eds), *Princes, Patronage and the Nobility: the Court at the Beginning of the Modern Age c.1450–1650* (Oxford: Oxford University Press,1991).

Ashley, Maurice, *Charles II: the Man and the Statesman* (London: Weidenfeld and Nicholson, 1971).

Avery, Charles, 'The collector earl and his modern marbles: Thomas Howard and Francois Dieussart', *Apollo*, June 2006, pp. 46–53.

Aylmer, Gerald, *The Crown's Servants: Government and Civil Service under Charles II, 1660–85* (Oxford: Oxford University Press, 2002).

Aylmer, Gerald, *The King's Servants: The Civil Service of Charles I* (London: Routledge & Kegan Paul, 1961).

Baillie, Hugh Murray, 'Etiquette and the planning of the state apartments in Baroque palaces', *Archaeologia*, 101 (1961), pp. 169–99.

Bak, Janos M., *Coronations: Medieval and Early-Modern Monarchic Ritual* (Berkeley: University of California Press, 1990).

Baldwin, David, *The Chapel Royal Ancient and Modern* (London: Duckworth, 1990).

Barbour, Violet, *Henry Bennet, Earl of Arlington, Secretary of State to Charles II* (Washington and London: Oxford University Press, 1914).

Barclay, Andrew, 'Charles II's failed restoration: administrative reform belowstairs 1660–4' in Eveline Cruickshanks (ed.), *The Stuart Courts* (Stroud: Sutton, 2000), pp. 158–70.

Barclay, Andrew, 'The rise of Edward Colman', *Historical Journal*, 42, I (1999), pp. 109–31.

Barlow, Frank 'The King's Evil', *English Historical Review*, XCV, no. 374 (January, 1980), pp. 3–27.

Battifol, Louis, *Le Louvre sous Henri IV et Louis XIII la vie de la Cour de France au xviie siècle* (Paris, 1930).

Battifol, Louis, *Marie de Médicis and the French Court in the XVIIth Century*, Mary King trans., H. W. Carless Davis (ed.) (London: Chatto and Windus, 1908).

Baxter, Stephen B., *William III* (London: Longman, 1966).

Bayne, C. G., 'The coronation of Queen Elizabeth', *English Historical Review*, XXV, 1910, pp. 550–2.

Beattie, John M., *The English Court in the Reign of George I* (Cambridge: Cambridge University Press, 1967).

Beddard, R., 'Cathedral furnishings of the Restoration period: a Salisbury Inventory of 1685', *The Wiltshire Archaeological and Natural History Magazine*, 66 (1971), part B, pp. 147–55.

Beer, E. S. de, 'King Charles II's own fashion: an episode in Anglo-French relations 1666–1670', *Journal of the Warburg Institute*, II (1938–9).

Bergeron, David, *English Civic Pageantry* (Columbia and London: Edward Arnold, 1971).

Bergeron, David, 'Charles I's royal entries into London', *The Guildhall Miscellany* III, 2 (April, 1970), pp. 91–8.

Bergeron, David, 'Elizabeth's coronation entry (1559): new manuscript evidence', *English Literary Renaissance*, 8 (1978), pp. 3–9.

Beier, L. M., *Sufferers and Healers: the Experience of Illness in 17th-century England* (London: Routledge and Kegan Paul, 1987).

Beltz, G. F., *Memorials of the Most Noble Order of the Garter* (London, 1841).

Bloch, Marc, *The Royal Touch: Sacred Monarchy and Scrofula in England and France*, J. E. Anderson, trans. (London and Montreal: Routledge and Kegan Paul, 1973).

Bosher, Robert S., *The Making of the Restoration Settelement: the Influence of the Laudians 1649–1662* (London: Dacre Press 1951).

Bottineau, Yves, 'Aspects de la cour d'Espagne au XVIIe siècle: l'étiquette de la chambre du roi', *Bulletin Hispanique*, LXIV (1972), nos 1–2, pp. 138–58.

Boulton, D. J. D, *The Knights of the Crown* (Woodbridge: Boydell, 1987).

A Brief Historical Relation of the Life of Mr John Livingstone, Thomas Houston (ed.) (Edinburgh, 1848).

Browning, Andrew, *Thomas Osborne, Earl of Danby and Duke of Leeds, 1632–1712*, 3 vols (Glasgow: Jackson Son & Company, 1951).

Bryant, Arthur, *King Charles II* (London: Longman, 1931).

Bucholz, R. O., *The Augustan Court: Queen Anne and the Decline of Court Culture* (Stanford: Stanford University Press, 1993).

Bucholz, R. O., '"Nothing but Ceremony": Queen Anne and the limitations of royal ritual', *Journal of British Studies*, XXX (1991), pp. 288–323.

Bucholz, R. O., 'Going to court in 1700: a visitor's guide', *The Court Historian*, 5, 3 (December, 2000), pp. 181–217.

Buisseret, David, *Henry IV* (London: Allen and Unwin, 1984).

Burke, Peter, *The Fabrication of Louis XIV* (London and New Haven: Yale University Press, 1992).

Callow, John, *The Making of King James II: the Formative Years of a Fallen King* (Stroud: Sutton, 2000).

Campbell Orr, Clarissa, *Queenship in Britain 1660–1837: Royal Patronage, Court Culture and Dynastic Politics* (Manchester: Manchester University Press, 2002).

Cannadine, David and Simon Price (eds), *Rituals of Royalty: Power and Ceremony in Traditional Societies* (Cambridge: Cambridge University Press, 1987).

Chapman, Hester W., *The Tragedy of Charles II in the Years 1630–1660* (London, Jonathan Cape, 1964).

Chatenet, Monique, 'Cherchez le lit: the place of the bed in sixteenth-century French residences', *Transactions of the Ancient Monuments Society*, 24 (1999), pp. 7–24.

Clarke, J. S. (ed.), *The Life of James the Second King of England Collected out of Memoirs Writ of his Own Hand…Published from the original Stuart Manuscripts in Carlton-House*, 2 vols (London, 1816).

Clay, Christopher, *Public Finance and Private Wealth: the Career of Sir Stephen Fox, 1627–1716* (Oxford: Clarendon Press, 1978).

Clifton, R., *The Last Popular Rebellion* (London: Maurice Temple Smith, 1984).

Colvin, Howard (ed.), *The History of the King's Works*, 6 vols (London: Her Majesty's Stationery Office, 1963–82).

Corp, Edward, 'Catherine of Braganza and cultural politics', in Clarissa Campbell Orr (ed.), *Queenship in Britain 1660–1837: Royal Patronage, Court Culture and Dynastic Politics* (Manchester: Manchester University Press, 2002).

Cox, J. Charles and Alfred Harvey, *English Church Furniture* (London: Meuthen, 1907).

Crawfurd, Raymund, *The King's Evil* (Oxford: Clarendon Press, 1911).

Crawfurd, Raymond, *The Last Days of Charles II* (Oxford: Clarendon Press, 1909).

Cressy, David, *Birth, Marriage, and Death: Ritual, Religion, and the Life-Cycle in Tudor and Stuart England* (Oxford: Oxford University Press 1997).

Croft Murray, Edward, *Decorative Painting in England 1537–1837. Volume One: Early Tudor to Sir James Thornhill* (London: Country Life, 1962).

The Crown Jewels: the History of the Coronation Regalia in the Jewel House of the Tower of London, 2 vols (London: The Stationery Office, 1998).

Cruickshanks, Eveline (ed.), *The Stuart Courts* (Stroud: Sutton, 2000).

Cuddy, Neil, 'Reinventing a monarchy: the changing structure and political function of the Stuart Court, 1603–88' in E. Cruickshanks (ed.), *The Stuart Courts* (Stroud: Sutton, 2000), pp. 59–86.

Cuddy, Neil, 'The revival of the entourage: the Bedchamber of James I, 1603–1625', in Starkey, et al, *The English Court from the Wars of the Roses to the Civil War* (London and New York: Longman, 1987), pp. 173–226.

Davidson, Lillias Campbell, *Catherine of Bragança, Infanta of Portugal & Queen-Consort of England* (London: John Murray, 1908).

Davies, Horton, *Worship and Theology in England*, 3 vols (Michigan: W.B. Eerdmans, 1996).

Dornon, Armaud de Behault de, *Bruges séjour d'exil d'Edouard IV et de Charles II rois d'Angleterre* (Brussels, 1931).

Duindam, Jeroen, *Myths of Power: Norbert Elias and the Early Modern European Court* (Amsterdam: Amsterdam University Press, 1995).

Elias, Norbert, *The Civilizing Process. Volume One: The History of Manners*, Edmund Jephcott (ed.) (Oxford: Blackwell, 1978).

Elias, Norbert, *The Civilizing Process. Volume Two: State Formation and Civilisation*, Edmund Jephcott (ed.) (Oxford: Blackwell, 1982).

Farmer, J. E. *Versailles and the Court under Louis XIV* (New York: Centry Co, 1905).

Farquhar, Helen, 'Royal charities. Part I: Angels as healing pieces for the King's Evil', *British Numismatic Journal*, XII, 2nd series, II, 1916, pp. 39–137.

Farquhar, Helen 'Royal charities. Part II: Touchpieces for the King's Evil', *British Numismatic Journal*, XIII, 2nd series, III, 1917, pp. 95–165.

Feasey, H. J., *Ancient English Holy Week Ceremonial* (London, 1893).

Fincham, Kenneth (ed.), *The Early Stuart Church 1603–1642* (Basingstoke: Macmillan, 1993).

Fincham, Kenneth, 'William Laud and the exercise of Caroline Ecclesiastical patronage', *Journal of Ecclesiastical History*, 51, I (January 2000), pp. 69–93.

Fincham, Kenneth, '"According to Ancient Custom": the return of altars in the Restoration church of England', *Transactions of the Royal Historical Society*, 13 (2003), pp. 29–54.

Fraser, Antonia, *King Charles II* (London: Weidenfeld and Nicholson, 1979).

Fritz, Paul S., 'From "public" to "private": the royal funerals in England, 1500–1830' in Joachim Whaley (ed.), *Mirrors of Mortality: Studies in the Social History of Death* (London: Europa, 1981), pp. 61–80.

Fritz, Paul S., 'The trade in death: the royal funerals in England, 1685–1830', *Eighteenth Century Studies*, 15 (1981–82), pp. 291–315.

Gardiner, S. R., *Letters and Papers Illustrating Relations between Charles II and Scotland in 1650* (Edinburgh, 1894).

Garrison, Fielding H., 'A relic of the King's Evil in the Surgeon General's Library' (Washington DC), *Proceedings of the Royal Society of Medicine*, 7, 1914, pp. 227–34.

Gasc, Nadine, 'De l'apparat à la naissance de l'intime', in *Reves d'Alcôves: la Chambre au Cours des Siècles* (Paris, 1995), pp. 70–91.

Geertz, Clifford, *Local Knowledge: Further Essays in Interpretative Anthropology* (New York: Basic,1983).

Gibson, Katharine, 'The decoration of St George's Hall, Windsor, for Charles II: "Too resplendent bright for subjects' eyes"', *Apollo*, May 1998, pp. 30–40.

Girouard, Mark, *Life in the English Country House* (London: Pavillion, 1978).

Glanville, Philippa, 'Protocoles et usages des tables à la cour d'Angleterre' *in Versailles et les Tables Royales en Europe XVIIème-XIXème Siecle*, Musée Nationale des Châteaux de Versailles et de Trianon, 3 Novembre 1993–27 Fevrier 1994 (Paris, 1993), pp. 156–9.

Glassey, L. K. J. (ed.), *The Reigns of Charles II and James VII and II* (Basingstoke: Macmillan, 1997).

Goldie, Mark, 'Restoration political thought' in L. K. J. Glassey (ed.), *The Reigns of Charles II and James VII and II* (Basingstoke: Macmillan, 1997), pp. 12–36.

Gow, I., *The Palace of Holyroodhouse* (London: The Royal Collection, 1995).

Gray, Cecil and Margery, *The Bed or the Clinophiles Vade Mecum* (London: Weidenfeld and Nicholson, 1946).

Green, I. M., *The Re-Establishment of the Church of England 1660–1663* (Oxford: Oxford University Press, 1978).

Guizot, M., *History of Oliver Cromwell and the English Commonwealth*, Andrew R. Scroble trans. 2 vols (London, 1854).

Hamilton, Elizabeth, *Henrietta Maria* (London: Hamilton, 1976).

Hammond, Paul, 'The king's two bodies: representations of Charles II', in Jeremy Black and

James Gregory (eds), *Culture, Politics and Society in Britain 1660–1800* (Manchester and New York: Manchester University Press, 1991) pp. 13–48.

Hammond, Paul, 'Dryden's "Albion and Albanius": the apotheosis of Charles II', in David Lindley (ed.), *The Court Masque* (Manchester: Manchester University Press, 1984), pp. 169–83.

Hatton, Ragnhild, *George I: Elector and King* (London: Thames and Hudson, 1978)

Hatton, R. M., 'Louis XIV and his fellow monarchs', in John C. Rule (ed.), *Louis XIV and the Craft of Kingship* (Ohio: Ohio State University Press, 1969), pp. 155–96.

Harris, Barbara J., 'Women and politics in early-Tudor England', *The Historical Journal*, 33, 2 (1990), pp. 259–81.

Harris, J., *Catalogue of the Drawing Collection of the Royal Institute of British Architects. Volume One: Inigo Jones and John Webb* (Farnborough: Gregg, 1972).

Harris, Tim, *Politics under the Later Stuarts: Party Conflict in a Divided Society 1660–1715* (London and New York: Longman, 1993).

Harris, Tim, Paul Seaward and Mark Goldie (eds), *The Politics of Religion in Restoration England* (Oxford: Blackwell, 1999).

Harvey, Anthony and Richard Mortimer, *The Funeral Effigies of Westminster Abbey* (Woodbridge: Boydell, 1994).

Hautecoeur, Louis, *L'Histoire des châteaux du Louvre et des Tuileries sous le règne de Louis XIV* (Paris and Brussels, 1927).

Heal, Felicity, *Hospitality in Early Modern England* (Oxford: Clarendon Press, 1990).

Hildesheimer, Françoise, *Testament Politique de Richelieu* (Paris: Champion, 1995).

Hofmann, Christina, *Das Spanische Hofzeremoniell von 1500–1700* (Frankfurt, 1985).

Holman, Peter, *Four and Twenty Fiddlers: The Violin at the English Court 1540–1690* (Oxford: Oxford University Press, 1993).

Hoskins, S. Elliott, *Charles the Second in the Channel Islands*, 2 vols (London, 1854).

Howarth, David, *Images of Rule: Art and Politics in the English Renaissance, 1485–1649* (Basingstoke: Macmillan, 1997).

Hutton, Ronald *Charles II: King of England Ireland and Scotland* (Oxford: Oxford University Press, 1989).

Hutton, Ronald, *The Rise and Fall of Merry England* (Oxford: Oxford University Press, 1994).

Hutton, Ronald, *The Restoration* (Oxford: Oxford University Press, 1985).

Hutton, Ronald, 'The religion of Charles II', in M. Smuts (ed.), *The Stuart Court and Europe* (Cambridge: Cambridge University Press, 1996), pp. 228–46.

Jacob, W. M., and Nigel Yates, *Crown and Mitre: Religion and Society in Northern Europe since the Reformation* (Woodbridge: Boydell, 1993).

Jardine, Lisa, *On a Grander Scale: the Outstanding Career of Sir Christopher Wren* (London: Harper Collins, 2002).

Jones, J. R., *Charles II: Royal Politician* (London: Allen and Unwin,1987).

Jones, J. R. (ed.), *The Restored Monarchy 1660–1688* (London: Macmillan, 1979).

Kantorowicz, Ernst H., 'Oriens Augusti – lever du roi', *Dumbarton Oaks Papers*, 17 (Washington, 1963), pp. 117–79.

Kantorowicz, Ernst H., *The King's Two Bodies* (Princeton: Princeton University Press, 1957).

Keay, Anna, '"Toyes and Trifles" the destruction of the English Crown Jewels', *History Today*, 52 (7), July 2002, pp. 31–7.

Keay, Anna, 'The later Stuart portraits in the Suffolk Collection', *English Heritage Historical Review*, I (2006), pp. 62–74.

Keay, Anna, *The Crown Jewels*, official guidebook (London: Historic Royal Palaces, 2002).

Keens-Soper, Maurice, 'Francois Callieres and Diplomatic Theory', *The Historical Journal*, XVI, 2 (1973), pp. 485–508.

Kenyon, John, *The Popish Plot* (London: Heinemann, 1972).

A King's Feast: The Goldsmith's Art and Royal Banqueting in the 18th Century, catalogue to an exhibition at Kensington Palace, 5 June–29 September 1991.

Kisby, F., '"When the King Goeth a Procession": chapel ceremonies and services, the ritual year and religious reforms at the early Tudor court, 1485–1547', *Journal of British Studies*, 40 (January 2001), pp. 44–75.

Kishlansky, Mark, *A Monarchy Transformed: Britian 1603–1714* (London: Allen Lane, 1996).

Kishlansky, Mark, 'Charles I: a case of mistaken identity', *Past and Present*, 189 (Nov. 2005), pp. 41–80.

Klingensmith, S. J, *The Utility of Splendor* (Chicago and London: University of Chicago Press, 1993).

Knights, Mark, 'London's 'monster' petition of 1680', *The Historical Journal*, 36, I (1993), pp. 39–67.

Knowles Middleton, W. E., 'Marchese Francesco Riccardi and Alessandro Segni in England 1668–69 – Segni's Diary', *Studi Secenteschi*, 21 (1980), pp. 187–279.

Lachs, Phyllis S., *The Diplomatic Corps under Charles II and James II* (New York: Rutgers University Press, 1965).

Langen, Ulrik, 'The meaning of "Incognito"', *The Court Historian*, 7, 2 (December 2002), pp. 145–55.

Law, Ernest, *The History of Hampton Court Palace*, 3 vols (London, 1898).

Le Roy Ladurie, Emmanuel, *Saint-Simon and the Court of Louis XIV* (Chicago and London: University of Chicago Press, 2001).

Lindley, David (ed.), *The Court Masque* (Manchester: Manchester University Press, 1984).

Lemaire, L., 'L'ambassade du Comte D'Estrades à Londres en 1661: l'affaire "du pas"', *Annuaire-Bulletin de la Société de l'Histoire de France*, 1934, pp. 181–226.

Levin, Carole '"Would I could give you help and succour": Elizabeth I and the politics of touch', *Albion*, 21, 2 (Spring 1989), pp. 191–205.

Levron, J., *Daily Life at Versailles in the Seventeenth and Eighteenth Centuries*, Claire Eliane Engel, transl. (London: Allen and Unwin, 1968).

The Life, Amours, and Secret History of Francelia, late D[uche]ss of P[ortsmou]th Favourite Mistress of King Charles II (London, 1734).

Loach, Jennifer, 'The function of ceremonial in the reign of Henry VIII', *Past and Present* 142 (1994), pp. 43–68.

Loomie, Alfred J., 'The conducteur des ambassadeurs of seventeenth-century France and Spain', *Revue Belge de Philologie et d'Histoire*, LIII, 1975 (2), pp. 333–57.

Macaulay, T. B., *The History of England from the Accession of James the Second*, 5 vols (London, 1849).

McCullough, P. *Sermons at Court: Politics and Religion in Elizabethan and Jacobean Preaching* (Cambridge: Cambridge University Press, 1998).

MacDonald Ross, George 'The royal touch and the Book of Common Prayer', *Notes and Queries*, October 1983, pp. 433–5.

McKean, Charles, *The Scottish Chateau: Country Houses of Renaissance Scotland* (Stroud: Sutton, 2001).

MacLean, Gerald, *Culture and Society in the Stuart Restoration: Literature, Drama, History* (Cambridge: Cambridge University Press, 1995).

Maguire, Nancy Klein, 'The duchess of Portsmouth: English royal consort and French politician, 1670–85', in Smuts (ed.), *The Stuart Court and Europe*, pp. 259–61.

Marshall, Alan, *The Age of Faction: Court Politics 1660–1702* (Manchester: Manchester University Press, 1999).

Mattingly, Garrett, *Renaissance Diplomacy* (London: Jonathan Cape, 1955).

Millar, Oliver, *The Tudor, Stuart and Early Georgian Pictures in the Collection of Her Majesty the Queen*, 2 vols (London: The Phaidon Press, 1963).

Millar, Oliver, *The Queen's Pictures* (London: Weidenfeld and Nicholson, 1977).

Miller, John, *Charles II* (London: Weidenfeld and Nicholson, 1991).

Miller, John, *James II* (New Haven and London: Yale University Press. 1978. Second edition, 2000).

Miller, John, *Bourbon and Stuart: Kings and Kingship in France and England in the Seventeenth Century* (London: Philip, 1987).

Milton, Anthony, '"That Sacred Oratory": religion and the Chapel Royal during the personal rule of Charles I', in A. Ashbee (ed.), *William Lawes (1602–1645): Essays on his Life, Times and Works* (Aldershot: Ashgate, 1998), pp. 69–96.

Morrah, Patrick, *Prince Rupert of the Rhine* (London: Constable, 1976).

Murdoch, Tessa, *Boughton House: the English Versailles* (London: Faber and Faber, 1992).

Mylne, Robert Scott, *The Master Masons to the Crown of Scotland and their Works* (Edinburgh, 1893).

Nelson, Janet, *Politics and Ritual in Early Medieval Europe* (London: Hambledon, 1986).

Nicholas, Donald, *Mr Secretary Nicholas 1593–1669: His Life and Letters* (London: Bodley Head, 1955).

Nichols, J. C., *London Pageants* (London, 1831).

Ogg, David, *England in the Reign of Charles II*, 2 vols (Oxford: Clarendon Press, 1934).

Ollard, Richard, *The Image of the King: Charles I and Charles II* (London, 1979).

Oman, Carola, *Mary of Modena* (London, 1962).

Oxford Dictionary of National Biography, Colin Matthew, Brian Harrison and Lawrence Goldman (eds), (Oxford: Oxford University Press, 2004).

Parry, Graham *The Golden Age Restor'd: The Culture of the Stuart Court 1603–1642* (Manchester: Manchester University Press, 1981).

Peck, Linda Levy, *Court Patronage and Corruption in Early Stuart England* (London: Unwin Hyman, 1990).

Peck, Linda Levy, *Consuming Splendor* (Cambridge: Cambridge University Press, 2005).

Phillips, J. R., *Memoirs of the Civil War in Wales*, 2 vols (London, 1874).

Pocock, Nicholas, *Life of Richard Steward, Dean Designate of St Paul's* (London, 1908).

Potter, D. and Roberts, P. R., 'An Englishman's view of the court of Henri III, 1584–5: Richard Cook's "Description of the Court of France"', *French History*, 2:3 (1988), pp. 312–44.

Procter, Francis and Walter Howard Frere, *A New History of the Book of Common Prayer with a Rationale of its Offices* (London, 1902).

Ratcliffe, E. E., *The Royal Maundy: a Brief Outline of its History and Ceremonial* (London, 1936).

Reedy, Gerard, 'Mystical politics: the imagery of Charles II's coronation', in Paul J. Korshin (ed.), *Studies in Change and Revolution: Aspects of English Intellectual History, 1640–1800* (Menston: Scolar Press, 1972), pp. 19–42.

Ribeiro, Aileen, *Fashion and Fiction: Dress in Art and Literature in Stuart England* (London and New Haven: Yale University Press, 2005).

Richards, Judith, '"His Nowe Majestie" and the English monarchy: the kingship of Charles I before 1640', *Past and Present*, 113, November, 1986, pp. 70–96.

Richardson, Thomas, 'H. R. Robinson's 'Dutch armour of the 17th century'', *The Journal of the Arms and Armour Society* XIII, 4 (March, 1991), pp. 256–78.

Robinson, Brian, *Silver Pennies and Linen Towels: the Story of the Royal Maundy* (London: Spink, 1992).

Rodger, N. A. M., *The Command of the Ocean: a Naval History of Britain, 1649–1815* (London: Allen Lane, 2004).

Roosen, William J., *The Age of Louis XIV: The Rise of Modern Diplomacy* (Cambridge, Massachusetts: Schenkman, 1976).

Roosen, William J., 'Early diplomatic ceremonial: a systems approach', *Journal of Modern History*, 52, September 1980, pp. 452–76.

Routledge, F. J., *England and the Treaty of the Pyrenees* (Liverpool: Liverpool University Press, 1953).

Le Roux, Nicolas, 'La cour dans l'espace du palais: l'exemple du Henri III', in Marie-France Auzepy *et al.*, *Palais et Pouvoir: de Constantinople à Versailles* (Saint-Denis: Universitaire de Vincennes, 2003), pp. 229–67.

St John Hope, W. H., *Windsor Castle: an Architectural History*, 2 vols (London, 1913).

Sainty, J. and Bucholz, R., *Officials of the Royal Household 1660–1837, Part I: Department of the Lord Chamberlain and Associated Offices* (London: University of London, 1997).

Satow, E., *Guide to Diplomatic Practice*, 2 vols (London, 1922).

Saule, B., *Versailles Triomphant: Une Journée de Louis XIV* (Paris: Flammarion, 1996).

'Scarce tracts on the touch for the King's Evil', *The Gentleman's Magazine*, 81, 1811, p. 125.

Schramm, P. E., *A History of the English Coronation* (Oxford: Clarendon Press, 1937).

Scott, Eva, *The King in Exile: the Wanderings of Charles II from June 1646 to July 1654* (London: Archibald Constable and Company, 1905).

Scott, Eva, *The Travels of the King: Charles II in Germany and Flanders 1654–1660* (London: Constable, 1907).

Sharpe, Kevin, *The Personal Rule of Charles I* (New Haven and London: Yale University Press, 1992).

Sharpe, Kevin and Peter Lake, *Culture and Politics in Early Stuart England* (London: Macmillan, 1994).

Sharpe, Kevin, 'The image of virtue: the court and household of Charles I, 1625–1642', in D. Starkey, *et al.*, *The English Court: from the Wars of the Roses to the Civil War* (London and New York: Longman,1989), pp. 226–60.

Sherwood, Roy, *The Court of Oliver Cromwell* (London: Croom Helm, 1977).

Sherwood, Roy, *Oliver Cromwell: King in all but Name* (Stroud: Sutton, 1997).

Sheppard, Edgar, *Memorials of St. James's Palace*, 2 vols (London, 1894).

Slaughter, Thomas P., *Ideology and Politics on the eve of the Restoration: Newcastle's Advice to Charles II* (Philadelphia: American Philosophical Society, 1984).

Smith, Geoffrey *The Cavaliers in Exile 1640–60* (Basingstoke: Palgrave Macmillan, 2003).

Smuts, R. Malcolm, *Court Culture and the Origins of a Royalist Tradition in Early Stuart England* (Philadelphia: University of Pennsylvania Press, 1987).

Smuts, R. Malcolm, 'George Wentworth goes to court, March 1634', *The Court Historian*, 6, 3 (December, 2001), pp. 213–25.

Smuts, R. Malcolm, 'The political failure of Stuart cultural patronage', in *Patronage in the Renaissance*, Guy Fitch Lytle and Stephen Orgel (eds) (Princeton: Princeton University Press, 1981), pp. 165–91.

Smuts, R. Malcom (ed.), *The Stuart Court and Europe* (Cambridge: Cambridge University Press, 1996).

Smuts, R. Malcolm, 'Public ceremony and royal charisma: the English royal entry in London, 1495–1642', in *The First Modern Society: Essays in English History in Honour of Lawrence Stone*, A. L. Beier, David Cannadine and James M. Rosenheim (eds) (Cambridge: Cambridge University Press, 1989), pp. 65–94.

Souvenirs 'Britain in Bruges' Exhibition Organized by the City of Bruges ... Catalogue (Bruges, 1966).

Spurr, John, *England in the 1670s: 'This Masquerading Age'* (Oxford: Blackwell, 2000).

Sparrow Simpson, W., 'On the forms of prayer recited "at the healing" or touching for the King's Evil', *Journal of the British Archaeological Association*, XXVII, 1871, pp. 282–307.

Starkey, David, et al, *The English Court: from the Wars of the Roses to the Civil War* (London and New York: Longman, 1987).

Starkey, David, 'Representations through intimacy: a study in the symbolism of monarchy and court office in early-modern England', in I. Lewis (ed.), *Symbols and Sentiments: Cross Cultural Studies in Symbolism* (London: Academic Press, 1977), pp. 187–224.

Stevenson, David, 'The English devil of keeping state: élite manners and the downfall of Charles I in Scotland', in R. Mason and N. Macdougall (eds), *People and Power in Scotland: Essays in Honour of T. C. Smout* (Edinburgh: John Donald, 1992), pp. 126–44.

Stone, Lawrence, *The Crisis of the Aristocracy 1558–1641* (Oxford: Clarendon Press, 1965).

Strickland, A. *Lives of the Queens of England: Volume VIII* (London, 1845).

Strong, Roy, *Feast: a History of Grand Eating* (London: Jonathan Cape, 2002).

Strong, Roy, *The Tudor and Stuart Monarchy: Pageantry, Paintings, Iconography. Volume II* (Woodbridge: Boydell, 1995).

Strong, Roy, *Coronation: A History of Kingship and the British Monarchy* (London: Harper Collins, 2005).

Strype, John, *Ecclesiastical Memorials, Relating Chiefly to Religion* (Oxford, 1822).

Stuart, John, Marquis of Bute, *Scottish Coronations* (London: Alexander Gardner, 1902).

Sturdy, David, 'The Royal Touch in England', in Duchardt, Jackson and Sturdy (eds), *European Monarchy* (Stuttgart: F. Steiner, 1992), pp. 171–84.

Sturdy, David, '"Continuity" versus "change": historians and English coronations of the medieval and early modern periods', in Janos M. Bak (ed.), *Coronations: Medieval and Early Modern Monarchic Ritual* (Berkeley: University of California Press, 1990), pp. 228–42.

Sutch, Victor D., *Gilbert Sheldon, Architect of Anglican Survival, 1640–1675* (The Hague: Martinus Nijhoff, 1973).

Tanner, Lawrence E., 'Lord High Almoners and Sub-Almoners 1100–1957', *Journal of the British Archaeological Association*, 3rd Series, XX, 1957–58, pp. 72–83.

Thomas, Keith, *Religion and the Decline of Magic* (London, 1971. Edition London: Penguin, 1991).

Thompson, G. S., *Life in a Noble Household 1641–1700* (London: Jonathan Cape, 1937).

Thompson, Michael, *The Medieval Hall: the Basis of Secular Domestic Life, 600–1600 AD* (Aldershot: Scolar Press, 1995).

Thornton, Peter, 'The Royal State Bed', *The Connoisseur*, CXCV, January 1977, pp. 137–47.

Thurley, Simon, *Hampton Court: a Social and Architectural History* (New Haven and London: Yale University Press, 2003).

Thurley, Simon, *The Lost Palace of Whitehall*, catalogue of an exhibition at the RIBA Heinz Gallery (London: RIBA, 1998).

Thurley, Simon, 'The Stuart kings, Oliver Cromwell and the Chapel Royal 1618–1685', *Architectural History*, 45, 2002, pp. 238–74.

Thurley, Simon, 'A country seat fit for a King: Charles II, Greenwich and Winchester', in E. Cruickshanks (ed.), *The Stuart Courts* (Stroud: Sutton 2000), pp. 214–40.

Thurley, Simon, *Whitehall Palace: An Architectural History of the Royal Apartments, 1240–1690* (New Haven and London: Yale University Press, 1999).

Thurley, Simon, *The Royal Palaces of Tudor England* (New Haven and London: Yale University Press, 1993).

Tinniswood, Adrian, *By Permission of Heaven: The True Story of the Great Fire of London* (New York: Riverhead, 2004).

Trevelyan, G. M., *England under the Stuarts* (London: Meuthen, 1925).

Varley, J. F., *The Siege of Oxford* (Oxford: Oxford University Press, 1932).

Walker, James, 'The Secret Service under Charles II and James II', *Transactions of the Royal Historical Society*, fourth series, XV (1932), pp. 211–43.

Wagner, Sir Anthony, *Heralds of England: A History of the Office and College of Arms* (London: Her Majesty's Stationery Office, 1967).

Watkin, David, *The Royal Interiors of Regency England* (London and Melbourne: Dent, 1984).

Watson, J. N. P., *Captain-General and Rebel Chief: The Life of James, Duke of Monmouth* (London: Allen and Unwin, 1979).

Weber, Harold, *Paper Bullets: Print and Kingship under Charles II* (Kentucky: University Press of Kentucky, 1996).

Weiser, Brian, 'A call for order: Charles II's ordinances of the household (BL Stowe 562)', *The Court Historian*, 6, 2 (October, 2001), pp. 151–6.

Weiser, Brian, *Charles II and the Politics of Access* (Woodbridge: Boydell, 2003).

White, Christopher, *The Dutch Pictures in the Collection of Her Majesty the Queen* (Cambridge: Cambridge University Press, 1982).

White, Michelle Anne, *Henrietta Maria and the English Civil Wars* (Aldershot: Ashgate, 2006).

Wickham Legg, L. J., *English Church Life from the Restoration to the Tractarian Movement* (London, 1914).

Wickham Legg, L. J., *English Coronation Records* (London and New York, 1901).

Wilentz, Sean, *Rites of Power: Symbolism, Ritual and Politics since the Middle Ages* (Philadelphia: University of Pennsylvania Press, 1985).

Willcock, John, *The Great Marquess: the Life and Times of Archibald 8th Earl and 1st (and only) Marquess of Argyll* (Edinburgh and London, 1903).

Winn, James Anderson, *John Dryden and his World* (New Haven and London: Yale University Press, 1989).

Withington, Robert, *English Civic Pageantry: An Historical Outline*, 2 vols (Cambridge, Mass.: Harvard University Press, 1918–20).

Woodward, Jennifer, *The Theatre of Death: the Ritual Management of Royal Funerals in England 1570–1625* (Woodbridge: Boydell, 1997).

Wolf, John B., *Louis XIV* (London: Victor Gollancz, 1968).

Wortman, Richard S., *Scenarios of Power: Myth and Ceremony in Russian Monarchy* (Princeton: Princeton University Press,1995).

Wright, Lawrence, *Warm and Snug: a History of the Bed* (London: Routledge and Kegan Paul, 1962).

Wrigley, E. A. and R. Schofield, *The Population History of England 1541–1871: A Reconstruction* (London: Edward Arnold, 1981).

Yates, Nigel, *Buildings, Faith and Worship: the Liturgical Arrangement of Anglican Churches 1600–1900* (Oxford: Oxford University Press, 2000).

Yates, Nigel, 'Unity in diversity: attitudes to the liturgical arrangement of church buildings between the late seventeenth and early nineteenth centuries', in W. M. Jacob and Nigel Yates, *Crown and Mitre: Religion and Society in Northern Europe since the Reformation* (Woodbridge: Boydell, 1993), pp. 45–63.

DOCTORIAL THESES

Barclay, Andrew, 'The Impact of King James II on the Departments of the Royal Household', unpublished PhD thesis, Cambridge University, 1993.

Clayton, Roderick, 'Diplomats and Diplomacy in London 1667–72', unpublished PhD thesis, Oxford University, 1995.

Gibson, Katharine, '"Best Belov'd of Kings": The Iconography of King Charles II', unpublished PhD thesis, University of London, 1997.

Reynolds, N.A.C., 'The Stuart Court and Courtiers in Exile 1644–1654', unpublished PhD thesis, Cambridge University, 1996.

Shaw, Dougal, 'The Coronation and Monarchical Culture in Stuart Britain and Ireland 1603–1661', unpublished PhD thesis, Cambridge University, 2002.

Weiser, Brian, 'The reconstruction of monarchy, the matter of access in the reign of Charles II', PhD thesis, Saint Louis, 1999.

Index

Monck, George, 1st Duke of Albemarle, 78–9,
  81–4, 86–7, 145
Monmouth, Duke of, *see* Scott
Montagu, Admiral Edward, 2nd Earl of
  Manchester, 86, 93, 123
    Edward, 1st Earl of Sandwich, 81, 91, 128,
    262
Montrose, Marquess of
  see Graham
Moray Firth, the, 46, 54
Morgan, William, 226
Morland, Sir Samuel, 101
Morley and Monteagle, Lord, 101
Morley, George, Bishop of Winchester and
  Dean of the Chapel Royal, 148, 150, 157
Morley, John, 226
Morris, Mr, 226
Motteville, Madame de, 65, 71, 73
Mounbadiac, Françoise, royal nurse, 10–11
Munson, John, 226
Murray, Alastair, 226
Murray, Sir David, 57
Mushey, John, 226

Napier, John, 226
Naseby, battle of, 41, 81
National Covenant of Scotland, the, and
  the Solemn League and Covenant, 29, 57,
  68, 69
Nayler, Mr, 226
Netherlands, United Provinces of the, 12, 18,
  35, 134, 136
    see also Spanish Netherlands
New Amsterdam, 134
New Exchange, the, 18
New Model Army, the, 1, 41
New York, 134
Newburgh, Lord, 227
Newcastle, Earl of, *see* Cavendish
Newmarket, Palace of, 35, 117, 129, 153, 155,
  182
Nicholas, Sir Edward, Secretary of State, 33,
  48–9, 68, 227
Northamptonshire, 41

Norwich, 48
  Earl of, *see* Goring
Nottingham Castle, 36

Oates, Titus, 183, 185, 190
Oatlands Palace, 32–3
Ogilvy, Lord, 56
Olivares, Duke of, 64
O'Neil, Daniel, 227
Ordnance Office, 17
Orfley, Robert, 227
Orléans, Duchess of, *see* Henriette Anne
Ormond, Duke of, *see* Butler
Osborne, Thomas, Earl of Danby, 186, 287
Oxford, 1, 14, 37–40, 66, 93, 100, 112, 115,
  133, 147–50, 160, 169, 187, 190

Palatinate
  Prince Charles of the, 174–5, 177
  Prince Edward of the, 72
  Prince Maurice of the, 72
Palden, Thomas, 227
Palmer
  Barbara, Countess of Castlemaine and
    Duchess of Cleveland, 122, 125–6,
    129–30
  Philip, 37, 42
  Richard, 227
  Roger, Earl of Castlemaine, 122
Parliament, 5, 7–8, 13, 29–30, 32, 35, 38, 46,
  53, 55, 62–3, 75, 78–9, 110, 123, 134, 145–6,
  163–4, 185–90
Pegge, Catherine, 77
Pembroke, Earl of, *see* Herbert
Pendennis Castle, 41–2
Pennicooke, James, 227
Penning, Thomas, 227
Penriddock, Mr, 227
Pepys, Samuel, 3, 7–8, 81, 103, 108, 117, 122,
  126, 128, 130, 134, 136, 138, 140, 142, 158,
  160, 162, 166
Percy, Lord Henry, 49, 51, 227
Peronne, Madame, royal midwife, 11
Perth, 63, 88